Information Modeling
the EXPRESS Way

Information Modeling the EXPRESS Way

DOUGLAS SCHENCK
PETER WILSON

New York   Oxford
OXFORD UNIVERSITY PRESS
1994

Oxford University Press

Oxford   New York   Toronto
Delhi   Bombay   Calcutta   Madras   Karachi
Kuala Lumpur   Singapore   Hong Kong   Tokyo
Nairobi   Dar es Salaam   Cape Town
Melbourne   Auckland   Madrid

and associated companies in
Berlin   Ibadan

Copyright © 1994 by Oxford University Press, Inc.

Published by Oxford University Press, Inc.,
200 Madison Avenue, New York, New York 10016

Oxford is a registered trademark of Oxford University Press

Library of Congress Cataloging-in-Publication Data
Schenck, Douglas (Douglas A.)
Information Modeling: The EXPRESS Way / Douglas Schenck and Peter Wilson.
p. cm. Includes bibliographical references.
ISBN 0-19-508714-3
1. Data base design 2. EXPRESS (Computer program language)
3. Object-oriented programming. I. Wilson, Peter (Peter R.) II. Title
QA76.9.D26S34 1993 005.13'3--dc20 93-11558

9 8 7 6 5 4 3 2 1

Printed in the United States of America
on acid-free paper

Contents

Preface   xix

Introduction   xxiii
    Typographic conventions   xxv

Definitions   xxvii

I   Information Modeling   1

1 Information and communication   5
    1.1 What is information?   5
    1.2 Information models   10
    1.3 Exercises   11
    1.4 Further reading   11

2 Models and representations   12
    2.1 Organizing principles   13
        2.1.1 Categorization   13
        2.1.2 Grouping   13
        2.1.3 Shielding from details   13
        2.1.4 Aggregations and ordering   14
    2.2 Terminology   14
    2.3 Representations   15
    2.4 Graphical representations   17
        2.4.1 Entity-Relationship   18
        2.4.2 EXPRESS-G   19
        2.4.3 IDEF1X   20
        2.4.4 NIAM   21
        2.4.5 OMT   22
        2.4.6 Shlaer-Mellor   23
    2.5 Lexical representations   24
        2.5.1 DAPLEX   24

        2.5.2   EXPRESS   25
        2.5.3   GEM   26
        2.5.4   SQL   26
   2.6 Graphical vs. lexical representations   27
   2.7 Exercises   28
   2.8 Further reading   29

3 The modeling process   31
   3.1 The team   31
   3.2 Phase 1: Basic objects   33
   3.3 Phase 2: Relationships and attributes   35
   3.4 Phase 3: Completion of constraints   36
   3.5 Phase 4: Model integration   37
   3.6 Further reading   37

4 A worked example   39
   4.1 The starting specification   39
        4.1.1   Scope   39
        4.1.2   Description   40
   4.2 The base model   41
        4.2.1   Categorization and specialization   42
        4.2.2   Attributes   43
        4.2.3   Uniqueness constraints   45
        4.2.4   Local constraints   46
        4.2.5   Existence constraints   47
        4.2.6   Documentation   48
        4.2.7   Basic example model   48
   4.3 Relationships and attributes   50
        4.3.1   Use of simple types   50
        4.3.2   Subtypes revisited   52
        4.3.3   Redundancy elimination   54
        4.3.4   Local constraints   56
        4.3.5   Module structure   58
        4.3.6   Refined model   59
   4.4 Model completion   63
   4.5 Exercises   65
   4.6 Further reading   67

5 Modeling principles   68
   5.1 Readability   68
   5.2 Scoping   69
   5.3 The nym principle   70
   5.4 Context independence   70
   5.5 Implementation independence   72
        5.5.1   Abstraction   73

5.6   Invariance   73
5.7   Constraint   75
   5.7.1   Structure   75
   5.7.2   Constraint functions   77
5.8   Reality   78
5.9   Redundancy   79
5.10 Concepts   79
   5.10.1 Syntax   79
   5.10.2 Implied correspondence   80
   5.10.3 Optional and default values   81
5.11 Hierarchies   82
   5.11.1 Inheritance   82
   5.11.2 Data aggregation   82
5.12 Simple types   83
5.13 Exercises   83
5.14 Further reading   85

6   **Integration and specialization**   **86**
6.1   Supertypes and subtypes   86
6.2   Schema interfacing   89
6.3   Model integration   91
   6.3.1   Cosmetic integration   92
   6.3.2   Editorial integration   92
   6.3.3   Continuity integration   94
   6.3.4   Structural integration   94
   6.3.5   Core based integration   95
   6.3.6   Evolutionary based integration   95
   6.3.7   Model quality   95
6.4   Subsets and specialization   96
   6.4.1   Subsetting   96
   6.4.2   Specialization   98
   6.4.3   ASIM structure   99
6.5   Exercises   101
6.6   Further reading 103

7   **Model documentation**   **104**
7.1   General 104
7.2   Embedded style 105
7.3   Partitioned style   107
7.4   Putting it together 107
7.5   Exercises   111
7.6   Further reading 111

8   EXPRESS information bases   **113**
  8.1   Information bases   113
  8.2   The EXPRESS connection   115
  8.3   The computer connection   116
     8.3.1   Environment   116
     8.3.2   Editor   117
     8.3.3   Capitalizer and pretty printer   117
     8.3.4   Parser   117
     8.3.5   Semantic analyzer   117
     8.3.6   Visualizer   118
     8.3.7   Compiler   118
     8.3.8   Documenter   118
  8.4   Further reading   118

II   The EXPRESS Language   **121**

9   Basic elements   **127**
  9.1   Composing the source   127
  9.2   The character set   128
  9.3   Remark   130
     9.3.1   Embedded remark   130
     9.3.2   Tail remark   130
  9.4   Symbols   131
  9.5   Reserved words   131
  9.6   Identifiers   132
  9.7   Literals   133
     9.7.1   Binary literal   133
     9.7.2   Integer literal   133
     9.7.3   Real literal   134
     9.7.4   String literal   134
     9.7.5   Logical literal   135
     9.7.6   Aggregate literal   135
     9.7.7   Entity literal   136
  Answers to Exercises   137

10 Datatypes   **139**
  10.1 Pseudotypes   140
     10.1.1 Generic pseudotype   140
     10.1.2 Aggregate pseudotype   140
  10.2 Simple datatypes   141
     10.2.1 Number datatype   141
     10.2.2 Real datatype   142
     10.2.3 Integer datatype   142
     10.2.4 Logical datatype   143

10.2.5 Boolean datatype 143

10.2.6 String datatype 143

10.2.7 Binary datatype 144

10.3 Collection datatypes 145

10.3.1 Array datatype 146

10.3.2 Bag datatype 147

10.3.3 List datatype 147

10.3.4 Set datatype 148

10.4 Enumeration type 149

10.5 Select type 150

Answers to Exercises 151

11 Declarations **152**

11.1 Schema 153

11.2 Constant 153

11.3 Type 154

11.4 Entity 156

11.4.1 Attribute 157

11.4.2 Local rule 162

11.4.3 Supertypes and subtypes 165

11.4.4 Interpreting supertype relationships 170

11.4.5 Implicit declarations 170

11.5 Algorithm 171

11.5.1 Formal parameter 171

11.5.2 Local variable 173

11.5.3 Function 173

11.5.4 Procedure 174

11.6 Rule 175

Answers to Exercises 177

12 References **179**

12.1 Names, scope and visibility 179

12.2 The anatomy of a name 181

12.3 References in general 182

12.4 Entity references 182

12.5 Type references 183

12.6 Attribute references 183

12.7 Enumeration item references 183

12.8 Function references 184

12.9 Variable references 184

Answers to Exercises 185

13 Executable statements   **187**

13.1   Null (statement) 187

13.2   Alias statement 188

13.3   Assignment statement 188

13.4   Case statement 189

13.5   Compound statement 190

13.6   If . . . Then . . . Else Statement 190

13.7   Procedure call statement 191

13.8   Repeat statement 191

       13.8.1   Increment control 193

       13.8.2   While control 193

       13.8.3   Until control 194

       13.8.4   Escape statement 194

       13.8.5   Skip statement 194

13.9   Return statement 195

Answers to Exercises 195

14 Expressions   **196**

14.1   Numeric valued operations 197

14.2   Logical and boolean valued operations 198

       14.2.1   NOT operator 199

       14.2.2   AND operator 199

       14.2.3   OR operator 199

       14.2.4   XOR operator 199

       14.2.5   Comparison 200

       14.2.6   Interval 202

       14.2.7   IN operator 203

       14.2.8   LIKE operator 203

       14.2.9   Subset operator 204

       14.2.10 Superset operator 204

14.3   String and binary valued operations 204

14.4   Aggregate valued operations 205

       14.4.1   Intersection operator 205

       14.4.2   Union operator 205

       14.4.3   Difference operator 206

       14.4.4   Query expression 206

14.5   Function call 207

Answers to Exercises 209

15 Interfacing   **211**

15.1   The interface specification 212

       15.1.1   Use 213

       15.1.2   Reference 213

15.2   Multiple specifications 214

15.3   Chaining 214

15.4 Implicit references 214
15.5 Subtype pruning 215
15.6 Independent existence 216
15.7 Putting it all together 217

16 EXPRESS Syntax **220**

17 A graphical form of EXPRESS **235**
17.1 Graphics requirements 236
17.2 Model forms 236
17.3 Example model 236
17.4 Further reading 238

18 Symbols **239**
18.1 Definition symbols 239
    18.1.1 Simple type symbols 239
    18.1.2 Type symbols 239
    18.1.3 Entity symbol 240
    18.1.4 Schema symbol 240
    18.1.5 Algorithm symbols 240
18.2 Relationship symbols 241
18.3 Composition symbols 242
    18.3.1 Page references 242
    18.3.2 Inter-schema references 244

19 EXPRESS-G models **245**
19.1 Schema level model 245
19.2 Entity level model 246
    19.2.1 Role names and cardinalities 246
    19.2.2 Constraints 247
    19.2.3 Type modeling 247
    19.2.4 Entity modeling 248
    19.2.5 Inter-schema references 250
19.3 Complete and partial models 250
    19.3.1 Complete models 251
    19.3.2 Partial models 251

20 Sample Models **253**

21 The EXPRESS-I Language **259**
21.1 Governing principles 260
21.2 Basic values 262
    21.2.1 Numbers 262
    21.2.2 Strings 263
21.3 Enumeration items 263

21.4 Select values 264
21.5 Aggregate values 264
21.6 Entity values and representations 265
      21.6.1 Attribute values 266
      21.6.2 Supertypes and subtypes 267
21.7 Constant values 268
21.8 Schema data instance 268

22 Usage notes   270
22.1 EXPRESS data examples 270
22.2 Abstract test cases 271
22.3 Object bases 271
      22.3.1 Input 271
      22.3.2 Output 272
      22.3.3 Code testing 272
22.4 Non-EXPRESS data examples 272

23 EXPRESS-I Syntax   273

A EXPRESS example model   280
A.1 Scope 280
A.2 Model overview 280
A.3 Authority schema 281
     A.3.1 Entity definitions 282
     A.3.2 Function and procedure definitions 284
     A.3.3 Entity classification structure 287
A.4 Support schema 287
     A.4.1 Type definitions 287
     A.4.2 Entity definitions 289
     A.4.3 Function and procedure definitions 295
     A.4.4 Entity classification structure 297
A.5 Calendar schema 297
     A.5.1 Type definitions 298
     A.5.2 Entity definitions 298
     A.5.3 Function and procedure definitions 299
     A.5.4 Entity classification structure 301

B Example model instance   302
B.1 The authority schema instance 303
B.2 The support schema instance 304
B.3 The calendar schema instance 307

C Interpreting supertype relationships   309

D Relationships and cardinality   **316**
  D.1 Forward cardinality of [1:1] 317
      D.1.1 Inverse cardinality of [1:1] 318
      D.1.2 Inverse cardinality of [0:1] 319
      D.1.3 Inverse cardinality of [1:?] 320
      D.1.4 Inverse cardinality of [0:?] 320
  D.2 Forward cardinality of [0:1] 321
      D.2.1 Inverse cardinality of [1:1] 321
      D.2.2 Inverse cardinality of [0:1] 322
      D.2.3 Inverse cardinality of [1:?] 323
      D.2.4 Inverse cardinality of [0:?] 323
  D.3 Forward cardinality of [1:?] 324
      D.3.1 Inverse cardinality of [1:1] 324
      D.3.2 Inverse cardinality of [0:1] 325
      D.3.3 Inverse cardinality of [1:?] 325
      D.3.4 Inverse cardinality of [0:?] 326
  D.4 Forward cardinality of [[0:?] 326
      D.4.1 Inverse cardinality of [1:1] 326
      D.4.2 Inverse cardinality of [0:1] 327
      D.4.3 Inverse cardinality of [1:?] 328
      D.4.4 Inverse cardinality of [0:?] 328

E An EXPRESS Meta-model   **330**
  E.1 Scope 330
  E.2 The metaEXPRESS Schema 331
  E.3 Support Schema 332

F Resources   **354**
  F.1 Standard constants 354
      Constant E 354
      Indeterminate 354
      False 355
      Pi 355
      Self 355
      True 355
      Unknown 355
  F.2 Standard functions and procedures 355
      Abs 355
      ACos 356
      ASin 356
      ATan 356
      BLength 357
      Cos 357
      Exists 357
      Exp 358

Format 358
HiBound 359
HiIndex 360
Insert 361
Length 361
LoBound 361
Log — Log2 — Log10 362
LoIndex 362
NVL 363
Odd 363
Remove 364
RolesOf 364
Sin 365
SizeOf 365
Sqrt 366
Tan 366
TypeOf 366
UsedIn 367
Value 368

Bibliography   **369**

Index   **381**

List of Figures

2.1   Entity-Relationship representation of the car example. . . .   18

2.2   EXPRESS-G representation of the car example.   19

2.3   IDEF1X representation of the car example.   20

2.4   NIAM representation of the car example.   21

2.5   OMT representation of the car example.   22

2.6   Shlaer-Mellor representation of the car example.   23

2.7   DAPLEX representation of the car example.   24

2.8   EXPRESS representation of the car example.   25

2.9   GEM representation of the car example.   26

2.10   SQL representation of the car example.   27

4.1   Partial entity-level model of the initial owner subtype tree (Page 1 of 1).   43

4.2   Partial entity-level model for a car (Page 1 of 1).   44

4.3   Partial entity-level model of the initial car_model (Page 1 of 1).   45

4.4   Partial entity-level model for transfer history (Page 1 of 1).   48

4.5   Partial entity-level model of some types (Page 1 of 1). . . .   52

4.6   Partial entity-level model of the refined owner subtype tree (Page 1 of 1).   54

4.7   Base model ambiguity between car, model, and manufacturer.   55

4.8   Complete schema-level model for Registration Authority refined model (Page 1 of 1).   58

7.1   Main schema for a simple model of the embedded document style.   105

7.2   Support schema for a simple model of the embedded document style.   106

7.3   Algorithm to strip remarks from EXPRESS source.   108

7.4   Sample LaTeX source.   109

7.5   Processed sample LaTeX source.   110

11.1   Inheritance alternatives   168

12.1 Scope 180
12.2 An inventory of full names 180
12.3 Full names and simple names 181

13.1 Repeat control logic 192

17.1 Complete entity-level model of Example 20.1 (Page 1 of 2). 237
17.2 Complete entity-level model of Example 20.1 (Page 2 of 2). 237

18.1 Simple type symbols. 240
18.2 Type definition symbols. 240
18.3 Entity and schema definition symbols. 240
18.4 Relationship Line Styles 241
18.5 Partial entity-level model showing relationship directions from
     Example 20.2. (Page 1 of 1) 242
18.6 The composition symbols. 243

19.1 Complete schema-level model of Example 20.5. (Page 1 of 1) 246
19.2 Complete entity-level model of Example 20.2. (Page 1 of 1) 247
19.3 Complete entity-level model of the Supertype tree from Ex-
     ample 20.3. (Page 1 of 1) 249
19.4 Complete entity-level model of Example 20.4 showing at-
     tribute redeclarations in subtypes. (Page 1 of 1) 249
19.5 Complete entity-level model of the fem schema of Exam-
     ple 20.5 illustrating inter-schema references. (Page 1 of 1). . 250
19.6 Partial entity-level model showing an abstraction of an Owner
     entity. (Page 1 of 1) 251

21.1 The major elements of the EXPRESS-I language. 261

A.1 Complete schema-level model for Registration Authority ex-
    ample (Page 1 of 1). 281
A.2 Complete entity-level model of the Authority schema (Page
    1 of 1). 282
A.3 Complete entity-level model of the Support schema (Page 1
    of 2). 288
A.4 Complete entity-level model of the Support schema (Page 2
    of 2). 290
A.5 Complete entity-level model of Calendar schema (Page 1 of 1). 297

D.1 EXPRESS-G representation of [1:1] cardinalities. 318
D.2 EXPRESS-G representation of [0:1] cardinalities. 321
D.3 EXPRESS-G representation of [1:?] cardinalities. 324
D.4 EXPRESS-G representation of [0:?] cardinalities. 327

List of Tables

2.1   Classes, objects, entities and instances.   15

9.1   The EXPRESS character set 128
9.2   EXPRESS character classes 129
9.3   Whitespace Characters 129
9.4   EXPRESS Symbols 131
9.5   EXPRESS Keywords 132

10.1 Datatype context usage. 140
10.2 String definition formats 144

14.1 Operator Precedence 196
14.2 Pattern matching characters 203
14.3 Union operation results 205
14.4 Difference operator results 206

15.1 An inventory of schema resources 219

C.1   Supertype operators 311

D.1   Cardinality constraint matrix 317

Preface

The language which is the subject of this book began life during the PDDI Program sponsored by the US Air Force during the early 80's — although it (the language) didn't know it at the time. When STEP development got under way the then anonymous language was adopted as a starting point as the way to *formally display* the models that were to be developed for the computer based exchange of mechanical product data. The name EXPRESS (which is supposed to conjure up the idea of expressiveness) was coined in Zurich in the spring of 1986 when Bernd Wenzel and I first started working on the problem. Not much of the language we started with has survived except for some of the broad principles we thought were important at the time (and still do).

For myself at least, the opportunity to develop EXPRESS was a chance to improve upon what seemed to be an inadequate way of thinking about and documenting what we know about information, which influences our lives so greatly. We were pushed into either of two corners: one that dealt with data and relationships only and another that entangled information with every conceivable computer application development detail. From my point of view, information is certainly more than the former and definitely should be kept apart from the latter.

A lot of people had a hand in the development effort. Here is a fairly comprehensive list of them: Jeffrey Altemueller, Edward Barkmeyer, Dave Briggs, Steve Clark, Rich Cochran, Joe Eggers, Philip Kennicott, Takeshi Kishinami, András Márkus, Sabine Mullenbach, Jon Owen, Doug Schenck, Ernst Schlechtendahl, Nigel Shaw, Chai-Hui Shih, Philip Spiby, Robert Strong, Max Ungerer, Robert Venderley, Jan Van Maanen, Bernd Wenzel, Peter Wilson and Mike Yinger.

The people who made the most significant contributions to the development of EXPRESS deserve special recognition: Joe Eggers built the first experimental parsers which tested the syntax and semantic validity, Steve Clark later also built test parsers, Nigel Shaw preserved my sanity and enthusiasm through some hard times, Phil Spiby took over as the editor and resident expert when other duties prevented me from doing the job, Bernd Wenzel of course is one of the founders of the language, Peter Wilson developed EXPRESS-G and EXPRESS-I, and Mike Yinger managed to complain about things that were (and still are in some cases) wrong with the language while staying a friend.

We should consider EXPRESS, and the development of STEP, in light of the following quote:

> Science and technology, and the various forms of art, all unite human-
> ity in a single and interconnected system. As science progresses, the
> worldwide cooperation of scientists and technologists becomes more
> and more of a special and distinct intellectual community of friend-
> ship, in which, in place of antagonism, there is growing up a mutually
> advantageous sharing of work, a coordination of efforts, *a common
> language for the exchange of information* and a solidarity, which are
> in many cases independent of the social and political differences of
> individual states.

The Medvedev Papers
Zhores Aleksandrovich Medvedev

The italics are mine. Then, on the other hand we should never forget this:

> Beware of language, for it is often a cheat.

Peter Mere Latham

D.A.S
St. Louis, MO
1993

I first became seriously aware of EXPRESS when I started developing in-formation models in the early days of STEP. That was a delightful time. Here, at last, was a language that allowed me to express what I wanted to say in the way that I wanted to say it. If it didn't, then I could always add my own constructs to the language to make my life easier as we were not constrained by what the compiler would allow — there were no compilers then. This had the added benefit that any code that I wrote was bug-free by definition!

However, all good things must come to an end, and it happened in this case. As the number of users grew there was less opportunity for experimentation, and parsers and compilers came along to spoil the fun. One of the strengths of EXPRESS is that it has been developed in parallel with its usage. On my filing cabinet I have a stack of reports over two feet high; these are all the prior language specification documents. Looking back, I am amazed at the forbearance of our users as the language kept changing on them, sometimes at our insistence, sometimes at their request, and sometimes not changing at all in spite of their pleas. Development in conjunction with the users has meant that the language is pragmatic —

that is, it has been developed to solve real information modeling problems in a manner that satisfies both the users and the language developers (well, most of the time, anyway). This has also been a drawback, in that the nice clean original design of the language has been overtaken by events. Nevertheless, it serves its purpose well.

This last statement is not merely prejudice on my part, as there is evidence to back it up. The original context in which EXPRESS was developed was the definition of information pertinent to mechanical products. The language is now used in a variety of contexts that we never dreamt of. These range from electrical product applications, laboratory chemical analysis, the petroleum exploration and production industry, and stock exchange asset management, through to applications in the human genome project and the interfacing of genomic databases.

I would like to acknowledge the unwitting contributions to this book by the members of the EXPRESS User Group whose questions and discussions have illuminated many of the perceived shortcomings of the EXPRESS Language Reference Manual. I also thank STEP Tools, Inc. for the use of their EXPRESS and EXPRESS-G compilers for checking the models in the Appendices.

We can always wish for more than we have. There are many directions in which the language might be improved and extended, but as the proverb says, 'Make haste slowly'. The version of EXPRESS described here took eight years to complete rather than the expected 18 months. Any future enhancements will also require a considerable time before they see the light of day.

P.R.W
Scotia, NY
1993

Introduction

EXPRESS is an object-flavored information model specification language which was initially developed in order to enable the writing of formal information models describing mechanical products. It is one of the technologies that has been developed as part of the STEP standard for product model data exchange. Although designed to meet the needs of STEP it has also been used in a variety of other large scale modeling applications. Examples include product, process and organization modeling for concurrent engineering; the specification of information pertinent to data exchange for electronic products; the modeling of petrochemical plants and other aspects of the petrotechnical industry; and stock exchange asset management applications, to name just a few. In a different vein it has also been used as a software specification language for CAD packages; to define compiler data structures; and as a neutral data specification language for a variety of database packages, for example.

The purpose of EXPRESS is to describe the characteristics of information that someday might exist in an *information base.* We call that process *information modeling.* Information modeling deals with things, what properties those things have (or that we care about), how they behave and how they interact together.

Building an information model is often a prelude to building an *information system,* including an information base. The information base deals with storing and accessing (values of) things, and other questions of consistency, behavior, etc. The information system interacts with users, carries out the mission of the system, reacts to and reports problems and deals with other questions of operation and environment.

One of the main tenets of EXPRESS is that a clear separation should be made between the information model and the information system environment. The reasoning is simple: *a piece of information is not tied to a single application that uses it.* Putting the argument the other way around we could say: *when a piece of information is tied to a single application there is much less chance that it can or will be shared.*

Another part of the reasoning is: *a piece of information does not (should not) care about the environment in which it lives.* This is an outgrowth of the idea that information should be shared (or at least sharable). In principle it should not matter whether information lives on a piece of paper or in a mainframe, workstation or personal computer; is operated on interactively or in a batch mode; or is stored in a relational database or a flat file. Moreover, we reasonably would expect different responses from interactive and batch systems when a problem is diagnosed, but those responses have nothing to do with the information itself.

In other words, environment and information are different things, which require different definition techniques and that should be as separate as possible from one another. Nevertheless, a fair amount of cooperation between them are needed when the implementation is finally put together.

This book is intended for both professionals and students. The reader will learn about why we need information modeling, what it is, and how to develop information models. Further, the EXPRESS family of information modeling languages is described in detail and many examples are given of how to use the different aspects of the languages. Exercises are provided throughout the book, sometimes with answers. These are intended to stimulate your imagination and also to emphasize certain technical points. Two relatively small, but non-trivial, examples of EXPRESS specified information models are described in detail to act as exemplars for your own work.

Here is a summary of what you will find in this book:

- Part I (Chapters 1–8) covers information modeling.

    - Chapters 1–3 provide an introduction to information modeling in general.
    - Chapter 4 consists of a worked example of creating a model and introduces the EXPRESS language family.
    - Chapters 5–7 consider more advanced aspects of information modeling and model documentation.
    - Chapter 8 discusses the connection between information models and information bases.

- Part II covers the family of EXPRESS languages.

    - Chapters 9–16 explain the written EXPRESS language.
    - Chapters 17–20 explain the EXPRESS-G graphics language.
    - Chapters 21–23 explain the EXPRESS-I instance language.

- Several appendices provide examples and additional information

    - Appendix A presents a complete example of an EXPRESS information model about car registration.
    - Appendix B shows instances of those models using EXPRESS-I notation.
    - Appendix C explains how to 'interpret' supertype lattices in a formal way.
    - Appendix D provides guidelines for representing various kinds of relationship cardinalities.

- Appendix E presents a metamodel of EXPRESS written in EXPRESS.
- Appendix F covers the standard constants, functions and procedures that can be used with EXPRESS and EXPRESS-I.

It turns out that information modeling, at least when EXPRESS is used, partakes of aspects from both data modeling and object-oriented programming. Some knowledge of either of these disciplines would be helpful to the reader, but such expertise is not presupposed by the authors. The book is self-contained, although there are plenty of pointers to other pertinent literature.

When we first started writing this book EXPRESS was an ISO Draft International Standard and was in the balloting process for upgrade to International Standard status. At the end of May 1993 the language passed this hurdle and was approved for registration as an ISO International Standard. Part II of the book provides a more readable description of the EXPRESS language family than is given in the somewhat stilted and spare formal definition document, which is Part 11 of ISO 10303. Every effort has been made to be consistent with Part 11 but, should there be any discrepencies, then the language definition in ISO 10303-11 is the primary description.

The EXPRESS-I language has not yet completed the standardization process. Our coverage of the language is limited to the most stable part of EXPRESS-I. The reader is cautioned that the final form of this part of the language may differ from the presentation here.

Typographic conventions

This book was typeset using the LaTeX document preparation system. The main body is displayed in a typeface like the one you are now reading. Other typefaces are used to set off certain parts of the presentation.

- *An italic typeface is used to set off individual words or phrases for emphasis. It is also used for exercises and their answers.*
- `Examples of source will look like this` and the narrative that accompanies them will have this appearance.
- EXPRESS reserved words are written in typewriter style, like this: `Schema`.

Definitions

"When I use a word," Humpty Dumpty said in rather a scornful tone, "it means just what I choose it to mean—neither more nor less."

Alice in Wonderland
Lewis Carroll

ASIM: Application Specialization Information Model.

Attribute: A trait, quality or property that is a characteristic of an entity.

Chunk: One of the several discrete entities that make up a complex entity.

Complex entity: An entity that has subtypes.

Conceptual Schema: A schema that is not configured for a specific implementation.

Constant: A value that does not change over time.

Data: Symbols which represent information for processing purposes, based on explicit or implicit agreements about the meaning of the data.

Datatype: A representation of a value domain. Datatype and type are not used interchangeably; see type.

Entity: A type which represents a collection of conceptual or real world physical objects which have common properties.

Function: An algorithm that operates on parameters and produces a result value of a specified type. In EXPRESS, the values of the parameters may not be modified.

IIM: Integrated Information Model.

Information: Knowledge of facts, processes or ideas.

Information Base: The collection of all values of all types corresponding to its conceptual schema.

ISO: International Organization for Standardization (which is also referred to as the International Standards Organization).

Object: A concept or physical thing which may exist in the real world.

OO – OOP: Object Oriented, Object Oriented Programming.

Part 11: The ISO definitive EXPRESS and EXPRESS-G language reference manual [ISO92b, ISO93].

Part 12: The EXPRESS-I language reference manual [Wil92c].

Population: The contents of an information base.

Procedure: An algorithm that operates on parameters and produces a specific end state. The values of the parameters may be modified.

Proposition: An assertion or denial that a particular state is valid for a value or collection of values.

Rule: A specification of one or more constraints on or between entity values.

Schema: A collection of items forming part or all of a model.

Sparse array: An EXPRESS array which contains unknown values. Note that this is not the typical mathematical definition.

STEP: The ISO 10303 international standard for the exchange of product model data [ISO92c]. See also [Wil93] for an overview of the history and technology of STEP.

TIM: Topical Information Model.

Token: A non-decomposable meaningful lexical element of a language.

Type: A representation of a thing of interest.

Value: A specific occurrence in the domain of some type.

Part I

Information Modeling

This Part provides an introduction to information modeling — why we need it, what it is, how a model may be represented, and a methodology for developing a model. We discuss information modeling principles and lightly touch on the connection between computer systems and information models.

We start in Chapter 1 from a general view of how we describe the world and the difficulties when using natural language for describing the things that we wish to communicate about precisely. This leads to the notion of formal languages for descriptive purposes, and hence models of relevant portions of the real world.

In Chapter 2 we briefly note some organizing techniques that we apply when talking and thinking about things. The main emphasis, though, is on providing examples of several different formal modeling notations. As well as the EXPRESS and EXPRESS-G languages, we show notations drawn from both the data modeling and the Object-Oriented software design worlds. Both lexical and graphical model representations are considered.

A general methodology for creating an information model is presented in Chapter 3. The discussion includes both the human aspects related to the modeling team, and the modeling process.

The methodology is demonstrated in Chapter 4 by an extensive worked example, using the EXPRESS, EXPRESS-G, and EXPRESS-I formal languages for model representation. This helps both to fix ideas and provide an introduction to the languages.

Following this exposure to modeling, some general modeling principles are enumerated in Chapter 5. EXPRESS code is used to illustrate the principles and acts as a further introduction to the language.

A complete information model is often composed from smaller models. Chapter 6 describes several strategies for integrating individually developed models into a cohesive whole. The inverse problem is creating a smaller, but complete, model from a larger one. Methods for accomplishing this are also discussed. Some further aspects of EXPRESS, namely subtyping and schema interfacing, are considered in more detail at this point.

It is not sufficient to just represent an information model using a formal notation; it is also necessary to provide as much assistance to the reader of the model as possible by providing comprehensive explanations. Documentation of a model is the subject of Chapter 7.

The major theme of the book is information modeling and the EXPRESS family of information modeling languages. However, there is also the question of how data representative of a model can be stored. In Chapter 8 we briefly discuss information bases in general, and the EXPRESS view of these in particular. We do no more than skim the surface as this is a major topic in its own right because information modeling partakes of aspects of both data and Object-Oriented modeling and, as well, impinges upon Artificial Intelligence styles of knowledge representation. We also touch upon the subject of computer tools for processing EXPRESS.

Although much of the material and examples are based on the use of the EXPRESS family of languages, the principles and methodology described are generic in nature. Exercises are provided, partly to encourage you to consider more deeply the discussion points in the text, and partly to enable you to practice modeling. In the latter case, you may find it necessary to study the material in the second part of the book which explains the EXPRESS language family in much greater depth.

Chapter 1

Information and communication

The central theme of this book is the representation of information in a
formal and precise manner. We therefore have to try and describe what
information is before we can go on and talk about its representation. Also,
we need to indicate why we want to utilize a formal means of representation.

We are all experts in the subject of information — we use it every day.
Unfortunately, information is an intangible and it is difficult to talk about
intangibles; most of the time we do not even think about such matters but
rest comfortably with an intuitive feel for such things.

1.1   What is information?

Good question!

According to Webster's, information is, among other things,

> **1:** The communication of or reception of knowledge or intelligence

> **2a:** Knowledge obtained from investigation, study or instruction

5

2b: The attribute inherent in and communicated by one or two
or more alternating sequences or arrangements of something (as nucleotides in DNA or binary digits in a computer
program) that produces specific effects

2c: A signal or character (as in a communication system or
computer) representing data.

From the same source, we learn that data is

Factual information (as measurements or statistics) used as a
basis for reasoning, discussion, or calculation.

The salient words that we are concerned with are *knowledge, communication* and *data*.

In general we are concerned about information in the real world. To make
matters more precise, we introduce our own definition of information.

Definition 1 *Information is knowledge of ideas, facts and/or processes.*

Information can be communicated, that is it may be transferred between
two or more partners. (Strictly speaking, as the producer and user of information may be one and the same, only a single 'partner' may be involved.)
This may be done in real time or there may be a delay between one partner
sending the information and another receiving it. For example, the authors wrote this document long before anyone else read it. Consequently,
information storage is just a special case of communication.

The ultimate goal in information modeling is to formulate descriptions
of real world information so that it may be processed and communicated
efficiently without any knowledge of its source and without making any assumptions. These requirements are difficult enough to meet if the partners
are intelligent. It is far more difficult if the partners are computer systems.

Information is communicated by means of *signals* of some sort. As humans those signals must be of such a nature that they impinge on our senses
in one form or another (vision, taste, touch, hearing, smell). For computers
the signals are, at the lowest level, in the form of electrical voltages and cur-
rents. However, we are not concerned here with such low level signals but
rather signals that are cast in some human-level communication medium.
That is, essentially communication through the medium of language.

The communication of information brings its own problems. Typically
we communicate using natural language, but consider the following well
formed sentences:

- Time flies like an arrow.
- Fruit flies like a banana.

These can only be interpreted by applying some knowledge of the real
world things mentioned in the sentences. The words 'flies' in the first sentence is a verb whereas it is a noun in the second sentence. Likewise the
word 'like' is a preposition in the first sentence while it is a verb in the second. These usages can only be disambiguated through context knowledge.

The meaning of a single sentence, such as 'The chicken is ready to eat.', may be inherently ambiguous without a surrounding context.

Even single words may be ambiguous, for example 'braces'. In England men use braces to hold up their trousers but in America they are used to straighten ones teeth.

Another example of ambiguity is the representation of a date (calendar, not fruit). Suppose that a letter was mailed on 1-3-91 and delivered 1-5-91. If the mailing and delivery took place in America then a valid supposition is that delivery took 2 days (from 3rd to 5th January). In England the delivery time would be 2 months (from 1st March to 1st May). If the letter had been mailed from England to America, then a valid supposition would be that it had taken just under a hundred years (March 1891 to January 1991) to be delivered!

In order to extract information from the signals used for communication we have to interpret the signals. When we see a swimmer waving, is he trying to communicate that he has seen us and the water is warm and we should swim as well, or is he drowning and needs help?

Definition 2 *Data are symbols (or functions) which represent information for processing purposes, based on implicit or explicit interpretation rules.*

Or, as Mary Loomis puts it:

Information is data placed in context.

We have already seen some of the problems associated with implicit interpretation rules — the speaker or writer may not realize that the hearer or reader has used a different form of English, for example, or organizes the components of a date in a different order.

Homonyms form a fruitful source of misinterpretation. For example, mentioning the word 'bridge' to a group of people might evince the following mental images.

- The dentist thinks of some bridge-work he has to do on a patient the following day.
- The film enthusiast thinks of the River Kwai.
- The lady thinks of the hand that her partner lost for her last night at the bridge club.
- The engineer thinks of Brooklyn.
- The lover of Victorian poetry thinks of *The Tay Bridge Disaster*.
- The child goes off to play Poohsticks.

Often, classes of things are not distinguished from instances.

- Roger Knutson is the author of the book *Flattened Fauna*.
- Peter Wilson is the owner of the book *Flattened Fauna*.

If you ask me how many books I have got, I will reply with a number. If you ask the same question of the owner of a bookshop, then the answer will also be a number. Do the two numbers have the same meaning? As a private individual I am unlikely to have more than a single copy of each book. A bookshop is likely to have several copies of the current bestsellers. In that case, should you understand the owner's response to be in terms of the number of titles that are in stock, or the number of individually bound items that are in stock? If you asked someone how many book titles they owned, the answer would typically be none, even if they had many books, on the grounds that it is authors and publishers who own book titles.

Sometimes precision is lacking. For example, 'Crimson is red' and 'Scarlet is red', but crimson is not scarlet (nor O'Hara). While at other times there may be too much precision:

> 'A road plan passing one highway over another and routing turning traffic onto connecting roadways which branch only to the right and lead around in a circle to enter the other highway from the right and thus merge traffic without left-hand turns or direct crossings.'

This is the definition of *cloverleaf* given in Webster's, but it only applies to countries that drive on the right-hand side of the road; there are many countries that have drive on the left rules. Sometimes both precision and imprecision can be mixed. Again from Webster's, this is a definition for a clock:

> 'A registering device with a dial and indicator attached to a mechanism to measure or gauge its functioning or to record its output.'

In general, the sender of information attempts to encode the information in such a manner that it will be understood precisely by the intended recipients[1]. That is, the sender has to estimate the implicit interpretation rules that the receiver will use and then encode the information according to his perception of those rules. The receiver then decodes the transmission according to either his actual set of implicit interpretation rules (which probably differ from the set assumed by the sender) or according to the receiver's estimate of the sender's rules (which the sender may not have used anyway). In any event, there is a high probability of miscommunication.

Using a more formal approach, let I and D stand for information and data respectively; also let R be the set of interpretation rules that produce information from data. Symbolically we can then write

$$R(D) \mapsto I$$

to mean that applying the interpretation rules R to the data D produces the (interpreted) information I. There is also the inverse process required which is necessary to define the data which represents some information. We write this as

$$R_{-1}(I) \mapsto D$$

---

[1] As with every generalization, there are exceptions; notably politicians in this case.

Combining the above, *provided R is invariant in an information system,* then

$$R(R_{-1}(I)) \mapsto I$$

i.e., provided the interpretation rules are constant and complete, it is possible to exchange information with no loss.

What are the problems? In general, information will be encoded in terms of data by a 'sender'; a 'receiver' will get the data and decode it into information. Using subscripts s and r for sender and receiver respectively, this can be denoted as

$$R_r(R_{-1_s}(I_s)) \mapsto I_r$$

The question is: does $I_r = I_s$? And the answer is: probably not! There are several cases to consider in explaining the answer. In the explanation we introduce one more symbol, $\mathcal{R}$ to denote an estimated set of interpretation rules.

1. Sender and receiver use the same rules (i.e., $R_s = R_r = R$).

$$R(R_{-1}(I_s)) \mapsto I_r$$

   In this case, then, $I_r = I_s$.

2. Sender and receiver have no knowledge of each others rules and these are probably different (i.e., $R_s \neq R_r$).

$$R_r(R_{-1_s}(I_s)) \mapsto I_r$$

   and $I_r \neq I_s$ except when coincidently $R_s = R_r$.

3. The sender tries to improve the communication by estimating the receiver's rules and uses these for encoding.

$$R_r(\mathcal{R}_{-1_r}(I_s)) \mapsto I_r$$

   and $I_r \neq I_s$ except when coincidently $R_r = \mathcal{R}_r$.

4. The receiver tries to improve communication by estimating the rules used by the sender and uses these for decoding.

$$\mathcal{R}_s(R_{-1_s}(I_s)) \mapsto I_r$$

   and $I_r \neq I_s$ except when coincidently $R_s = \mathcal{R}_s$.

5. Both sender and receiver try to improve communication by estimating the other's rules and use these for encoding and decoding.

$$\mathcal{R}_s(\mathcal{R}_{-1_r}(I_s)) \mapsto I_r$$

   and $I_r \neq I_s$ except when coincidently $\mathcal{R}_s = \mathcal{R}_r$.

Out of these various scenarios, only one out of the five appears to offer any hope of reliable information communication. This is case (1) where both sender and receiver knowlingly use the same rules. However, even this is optimistic in the real world, as anyone who has written a computer program and then revisits it some months later can testify — we don't always remember what we meant when we said something.

1.2   Information models

In order to be able to exchange information we need both the data that represents the information together with the interpretation rules. To exchange information reliably, all parties in the communication process need to operate with the same set of interpretation rules. In order to ensure this, it is necessary to reach agreement on the interpretation rules. Thus they need to be made explicit, rather than implicit.

Definition 3 *An information model is a formal description of types of ideas, facts and processes which together form a model of a portion of interest of the real world and which provides an* explicit set of interpretation rules. *(If an information model is written in* EXPRESS *or any other computer sensible representation, it has the additional quality of being computer processible.)*

By type we mean to imply a general form of a 'thing'. For example, a *car* brings to mind a four-wheeled motorized vehicle that has at least one seat. On the other hand, the *red Honda CRX Si, license plate SNM 467* is a particular *instance* of a car.

We insist that an information model has a formal description rather than an informal description. That is, a description built from some limited set of primitive concepts each of which has a precise meaning. The primitive concepts can be built into more complex constructs via a defined set of rules to produce, in turn, further items which also have precise meanings. Ideally, an information model is a complete, precise and *unambiguous* representation. We wish to avoid, as far as possible, the vagaries associated with our normal means of communication.

Information modeling is an outgrowth of data modeling and the question of classifying a model as being an information or a data model can be somewhat fuzzy. Data modeling is concerned with specifying the appearance and structure within a computer system of the data which represents particular types of information. Information modeling, as we implied earlier, has a goal of describing information so that the representative data *could* be computer processed. Note that this does not require that it be processed or even that it should be so processed. Thus, one distinction between data and information modeling is that one is explicitly targeted for computer processing of the data while the other has the potential (which may, of course, be realized) for such processing.

The other major distinction is in the treatment of the interpretation rules. In an information model these must be made explicit and formally documented. In a data model, the rules are typically implicit; even if they are made explicit, they are informally documented.

1.3 Exercises

1.1 Write three sentences that are ambiguous along the lines of 'The chicken is ready to eat'. Can you think of more?

1.2 How many ways can a date be written? Are they all in use? What other sorts of dating sytsems are there in addition to Anno Domine style dates?

1.3 Ouida is said to have said 'All rowed fast but none so fast as stroke'. The word 'stroke' has many other meanings than in this quotation. How many ways can you interpret the word 'stroke'? Write sentences which provide examples for each meaning.

1.4 How many descriptions can you think of for a timepiece? List them.

1.5 Write a more general definition for 'cloverleaf' that makes no assumptions about which side of the road people drive on.

1.4 Further reading

William Kent [Ken78] provides a stimulating introduction to the nature and description of information and its representation in computer systems. The emphasis is on the ambiguity of natural language and he poses many thought provoking questions. Bernd Wenzel [Wen91] has applied some of these to the question of information modeling.

Mary Loomis [Loo87, page 3] is one of the few authors from the database community who make clear the important distinction between information and data.

The use of (the English) language in general is admirably treated by H. W. Fowler [Fow65] and by Sir Ernest Gowers [Gow73] in their classic texts on the subject.

We have used *Webster's Ninth New Collegiate Dictionary* [Web85] for the definitions stated as being from Webster's.

Poohsticks is the game of throwing sticks into a stream from a bridge and seeing which comes out first on the other side. This was described and named by A. A. Milne [Mil28]. Readers who are interested in the other two literary works mentioned can find them in the Bibliography as items [Knu87] and [McG34].

Chapter 2

Models and representations

Entities are a state of mind. No two people agree on what the real world view is.

Metaxides

A model is a representation of something; it is an abstraction. The thing being modeled need not be real — think of plastic models of the starship *Enterprise*. In this case the thing is imaginary while the model is real. Models are typically built to aid understanding. Also, because they are abstractions that omit inessential details, they are often easier to construct and manipulate than the thing they represent. However, as we shall see, an information model is not necessarily simple, either to create or to manipulate.

We distinguish two sorts of model here, namely a conceptual model and a concrete model.

Definition 4 *A conceptual information model is independent of any particular instantiation form.*

Definition 5 *A concrete model is an information model that is specialized to take account of a particular instantiation method. (This is what is typically known as a data model.)*

An information (data) model may be *instantiated* or *populated* to represent collections of **particular** ideas, facts or processes.

Definition 6 *An instantiated model consists of the data that represents instances of the things defined in an information model.*

We are principally concerned with conceptual information models. A conceptual model is a view about real world information and is itself, therefore, communicable information. The model needs to be organized in such a manner to aid understanding by the recipient, which will essentially be a human as opposed to a computer system; even if the intended recipient is a software system this is still a human artifact.

Before examining ways of representing models it is useful to look briefly at some of the methods that we humans use to organize our thoughts.

2.1 Organizing principles

There are some organizing principles and concepts that we seem to use time after time, whether consciously or unconsciously.

2.1.1 Categorization

We tend to group things into categories or classes. Each member of a category has some aspects that are common to other members and some individual aspects. For example, we can talk about vehicles in general with one common aspect being that a vehicle provides a means of transportation. Within the general vehicle class we might split it up into sub-categories of truck, bus and car. The car category may be further subdivided into limousines, sedans, wagons and sports cars. And so on.

The higher levels are more general than the lower levels. Sometimes categorization is referred to as generalization-specialization. Thinking of things in the real world, the number of actual examples of things in the higher categories is greater than the number of things in a lower category — there are more cars than there are sports cars, for example.

Categorization provides one means of controlling the level of detail which is required to describe something; it is a form of abstraction.

2.1.2 Grouping

We tend to put like things together. Think of a library. There are many ways in which the books in a library may be organized on the shelves. They could be grouped by size (the largest books on the lowest shelves and the smallest books on the highest shelves). They could be grouped alphabetically by author — all the A's in one bookcase, all the B's in another. They could be grouped by subject — the books on a particular topic are placed in one location.

Grouping provides a means of partitioning a wide variety of things into smaller clumps of things that are relevant to some sub-topic within an overall topic. Grouping may be based on some categorizations but provides no abstraction.

2.1.3 Shielding from details

When describing something we typically postpone talking about the details of the thing. In describing a room, for example, we may talk about the ceiling, the floor, the walls, the windows and doors — it has one ceiling, one floor, four walls, three windows and two doors. If someone didn't understand what a window was, then we would then describe the window. We wouldn't normally describe rooms and windows together.

In general, detail is only introduced when necessary. In other words, descriptions of things are often given in terms of other things, which are in turn described by yet other, more detailed items. Eventually this process stops at some atomic level where items can no longer be decomposed. The atomic level in information models is typically character strings and numbers.

This is another form of abstraction.

2.1.4 Aggregations and ordering

Consider a text book. These are normally composed of several different kinds of things — a table of contents, an index, and a number of chapters. Each chapter is composed of a number of sections. Within the book the ordering of the chapters is important — earlier chapters typically provide the foundation for topics discussed in later parts of the book.

The concept that something is composed of a bunch, or more formally an *aggregation*, of like things, and that they may be sequenced, is an important concept.

2.2   Terminology

We will shortly be looking at various ways of formally representing a model, but first we need to define the terminology that we will be using. Information modeling, as practised via EXPRESS, has connections with both data modeling, as practised by the database community, and some aspects of the design of Object-Oriented systems. Models are abstracts of the real world, so real world things also come into play.

We will call a specific, identifiable thing in the real world an *object*. An example of a real world object is the particular chair you are sitting in as you read this. Moving from the particular to the generic, we will use the word *class* to refer to the kind, or type, of a particular object. Thus 'chair' can be a class when no particular chair is intended. There can be many objects in a class — your chair, my chair, my grandfather's rocking chair, etc. An object can be considered to be an instance of a class.

In the model abstraction of the real world, we will call the thing that represents a class an *entity*. Just as real world objects are instances of real world classes, we can consider that there are instances of entities, which we will call *instances*.

As we have implied, there are parallels between creating an OO program and creating a model. The OO world has its own terminology, although there appears, as yet, to be no general consensus on exactly what it is. How-

Table 2.1: Classes, objects, entities and instances.

	Real world	Modeling	OO Programming
Generic	Class	Entity	Class
Particular	Object	Instance	Object

ever, the OO community appears to use the word 'class' when we would use 'entity', and they use the word 'object' where we use 'instance'. Table 2.1 shows the different uses of the words. We prefer our terminology as it clearly distinguishes between real world things and modeling constructs.

2.3 Representations

Having stated that an information model must have a formal description there arises the question of how to represent such a thing. Obviously there must be some more precise means of doing this than via natural language. As might be expected there are two natural means of representing abstract things — either by a written language or by pictures. In either case, the representation uses a finite structured collection of predefined symbols which, hopefully, provide a rich enough vocabulary for stating everything that needs to be said.

The graphics vocabulary includes icons for representing the major items comprising a model together with a means of connecting the icons in a meaningful manner. The written, or lexical, forms includes a basic set of symbols (words) and rules (grammar) about how these may be combined to produce 'sentences' describing the things of interest in the model.

In an information model, the things of particular interest are ideas, facts and processes, together with the relationships between these. We will use the generic term *item* to refer to these. Also of major interest are restrictions on and between these items. For example, we may be creating a model about people. A person has ancestors and may have descendants, but one restriction is that a person cannot be his own ancestor. We use the term *constraints* when talking about restrictions.

Historically the means of representing a model have been linked with the data structures used within the concrete model together with likely questions that may be asked of the data. Thus, typically both a Data Specification Language (DSL) and a Data Manipulation Language (DML) have been created as a pair. A DML is also referred to as a Query Language (QL). Given this fact, the languages then tend to be configured more towards the data representation paradigm envisaged by the language creator than the real world that the model is an image of.

The most ubiquitous paradigm has been the relational data model. In this model a table is the underlying construct, where a table corresponds to some real world class of objects, or at least as much of a real world object that a table is able to represent. A table consists of a number of columns, each corresponding to some simple property of the class of object in question. A row in a table provides the specific data values for one instance of the class (i.e., a row corresponds to a real world object). The set of data values in each row in a table must be unique and an object instance is identified by its set of defining values. These values must be simple (e.g., a character string or a number). We can argue, though, that these *simple* representation types might not be as simple as they appear. A string, for example, is an aggregate value — a list of characters.

A relational model may be more or less rigorously constructed. There are varying levels of rigor which are called *normal form*. Suffice it to say here that different normal forms have an effect on the required structuring of the tables and columns in a model.

This model has proved to be adequate for modeling simple portions of the world, such as a personnel database, but are inadequate for more complex environments, such as engineering data.

The relational model has been extended in various ways, for example by the Entity-Relationship model which specifically represents associations between objects. A somewhat different approach has been taken by considering a model in terms of entities and the functions that may be applied to the entities.

More recently interest has moved to the Object-Oriented paradigm. Here object instances have (possibly complex) properties and are identifiable by some means other than a data value. Most of the ideas in this area have come from the OO programming field. In this case the intent of the models has been to represent the objects and their behavior as they would appear in some algorithmic application. These models typically support the notion of *classes* (which correspond to entities in the data oriented world) together with the idea of inheritance (i.e., properties of a class can be inherited from a super-class).

The following sections provide a brief overview of the some of the languages that are used for data and information modeling. In each case a representation of a very simple model is presented. This model is, in words:

> *A car is made by a manufacturer. Each manufacturer has a unique name. A manufacturer constructs cars in several models and a car is of a particular model. A manufacturer gives a serial number to each car he produces and this is unique across all cars produced by that manufacturer. Each model also has a name, and this is unique across all models. A car has a year of production.*

The terms that we use may not exactly correspond to those used in the definitions of the languages but rather have been chosen to provide a consistent terminology. Likewise, due to the graphics limitations of the processor used, some of the language graphics symbols have been changed.

Before delving into details we need to define some more terminology.

Entity: An entity is a modeling construct that is a representation of some item of interest in the real world.

Property: Entities have properties. A property is a particular aspect of an entity. Properties may represent values, constraints, behavior, etc.

Attribute: An attribute is a particular kind of property that identifies an interesting trait and how it is represented.

Constraint: A constraint is a particular kind of property that specifies a restriction on other properties of an entity, or the entity taken as a whole, or on relationships.

Simple type: A simple type is an elementary representation that cannot be further subdivided. Typical simple types are numbers, strings of characters, and boolean values (i.e., true or false).

Relationship: An association between two constructs in a model. A relationship may be implied or explicitly identified.

Cardinality: The specification of the number of instances of one construct that can be associated with one instance of a related construct. This is described in more detail later, but some examples may clarify the concept for now.

- A person has one head and a head can only belong to one person.
- A person has two legs and a leg can only belong to one person.
- A person can have many addresses and an address may be for zero or more people.

2.4 Graphical representations

A graphical model representation utilizes symbols or icons of various shapes to represent the major items in a model. These icons are labeled with the 'name' of the particular type of item that is being represented. For example, a rectangular box may represent a 'thing' in a language. In a particular model about vehicles, we may wish to describe cars and trucks and buses. In this case there would be three rectangular boxes, one labeled 'car', one labeled 'truck', and one labeled 'bus'.

Lines drawn between the icons are used to indicate that the items represented by the icons are connected or related in some manner. Typically, these connecting lines are also labeled in some manner to indicate the type or meaning of the connection. Continuing the vehicle example, all vehicles (at least of the types described above) have wheels. Hence we may wish to include wheel among the things of interest in our model. This means another box labeled 'wheel' and a connection between this and the car, truck and bus boxes. The line would then be labelled in some manner to indicate that a car has wheels, a truck has wheels, etc. Also, an indication that a wheel may belong to a car, a truck, or a bus. Some graphical languages use

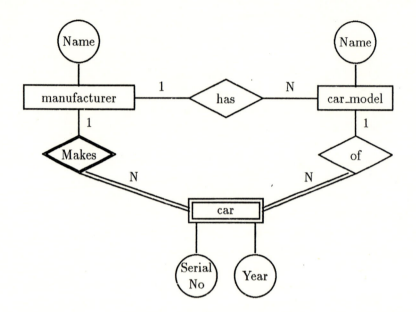

Figure 2.1: Entity-Relationship representation of the car example.

special icons for describing the form of a relationship while others just use labeling techniques.

In graphical models the constraints that can be represented are usually fairly restricted, and are typically limited to counting types of constraints (e.g., cardinalities). For example, every vehicle has at least four wheels, but trucks and buses may have more. On the other hand, a particular wheel can only be used by one car or one truck or one bus, or may not be used by any of these (e.g., it is in the garage waiting to be sold).

2.4.1 Entity-Relationship

The Entity-Relationship (ER) model was introduced by Chen in 1976 as a generalization of network, relational and set models. Figure 2.1 illustrates an ER rendition for the example model.

ER adopts the view that the real world consists of entities and relationships and incorporates some of the semantics of the real world. An *entity* is a 'thing' that can be distinctly identified. This is represented by a rectangular box. A *relationship* is an association among entities. These are represented by diamond shaped boxes. Lines are used to connect entities and relationships. Cardinality constraints can be specified on the lines joining entity and relationship symbols. Entities may have attributes. An *attribute* is a simple type, such as a number or a string. These are indicated

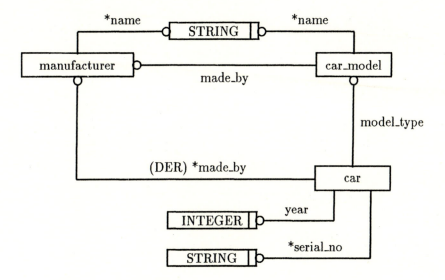

Figure 2.2: EXPRESS-G representation of the car example.

by the circles.

ER does not support inheritance hierarchies, although later extensions have added this concept.

2.4.2 EXPRESS-G

EXPRESS-G, which is one of the subjects of this book, was created in 1990 as a means of graphically displaying models written in the EXPRESS lexical language. An example is shown in Figure 2.2.

Rectangular boxes are used to represent entities, which correspond to the real world items of interest. An entity may have attributes, which are the specific properties of interest. These may be either simple (e.g., numbers or strings) or complex (e.g., another entity) types. Lines are used to connect an entity with its attributes. The lines are labelled with the name of the attribute, together with any cardinality constraints. There is an implicit relationship between an entity and its attributes.

Supertype/subtype inheritance hierarchies are supported.

An EXPRESS-G model may stand by itself, in which case any additional constraints should be described by accompanying text. More typically, there would be a full EXPRESS model which contained all the constraints explicitly.

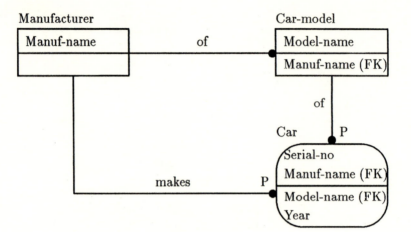

Figure 2.3: IDEF1X representation of the car example.

2.4.3 IDEF1X

IDEF1X is a formally specified graphical language developed by the US Air
Force ICAM project for relational data modeling. The language is most
popular in the USA. The basic constructs are the *entity*, the *attribute* and
the *relationship*. An IDEF1X model of the example is shown in Figure 2.3.

Boxes represent entities, with the name of the entity being placed on top
of the box. An entity is defined as a set of attributes, where each attribute
is in a one-to-one correspondence with the entity. Attributes are limited to
simple types and are listed inside the entity box. A relationship associates
two entities and is drawn as a line connecting the entity boxes. A role name
or phrase, conveying the meaning of the relationship is placed by the line.
Also specified is the cardinality of the child entity to exactly one parent
entity (child entities are those at the circled end of the relationship line).
One or more attributes must be selected to form a *key* whose value set can
uniquely identify any instance of a particular entity. The attributes forming
the key are listed in the top half of the entity box.

Supertype/subtype hierarchies are supported.

IDEF1X entails an underlying methodology which guides the modeling
process, particularly by imposition of third normal form, thus IDEF1X
models have a strong relational feel. The methodology suggests that things
which are inexpressible in the graphical language should be described using
some form of structured text. Structured text is also used to explicate the
graphical representation.

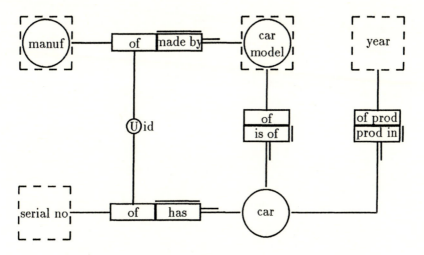

Figure 2.4: NIAM representation of the car example.

2.4.4 NIAM

NIAM (Nijssen's Information Analysis Method) is a formal graphical language that was originally developed for the analysis of natural language sentences. The language is in widespread use within Europe for data modeling. A NIAM model of the example is shown in Figure 2.4.

Each noun in a sentence is represented as a node in a network. The relationships are the bi-directional edges of the network. The emphasis in a model is on the relationships; both the meaning of the relationship and the constraints on it. Each constraint either refines the relationship between two nodes or specifies a restriction among two or more relationships. Grouping on the constraints can generate an equivalent relational model.

The nodes are either *lexical object types (lots)* or *non-lexical object types (nolots)*. Lexical (lots) refers to language; the means of representation and communication, or the naming of things. Non-lexical (nolots) refers to physical things or mental concepts; the things which we communicate about. We represent lots by dashed boxes and nolots by circles. A *fact* is a relationship between two nodes. An *idea fact* connects two nolots and a *bridge fact* connects a nolot and a lot. Each fact contains two *roles*. A role describes the meaning or nature of the relationship of its adjacent node to the other node in the relationship. Facts and roles are represented by the paired boxes.

Supertype/subtype hierarchies are supported and constraints may be placed on the allowable combination of subtype instances.

In the terminology introduced earlier, a nolot is equivalent to an entity. There is no equivalent idea to an attribute.

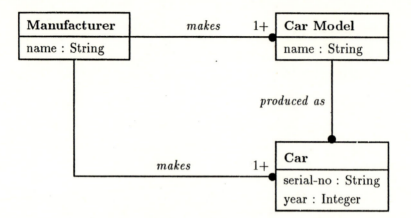

Figure 2.5: OMT representation of the car example.

NIAM entails an underlying methodology which imposes fifth normal form, thus NIAM models have a strong relational feel. The methodology suggests that things not expressible in the language should be described through structured text. The graphical model is normally explicated by associated textual descriptions.

2.4.5   OMT

The *Object Modeling Technique* (OMT) was originally a graphical notation for the modeling of classes for Object-Oriented Programming (OOP) applications. The meaning has since been expanded to include a methodology for Object-Oriented modeling, and the notation has also been expanded to cater for dynamic and functional modeling as well as the original object modeling. Here, we concentrate on the object modeling notation.

An OMT model of the example is shown in Figure 2.5.

The basic constructs are the *object class*, the *attribute*, the *operation* and the *association*. For the sake of consistency, the word *entity* will be used instead of class. An entity describes a group of objects with similar properties (i.e., attributes), common behavior (i.e., operations), common relationships to other entities (i.e., associations), and common semantics. An attribute is a data value held by the entity instances. An attribute must be a pure data value (e.g., an integer or a string) and must not be an entity instance. Operations describe the behavior of an entity. An association (i.e., relationship in the terms described earlier) describes a physical or conceptual connection between entities. A relationship may contain attributes.

Supertype/subtype inheritance hierarchies are supported.

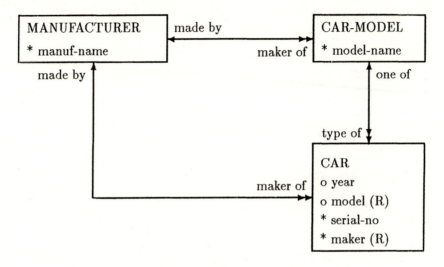

Figure 2.6: Shlaer-Mellor representation of the car example.

2.4.6 Shlaer-Mellor

Shlaer and Mellor in their book *Object-Oriented Systems Analysis* discuss a methodology for information modeling. During their discussions they suggest various forms for describing a model. These include the use of example relational tables, a graphical language, and structured text. All of these are specified in a semi-formal manner, but not with the rigor of the other languages — the specifications are cast in the form of suggestions rather than requirements. We limit our focus to their graphical form, which will be denoted as the SM language for brevity.

The basic constructs are the *object*, the *attribute* and the *relationship*. In the following descriptions we will use the term *entity* instead of the SM term *object* to match the usage in other languages. An SM model of the example is shown in Figure 2.6.

An entity is defined as a set of attributes, where each attribute in an entity captures a separate aspect of the entity and the attributes are mutually independent (that is, they take on their values independently of one another). Like IDEF1X, the SM language requires that there be a set of key attributes; these are prefixed by an asterisk. Non-key attributes are prefixed by a small circle. A relationship is the abstraction of a set of associations that hold systematically between different kinds of things. The relationship is stated in terms of the entities that represent objects, verb phrases conveying its meaning (roles) and the cardinality of the entities. Relationships may have attributes.

Supertype/subtype hierarchies are supported.

The methodology requires normalization into at least second normal

```
DECLARE Manufacturer() ==> ENTITY
DECLARE Name(Manufacturer) ==> STRING

DECLARE CarModel() ==> ENTITY
DECLARE Name(CarModel) ==> STRING
DECLARE MadeBy(CarModel) ==> Manufacturer

DECLARE Car() ==> ENTITY
DECLARE SerialNo(Car) ==> STRING
DECLARE Year(Car) ==> INTEGER
DECLARE Model(Car) ==> CarModel
DEFINE  MadeBy(Car) ==> MadeBy(Model(Car))
```

Figure 2.7: DAPLEX representation of the car example.

form. Therefore, SM models have a relational flavour.

2.5   Lexical representations

A lexical language uses words and mathematical symbols to represent the
items within a model. Particular symbols (or tokens) in the language have
precisely defined meaning (semantics). The ways that these can be combined are formally specified. In essence, that means that algorithms can be
written to check the validity of the statements in the model, and that the
language is 'computer processible'. That is, software tools may be written
to assist in model creation and checking.

A model consists of both the items of interest and the constraints on
those items. Lexical languages typically have some portion devoted to
means of specifying constraints. If a complete programming language is
included, then very complex constraints can be formally specified, although
whether this is always practical is another matter.

2.5.1   DAPLEX

The DAPLEX language, published in 1981, is an example of a *functional*
model representation. Figure 2.7 illustrates the representation of the example model.

The basic constructs are the *entity* and the *function*. These are used to
represent conceptual objects and their properties. A function has a name,
may take some parameters, and returns a set of entities of a given type.
The language has a built in set of defined types, including ENTITY and
simple types such as STRING and INTEGER. An entity is specified via a
function taking no parameters. The components of an entity are specified
by declaring functions that take the entity as a parameter.

```
ENTITY manufacturer;
  name : STRING;
UNIQUE
  ur1 : name;
END_ENTITY;

ENTITY car_model;
  name    : STRING;
  made_by : manufacturer;
UNIQUE
  ur1 : name;
END_ENTITY;

ENTITY car;
  model         : car_model;
  serial_number : STRING;
  year          : INTEGER;
DERIVE
  made_by : manufacturer := model.made_by;
UNIQUE
  ur2 : made_by, serial_number;
END_ENTITY;
```

Figure 2.8: EXPRESS representation of the car example.

Some constraints may be specified via the functional programming language provided. However, unlike a lot of the other languages, cardinality constraints are not straightforward to compose.

2.5.2   EXPRESS

EXPRESS was developed by the international standards community for the purposes of information modeling as applied to describing the information required to design, build and maintain products. It was developed after both NIAM and IDEF1X had been applied to the problem and were found lacking. The initial versions of the language, then called DSL, were developed in the early eighties within the US Air Force funded PDDI program by Doug Schenck of McDonnell Douglas. It is a formally specified structured language, together with a formally defined graphical language called EXPRESS-G for representing a subset of the textual form, and an instance language called EXPRESS-I for showing how values of entity declarations might be written. The basic constructs are the *entity* and the *attribute*. An EXPRESS model of the example is shown in Figure 2.8.

An entity is defined as a set of attributes. An attribute specifies a *data type* (and hence a *domain*) and a cardinality. A data type may be a primi-

```
MANUFACTURER(Name: c) key(Name);

CAR_MODEL(Name: c, MadeBy: MANUFACTURER) key(Name);

CAR(Model: CAR_MODEL, SerialNo: c, Year: i2,
    MadeBy: MANUFACTURER) key(SerialNo, MadeBy);
```

Figure 2.9: GEM representation of the car example.

tive of the language such as *number, real, string,* etc. or it may be an entity (i.e., reference to another entity). The relationship between entities is subsumed in the *entity data type* or the domains of the attributes; the roles are represented by the names of the attributes. The entity or its attributes (and relationships) can be further described or refined by constraints written in a procedural language form.

Supertype/subtype hierarchies are supported, together with constraints on the allowable combinations of subtypes.

EXPRESS does not mandate a methodology and is not constrained by normalization, although models may be written in a normal form if desired. EXPRESS models typically have an object oriented flavor. The formal language is usually explicated by structured explanatory text.

2.5.3   GEM

GEM was created in 1983 and belongs to the ER model representation family. A rendition of the example model is given in Figure 2.9.

The basic elements in a GEM model are the *entity* and *attribute*. An entity represent a real world object. It is composed of attributes. The attributes may be single valued, a reference to an entity, or be set-valued. Attributes may also represent a hierarchy.

A GEM model is somewhat richer than a relational model as it allows for complex attributes.

2.5.4   SQL

SQL, typically pronounced 'sequel', originally stood for 'Structured Query Language'. It consists of a set of facilities for defining, manipulating and controlling data in a relational database. The current version of the language is described in a 1989 ANSI and ISO standard. Work is in progress to extend the language and enhaced versions should be standardized during the nineties. Figure 2.10 gives the SQL version of the example model.

The fundamental concept in SQL is the *table*, which corresponds more or less to the *entity* in our terminology. A table is composed of columns of values, which must be of simple types. A column corresponds to an

```
CREATE TABLE MANUFACTURER
     ( NAME        CHAR(20) NOT NULL,
       PRIMARY KEY (NAME) )

CREATE TABLE CAR_MODEL
     ( NAME        CHAR(20) NOT NULL,
       MADE_BY     CHAR(20) NOT NULL,
       PRIMARY KEY (NAME),
       FOREIGN KEY (MADE_BY) REFERENCES MANUFACTURER )

CREATE TABLE CAR
     ( SERIAL_NO   CHAR(50) NOT NULL,
       YEAR        SMALLINT NOT NULL,
       MODEL       CHAR(20) NOT NULL,
       MADE BY     CHAR(20) NOT NULL,
       PRIMARY KEY (SERIAL_NO, MADE_BY),
       FOREIGN KEY (MADE_BY) REFERENCES MANUFACTURER,
       FOREIGN KEY (MODEL) REFERENCES CAR_MODEL )
```

Figure 2.10: SQL representation of the car example.

attribute. A primary key consists of one or more attributes whose values uniquely identify an instance of an entity (i.e., a row in a table). The data specification part of SQL does not recognize the concept of a relationship. Constraints between attribute values in a table may be specified by logical expressions according to the DML portion of the language.

Following from the underlying relational model, supertype/subtype hierarchies are not supported.

2.6 Graphical vs. lexical representations

Both forms of model representation have their advantages and disadvantages. In general we have found that using a mix of representations during the modeling process has some significant benefits. Each representation implies a particular view of the world (or at least modeling of the world). Using multiple representations provides a multi-view thus helping to ensure an unbiased and complete model.

Graphical models are excellent for group explanations and work — it is much easier to sketch a few boxes and lines on a blackboard than it is to write reams of text. The associations between the items in the model are also easy to follow — just follow the lines. The down side to this is that models can get very complex and take up a lot of wall space. It then becomes more difficult both to layout the model and to follow the connections.

A danger to be guarded against with graphical models is that model development may be superficial (e.g., it looks right, so it must be). Further, a large part of modeling is documenting the constraints and it is notoriously difficult to provide a graphical language with enough richness to capture all that needs to be said in this regard.

Some software tools may exist to help generate the model drawings. However, these are unlikely to be able to offer much, if anything, in the way of checking the correctness of the model. Effectively, a graphical model is not computer processable — what you see is all you've got!

On the other hand, lexical model representations are typically designed to be computer processable. There may be, then, a plethora of tools available to assist the modeler, ranging from specialized text editors and parsers to compilers and complete modeling support systems. There is also the possibility for automatic translation from one model representation to another, and for the generation of implementations of the model for simulation and test purposes and quality assurance.

Lexical representations often have good formal definitions of the semantics and, depending on the language, mathematical underpinnings. In some cases, though, the models may be non-intuitive; for example when the representation is in formal mathematical terms such as predicate logic which is not within the typical skill set of the putative modeler.

Complex constraints and rules are possible to describe using a lexical language if it includes some algorithmic capabilities.

Lexical models, though, are not necessarily easy to follow; in some sense they are like procedural code which is not the easiest thing in the world to read without plentiful comments.

Summarizing, the strengths of graphical representations lie in their ability to display the structure of a model, while those of lexical representations lie in their ability to formally document the details and constraints of a model.

In general it is essential, whatever model representation form is chosen, to document the formal model with as much explanatory material as possible.

2.7   Exercises

2.1 Develop a categorization system for non-fiction books. (Hint — think how they are organised in a library).

2.2 Develop a categorization scheme for the goods sold in your local grocery store.

2.3 A book is written by one or more authors and is printed by a single publisher. A book is owned by a person. Create a model using firstly EXPRESS-G and secondly using EXPRESS that captures these statements.

2.4 Create EXPRESS-G and EXPRESS models of a bicycle. Assume that a bicycle consists of a frame, a saddle, handlebars, pedals, and two wheels.

2.5 How does your model change if you include a chain connecting the pedals to the rear wheel, and also if you consider that a wheel has a hub, spokes, a rim and a tire?

2.6 Use any two other languages to represent the book and bicycle models.

2.8 Further reading

Stonebraker [Sto88] provides a wide ranging compendium of reprints of papers on database systems and modeling representations. This includes the original papers by Chen on the Entity-Relationship model [Che76], by Shipman on DAPLEX [Shi81], and by Zaniolo [Zan83] on GEM. A somewhat later view of database languages is given by Bancilhon and Buneman [BB90]. These early database language forms are still being developed; Mannino, for example, has described an Object-Oriented functional database language called O^2FDL [MCB90] while Poulovassilis [Pou92] has recently discussed the implementation of the FDL functional language.

The original Entity-Relationship model has been extended by several authors, for example Misic, Velasevic and Lazarevic [MVL92]. Perhaps the most interesting extension from our viewpoint is by Elmasri and Navathe [EN89] which adds in super- and subtyping and inheritance.

The original IDEF1X specifications are given in [IDE85]. A commercial variant is described by Mary Loomis [Loo87] and more recently the application of IDEF1X to database design has been published by Bruce [Bru92].

Nijssen first introduced NIAM in the early eighties [NV82]. The most accesible source is by Nijssen and Halpin [NH89].

Normalisation is described in any book on relational databases. As well as the ones cited above, several others are noted in the Bibliography. Ceri and Gottlob [CG86] provide a Prolog algorithm for the automatic normalisation of a database schema.

The first widely read publication of OMT was in the Communications of the ACM [BPR88]. Since then the methodology has been broadened extensively by Rumbaugh and his co-workers [RBP+91]. One chapter in their book describes the application of their techniques in developing a compiler for their model representation language. Perhaps unintentionally, this highlights some of the problems with graphical languages versus lexical languages. A case study of the application of OMT is given by Bruegge *et al* [BBJS92].

Shlaer and Mellor [SM88a] present a variety of informal and semi-formal data modeling techniques and representations. Fayad and his colleagues have described how they applied these methods to engineer the requirements of a mission planning system [FHRK93].

Date [Dat89] provides an insiders view of SQL, warts and all.

An ISO Technical Report [ISO87] utilises several different kinds of modeling languages to represent conceptual models of a particular example.

The PDDI project, which saw the birth of EXPRESS, is described by Birchfield [BK85] with more detail given in [PDD84]. In May 1993 EXPRESS passed the international ballot for upgrade from a Draft International Standard [ISO92b] to an International Standard [ISO93]. The standard document also includes the specification for the EXPRESS-G language. The companion EXPRESS-I language is also being developed as an ISO standard, but is at a much earlier stage in the process [Wil92c]. The principal use of these languages has been to formally represent information of products within the STEP standard [Tra93, Wil93], although they have also been used in many other modeling projects.

There are other languages that we have not touched on here, principally those used, or being developed by, the artificial intelligence community. Typically these languages are based on first order logic. Examples include Conceptual Graphs, which was mainly developed by John Sowa [Sow84, Sow91, NNGE92], and the Knowledge Interchange Format (KIF) [GF92, P+92]. This latter effort, though, has its critics [Gin91]. Even more exotic is situation theory where the developers are inventing new mathematics [Dev91]. There are also the formal specification languages such as VDM [Jon86, PL92] and the Z language developed by Spivey [Spi92] which are used in software specifications. Like the logic languages, these tend towards mathematical notations. Even so, Misic and his co-workers [MVL92] have used Z as the formal specification for an extended ER graphical language.

Several authors have compared modeling languages from different aspects. For example, Wilson [Wil91b] provides a detailed technical comparison between several of the languages described here while Batra [BHB90] descibes a human factors comparison between relational and EER modeling.

It is possible to map between models developed for different implementation technologies. Between them, Elmasri [EN89] and Batini [BCN92] describe algorithms for mapping between their EER model and relational, hierarchical, and network models. Sanderson [SS92] has extended this by developing mapping algorithms between EXPRESS and the EER model, and by extension also to the other models.

Research has recently started on developing kinds of meta-languages that will enable general mapping between lower level languages. Both KIF and Conceptual Graphs have been proposed as contenders. Another contender is a higher order logical language, known as the SUMM (Semantic Unification Meta Model) [F+92], being developed by James Fulton and others [ZW91, Ful92b, Ful92a]. This started as a project to unify EXPRESS, IDEF1X and NIAM but has since been significantly extended in scope.

Chapter 3

The modeling process

> A theory has only the alternative of being
> right or wrong. A model has a third
> possibility: it may be right but irrelevant.

Manfred Eigen

Each information model is unique, as is the process of developing that model. In this Chapter we provide some broad guidelines to assist you in creating a quality model. We are basically recommending a policy of progressive refinement when modeling but the actual process usually turns out to be iterative. So, although one might start out with good intentions of using a top-down approach, one often ends up with a mixture of top-down, bottom-up, and middle-out strategies.

The recommendations are principally cast in the form of check lists and give a skeleton outline of the process. Chapter 4 provides a complete worked example which puts some flesh on the bones.

3.1 The team

An information model may be created by a single person, given sufficient knowledge, or preferably and more likely by a team of people.

An information model represents some portion of the real world. In order to produce such a model an obvious requirement is knowledge of the particular real world aspects that are of interest. People with this knowledge are called *domain experts*. The other side of the coin is that knowledge of information modeling is required in order to develop an information model. These people are called *modeling experts*.

Typically, the domain experts are not conversant with information modeling and the modeling experts are not conversant with the subject. Hence the usual need for at least two parties to join forces. Together the domain and modeling experts can produce an information model that satisfies their own requirements.

However, an information model is typically meant to be used by a larger audience than just its creators. There is a need to communicate the model to those who may not have the skills and knowledge to create such a model but who do have the background to utilize it.

Thus the requirement for a third group to review the model during its formative stages to ensure that it is understandable by the target audience. This is the review team who act somewhat like the editors in a publishing house, or like friendly quality control inspectors.

The modeling experts will have to become conversant with the technical terms used by the domain experts. Both the domain experts and the reviewers will need to learn about modeling techniques, but the reviewers need not have the in-depth knowledge that will eventually be required of the domain experts — one can read a book and sensibly critique it without necessarily having the skills to have written it.

The initiation phase in an information modeling project basically consists of assembling the entire team, providing sufficient training to the members so that they can work efficiently on the project, and defining the scope of the model that is the end goal. At the end of this phase everyone, it is hoped, will be talking the same language (but it will usually turn out that they are using the same words but with different understandings; these mismatches will clear as the work progresses).

The scope of the information model should be briefly described. The scoping statement should be no longer than two pages, and may be shorter (an example scope is given in Section 4.1.1). During the course of the project the scope may well be refined and modified as more details of the work become apparent (e.g., the example scope is further detailed in Section 4.1.2).

All the domain experts, whether they will be on the modeling or review teams should be given an introduction to information modeling principles. Utilizing a graphical modeling language such as EXPRESS-G provides a useful medium for this. The modeling team will require further in-depth training in the use of any other modeling languages that will be used. The reviewers will need to have some lighter knowledge of these languages in order to effectively review the work of the modeling team.

A review schedule must be developed as one of the initial work items. This will add discipline to the project. The modeling team will be working together continuously throughout the project, but the review team need only be involved during the review periods.

Once the modeling team is assembled, trained, and have decided on what to do, then the actual modeling can start. We recommend a three phase approach, with possibly a fourth phase for a large project. These phases are:

- Basic objects;
- Relationships and attributes;

- Constraints; and

- Model integration.

We recommend that initial model concepts be developed using a graphical language such as EXPRESS-G and then detailed using a lexical language like EXPRESS. The use of an instance language such as EXPRESS-I is also beneficial in order to develop some small populated models to check the information model.

A high level summary of the modeling phases is given below. These are expanded later throughout this Part. As usual, the whole modeling process is iterative. The process as described should be treated as a guide rather than as a hard and fast set of rules. For example, if something that appears in a later phase is obvious at an earlier phase it can be dealt with when recognized rather than postponed.

3.2 Phase 1: Basic objects

The principal objective of this task is to develop the major aspects of the items in, and the general structure of, the model. This lays the groundwork for the later phases which are more concerned with refining the details.

This is, perhaps, the most difficult part of developing a model. Unless the team has worked together before, there is an initial period during which they are getting to know each other and getting to know each other's terminology (jargon) and viewpoint. Further, it usually becomes rapidly apparent that the domain experts do not agree on numerous aspects of the domain that they are trying to represent. All this confusion takes time to resolve.

The modeling process starts by getting agreement on the real world things that are to be represented in the model and naming them. It is essential to reach agreement on the meaning of each name. It may take several discussion meetings before consensus is reached. The following rules of thumb are useful in this regard.

1. When talking about things we often move between the general and the specific. For example we might say 'I communicated with Fred.' when in fact we wrote a letter or made a telephone call. It is important to try and be as precise about things as necessary while being as general as possible, and to be consistent in our level of precision. We might say 'communicate' for the general term and use 'talk' or 'write' when we need to be more specific and perhaps 'wrote a letter' or 'sent a Fax' to be even more precise.

2. In general conversation and in writing we use many different ways of saying the same thing. This is considered to be good style as it adds interest. However, the opposite is true in modeling. Stylish variations

should be avoided in modeling as it can be unclear whether descriptions differ for effect or whether different descriptions are intended to describe different things.

3. Be alert for synonyms and homonyms. A homonym is a word that has multiple meanings while synonyms are two or more words that have the same meaning. Homonyms cause much more trouble than synonyms and are a fruitful source of misunderstanding.

4. Developing a glossary of terms is a good way of documenting the common vocabulary that is being developed. Each entry in the glossary should include the name of the term and a short definition of, say, five to twenty words. Do not spend a long time wordsmithing the definitions. It can also be useful to include possible synonyms and related words. One of the purposes of the glossary is to eliminate homonyms from the working vocabulary.

For the modeling aspects of this phase, the use of a graphical language is generally recommended. Typically, only a single review cycle is needed for completion of the phase.

The major questions that need to be answered include the following.

- What are the entities according to the scope?

  This entails recognizing the major items that need to be represented in the model and at least naming them. A previously developed glossary can be helpful here. On the other hand, this process can assist in developing the glossary.

- What do we know about the attributes of the entities?

  Describe the major aspects of the classes. These may be simple, like a name or something that could be represented by a number, or may be complex and require some other object for its representation.

- Can we categorize the entities? Are there specialization relationships between the entities?

  This involves recognizing that some entities may be a special type of another entity. Perhaps that more general entity does not yet exist and should be added to the model.

- What local consistency constraints apply to the entities?

  An information model is as much about limitations as it is about descriptions. If there are readily identifiable constraints that apply to every instance of an entity, then these should be documented. For example, if a number represents the age of something, then that number should be constrained to be positive.

- Are all the entities and attributes documented?

  The model must be documented in natural language describing the intended meaning of all the constructs in the model.

- Is the use of simple types (integer, string, etc.) correct?

  The simple types in a model carry virtually no semantics. Their use and meaning must be carefully documented.

Minor concerns include:

- Which, if any, combinations of attribute values uniquely identify an entity instance?

  In some cases it may be possible to identify some combination of attributes whose values would uniquely identifier instances of the entity. For example, in the USA a social security number uniquely identifies an individual. In other cases there may be no attribute set that can perform this function.

- Is the existence of an instance of one entity dependent on its usage by another entity?

  For example, if we are modeling a library, then only books that are owned by the library are of interest. Books in bookstores are irrelevant to this particular application.

- Are the values of some attributes deriveable from other attribute values?

  The attribute set for an entity should be both minimal and complete. Often there can be many attribute sets, some of whose values can be calculated from others. For example, the perimeter of a rectangle can be calculated from the length of its sides. Thus a rectangle can be described by any two of length, width and perimeter. Having all three may lead to ambiguity in data instances.

At the end of this phase the model should be reviewed. If serious concerns are raised by the review team then the model must be reworked. It may also turn out that the scope statement needs revisiting due to the experience gained. Minor review team concerns may be addressed in the next phase.

3.3 Phase 2: Relationships and attributes

This phase is essentially refining the model developed in the first phase. The utilization of a graphical language is especially useful at this stage, particularly if there is not a sufficient core of experienced information modelers in the project. However, by the end of the phase the model should also be fully represented in a lexical language, such as EXPRESS.

- What are the relationships between the entities?

  Decide the manner in which entities are associated with each other, if at all. Define any constraints on these relationships.

- Can we categorize the entities? Are there inheritance, subset or specialization relationships between the entities?

  Review and refine the categorization structures in the model.

- Is the use of simple types correct?
- Are additional attributes required to characterize an entity?
- Are the values of some attributes deriveable from other attribute values?
- Is the existence of an instance of one entity dependent on its usage by another entity?
- Which, if any, combinations of attribute values uniquely identify an entity instance?
- What local consistency constraints apply to the entities?
- Are all the entities, relationships, and attributes documented?

Minor concerns include:

- For a complex model, is it partitioned into topic areas?

During this phase, entities and types are added to the schema. Consequently, the phase must be iterated until the model has reached the desired level of detail.

If the end of phase review reveals serious problems with the model, then it is advisable to go back to the beginning of phase 1 again. Typically, problems are caused by the model being poorly structured and/or not adequately reflecting the real world; these must be fixed rather than trying to band-aid in the detailing stage.

3.4   Phase 3: Completion of constraints

To avoid a lot of rework, it is advisable to postpone defining the global constraints until the model is sufficiently mature and stable. If, on the other hand, a global constraint is identified during an earlier phase, then it should be documented immediately. If you are using EXPRESS, then a rule with an empty body and some comments to indicate the semantics is a good way of doing so.

- What are the global consistency rules?
  Global rules are constraints that either apply between entities in a model, or apply to some instances of a particular entity. These should now be documented.
- Are all existence dependencies captured?
- Are all the uniqueness constraints captured?
- Are all other cardinality constraints captured?
- Are there any missing local consistency rules?
- Is the model well partitioned?

At the end of this phase all constraints must be formally documented. For simple projects this is the final phase.

3.5 Phase 4: Model integration

When developing a large information model, the work is often broken down into parts, such that small modeling groups can work on the individual pieces in parallel. This facilitates the rate of progress, but at a cost. The cost is that the end result of these individual modeling efforts, called here *Topical Information Models* (TIMs), do not necessarily fit well together to form an *Integrated Information Model* (IIM). An IIM is intended to be a complete, minimally redundant, unambiguous, implementation independent information model, therefore it is important to plan for the day when all of the pieces will come together. This requires considerable project management attention and frequent meetings between the development teams to ensure that integration is practical.

In an ideal world, the TIMs would be developed concurrently and harmoniously, but this is not usually the case in real life. Some of the characteristics of TIMs in the real world are:

- Developed (semi-)independently.

- Developed using different methodologies and representation methods.

- Developed to differing levels of detail (abstraction).

In some sense, information model integration is analogous to system optimization. Unfortunately, optimization is not distributive. That is, if a system S is composed of a set of subsystems $a, b, c, \ldots$ as $S = (a, b, c)$ and $\mathcal{O}()$ is an 'optimization function' then, in general

$$\mathcal{O}(S) \neq (\mathcal{O}(a), \mathcal{O}(b), \mathcal{O}(c))$$

and, further

$$\mathcal{O}(S) \geq (\mathcal{O}(a), \mathcal{O}(b), \mathcal{O}(c))$$

where the symbol $\geq$ is to be understood to mean 'better than or same as'. In other words, the individual optimization of each of the subsystems in a system does not necessarily lead to an overall optimization of the system. For overall system optimization it may be necessary to have some subsystems that are sub-optimal when viewed individually.

There are several levels of difficulty in integrating models. These are described in detail in Chapter 6.

3.6 Further reading

We have described a generic modeling methodology; it should be modified to meet individual requirements. There are many more specialised methodologies espoused in the literature. These basically fall into two categories; one deals with the design of databases and the other with the design of software systems. Our methodology uses concepts from both of these.

Booch [Boo91] discusses Object-Oriented system design with a wealth of examples in different OO languages. He provides some graphical notations to assist in the design process. Meyer is more concerned with the Eiffel language [Mey88], but has interesting remarks on design aspects. Both Rumbaugh and his co-workers [RBP+91], and Shlaer and Mellor [SM88a] provide general methodologies and notations for OO system design. Authors such as Yourdon [YC79, You89] give very detailed and wide ranging methodologies for the design and analysis of software sytems in general.

Most books on databases discuss methodologies. These, though, are usually biased towards a particular database technology — typically relational. Authors include Date [Dat90], Loomis [Loo87], and Nijssen and Halpin [NH89]. The original IDEF1X report also includes a detailed methodology [IDE85]. Batini *et al* [BCN92] are principally concerned with the use of EER as a conceptual modeling tool for databases and are less concerned with implementation aspects than many other authors are.

There is a large literature on design methodologies. In addition to the above the following works are a sampling of recent publications: de Champeuax [dC90, dCLF92], Fichman and Kemerer [FK92], Holibaugh [Hol92], Karam and Casselman [KC93], Monarchi and Puhr [MP92], Navathe [Nav92], Song and Osterweil [SO92], Ward [War89], Wegner [Weg90, Weg92], and Wirfs-Brock and Johnson [WBJ90].

Chapter 4

A worked example

> I pass with relief from the tossing sea of
> Cause and Theory to the firm ground of
> Result and Fact.

The Story of the Malakand Field Force
Sir Winston Churchill

In this Chapter we provide a complete worked example of the development
of an information model. The initial model specification is taken from an
ISO report, TR 9007, which, among other things, describes several means
of representing this particular example.

The model representations used here are the EXPRESS-G and EXPRESS
languages, and this also serves as an introduction to some aspects of the
languages. Minor use is also made of EXPRESS-I. For explanatory purposes
we do not strictly adhere to the methodology described earlier. The principal difference being that we develop simultaneously both a graphical and
a lexical version of the model.

4.1   The starting specification

The initial model statement for the worked example is given in Section 4.1.1
and 4.1.2 and is taken from ISO TR 9007. In our modeling methodology
this would be developed by the modeling team as the initial step in the
modeling process. By the time the team is in a position to be as clear on
the specification as given in 4.1.2 about the real world aspects of the problem, then the majority of the modeling work has been accomplished. The
remaining task, which is what we will be concentrating on, is to formally
describe and document the model.

4.1.1   Scope

The scope of the model to be described has to do with the registration of
cars and is limited to the scope of interest of the Registration Authority.

The Registration Authority exists for the purpose of:

- Knowing who is or was the registered owner of a car at any time from construction to destruction of the car.

- To monitor certain laws, for example regarding fuel consumption of cars and their transfer of ownership.

4.1.2 Description

Manufacturers of cars

There are a number of manufacturers, each with one unique name. Manufacturers may start operation, with the permission of the Registration Authority (which permission cannot be withdrawn). No more than five manufacturers may be in operation at any time. A manufacturer may cease to operate provided he owns no cars, in which case permission to operate lapses.

Cars

A car is of a particular model and is given a serial number by its manufacturer that is unique among the cars made by that manufacturer. The manufacturer is registered as owner of the car as soon as practicable. At this time it is given one registration number, unique for all cars and for all time. The year of production is also recorded. During the month of January only, a car can be declared to have been produced in the previous year. Eventually a car is destroyed and the date of destruction is registered. The history of the car must be kept until the end of the second calendar year following its destruction.

Car models

A model of car has one universally unique name. Cars of each model are made by only one manufacturer. New models may be introduced without limit. All cars of one model are recorded as having the same fuel consumption.

Fuel consumption

Fuel consumption is the number of liters of hydrocarbon fuel per 100 kilometers, which will be between 4 and 25 liters. The fuel consumption averaged over all registered cars produced by a particular manufacturer in a particular year is required not to exceed a maximum value, which is the same for each manufacturer and may change from year to year. At the end of each January an appropriate message is sent by the Registration Authority to each manufacturer which has failed to meet this requirement.

Garages

There are a number of garages[1], each one with a unique name. New garages may start trading. Garages may own cars, but at any time the cars they own must have originated from no more than three manufacturers (which three is unimportant, and may vary with time). A garage cannot cease to trade as long as it owns cars.

Persons

There are a number of persons who can own one or more cars. Each person has one unique name. Only those persons are of interest who own, or have at some time owned, a car still known to the Registration Authority.

Car ownership

At any one time a car may be owned by either its manufacturer, or a trading garage, or a person or a group of persons. If a car is owned by a group of persons, each is regarded as an owner.

Transfer of ownership

Ownership of a car is transferred by registration of the actual transfer, including the date. A manufacturer can only transfer to garages, and cannot be a transferee. A garage can transfer only to people. After destruction of the car it cannot be transferred anymore. Earlier transfer though still can be recorded.

4.2 The base model

Where do we start modeling? Developing an information model is akin to developing an Object Oriented (OO) program. The items that are of major interest in an information model are the things that occur or are conceived of in the real world, as limited by the intended scope of the model. These things may be facts, physical objects, ideas, relationships, and so on.

The first task is to determine what sorts of real world things are of interest. The problem of finding the initial set of things to be modeled is known in the OO world as 'Finding the objects'. But, before doing that, we need to recall the terminology that we will be using. This was summarised in Table 2.1. We use the words 'class' and 'object' to refer to real world items and 'entity' and 'instance' to refer to the modeling constructs that represent the respective real world items.

The desired (real world) classes may often be found by reading the natural language scope statements and extracting the nouns and verbs. Each

---

[1] Dealerships in American English.

individual noun or verb is a potential class. The information modelers can
also generate a list of potential classes by listening to the domain experts
describing their work and noting the words that occur most frequently in
their conversation. Nouns often correspond to real world physical objects
and ideas. Verbs often indicate relationships among these things. Relationships are, in some sense, ideas and hence are also candidates for classes. In
EXPRESS there is no distinction between an entity representing a real object
and an entity representing a relationship —they are both modeled using the
Entity construct. However, typically the first collection of classes is heavily
biased towards real world objects and ideas rather than relationships.

From the example in Section 4.1.2 the following list of potential classes
can be garnered:

> Registration authority, Manufacturer, Car, Model, Fuel consump-
> tion, Garage, Person, Ownership, Transfer, Permission, Year, Month,
> Name, Destruction, Date.

4.2.1   Categorization and specialization

This is quite a lengthy list, and we need to start collecting together some
of the items noted. For instance, reading again the example, it becomes
clear that an 'owner' is an important concept and, further, that there can
be different kinds of owners. In EXPRESS-G and EXPRESS, the Subtype
concept is used for modeling this.

A supertype is a generalization of its subtypes and, conversely, a subtype
is a specialization of its supertype(s); that is, a subtype is a particular more
limited kind of its supertype.

Figure 4.1 shows an EXPRESS-G representation of the subtype tree where
an entity called owner is a supertype of the entities called manufacturer,
garage, person and group. These latter are all subtypes of the owner
entity.

In EXPRESS-G an entity is denoted by a solid rectangular box enclosing
the name of the entity. Supertypes and subtypes are connected by a thick
line, with the subtype end of the line denoted by a circle.

The following is the same model, only written in EXPRESS instead.

```
ENTITY owner; END_ENTITY;

ENTITY manufacturer SUBTYPE OF (owner); END_ENTITY;

ENTITY garage SUBTYPE OF (owner); END_ENTITY;

ENTITY person SUBTYPE OF (owner); END_ENTITY;

ENTITY group SUBTYPE OF (owner); END_ENTITY;
```

An entity declares itself to be a subtype by saying what it is a subtype of.
In the above the entities called manufacturer, garage, person and group

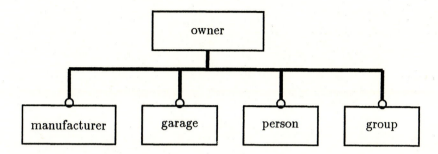

Figure 4.1: Partial entity-level model of the initial owner subtype tree (Page 1 of 1).

are all subtypes of the entity called **owner**. Conversely, the entity **owner** is a supertype by virtue of the fact that some other entity has identified it as such via its subtype statement.

One further point about the supertype/subtype hierarchy: a subtype inherits all the attributes and constraints of its supertype.

4.2.2 Attributes

The attributes of a class are those traits or characteristics which distinguish one class from another and also whose values will distinguish one object in a class from another object in the same class.

For example, picking the idea of a car as being a useful class, we are told that a car is a manufactured item of a particular model type, is given a serial number by its manufacturer, has a year of production, and is given a registration number. We are also told that a car is owned by only one owner at any given time. Thus, we could make a first pass at modeling a car as given in the EXPRESS-G representation in Figure 4.2.

An entity icon is connected to the icons representing its attributes by thin lines. The circled end of the line indicates the 'attribute end' of the connection. The name of the attribute is placed adjacent to the connecting line.

The EXPRESS-G icon for a simple type is a solid rectangular box, with a vertical line at the right-hand end, enclosing the name of the simple type in upper-case characters. The simple types in both EXPRESS and EXPRESS-G are: **Binary**, **Boolean**, **Integer**, **Logical**, **Number**, **Real** and **String**.

An entity in EXPRESS may have attributes. An attribute declaration consists of a name for the attribute and the *domain* of the attribute. A domain can be considered to specify the type of value that the attribute will have in an instance of the entity. The name of the attribute should be indicative of its role within the description of the entity, as shown in the following EXPRESS code.

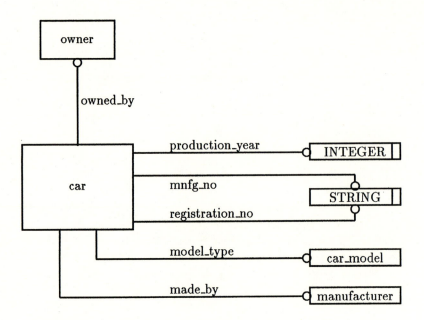

Figure 4.2: Partial entity-level model for a car (Page 1 of 1).

```
ENTITY car;
   model_type       : car_model;
   made_by          : manufacturer;
   mnfg_no          : STRING;
   registration_no  : STRING;
   production_year  : INTEGER;
   owned_by         : owner;
END_ENTITY;
```

Here, the attributes named **model_type**, **made_by** and **owned_by** will be represented by other classes in the model. The **production_year** will be represented by an **Integer**, which is one of the atomic simple types in EX-PRESS. Both of the numbers allocated to the car will be represented by another simple type, namely a **String** (of characters), as often these types of 'numbers' are mixtures of alphanumeric characters and other symbols.

Similarly we could model a **car_model** class as shown via EXPRESS-G in Figure 4.3, and in EXPRESS as below.

```
ENTITY car_model;
   name        : STRING;
   made_by     : manufacturer;
   consumption : REAL;
END_ENTITY;
```

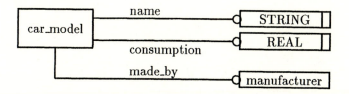

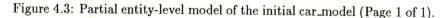

Figure 4.3: Partial entity-level model of the initial car_model (Page 1 of 1).

4.2.3 Uniqueness constraints

The values of some attributes, or combination of attribute values, may be unique across all instances of a class. In other words, they could be used to identify objects. The model should be examined to see if there are any occurrences of this form of behavior.

Note that in the OO world, of which EXPRESS can be considered to be a member, each object is uniquely identifiable by a method that does not depend on attribute values. Typically this is done in an object-base by providing a unique 'object identifier' (OID) with each instance. In the relational world, instances are identified via uniqueness among attribute values.

For information modeling purposes, it is assumed that instance identification utilizes the OID paradigm. Nevertheless, attribute value uniqueness, if it exists, is a constraint that must be captured within the model.

In the example model, there are several occurrences of this type of constraint. To begin with, let us revisit the **owner** class. Most of the owner subtypes have names, which are declared to be unique. Thus, we can extend the model a little, as

```
ENTITY manufacturer
   SUBTYPE OF (owner);
   name : STRING;
UNIQUE
   un_mfg_name : name;
END_ENTITY;
```

and so on for the other owners with names (but note that a group is not required to have a name).

Uniqueness constraints are included in an entity description after listing the entity's attributes, and are introduced by the **Unique** keyword. A label, un_mfg_name in this case, is used to identify the constraint. The attribute(s) whose value is being constrained follows.

Also, returning to the definition of a **car**, we are told that each manufacturer gives his own unique number to a car (but there is no requirement that different manufacturers have to have unique numbers), and also that the number given by the Registration Authority is unique across all cars. Therefore, we can model this as:

```
ENTITY car;
   model_type        : car_model;
   made_by           : manufacturer;
   mnfg_no           : STRING;
   registration_no : STRING;
   production_year : INTEGER;
   owned_by          : owner;
UNIQUE
   joint  : made_by, mfg_no;
   single : registration_no;
END_ENTITY;
```

The unique constraint labelled **single** states that the value of the attribute called **registration_no** must be unique across all instances of **car**.

The constraint labelled **joint** states that the values of **made_by** and **mnfg_no** taken as a pair must be unique across all instances. Note that this permits different cars to be made by the same manufacturer and also that different cars could have identical manufacturer's number.

4.2.4   Local constraints

It often occurs that the values of attributes are constrained to be within some range. That is, for a particular usage of the attribute type, not all possible values are legal. The model needs to be examined for these types of constraint.

Turning to a different aspect of the example model, a **date** appears to be a useful concept. Ignoring for now the full complexity of the problem, we can represent this as:

```
ENTITY date;
   day    : INTEGER;
   month : INTEGER;
   year   : INTEGER;
WHERE
   days_ok    :
     {1 <= day <= 31};
   months_ok :
     {1 <= month <= 12};
END_ENTITY;
```

where the range of permissible integer values for the **day** and **month** are limited to be at least one in each case and not more than 31 and 12 for the day and month respectively.

Local constraints in EXPRESS follow the **Where** keyword. Like the uniqueness constraints they can be labelled. The constraint takes the form of a logical expression. An entity instance is invalid if, at the time of checking the constraint, the expression evaluates to FALSE. Labelling is useful as it provides a means for an instance validation system to report exactly which constraint, or constraints, may not have been satisfied in a particular entity instance.

Other more complex constraints may have to be specified in other parts of the model, and we will come across some of these later.

EXPRESS-G, unlike EXPRESS, cannot be used to represent constraints in general. However, an entity or attribute that is constrained may be flagged with an asterisk to indicate that there is some constraint on it, the nature and description of which must be sought elsewhere.

4.2.5 Existence constraints

A further type of constraint to be considered is that of existence. The question here is whether the existence of an instance of one class is dependent on the existence of an instance of another related class.

Consider another aspect of the example model that we have not yet discussed, namely the transfer history that the Registration Authority has to maintain. A history is a record of all the transfers of ownership of a car. This can be modeled as:

```
ENTITY history;
   item     : car;
   transfers : LIST [0:?] OF transfer;
END_ENTITY;
```

EXPRESS supports the notion of aggregations and ordering. Three dynamic aggregates are provided, **Bag**, **List** and **Set**, each with differing semantics. A **List** is ordered while the others are not. A **Set** cannot have duplicate members while the others can. The potential number of elements in the aggregation is given by the lower and upper bounds (the numbers within the square brackets). The question mark symbol is used to denote an indefinite upper bound (e.g., in the list above there may be an unlimited number of **transfer** values). There is also a static aggregation construct called an **Array**. This is fixed in size.

The expected behavior is that if the transfer history of a car is destroyed then all the referenced individual transfers will also be destroyed. Thus, an instance of **transfer** is existent dependent on it being referenced by an instance of **history**.

One EXPRESS method of declaring this constraint is by the use of an **Inverse** clause.

```
ENTITY transfer;
   item   : car;
   prior  : owner;
   new    : owner;
   on     : date;
INVERSE
   must_be_in_history : history FOR transfers;
END_ENTITY;
```

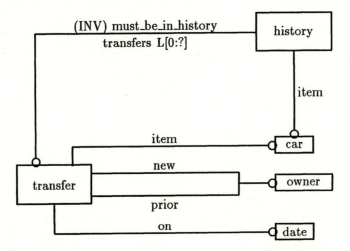

Figure 4.4: Partial entity-level model for transfer history (Page 1 of 1).

This stipulates that each instance of a **transfer** must be referenced by one and only one instance of **history** through the **transfers** attribute.

Figure 4.4 shows the EXPRESS-G representation of this portion of the model.

In EXPRESS-G an aggregation is denoted by following the attribute name with an indication of the type and range of the aggregation in question. To save space on the diagram only the initial letter of the aggregation type is used (i.e., A, B, L or S).

One of the few forms of constraint that EXPRESS-G supports is the notion of an inverse constraint. This is indicated on the relevant attribute line by qualifying the name of the inverse by the symbol '(INV)'. Note that the attribute name refers to the entity at the circled end of the line, while the inverse refers to the entity at the end of the line that is not circled.

4.2.6   Documentation

The model has to be documented in natural language; it is not sufficient to just have the formal model specification. The documentation must be sufficiently comprehensive to enable the review team to understand the objects and their attributes. Chapter 7 describes how to document a model.

The fully documented final example model is presented in Appendix A.

4.2.7   Basic example model

The following EXPRESS shows the completed basic model for the running example.

```
SCHEMA base;

ENTITY history;
   item     : car;
   transfers : LIST [0:?] OF transfer;
END_ENTITY;

ENTITY transfer;
   item  : car;
   prior : owner;
   new   : owner;
   on    : date;
INVERSE
   must_be_in_history : history FOR transfers;
END_ENTITY;

ENTITY date;
   day   : INTEGER;
   month : INTEGER;
   year  : INTEGER;
WHERE
   days_ok   :
      {1 <= day <= 31};
   months_ok :
      {1 <= month <= 12};
END_ENTITY;

ENTITY car;
   model_type      : car_model;
   made_by         : manufacturer;
   mnfg_no         : STRING;
   registration_no : STRING;
   production_year : INTEGER;
   owned_by        : owner;
UNIQUE
   joint  : made_by, mfg_no;
   single : registration_no;
END_ENTITY;

ENTITY car_model;
   name        : STRING;
   made_by     : manufacturer;
   consumption : REAL;
END_ENTITY;

ENTITY owner
END_ENTITY;

ENTITY manufacturer
```

```
   SUBTYPE OF (owner);
   name : STRING;
UNIQUE
   un1 : name;
END_ENTITY;

ENTITY garage
   SUBTYPE OF (owner);
   name : STRING;
UNIQUE
   un1 : name;
END_ENTITY;

ENTITY person
   SUBTYPE OF (owner);
   name : STRING;
UNIQUE
   un1 : name;
END_ENTITY;

ENTITY group
   SUBTYPE OF (owner);
   members : SET [1:?] OF person;
END_ENTITY;

END_SCHEMA;  -- base schema
```

One further note about an EXPRESS construct that we have not met before, that of Schema. A complete EXPRESS model consists of one or more partitions, or schemas. A Schema must be named and the contents of a schema is some set of items that are grouped for some purpose.

4.3   Relationships and attributes

This phase of information modeling is principally a refinement of the basic model developed during the previous phase. A complete review of the basic model should be undertaken before starting on the refinement process. It is essential that if serious problems with the basic model are raised by the review team, then the model should be re-worked until these are solved.

4.3.1   Use of simple types

Modeling languages usually offer some basic simple types which can be used to build more complex types. In EXPRESS, for example, these are numbers (which includes integers and reals), strings of characters, logical types (both two and three valued logic), and a binary type. Of themselves, these effectively carry no semantics.

The model should be examined to determine whether the use of these simple types as attributes has semantic implications. If so, then new classes should be defined to convey the semantics explicitly. Typically, character strings serve particular roles in a model which could be made explicit. Integers are also often used as 'flags' which have associated semantics.

EXPRESS provides a **Type** construct for this purpose. It is used to extend, and add semantics to, the simple types provided in the language.

Examining the basic example model for the use of **String** as an attribute we see that it is often used in the role of something's name. Another use of **String** is as a serial or registration number. The semantics of the **String** in these two cases is different, and may be captured by defining two **Types**.

```
TYPE name = STRING;
END_TYPE;


TYPE identification_no = STRING;
END_TYPE;
```

Real values are often used as the 'measure' of something. In this case, **Types** should be defined to capture the semantics of the measure. In the example, fuel consumption is an instance of this. We also notice that the range of values is limited (a constraint that was not incorporated into the base model).

```
TYPE fuel_consumption = REAL;
WHERE
  range :
    {4.0 <= SELF <= 25.0};
END_TYPE;
```

A different form of the use of simple types is shown in the **date** entity, where the **month** attribute is specified as **Integer**. In this case the values take on a known, limited range (1–12). This can be replaced by an enumeration of the months, as:

```
TYPE months = ENUMERATION OF
      (January,    February,      March,
        April,     May,           June,
        July,      August,        September,
      October,     November,      December);
END_TYPE;
```

Figure 4.5 shows the EXPRESS-G representation of the types that we have been discussing.

The icon for a non-simple type is a dashed box enclosing the name of the type. EXPRESS-G provides no means of displaying the contents of an enumeration type, such as the **months** type. It treats this in a similar manner to a simple type which is why the box has a dashed vertical line at the right hand end.

Other types are defined in terms of what could be called type attributes. There are connection lines from the type icon to the attribute icon. These

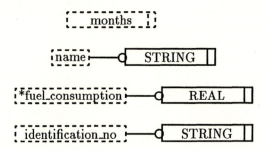

Figure 4.5: Partial entity-level model of some types (Page 1 of 1).

are not labelled with an attribute name (as those for entity attributes are) but may have an aggregation symbol placed on the line.

The asterisk on the `fuel_consumption` type name indicates that there is some constraint on the value; also, it can be seen that its value is a `Real` number.

4.3.2   Subtypes revisited

The base model should be examined to determine whether the supertype-subtype structures need adjusting. That is, are there any further specializations, categorizations, or generalizations that apply?

As an example of introducing a new specialization into the model, recall that cars may be destroyed. Thus, a 'destroyed car' may be considered to be a specialization of the general concept of `car`.

```
ENTITY destroyed_car
  SUBTYPE OF (car);
  destroyed_on : date;
END_ENTITY;
```

Because of inheritance a `destroyed_car` has all the attributes and constraints of its `car` supertype, with the additional attribute of the date on which it was destroyed.

In the example base model we note that of the different owners, three have a `name` attribute, while the `group` subtype does not. Introducing a further level into the supertype lattice allows us to group the owners with names, and make use of inheritance to slightly simplify the model, as illustrated in Figure 4.6.

Also, at this time, the behavior of the supertypes should be determined. There are two questions to be answered here:

1. Can a supertype be instanced without simultaneously instancing one of its subtypes?

2. Are there any constraints among the subtype instances of a supertype? That is, given two or more entities that are subtypes of a common

supertype, must the sets of instances of the subtypes be disjoint, can they be disjoint (i.e., they may or may not overlap), or must the sets be the same?

Reverting to the example **owner** supertype tree, we decide that the Registration Authority is only interested in the specific types of owners, therefore only the particular subtypes will be of interest. EXPRESS provides a means of specifying whether a supertype can or cannot be instantiated without instantiation of one of its subtypes. In the normal case nothing needs to be done. If, on the other hand, a supertype cannot be instanced without instancing a subtype, then the supertype must be declared as being **Abstract**.

We are also told that at any one time a car is owned by a manufacturer, or a garage, or a person, or a group of people. In other words an owner cannot simultaneously be both a manufacturer and a garage, for example. EXPRESS enables this to be declared via a **OneOf** relationship among the subtypes. Other subtype relationship constraint relationships are **AndOr** and **And**. If no constraint is specified then the relationship among the subtypes is **AndOr**. For example, if a person is a supertype of both a student and a teacher and there is no constraint specified, then a particular person could be a student, or a teacher or a student-teacher.

The resulting modifications to the owner portion of the model gives the following partial EXPRESS rendition where the subtype naming attribute has been moved up into their supertype.

```
ENTITY owner
   ABSTRACT SUPERTYPE OF (ONEOF(named_owner,
                                 group));
END_ENTITY;

ENTITY named_owner
   ABSTRACT SUPERTYPE OF (ONEOF(manufacturer,
                                 garage,
                                 person))
   SUBTYPE OF (owner);
   called : name;
UNIQUE
   un1 : called;
END_ENTITY;
```

The new subtype tree is shown fully in the EXPRESS-G model in Figure 4.6. Abstract supertypes are labeled with the symbol '(ABS)' before the name of the supertype. A **OneOf** constraint can be indicated by placing the digit '1' near the relevant junction in the subtype relationship lines.

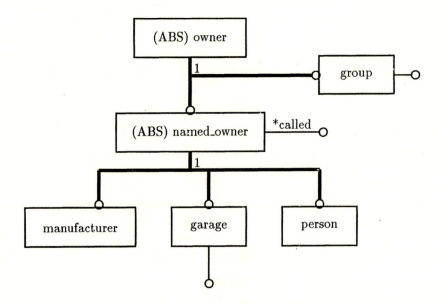

Figure 4.6: Partial entity-level model of the refined owner subtype tree (Page 1 of 1).

4.3.3   Redundancy elimination

One of the principles of information modeling is that a model should be unambiguous. Ambiguity often arises when the attribute values of a class are inter-related. Typically this occurs when the value of one attribute may be determined from the value of one or more other attributes. For example, if the attributes of a circle include both its radius and circumference, then there is redundancy between these as, given the value of one of these then the other may be calculated. Ambiguity could arise in an instance of a circle defined in this manner if the circumference value was not two pi times the radius — which value should be taken as the 'primary' value? These, and other, forms of redundancy should be eliminated from the model. Sometimes this can be done by modifying the structure, sometimes by adding constraints, and sometimes by explicitly permitting the redundancy but indicating which is the primary.

The example base model exhibits redundancy among the definitions of the car and car_model entities. Figure 4.7 illustrates the relevent portion of the model. Among the attributes of a car are the manufacturer and the model. A car_model also has an attribute which refers to the manufacturer. What happens if in the database the manufacturer of a car is different from the manufacturer of the model? The following EXPRESS-I code provides an

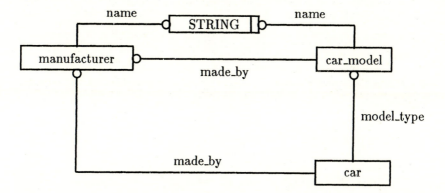

Figure 4.7: Base model ambiguity between car, model, and manufacturer.

example. Shown are two instances of **manufacturer** whose **name** attributes are 'Ford' and 'General Motors'. These instances have been given Object Identifiers (OIDs) of **ford** and **gm** respectively. There are also two instnaces of **car_model**, one identified as **mustang** which is made by the **ford** manufacturer and the other identified as **impala** which is made by the **gm** manufacturer. Finally, there are two instances of **car** entities, identified as **car1** and **car2**. Car1 is made by **ford** and is of model type **mustang** which is made by **ford**. However, **car2** is made by **gm** and is of model type **mustang** which is made by **ford**. This is the ambiguity! **Car2** should either be made by **ford** or it should be of model type **impala**.

```
ford = manufacturer{name --> 'Ford'; };
gm   = manufacturer{name --> 'General Motors'; };
mustang = car_model{name --> 'Mustang'; }
                    made_by --> @ford; };
impala  = car_model{name --> 'Impala';
                    made_by --> @gm; };
car1 = car{model_type --> @mustang;
           made_by     --> @ford; };
car2 = car{model_type --> @mustang;
           made_by     --> @gm; };     (* AMBIGUITY *)
```

The base model needs to be modified to eliminate this redundancy in the information model and potential ambiguity in the database.

One way of resolving this problem is to put an additional constraint on the **car** entity, as

```
ENTITY car;
   model_type       : car_model;
   made_by          : manufacturer;
   ....
WHERE
   same_mnfg :
```

```
            made_by :=: model_type.made_by;
        END_ENTITY;
```

Another approach is to eliminate the direct relationship between `car` and `manufacturer` by using a `Derive`d attribute instead. In EXPRESS a derived attribute is one whose value can be calculated from the values of other attributes of an entity. In this case, using a derived attribute means that the constraint shown above is not required.

```
        ENTITY car;
          model_type        : car_model;
             ....
        DERIVE
          made_by : manufacturer := model_type.made_by;
        END_ENTITY;
```

In EXPRESS-G a derived attribute is indicated by putting the symbol '(DER)' before the attribute name.

4.3.4   Local constraints

The classes in the base information model should be re-examined to determine whether all the local constraints on individual class instances have been defined. It is advisable to leave this task until after the class structure and relationships appear to be stable.

Taking a simple example of the `date` entity (suitably modified to take account of the new representation for the `month` attribute), we realize that we have only constrained the days not to exceed 31. What about months that have less than 31 days, what about leap years? Another general information modeling principal is that only formally specified constraints apply — computer systems have no common-sense.

```
        ENTITY date;
          day   : INTEGER;
          month : months;
          year  : INTEGER;
        WHERE
          days_ok :
            {1 <= day <= 31};
          year_ok :
            year > 0;
          date_ok :
            valid_date(SELF);
        END_ENTITY;
```

This revised definition now restricts the year to be greater than 0, hence this class is only applicable to years *Anno Domine*.

Specifying the more general constraint about matching days and months is more complicated than just restricting the range of a number. EXPRESS provides an algorithmic language, including functions, to assist in this.

The `date_ok` constraint is specified via a function named `valid_date`. The function signature for this is written as below together with the signature of a function for identifying leap years (the code for these functions is given in Appendix A).

```
FUNCTION valid_date (par : date) : BOOLEAN;
   (* returns FALSE if its input date is not a valid date *)
END_FUNCTION;

FUNCTION leap_year(year : INTEGER) : BOOLEAN;
   (* returns TRUE if its input is a leap year *)
END_FUNCTION;
```

Other classes in the base model also require additional constraints to be specified. For instance there are restrictions in the specification of the example model on which types of owner can participate in any particular transfer. Further, a car cannot be transferred after it has been destroyed.

```
ENTITY transfer;
   item  : car;
   prior : owner;
   new   : owner;
   on    : date;
INVERSE
   must_be_in_history : SET [1:1] OF history FOR transfers;
WHERE
   wr1 :
     NOT ('BASE.MANUFACTURER' IN TYPEOF(new));
   wr2 :
     (NOT ('BASE.MANUFACTURER' IN TYPEOF(prior))))
     XOR
     ('BASE.MANUFACTURER' IN TYPEOF(prior)
     AND
     'BASE.GARAGE' IN TYPEOF(new));
   wr3 :
     (NOT ('BASE.GARAGE' IN TYPEOF(prior)))
     XOR
     ('BASE.GARAGE' IN TYPEOF(prior)
     AND
     ('BASE.PERSON' IN TYPEOF(new) XOR
      'BASE.GROUP' IN TYPEOF(new)));
   not_destroyed :
     (NOT ('BASE.DESTROYED_CAR' IN TYPEOF(item))
     XOR
     (('BASE.DESTROYED_CAR' IN TYPEOF(item))
     AND
     days_between(on, item.destroyed_on) > 0);
END_ENTITY;
```

The constraint labelled `wr1` says that a car cannot be transferred to a manufacturer. That labelled `wr2` states that a manufacturer can only transfer

Figure 4.8: Complete schema-level model for Registration Authority refined model (Page 1 of 1).

a car to a garage, and that labelled **wr3** that a garage can only transfer to a person or a group. The constraint labelled **not_destroyed** says that if a car is a destroyed car then the date of transfer must be before the date of destruction (a new function **days_between**, which takes two dates and returns the number of days between the dates, has been introduced to help in this constraint definition).

4.3.5   Module structure

An information model can get large very quickly. Consideration should be given as to whether the model can be modularised, where closely related classes can be formed into groups. The recognition of significant groupings can occur at any time during the development process. Often the groupings are reasonably well understood at the start of model development, and work can proceed in parallel in fleshing out the contents of the individual groups. Other times, this recognition comes later in the process.

There are at least two reasons for partitioning. One is that there are natural divisions within the model that can be exploited for understandability and explanatory purposes. The other is that a subset of the model under development may have wider applicability than its immediate context.

In the case of our example, we may suppose that the 'stuff' related to dates could very well be reusable in another context, and thus could be broken out into a separate grouping. The EXPRESS Schema construct enables this kind of partitioning. Thus, we will divide the example model up into two schemas. One of these is called **authority** and the other is called **calendar**.

Figure 4.8 is an EXPRESS-G representation of the two schemas that we intend to have.

The icon for a schema is a rectangular solid box with a horizontal partition. The name of the schema is enclosed in the upper box. A dashed line connecting two schema icons indicates that one of them is referenced by the other. The circled end of the line indicates the schema that is being referenced.

4.3.6 Refined model

The end result of the above work on the example model leads to the following:

```
SCHEMA authority;
  REFERENCE FROM calendar;

TYPE name = STRING;
END_TYPE;

TYPE identification_no = STRING;
END_TYPE;

TYPE fuel_consumption : REAL;
WHERE
  range :
    {4.0 <= SELF <= 25.0};
END_TYPE;

ENTITY history;
  item : car;
  transfers : LIST [0:?] OF UNIQUE transfer;
UNIQUE
  un1 : item;
WHERE
  one_car  :
    single_car(SELF);
  ordering :
    exchange_ok(transfers);
END_ENTITY;

ENTITY transfer;
  item  : car;
  prior : owner;
  new   : owner;
  on    : date;
INVERSE
  must_be_in_history : history FOR transfers;
WHERE
  wr1 :
    NOT ('AUTHORITY.MANUFACTURER' IN TYPEOF(new));
  wr2 :
    (NOT ('AUTHORITY.MANUFACTURER' IN TYPEOF(prior)))
    XOR
    ('AUTHORITY.MANUFACTURER' IN TYPEOF(prior)
    AND
    'AUTHORITY.GARAGE' IN TYPEOF(new));
  wr3 :
    (NOT ('AUTHORITY.GARAGE' IN TYPEOF(prior)))
```

```
      XOR
      ('AUTHORITY.GARAGE' IN TYPEOF(prior)
      AND
      ('AUTHORITY.PERSON' IN TYPEOF(new)
      XOR
      'AUTHORITY.GROUP' IN TYPEOF(new)));
    not_destroyed :
      (NOT ('AUTHORITY.DESTROYED_CAR' IN TYPEOF(item))
      XOR
      (('AUTHORITY.DESTROYED_CAR' IN TYPEOF(item))
      AND
      days_between(on, item.destroyed_on) > 0);
END_ENTITY;


ENTITY car;
    model_type      : car_model;
    mnfg_no         : identification_no;
    registration_no : identification_no;
    production_date : date;
    production_year : INTEGER;
DERIVE
    made_by : manufacturer := model_type.made_by;
UNIQUE
    joint  : made_by, mnfg_no;
    single : registration_no;
WHERE
    jan_prod :
      (production_year = production_date.year)
      XOR
      (production_date.month = January
      AND
      (production_year = production_date.year - 1));
END_ENTITY;

ENTITY destroyed_car
    SUBTYPE OF (car);
    destroyed_on : date;
WHERE
    dates_ok :
      days_between(prod_date, destroyed_on) >= 0;
END_ENTITY;

ENTITY owner
    ABSTRACT SUPERTYPE OF (ONEOF(named_owner,
                                 group);
END_ENTITY;

ENTITY named_owner
```

```
      ABSTRACT SUPERTYPE OF (ONEOF(manufacturer,
                                   garage,
                                   person));
   called : name;
UNIQUE
  un1 : called;
END_ENTITY;

   ENTITY manufacturer
     SUBTYPE OF (named_owner);
   END_ENTITY;

   ENTITY authorized_manufacturer
     SUBTYPE OF (manufacturer);
   END_ENTITY;

ENTITY garage
   SUBTYPE OF (named_owner);
END_ENTITY;

ENTITY person
   SUBTYPE OF (named_owner);
END_ENTITY;


ENTITY group
   SUBTYPE OF (owner);
   members : SET [1:?] OF person;
END_ENTITY;

ENTITY car_model;
   called      : name;
   made_by     : manufacturer;
   consumption : fuel_consumption;
UNIQUE
   un1 : called;
END_ENTITY;

FUNCTION exchange_ok(par : LIST OF transfer) : BOOLEAN;
   (* returns TRUE if the "to owner" in the N'th transfer
      of a car is the "from owner" in the N+1'th transfer *)
END_FUNCTION;

FUNCTION single_car(par : history) BOOLEAN;
   (* returns TRUE if a history is of a single car *)
END_FUNCTION;

END_SCHEMA;  -- authority schema
```

```
SCHEMA calendar;

TYPE months = ENUMERATION OF
    (January, February, March,
     April,   May,      June,
     July,    August,   September,
     October, November, December};
END_TYPE;

ENTITY date;
  day   : INTEGER;
  month : months;
  year  : INTEGER;
WHERE
  days_ok :
    {1 <= day <= 31};
  year_ok :
    year > 0;
  date_ok :
    valid_date(SELF);
END_ENTITY;




FUNCTION valid_date (par : date) : BOOLEAN;
  (* returns FALSE if its input is not a valid date *)
END_FUNCTION;

FUNCTION leap_year(year : INTEGER) : BOOLEAN;
  (* returns TRUE if its input is a leap year *)
END_FUNCTION;

FUNCTION current_date() : date;
  (* This function returns the date when it is called.
     Typically, it will be implemented via a system
     provided procedure within the information base *)
END_FUNCTION;

FUNCTION days_between(d1, d2 : date) : INTEGER;
  (* returns the number of days between two input dates.
     If d1 is earlier than d2, a positive number is
     returned. *)
END_FUNCTION;

END_SCHEMA; -- calendar
```

4.4 Model completion

At the start of this stage, the review team will have closely examined the model for major structural flaws and missing local constraints. Any problems will have been resolved, either by iterating on the previous stage of model refinement, or going back and developing a new base model according to the experience gained.

The major items of concern within this modeling phase are the global constraints that apply to the entities, the existence and behavioral constraints, and the block structure of the model.

In the particular case of the running example, it is convenient to reconsider the existence constraints and the block structure together. From the viewpoint of the Registration Authority, the only 'things' that it cares about are those objects that appear in its records. We are told that the history of car transfers are only kept for a short period after the car has been destroyed. Therefore, we can assume that typically the data instances are dependent on their appearance in a history of transfers. The EXPRESS schema structuring and interface mechanism provides an elegant method of specifying this.

Definitions within one schema are invisible to another schema unless they are explicitly imported. The **Use** and **Reference** statements both enable the import of definitions from another schema. The definitions that are mentioned in a **Use** statements become *first-class* definitions within the importing schema. That is, in an instantiation of the model, these items may have an independent existence — instances can occur which are not utilized as attribute values of other items. Definitions that are imported via a **Reference** statement are *second-class*. That is, instances can only occur when required as attribute values.

Hence, if we partition the model into some primary schema that essentially contains only the **history** entity and **Reference** its supporting definitions into the primary schema from another, then we have effectively modeled the existence dependencies.

Turning now to some other parts of the model, we are told that there can be no more than five manufacturers in operation at any one time. This constraint can be modeled by the use of a global rule.

```
RULE max_number FOR (authorized_manufacturer);
WHERE
  max_of_5 :
    SIZEOF(authorized_manufacturer) <= 5;
END_RULE;
```

Two other behavioral aspects of the example have not yet been incorporated into the information model. The first of these is that a transfer **history** must be kept until the end of the second calendar year following the destruction of the car. The current version of EXPRESS has no facilities for modeling this kind of behavior as it is an information modeling language not a system modeling language. Hence it has no components for the modeling of behavior or activities. Nevertheless, modeling of the underlying decisional information is possible. In this case the relevant aspect is modeled by adding a derived `Boolean` attribute to the `history` entity which, when queried, will indicate whether the particular instance may be deleted or not.

```
ENTITY history;
  ....
DERIVE
  to_be_deleted : BOOLEAN := too_old(SELF);
WHERE
  ....
END_ENTITY;

FUNCTION too_old (par : history) : BOOLEAN;
  (* The function returns TRUE if the input history is
     outdated. That is, if it is of an item that was destroyed
     more than 2 years ago. *)
  IF 'AUTHORITY.DESTROYED_CAR' IN TYPEOF(par.item) THEN
    IF current_date.year - par.item.destroyed_on.year >= 2 THEN
      RETURN(TRUE);
    END_IF;
  END_IF;
  RETURN(FALSE);
END_FUNCTION;
```

The second behavioral element that has not been modeled is the fact that the Registration Authority sends a message to each manufacturer whose average fuel consumption exceeds a certain limit. Again, EXPRESS does not currently support this form of behavioral modeling, but we can invent an entity that does most of the job.

```
ENTITY send_message;
  max_consumption : fuel_consumption;
  year            : INTEGER;
  makers          : SET [0:?] OF authorized_manufacturer;
DERIVE
  excessives : SET [0:?] OF manufacturer := guzzlers(SELF);
END_ENTITY;

FUNCTION guzzlers (par : send_message) : SET OF manufacturer;
LOCAL
  result : SET OF manufacturer := [];
  mnfs   : SET OF manufacturer := par.makers;
  limit  : fuel_consumption := par.max_consumption;
  time   : INTEGER := par.year;
END_LOCAL;
  REPEAT i := 1 TO SIZEOF(mnfs);
```

```
      IF (mnfg_average_consumption(mnfs[i],time) > limit) THEN
        result := result + mnfs[i];
      END_IF;
    END_REPEAT;
  RETURN(result);
END_FUNCTION;
```

The entity **send_message** has attributes which consist of the maximum allowable fuel consumption for a particular year, and the set of authorized manufacturers for that year. It has a derived attribute which provides the list of manufacturers who have exceeded the fuel limit. These are calculated via the **guzzlers** function.

At this point we have essentially completed the example information model. The documentation of the model has been deliberately avoided in order to conserve space, but the fully documented final EXPRESS information model can be found in Appendix A; this also includes a complete EXPRESS-G rendition of the model.

4.5 Exercises

4.1 Do the following:

1. Write an information model that describes the logical content of a report. Assume that a report consists of a title and one or more authors, together with the publication date. It may have an abstract and may have a table of contents. The body of the report consists of at least two sections. Further divisions of the report are subsections and sub-subsections. Figures and tables may also be included within any sub-subsection, or higher level partitions. The report may have a bibliography.

2. Write an information model that describes a book. A book is similar to a report with the following exceptions. A book may consist of two or more parts, each of which must contain two or more chapters. Each chapter contains at least two sections. There is always a table of contents and there is never an abstract, although it may have a preface which serves the same purpose. A book may have an index.

3. Does the above description apply to all books?

4. Create an information model that supports both reports and books. Include anything extra that you feel is necessary that is missing from the above descriptions.

4.2 Write an information model corresponding to the following description.

An international company has a number of ongoing development projects. A project has a unique name and is located in a specific city.

There are a number of suppliers to the company. The suppliers have names and may have several branches, each in a different city. Suppliers with identical names do not have branches in the same city. A supplier may supply one or more different kinds of parts to the company. A part is identified by a catalogue number, and also has a short description. Projects purchase parts from the nearest location which stocks the part. The company keeps a record of the purchase orders (i.e.,part, supplier, and quantity) of each project.

4.3 Write an information model corresponding to the following description.

A University is organised into academic, research and administrative departments. Administrative staff may work in any kind of department, but neither academic staff nor research staff work in the administrative departments. Academic staff teach courses and may do research work. Research staff are limited to research work only. Administrative staff neither teach nor do research. All undergraduate and some graduate students attend courses. There is a fee for each course, the amount of which differs according to the course. Students are graded on each course they attend, with a grade having a value between 0 and 100. It is a tradition, however, of the University that no student has ever been graded at either 0 or 100. Some undergraduate students may be employed part-time to assist the administrative staff, but only if their grade is 75 or more. All staff get paid a salary, the amount of which depends on their position. Graduate students do research. They may teach not more than two courses, and are paid at a fixed rate per course. No person under the age of 18 may be paid, and the retirement age is 65.

4.4 Write an information model about the delivery of items according to the following description.

The currency of Fluidistan is the G. This is divided into the smaller p and z units, where G1 = 8p and 1p = 16z. The amount 190z, for example, is written as G1-7-12. Linear measures in Fluidistan are the inch and foot, where 1 foot equals 12 inches. The weight measures are the pound and ounce, where 1 pound is 16 ounces.

The government of Fluidistan operate a mail delivery service for certain kinds of item. There are also private delivery services which will accept any kind of item. The following are the regulations governing the Fluidistan mail service.

Post Cards: The card rate is 1p 3z. To qualify for the card rate a postcard must be of a uniform thickness and no thinner than 0.007 inches. It must be no larger than 4.25 by 6 inches and no smaller than 3.5 by 5 inches.

Letters: The letter rate is 1p 13z for letters weighing one ounce or less. The rate increases by 1p 6z for each additional ounce or part thereof. An item weighing more than 11 ounces cannot be sent at the letter rate. Letters less than one ounce are non-standard if the length is greater than 11.5 inches or the height is greater than 6.125 inches or the thickness is greater than 0.25 inches or the length to height ratio is not between 1.3 and 2.5 inclusive. Non-standard letters are subject to a surcharge of 10z in addition to the standard rate.

Parcels: The parcel rate is G2-4-2 for items not exceeding two pounds in weight. The rate increases by by 2p 11z for each additional pound or part thereof, provided the weight is not greater than ten pounds. Above ten pounds the rate increases by 2p 8z for each additional pound or part thereof. Note: Parcels weighing less than fifteen pounds and whose length plus girth exceeds seven feet are chargeable at the fifteen pound rate.

Size Standards: Items whose thickness is less than 0.007 inches are not accepted for delivery. Items less than 0.25 inches in thickness must be rectangular in shape and at least 3.5 inches high and at least 5 inches long. Items weighing more than 70 pounds are not accepted for delivery.

Environmental: Neither hazardous materials nor live or dead animals will be accepted for delivery. All items, except cards, must be enclosed in some wrapping. Items enclosed in environmentally sound and recycleable wrapping are entitled to a discount of ten percent of the applicable rate; if this results in a fraction of a z, the rate is rounded up to the nearest z.

4.6 Further reading

The specification for the worked example was taken from an ISO technical Report [ISO87]. This contains several renditions of the example using different kinds of representations including Entity-Relationship, a NIAM like approach and a formulation based on predicate logic.

Approaches to 'Finding the objects' are described by, among others, Peter Coad [Coa92a], Norman Kerth [Ker92], and Mark Whiting [WD90].

Chapter 5

Modeling principles

> Too servile a submission to the books and
> opinions of the ancients has spoiled many an
> ingenious man, and plagued the world with
> an abundance of pedants and coxcombs.
>
> *James Puckle*

We now look at some of the more general principles which should be applied
when creating an information model. These principles have evolved through
experience in creating a wide variety of models.

We have tried to separate the topics but, as with any non-trivial subject,
there are inevitably overlaps between these, and also some of the principles
exhibit a creative tension between them. That is to say that complete
adherence to one principle may prevent complete adherence to another;
there are trade-offs that can be made and these will vary according to the
modeling scope and purpose, and the choice of representation methods.

In general, an information model should be precise, complete, non-
ambiguous, minimally redundant and implementation independent. The
modeling should tend towards clarity rather than conciseness.

5.1 Readability

An information model, although if defined via EXPRESS is computer interpretable, should primarily be designed for a human reader. The modeling
constructs should be chosen to aid the reader rather than obfuscate understanding by using complex, intertwined or opaque definitional relationships,
particularly if they are comingled with obscure, pretentious, tautological
and circumlocutory prosody.

It is advantageous to present a model in more than one way, for example
using both lexical and graphical representations. This, though, raises a
potential ambiguity problem when the multiple representations are not in
agreement. Any model that involves multiple representations must be clear

about which representation is primary, so the 'legal' source is clear in case of disagreements between the various model forms.

5.2 Scoping

Define the scope *and assumptions* of the information model. This should be done at the start of the modeling project.

It may turn out that for a complex model, the overall scoping statement can be partitioned into several more detailed scopes each of which serves a particular purpose in the overall model.

A scope also defines a *context* in which the model items reside, thus providing a specific viewpoint in which the items are defined.

One view of a model is that it can be considered to consist of a set of scopes and contexts within which the details are represented. The model should be documented according to these aspects. A book or a report can be taken as an analogy — these are broken up into chapters or sections, each discussing a particular aspect. An information model should be structured and documented in a similar manner. As far as possible, each section should be self-contained with as few references as possible between the different topics. This makes for easier understanding by the reader and also assists in the potential re-usability of the several portions of the model.

Some model representation methods permit such divisions in a model to be made explicit. If these capabilities are present in the representation then full advantage should be taken of them. For example, both EXPRESS and EXPRESS-G have the `Schema` construct. Putting it simply, a `Schema` represents a context and a scope.

All entities are defined within a schema and that schema may be referenced from other schemas. Thus each entity exists within a scope defined by its schema. That scope also defines a context which implicitly involves the definitions and semantics of all the entities in the same scope. Consider the following pair of schemas.

```
SCHEMA some_topology;

  ENTITY shell;
    components : SET [1:?] OF face;
  END_ENTITY;

  ENTITY face;
    -- attributes of the entity
  END_ENTITY;

END_SCHEMA;  -- end some_topology schema

SCHEMA some_constraint;
  USE FROM some_topology (shell);
```

```
REFERENCE FROM some_topology (face);

ENTITY brep;
   boundary : LIST [1:?] OF UNIQUE shell;
END_ENTITY;

RULE rule_1 FOR (shell, face);
  (* some constraint on shells and faces *)
END_RULE;

END_SCHEMA;  -- end some_constraint schema
```

The internals of the two schemas are hidden from each other, except where
they are imported into the some_constraint schema via the Reference
and Use statements. Simplistically, these indicate that if a reference to a
definition cannot be found within a given schema, then the definition can
be searched for among the imported elements. Within the context of the
some_topology schema, there is no constraint on face or shell entities.
However, within the context of the some_constraint schema there is such
a constraint.

5.3 The nym principle

The EXPRESS language specifies that within each schema, the name of each
definition must be unique, but the same name can be used for different
definitions in different schemas. This reuse of names may lead to confusion
in the mind of the reader. The principle to be applied is 'one name, one
meaning, one definition'.

As a side effect, the application of this principle permits easy reconfigu-
ration (e.g., partitioning into a different set of schemas) of the information
model.

In more general terms, the 'one name, one meaning, one definition' can
be expanded to the *nym principle* of 'no synonyms, no homonyms'.

5.4 Context independence

Each entity exists in a context in which it may be used. This may vary from
extremely broad (the whole universe of discourse) to highly specific. Consequently, an entity definition should be as context independent as possible
and as context specific as required at the same time.

Each entity should include only those constraints that are independent
of the contexts in which it may be used. Context dependent constraints can
be specified either through a specialization of the entity (i.e., subtyping),
or by constraints within a 'referencing' entity.

There is an implicit relationship between an entity and its scope. An entity is defined in a particular context together with its own constraints. The principle of contextual independence states that each entity must have only those constraints which are independent of the specific context bound tightly to it. Any constraint which is a consequence of the context or relates the entity to the context must be given as part of the scope.

In EXPRESS terms this principle implies that only those constraints which apply to every usage of the entity should be stated in the local **Where** rules.

Any other constraints should be given either in a **Rule** or as a **Where** clause in an entity which references it. If necessary, a **Rule** need only reference the single entity type.

To illustrate, consider edges and loops in topology, where a loop is composed of a list of edges. In one form of topology there is a constraint which states that every edge must belong to two and only two distinct loops; in a slightly less restricted form of topology the constraint is that an edge must be used twice by the loops (i.e., either appear in two distinct loops or appear twice in a single loop). These effectively define a manifold geometry. In non-manifold geometry these restrictions are totally relaxed and an edge can belong to zero, one or many loops. Thus the constraint is context dependent. In EXPRESS the second constraint (that edges must be used twice by the loops) can be modeled using a **Rule** as:

```
ENTITY edge;
  p1 : point;
  p2 : point;
END_ENTITY;

ENTITY loop;
  edges : LIST [1:?] OF edge;
END_ENTITY;

RULE edge_loop FOR (edge, loop);
  (* edges must be used twice by loops *)
LOCAL
  edges_in_loops : BAG [0:?] OF edge := [];
END_LOCAL;
REPEAT i := 1 TO SIZEOF(loop);
  edges_in_loop := edges_in_loop + loop[i].edges;
END_REPEAT;
WHERE
  manifold : SIZEOF(edges_in_loop) = 2*SIZEOF(edge);
END_RULE;
```

There are of course alternatives to this. The constraint could be placed in the **edge** entity or in the **loop** entity. In both cases this has the attraction of being simpler to write and process for implementation. However it renders both entities possibly unusable in other contexts. The use of subtyping is, perhaps, the optimum solution in that it provides structural clarity while not violating the nym principle.

```
ENTITY edge;
  p1 : point;
  p2 : point;
END_ENTITY;

ENTITY loop;
  edges : LIST [1:?] OF edge;
END_ENTITY;

ENTITY manifold_edge
  SUBTYPE OF (edge);
INVERSE
  loops : BAG [2:2] OF loop FOR edges;
END_ENTITY;

ENTITY more_restricted_manifold_edge
  SUBTYPE OF (manifold_edge);
INVERSE
  loops : SET [2:2] OF loop FOR edges;
END_ENTITY;
```

It is worth noting that we do not wish to prevent any application from creating context dependent entity definitions. It is quite possible to envisage specialized entities with only one sensible context. Such entities should be clearly commented as such to show that they have resulted from a clear and considered decision.

5.5   Implementation independence

An information model defines the *information* necessary for an enterprise of interest; it is not defining the *data* structuring. The data and structuring will be different for different implementation technologies. Essentially, the information model defines the *what* and not the *how*.

One example is a model that was being created for the purposes of defining the data that needed to be exchanged between two Computer Aided Drafting (CAD) systems. The intended data exchange method was to be via a data file. The thinking of one group of modelers was dominated by the idea of efficiency in the file exchange process; 'efficiency' in this case being concerns about minimizing the number of data types to be transmitted and minimizing the number of data values. The resulting model made much use of default values and multiple meanings for the entities in the model. The other modeling group concentrated more on completeness and non-redundancy, leading to a model with many more entities.

For the purposes of information modeling, the second group had the correct approach. Although aimed at a data file implementation in the first place, the basic information model should be targeted at independence from implementation form. The basic reasoning being followed here is that of the ANSI/SPARC three level schemas:

- external schemas (application views)
- conceptual schema
- internal schemas (physical forms)

where the conceptual schema is intended to be independent of both usage and implementation.

An information model corresponds to the conceptual schema in this hierarchy. It is important to preserve independence from implementation both in detail and on larger scales.

In the example case, this was brought home to the 'efficient file' modelers when a different data exchange mechanism was proposed which negated much of their carefully crafted model as it did not support efficiency in the new environment.

The language selected to represent the model has a large part to play here. Some languages, such as SQL, are intimately bound up with a particular implementation method. Others, such as EXPRESS allow much greater freedom from a particular style of implementation.

5.5.1 Abstraction

Stemming from the implementation independence principle, the following type of constructs need special justification if used in an information model:

- Specification of the 'precision' of the base types (e.g., number of digits in a number, the length of a string, etc.).
- Specification of default values.
- Using fixed size aggregations instead of dynamic aggregations.

5.6 Invariance

Another principle is that of invariance. Again this follows from similar practice in the database area. It can be stated as follows: the meaning of an entity should not be dependent on the values of its attributes.

Where this typically shows up as a problem is in entities with attributes such as 'flag' or 'form'. The appropriate values for the remaining attributes often change with the value of flag or form, resulting in complex constraints which try to accommodate the changes. The code below, where the **sex** attribute acts as a flag, exhibits this behaviour. The problem in this case is that only females may have maiden names, so a constraint has to be written to ensure that males cannot have a value for the maiden name.

```
ENTITY person;
    sex        : enumeration_of_male_female;
    name       : STRING;
```

```
    ss_number     : INTEGER;
    maiden_name : OPTIONAL STRING;
    spouse        : OPTIONAL person;
    children      : SET [0:?] OF person;
  UNIQUE
    one_id : ss_number;
  WHERE
    WR1 : ((sex = male) AND (NOT EXISTS(maiden_name))) XOR
          (sex = female);
    WR2 : (EXISTS(spouse) AND (sex <> spouse.sex)) XOR
          NOT EXISTS(spouse);
  END_ENTITY;
```

The entity should be expanded into a number of subtypes if at all possible. The flag value (**sex** in this example) now becomes part of the subtype name (and its corresponding definition).

```
ENTITY person
  SUPERTYPE OF (ONEOF(female,
                      male));
  name       : STRING;
  ss_number : INTEGER;
  children   : SET [0:?] OF person;
UNIQUE
  one_id : ss_number;
END_ENTITY;

ENTITY female
  SUBTYPE OF (person);
  maiden_name : OPTIONAL STRING;
  husband     : OPTIONAL male;
END_ENTITY;

ENTITY male
  SUBTYPE OF (person);
  wife : OPTIONAL female;
END_ENTITY;
```

As this example shows, other entities in the model may now refer either to the generic **person** or to specific types of person without having to define constraints on the **sex** attribute as they would have had to do with the first definition. Note also that the original constraint specifying that spouses must not be of the same sex is no longer required as it is now part of the model structure.

In general, the invariance principle leads to a cleaner, simpler and more understandable model.

5.7 Constraint

An information model is permissive rather than restrictive. That is, domains and relationships may take any values unless these are restricted in some manner. The modeling of constraints is just as important as the modeling of objects.

For example, consider an object **age**. Typically this would be represented by a number. In a permissive model, the value of the number could lie anywhere between plus and minus infinity.

```
TYPE age = INTEGER;
END_TYPE;
```

This, though, does not match the semantic normally associated with **age** which is usually given in terms of a non-negative number value. Therefore, any use of number to represent an **age** should be constrained to be non-negative.

```
TYPE age = INTEGER;
WHERE
  non-negative : SELF >= 0;
END_TYPE;
```

5.7.1 Structure

An information model has a structure given by the relationships between the items in the model. Having said that constraints are an important part of any model, the question arises of how to best represent these. The ordering should be:

1. Structurally embedded

2. Local to an item

3. Global

The structural aspects of a model dictate what may and may not may go together. Other constraints have to take the form of some sort of rule or checking procedure. It is all too easy to break the law, either deliberately or inadvertently.

A real world example of a structural constraint comes from the jet engine industry. Because of the highly stressed environment within an engine special materials have to be used for the nuts and bolts. In the critical regions of an engine, these have unique sizes and thread forms depending on the material they are made from. This ensures that fasteners of the wrong material physically cannot be used in the wrong place. The same effect cannot be guaranteed via assembly instructions — the fitter may inadvertently select a bolt made from low performance material if it is the same shape as a high performance fastener.

Having structured the model to embody as many constraints as possible, the next best choice is to define constraints that are local to an item. These may then be checked when an instance of the item is created or queried.

Sometimes this is not sufficient, as when a constraint only applies to some instances of a given type. Then a global constraint must be specified.

Taking people as an example again, suppose we have

```
ENTITY female
  SUBTYPE OF (person);
  husband : OPTIONAL male;
END_ENTITY;

ENTITY male
  SUBTYPE OF (person);
  wife : OPTIONAL female;
END_ENTITY;
```

Structurally this says that a spouse must be someone of the opposite sex (the domains of the spouse attributes are of the opposite sex to the person with a spouse). By itself, this is not a sufficient constraint as we need to ensure that in any particular case, two people are each other's spouse. This could, in EXPRESS, be denoted by a global rule:

```
RULE marriage FOR (male, female);
  LOCAL
    s1 : BAG [0:?] OF male;
    s2 : BAG [0:?] OF female;
  END_LOCAL;
  s1 := QUERY(t <* male | EXISTS(t.wife) AND
                          t :<>: t.wife.husband);
  s2 := QUERY(t <* female | EXISTS(t.husband) AND
                            t :<>: t.husband.wife);
WHERE
  r1 : SIZEOF(s1) = 0;
  r2 : SIZEOF(s2) = 0;
END_RULE;
```

In order to check this some special procedure has to be developed. Further, it is easy to make an error in writing such a rule and conversely in reading it. Instead, in this case, local rules may be written in each entity, as:

```
ENTITY female
  SUBTYPE OF (person);
  husband : OPTIONAL male;
WHERE
  couple : NOT EXISTS(husband) XOR
           SELF :=: husband.wife;
END_ENTITY;

ENTITY male
  SUBTYPE OF (person);
  wife : OPTIONAL female;
WHERE
  pair : NOT EXISTS(wife) XOR
         SELF :=: wife.husband;
```

```
    END_ENTITY;
```

Again, some special procedure would have to be invoked to check the local constraint, and there is the possibility of errors in writing and reading the constraints.

The third, and recommended solution, is to use the structure of the model to enforce the constraint. Here we do it by adding a new entity to the model.

```
    ENTITY female
      SUBTYPE OF (person);
    END_ENTITY;

    ENTITY male
      SUBTYPE OF (person);
    END_ENTITY;

    ENTITY married;
      husband : male;
      wife    : female;
    UNIQUE
      no_polygamy  : wife;
      no_polyandry : husband;
    END_ENTITY;
```

No special procedures are called for in validating the constraint. Further, this structural solution leaves open the possibility of a simple modification to the model to take account of polygamous and/or polyandrous societies at a later date by modifying the description of married.

5.7.2 Constraint functions

EXPRESS provides functions as a means of specifying complex constraints. That is, code may be written in the body of the function to formally specify a constraint via some algorithmic procedure. Conceptually, any constraint that can be expressed in an algorithmic or logical manner can be catered for. However, experience has shown that the types of constraints that information modelers wish to specify fall into several classes.

1. Simple logical statement. For example that a number must be greater than zero.

2. Can be easily expressed as a simple algorithm. An example is checking a date for the correct days in the month, taking into account leap years.

3. Can be expressed as an algorithm, but this is complex and/or long and tedious. An example is determining whether a boundary representation solid model represents a 2-manifold[1] object — solid modeling

---

[1] Manifold is a mathematical term whose elucidation takes a textbook on topology.

system vendors have spent tens of hundreds of man-years developing such algorithms.

4. Cannot be expressed as an algorithm, either because given the current state of knowledge, there is no algorithm, or if there is it does not apply to every desired situation. An example of this category is determining whether an arbitrary geometric surface is manifold. This can be done for special cases, but not in general.

We firmly believe that all constraints should be present formally in an information model. Constraints in class 1 can be expressed either as an in-line logical statement or as a function call in a local or global rule. Constraints in the other classes should be documented via a function call; the presence of the call formally documents the existence of a constraint and provides a name for it (the function name). At a minimum, this enables the determination of those things which have identical constraints.

We recommend that for class 2 constraints the body of the function be present. That is, formally and precisely document the constraint. By their very nature, class 4 constraints cannot be formally documented. In this case only the function signature is required (that is, the name, formal parameters and return type of the function). A comment should be placed in the body of the function to explain in words what it would do if it could. Class 3 constraints can either be treated like class 2 or 4, depending on the inclinations of the model developers.

As an aside, functions in EXPRESS should be treated as pseudo-code by an implementor of the model. That is, they specify a means of obtaining a desired effect, but should not be taken as the only, or best, way of achieving the effect.

5.8   Reality

Create entities that have a strong correspondence to reality. Often these can be easily related to natural language sentences which are meaningful to the subject matter experts.

Do not create entities which are just a bunch of (unrelated) attributes.

```
ENTITY make;
   result : silk_purse;
   from   : sows_ear;
END_ENTITY;
```

Actually, this example shows how difficult it is to be pedantic about things. In normal circumstances the above is a nonsense combination of attributes, but could be reasonable if the model had something to do with proverbs.

5.9   Redundancy

Do not introduce redundancy into the model.   For example

```
ENTITY poor_circle_2d;
   center    : point;
   radius    : REAL;
   diameter  : REAL;
   perimeter : REAL;
WHERE
   w1 : radius > 0.0;
   w2 : diameter > 0.0;
   w3 : perimeter > 0.0;
END_ENTITY;
```

is redundant as there are well known mathematical relationships between the radius, diameter and perimeter of a circle. This can, instead be modeled as:

```
ENTITY circle_2d;
   center : point;
   radius : REAL;
DERIVE
   diameter  : REAL := 2.0*radius;
   perimeter : REAL := 2.0*PI*radius;
WHERE
   w1 : radius > 0.0;
END_ENTITY;
```

Redundancy leads to the possibility of ambiguities in model instances. In the case of the entity **poor_circle_2d** there is nothing to prevent a particular instance having incompatible values for the radius, perimeter and diameter.

Remember that redundancy is not limited to attributes within a particular entity, but may span several entities. We saw an example of this when developing the car registration authority model (see Figure 4.7).

5.10   Concepts

Model the underlying concepts not the surface appearance, description or data. There are several aspects to this principle.

5.10.1   Syntax

Do not model descriptions or syntactical structures. There is typically an underlying concept that should be made visible without the syntactic sugar.

EXPRESS may be used to model itself (i.e., use the language to produce a meta-model of itself). Remembering that entities have attributes, these could be described using code like

```
TYPE
separator_char = STRING(1) FIXED; WHERE
  SELF = ':';
END_TYPE;

TYPE eol_char = STRING(1) FIXED;
WHERE
  SELF = ';';
END_TYPE;

TYPE simple_id = STRING;
WHERE
  -- restrictions to ensure string is a simple identifier
END_TYPE;

ENTITY poor_attribute;
  id        : simple_id;
  separator : separator_char;
  domain    : attribute_domain;
  eol       : eol_char;
END_ENTITY;
```

The entity **poor_attribute** is principally representing the syntax of an EX-
PRESS attribute. The purpose of an information model is to capture the
underlying concepts of a thing — not its representation (which could take
many forms). So, a better model is:

```
TYPE name = STRING;
END_TYPE;

ENTITY better_attribute;
  role   : name;
  domain : attribute_domain;
END_ENTITY;
```

5.10.2   Implied correspondence

Do not use 'corresponding' arrays or lists. For example

```
ENTITY poor_exam_result;
  exam     : STRING;
  students : LIST [1:?] OF UNIQUE person;
  marks    : LIST [1:?] OF INTEGER;
WHERE
  corresponding : SIZEOF(students) = SIZEOF(marks);
END_ENTITY;
```

where the values in the two lists are meant to be in one-to-one correspondence (i.e., matching a student and a mark). If they *are* in one-to-one
correspondence then there is some (conceptual) relationship between them,
and this should be brought out in the model. A better representation is:

```
ENTITY student_mark;
   student : person;
   mark    : INTEGER;
END_ENTITY;

ENTITY better_exam_result;
   exam    : STRING;
   results : LIST [1:?] OF student_mark;
END_ENTITY;
```

5.10.3   Optional and default values

An entity with an optional attribute is possibly wrong. An entity with only optional attributes is almost certainly wrong.

The presence or absence of a value for an optional attribute in an entity instance has no effect on the meaning or other characteristics of the entity. There are actually few legitimate uses for an optional attribute. One of the cases happens to be when modeling a person and it may be desireable to take account of the fact that some people have nicknames, but this is not an essential characteristic of a person.

An information model should not provide for default values for missing values of optional attributes, even though some model representation languages have facilities for this. It presupposes knowledge about the use and implementation of the model which may not always be valid — it goes against the implementation independence principle.

EXPRESS does not have a facility for default values. However, there is the **NVL** function which, given an attribute will return the attribute value if present or, if the attribute has no value, returns a user-specified value. The intended use of this is for the specification of constraints which include optional attributes. A perverted use of this construct has been to provide default values. This is wrong, as in the example below.

```
ENTITY bad_graphic_attributes_entity;
   color  : OPTIONAL display_color;
   weight : OPTIONAL line_weight;
   style  : OPTIONAL line_style;
DERIVE
   default_color  : display_color := NVL(color, black);
   default_weight : line_weight := NVL(weight, 1.0);
   default_style  : line_style := NVL(style, plain);
END_ENTITY;
```

Effectively this is saying that there are always values for the graphic attributes. If there are always values, then the model should be written in that vein, as:

```
ENTITY better_graphic_attributes_entity;
   color  : display_color;
   weight : line_weight;
```

```
   style  : line_style;
END_ENTITY;
```

5.11   Hierarchies

Use hierarchies as an organizing principle among the concepts being modeled, where items higher in a hierarchy are a more general kind of thing than the lower items which are more specialized kinds of thing. These are one way of applying the invariance principle.

5.11.1   Inheritance

Some representation languages support inheritance of properties from entities higher in a hierarchy. In EXPRESS the existence of attributes is inherited by subtypes from their supertypes; subtypes also inherit all the constraints applied to their supertypes.

Common attributes should be migrated upwards as far as possible in the generalization structure. This reinforces the statement that the attributes are not only common but are the same!

Note that this does not imply that values are inherited between instances. Each instance of a subtype entity *is* an instance of the supertype. Therefore they share (have) the same value for any common attributes. In EXPRESS the **Derive** section can be used to model value inheritance between entities but this is independent of the generalization tree.

5.11.2   Data aggregation

Do not use inheritance hierarchies for data aggregation. For example, a straight line can be defined in terms of a point on the line and the direction vector of the line. One bad way of representing this is:

```
ENTITY point;
   coords : ARRAY [1:3] OF REAL;
END_ENTITY;

ENTITY vector;
   cosines : ARRAY [1:3] OF REAL;
WHERE
   unit_vector :
       cosines[1]**2 + cosines[2]**2 + cosines[3]**2 = 1.0;
END_ENTITY;

ENTITY bad_directed_line
   SUBTYPE OF (point,vector);
END_ENTITY;
```

Instead, the **directed_line** should be modeled as

```
ENTITY directed_line;
  location  : point;
  direction : vector;
END_ENTITY;
```

because, although a **directed_line** can be described or identified uniquely by a point and a vector, it *is not* a point and a vector at the same time — it cannot replace points and vectors.

5.12   Simple types

Simple types (e.g., strings and numbers) by themselves carry virtually no semantics. For example, a string representing a person's name is conceptuall different from a string representing the serial number of a piece of equipment. If the representation language permits, as EXPRESS and EXPRESS-G do, these should be modeled as different types so that their semantics are more easily discerned and their (mis)use more obvious. Here are some examples.

```
TYPE name = STRING; END_TYPE;
TYPE serial_number = STRING; END_TYPE;
TYPE length = NUMBER; END_TYPE;
TYPE area = NUMBER; END_TYPE;
```

5.13   Exercises

5.1 Section 5.4 mentions putting certain constraints in **edge** and **loop** entities. Write models embodying these constraints.

5.2 Explain the **marriage** rule given in Section 5.7.1.

5.3 The entity **poor_exam_result** (see 5.10.2) has an attribute **students** defined as LIST [1:?] OF UNIQUE person. What is the meaning of UNIQUE in this case, and how is the meaning of the entity changed if it was not present? Does the entity **better_exam_result** match with the entity **poor_exam_result**? If not, then how would you modify the second model to match the first?

5.4 Can you think of circumstances where value inheritance (see 5.11) would be important?

5.5 Create an information model for the following.
The BMD authority is responsible for recording births, marriages, divorces and deaths. At birth the name of the child, its sex, its date of birth, and its parents are recorded. The spouses and the date of the marriage are recorded. A similar record is kept for each divorce. The divorced couple and date are recorded. Deaths are recorded after the issuance of a death certificate. The date of death and the signatory of

the death certificate are recorded. The legal age for marriage is eighteen, but minors between the ages of sixteen and eighteen may marry
with their parents' consent. Upon request, the BMD authority will
provide information on the marital status of anybody (i.e., whether
they are single, married, divorced, widowed or deceased). They will
also provide, to the person concerned, a listing of all their ancestors.

5.6 Write a model that captures the following information about a very
simple bridge.

Simplistically, a bridge can be considered to be a simply supported
beam, of length l, with width b and depth h. The beam is of uniform
material having density d and modulus of elasticity E. As well as its
own weight, a bridge must support a uniformly distributed load L,
and a point load P at the center of the span. There are limits on the
maximum deflection, y, of the span under load and also limits on the
maximum stress, s, in the beam.

The moment of inertia, I, of the beam cross-section is given by

$$I = \frac{bh^3}{12}$$

and the maximum stress at any beam cross-section is given by

$$s = \frac{Mh}{2I}$$

where M is the bending moment.

For a beam of length l with a total uniformly distributed load of W,
the maximum bending moment is

$$M = \frac{Wl}{8}$$

while for a point load W at the center of the beam it is

$$M = \frac{Wl}{4}$$

The maximum deflection of a uniformly loaded beam is

$$y = \frac{5Wl^3}{384EI}$$

and for a center loaded beam is

$$y = \frac{Wl^3}{48EI}$$

Bending moments, deflections and stresses are additive with respect
to loading conditons. That is, the total bending moment is the sum
of the bending moments for the uniform load case and the point load
case.

5.7 Produce a model of the following cartesian geometry items.

A point is a location in space and is defined by its location with respect to the origin of a coordinate system The location is represented by the x, y and z coordinate values. A vector is a direction and is represented in terms of three numbers corresponding to its relative extent in the x, y and z coordinate directions.

A plane can be represented by a point through which it passes, and the direction of the normal to the plane surface.

A straight line can be represented by a point on the line and a vector denoting its direction.

A circle is a planar curve. It can be represented by a center point, the normal to the plane in which it lies, and a non-negative radius value.

An ellipse is a planar curve. It can be represented by a center point, the normal to the plane on which it lies, major and minor non-negative radius values, and the direction of the major radius.

A parabola is a planar curve. It can be represented by a vertex point, the normal to the plane on which it lies, a non-negative focal distance, and the direction of the focus from the vertex.

5.14 Further reading

Most database books describe the ANSI/SPARC three-schema architecture. A comprehensive presentation is given by Tsichritzis and Klug [TK78].

Chapter 6

Integration and specialization

> We are not fighting for integration, nor are we fighting for seperation.

Speech, Black Revolution
Malcolm X

The major topic of this Chapter is modeling in the large. By this we mean looking at methods to integrate several different models into a single cohesive whole, and also examining the inverse problem of extracting a small specialized model from a larger one.

Before we can sensibly discuss these, though, we need to look more closely at two aspects of EXPRESS, namely subtyping and schema interfacing.

6.1 Supertypes and subtypes

EXPRESS has a concept of `Supertype` and `Subtype` which taken together enable a type lattice to be constructed. A Subtype-Supertype relationship is typically called an 'Isa' relationship in data modeling terms. That is, a Subtype is a kind of its Supertype(s). For example, if we define an entity `pet` and also define two subtypes of this called `cat` and `goldfish` then an instance of `cat` is also an instance of `pet`, and similarly for a `goldfish`. The relationship, though, is asymmetrical, as a `pet` may be something other than a `cat` or `goldfish`; for instance a pet may also be a dog. A Subtype is a more specialized kind of thing than its Supertype and, conversely, a Supertype is a generalization of its Subtypes.

A Subtype inherits all the attributes and constraints of its Supertype(s). In EXPRESS an entity is a Subtype of another entity if it declares its Supertype entity within its `Subtype` declaration. A Supertype does not declare its Subtypes.

In general, an instance of a Subtype requires an instantiation of each of its Supertypes, while an instance of a Supertype does not require instantiation of its Subtypes. This later behavior may be modified by declaring the Supertype to be an **Abstract** Supertype, in which case an instance of the Supertype does require instantiation of at least one of its Subtypes.

In most data modeling and Object Oriented languages that support similar notions to Subtyping, if an instance of a Supertype requires instantiation of a Subtype, then one and only one Subtype can be instantiated. EXPRESS does not have this restriction. Unless otherwise constrained, an instance of a Supertype may be accompanied by one instance of each of its Subtypes. For example, given the following EXPRESS definitions

```
ENTITY super;
END_ENTITY;

ENTITY sub1
  SUBTYPE OF (super);
END_ENTITY;

ENTITY sub2
  SUBTYPE OF (super);
END_ENTITY;
```

then we can have, in EXPRESS-I instances, the following:

```
(* supertype only *)
suponly = super{};

(* supertype + one subtype *)
sup_and_sub1 = super{SUPOF(@sub1_1);};
sub1_1       = sub{SUBOF(@sup_and_sub1);};

(* supertype + one subtype *)
sup_and_sub2 = super{SUPOF(@sub2_1);};
sub2_1       = sub{SUBOF(@sup_and_sub2);};

(* supertype + both subtypes *)
sup_and_subs = super{SUPOF(@sub1_2, @sub2_2);};
sub1_2       = sub1{SUBOF(@sup_and_subs);};
sub2_2       = sub2{SUBOF(@sup_and_subs);};
```

This default relationship between Subtype instances is termed an **AndOr** relationship.

If the supertype is constrained to be **Abstract**

```
ENTITY super
  ABSTRACT SUPERTYPE;
END_ENTITY;
```

then the instance labelled *supertype only* in the EXPRESS-I model is no longer legal.

The relationship between Subtype instances can be constrained to be OneOf meaning that if an instance of a Supertype is accompanied by Subtype instances, then only one of those Subtypes mentioned can be instanced:

```
ENTITY super
  SUPERTYPE OF (ONEOF(sub1, sub2));
END_ENTITY;
```

In this case, the instance labelled *supertype + both subtypes* in the EXPRESS-I model is invalid.

The OneOf constraint is the most commonly used because most Subtype instances are disjoint. More rarely is the default AndOr constraint utilized. One example of its use, though, is when the roles that an object may play differ over the lifetime of the object. Perhaps a person is the prototypical example of this.

```
ENTITY person;
END_ENTITY;

ENTITY student
  SUBTYPE OF (person);
END_ENTITY;

ENTITY teacher
  SUBTYPE OF (person);
END_ENTITY;

ENTITY pensioner
  SUBTYPE OF (person);
END_ENTITY;
```

In this model, a person may be a student and/or a teacher and/or a pensioner, or none of these (say a house-painter, which category of person is outside the scope of the model). During a person's lifetime he may play any of these roles, sometimes simultaneously, as in the case of a graduate student at a university who also has some teaching duties; but he is the same person throughout.

As another example, consider the set of non-negative integers $(0, 1, \ldots)$. This set may be partitioned in many different ways:

- Even and odd numbers: $(0, 2, 4, 6, \ldots)$ and $(1, 3, 5, 7, \ldots)$
- Prime numbers: $(2, 3, 5, 7, \ldots)$
- Divisible by 3: $(3, 6, 9, 12, \ldots)$
- Divisible by 4: $(4, 8, 12, 16 \ldots)$

In EXPRESS terms, the natural numbers could be modeled as a supertype and the other sets of numbers as subtypes. It can readily be seen that while some of the sets of numbers corresponding to subtypes are non-overlapping (e.g., the even and odd subtypes) others do have some members in common (e.g., the sets 'Divisible by 3' and 'Divisible by 4' have the members $(12, 24, \ldots)$ in common).

The following code captures the relationships between even and odd and prime numbers. Numbers are either even or odd, so a `OneOf` constraint is declared between these two subtypes. A prime number may be either even or odd and hence the default (`AndOr`) relationship applies between primes and the even-odd numbers.

```
ENTITY natural
  SUPERTYPE OF (ONEOF(oddnum,evennum));
  val : INTEGER;
WHERE
  non-negative : SELF >= 0;
END_ENTITY;

ENTITY oddnum
  SUBTYPE OF (natural);
WHERE
  not_even : ODD(SELF\natural.val);
END_ENTITY;

ENTITY evennum
  SUBTYPE OF (natural);
WHERE
  not_odd : NOT ODD(SELF\natural.val);
END_ENTITY;

ENTITY prime
  SUBTYPE OF (natural);
  -- primality constraint
END_ENTITY;
```

This gives rise to the following possibilities for instances:

- Natural numbers: e.g., $0, 1, 2, 3, 4, 5, 6, 7, \ldots$
- Odd natural numbers: e.g., $1, 3, 5, 7, 9, 11, 13, 15, \ldots$
- Even natural numbers: e.g., $0, 2, 4, 6, 8, 10, 12, 14, \ldots$
- Prime natural numbers: e.g., $2, 3, 5, 7, 9, 11, 13, 17, \ldots$
- Odd prime natural numbers: e.g., $3, 5, 7, 9, 11, 13, 17, \ldots$
- Even prime natural numbers: i.e., 2

6.2 Schema interfacing

In EXPRESS a model may be partitioned into different schemas. The contents of one schema are invisible to other schemas unless they are imported. There is no provision for a schema to keep its contents private. Items defined within a schema are said to be *first-class*. That is, they can have instances within the information base that are independent of any use of the instances by any other entity instances. For example, given the following model

```
SCHEMA small;

  TYPE coord = REAL; END_TYPE;

  ENTITY point;
    x : coord;
    y : coord;
  END_ENTITY;

  ENTITY line;
    start : point;
    end   : point;
  END_ENTITY;
END_SCHEMA;
```

there may be **point** instances which are not used in the definition of any **line** instances.

Two constructs are provided for importing stuff from another schema — **Use** and **Reference**. Items that are imported via a **Use** become first-class in the importing schema. Items that are imported via a **Reference** become *second-class* within the importing schema. A second-class item is one which shall not be instanced unless it is referenced by another instance.

```
SCHEMA other;
  USE FROM small (line);
  REFERENCE FROM small (point);

TYPE pos_length = REAL;
WHERE
  non_negative : SELF >= 0.0;
END_TYPE;

ENTITY circle;
  center : point;
  radius : length;
END_ENTITY;
END_SCHEMA;
```

In this model, instances of **point** can only exist within schema **other** if they are required by instances of **line** or **circle**. An EXPRESS-I example of this model is:

```
MODEL a;
  SCHEMA_DATA small;
    p1 = point{x --> 0.0; y --> 0.0; };
    p2 = point{x --> 1.0; y --> -1.0; };
  END_SCHEMA_DATA;

  SCHEMA_DATA other;
    p3 = point{x --> 1.0; y --> 1.0; };
    p4 = point{x --> 2.0; 2.0; };
```

```
    l1 = line{start --> @p1; end --> @p3; };
    c1 = circle{center --> @p4; radius --> 1.0; };
(* Can't have p5 = point{x --> 3.0; y --> 3.0;};
    for example, as it is not part of the data of
    any line or circle instance *)
END_SCHEMA_DATA;
END_MODEL;
```

Any item imported into a schema will implicitly **Reference** the items it needs from the schema in which it was defined (see later for details). However, it is good modeling practice to explicitly import all the required definitions. Only items native to a schema or explicitly imported into a schema can be referenced within that schema.

```
SCHEMA third;
  REFERENCE FROM other (circle);
  REFERENCE FROM small (line);

  ENTITY ok;
    c : circle;
    l : line;
  WHERE
    w : (l.start = c.center) OR (l.end = c.center);
  END_ENTITY;

  ENTITY wrong;
    l : line;
    p : point;
  END_ENTITY;
END_SCHEMA;
```

The entity **wrong** in schema **third** is incorrect as it refers to the entity **point** which has not been explicitly imported into the schema, although it has been implicitly imported via the importation of the **circle** and **line**. The **point** can only be used as part of the instantiation of these entities.

6.3 Model integration

As we have noted earlier, the development of a large information model may have been partitioned among several modeling teams. At the end of the modeling project these Topical Information Models (TIMs) have to be integrated into a minimally redundant, non-ambiguous, and complete Integrated Information Model (IIM). It may also happen that there are a number of pre-existing IIMs that could be advantageously integrated to form a larger single IIM. The difference between these two scenarios is that in the first case the models will have been developed under the assumption that they would be integrated while there was no initial thoughts about integration in the second case. The practical difference in performing the model integration boils down to the fact that there is likely to be much more work involved in the second case than in the first, but the principles are the same.

There are different forms of integration which we have classed as below:

- Cosmetic — written by a single author.
- Editorial — elimination of synonyms and homonyms.
- Continuity — elimination of redundancies and identification of gaps.
- Structural — interfaces and 'meta-models'.
- Core based
- Evolutionary based

6.3.1 Cosmetic integration

The Cosmetic integration, although of importance, is of little concern here as it is about style rather than substance; the intent is to produce a consistently styled output so that it appears to be the result of a single mind and author rather than a plenitude of committees. In effect, both the modeling style and the documentation style should be consistent.

6.3.2 Editorial integration

Editorial integration is principally concerned with 'one name, one idea' (this is an application of the nym principle). That is, the same wording should be used to express the same idea throughout the model. The converse is that different names imply different ideas. It is also related to Cosmetics and is one method of performing Continuity integration. It can be considered to be 'integration in the small'.

Editorial integration applies both to the supporting model documentation and to the formal representation of the model.

For example, consider two models (schemas) that are to be integrated into a model about produce (i.e., fruit and vegetables). Assume that the schemas include the following definitions:

```
SCHEMA TimOne;
  ENTITY Date
    SUBTYPE OF (Fruit)
  END_ENTITY;

  TYPE DateAd = ARRAY [1:3] OF INTEGER;
  WHERE
    year_ad : SELF[3] > 0;
  END_TYPE;

  -- other definitions
END_SCHEMA;  -- end of schema TimOne
```

```
SCHEMA TimTwo;

  ENTITY Date;
    year   : INTEGER;
    month  : INTEGER;
    day    : INTEGER;
  WHERE
    ad : year > 0;
  END_ENTITY;

  -- other definitions
END_SCHEMA;  -- end of schema TimTwo
```

This poses some problems that have to be solved in order to integrate the schemas into a minimally redundant model. First, **Date** is a homonym between the two schemas; in one it is a fruit and in the other it is a calendar date. Note that the developers of the first schema, though, ensured that they did not have the homonym as they called the calendar date by the name **DateAd**. The homonym conflict between the two schemas must be resolved.

Secondly, the formal specification of a calendar date differs between the two schemas. In order for the integrated model to be minimally redundant, then one or other of these definitions should be eliminated.

A possible solution to these problems is to modify the two schemas as:

```
SCHEMA TimOne;
  USE FROM TimTwo (DateAd);

  ENTITY Date
    SUBTYPE OF (Fruit)
  END_ENTITY;

  -- other definitions
END_SCHEMA;  -- end of schema TimOne

SCHEMA TimTwo;

  ENTITY DateAd;
    year   : INTEGER;
    month  : INTEGER;
    day    : INTEGER;
  WHERE
    ad : year > 0;
  END_ENTITY;

  -- other definitions
END_SCHEMA;  -- end of schema TimTwo
```

In the first schema we have deleted the local calendar date definition and imported it instead. In the second schema we have changed the name of the calendar date definition to eliminate the homonym. There is, of course, another modification to be done, which is to check that all references to calendar dates refer to the name `DateAd`.

6.3.3 Continuity integration

Continuity checking is intended to identify redundancies between models (i.e., overlaps in scope or modeling) and, more importantly, to identify gaps between models, where X thinks that Y has provided something that he needs but Y was unaware of X's need.

The following example is a variant on the produce model in Section 6.3.2. In this scenario, the developers of `TimThree` were only concerned with fruit and vegetables, not calendar dates. Unfortunately, the developers of `TimFour` needed calendar dates and thought that these were going to be in `TimThree`, so they imported `Date` and got the fruit instead!

```
SCHEMA TimThree;

   ENTITY Date
     SUBTYPE OF (Fruit)
   END_ENTITY;

   -- other definitions
END_SCHEMA;  -- end of schema TimThree

SCHEMA TimFour;
   USE FROM TimThree (Date);

   -- other definitions
END_SCHEMA;  -- end of schema TimFour
```

In this case, the model is structurally sound, but does not reflect the modeler's intent. This is a more subtle problem than if, say, `TimFour` had imported `DateAd` from `TimThree` where there was no such definition.

6.3.4 Structural integration

Structural integration is essentially 'integration in the large', and is concerned with discovering general concepts underlying two or more TIMs. For example, an IIM is being created to specify the information within a windows-based graphical interface for a computer program. One group develops a TIM concerned with the textual aspects of the display. As part of the TIM they create a model for a text font library. A parallel group develops another TIM concerned with the graphical aspects; they create a model for a library of icons. The library concept is then common to the two TIMs, but its contents differ in the two cases. A schema describing the shared concept can be developed, and then specialised for use within the two models.

The other aspect of Structural integration is developing interfaces between different models. Continuing the example, it may have been decided that the library concept was important enough, or of such general applicability, that it should be a model in its own right. In this case, the text and graphical models both require an interface to the library model. Another example of interfacing is between a model that contains several different means of representing the shape of something, and application models that use shape. It is desireable that the application models should not be concerned with the particular details of shape representation. Therefore it is beneficial to define an interface to the shape model that hides the details.

6.3.5 Core based integration

Core based integration starts with developing a core information model (high level, very abstract and generic) to identify the major elements and the potential interfaces. The interfaces indicate the integration points where the individual TIMs interact. Further model development is then distributed among the modeling teams, based on these interfaces. This should make subsequent detailed integration easier. This is effectively taking a top-down approach to the development of a model.

Sometimes a bottom-up strategy has to be adopted, particularly when the models for integration are pre-existing and were not originally intended to be integrated with each other. In this case, the core model can be created as an abstraction of the original TIMs. This will give a framework that can assist in performing the integration.

6.3.6 Evolutionary based integration

If model development does not start from scratch but rather with an existing integrated model, then this predecessor version can be used in the same manner as the core model in the core based strategy.

This could also be considered to be a middle-out strategy. Typically, an IIM will be composed from several TIMs. One can either attempt to integrate all the TIMs simultaneously, or they could be integrated in a pairwise manner. That is, take two TIMs and produce an IIM corresponding to the pair. Then take another TIM and integrate it with the IIM; and so on until all the TIMs are dealt with.

6.3.7 Model quality

The global model is the sum of the modified partial models. To prove successful integration, the semantics of the partial models have to be deriveable from the global model. In other words, model integration must not lose any of the semantics associated with the TIMs, although the semantics may be represented in the IIM in a different manner.

6.4 Subsets and specialization

It may occur that once an Integrated Information Model (IIM) has been developed that, for certain purposes, a subset and/or a specialization of the model can be useful in its own right. In some sense, this is the converse of integration where individually developed TIMs are being merged into an IIM. We will call a specialized model an *Application Specialization Information Model* (ASIM).

The method for creating an ASIM from an IIM is to define a set of schemas for the ASIM which import from the IIM schemas. The items to be imported are only those that are relevant to the ASIM.

6.4.1 Subsetting

A subset of a model is one where some, but not all, the modeled objects in the original model are utilized in the new model. In EXPRESS terms, this effectively means a subset of the entities within the original model (which for completeness also have to 'bring along' any other entities or types which are used as attributes of these entities, together with any functions or rules that act as constraints on the entities).

The desired entities should be imported via Use statements. Their supports should be imported via Reference statements.

Subtype pruning

When a Subtype is Use imported, only its Supertypes are implicitly imported as well — its Subtypes are not imported unless either explicitly called for or are implicitly imported via their use as the domain of an attribute of another imported entity. This enables pruning of the Supertype lattice. Consider the following IIM schema.

```
SCHEMA iim;
  ENTITY e1 SUPERTYPE OF (ONEOF(e2,e3,e5));
  END_ENTITY;

  ENTITY e2 SUBTYPE OF (e1);
  END_ENTITY;

  ENTITY e3 SUBTYPE OF (e1);
  END_ENTITY;

  ENTITY e4 SUBTYPE OF (e1);
  END_ENTITY;
```

```
      ENTITY e5 SUBTYPE OF (e1);
      END_ENTITY;
  END_SCHEMA;
```

With this schema in hand, we show several subsets that could be produced. We display not only how a model subset can be extracted from a larger model, but also give examples of how the subset may be expanded into a self-contained model.

Firstly, suppose that only entity **e1** was wanted in the ASIM. All we need to do is import **e1**; none of the subtypes will be imported.

```
  SCHEMA subset;
    USE FROM iim (e1);
  END_SCHEMA;

  (* IS EQUIVALENT TO *)

  SCHEMA long_form_subset;
    ENTITY e1;
    END_ENTITY;
  END_SCHEMA;
```

Secondly, if **e1**, **e3**, **e4** and **e5** were needed in the subset, then they all have to be imported.

```
  SCHEMA subset;
    USE FROM iim (e1, e3, e4, e5);
  END_SCHEMA;

  (* IS EQUIVALENT TO *)

  SCHEMA long_form_subset;
    ENTITY e1 SUPERTYPE OF (ONEOF(e3, e5));
    END_ENTITY;

    ENTITY e3 SUBTYPE OF (e1);
    END_ENTITY;

    ENTITY e4 SUBTYPE OF (e1);
    END_ENTITY;

    ENTITY e5 SUBTYPE OF (e1);
    END_ENTITY;
  END_SCHEMA;
```

Finally, if only **e3**, **e4** and **e5** were desired in the subset, then again we import these. The difference between this case and the prior ones is that the supertype **e1** is implicitly imported as well. We show two means of representing the expansion of the model.

```
  SCHEMA subset;
    USE FROM iim (e3, e4, e5);
```

```
END_SCHEMA;

(* IS EQUIVALENT TO *)

SCHEMA long_form_1_subset;
  ENTITY e1 ABSTRACT SUPERTYPE OF (ONEOF(e3, e5));
  END_ENTITY;

  ENTITY e3 SUBTYPE OF (e1);
  END_ENTITY;

  ENTITY e4 SUBTYPE OF (e1);
  END_ENTITY;

  ENTITY e5 SUBTYPE OF (e1);
  END_ENTITY;
END_SCHEMA;

(* AND IS ALSO EQUIVALENT TO *)

SCHEMA long_form_2_subset;
  REFERENCE FROM auxiliary (e1);

  ENTITY e3 SUBTYPE OF (e1);
  END_ENTITY;

  ENTITY e4 SUBTYPE OF (e1);
  END_ENTITY;

  ENTITY e5 SUBTYPE OF (e1);
  END_ENTITY;
END_SCHEMA;

SCHEMA auxiliary;
  REFERENCE FROM long_form_2_subset (e3, e5);

  ENTITY e1 SUPERTYPE OF (ONEOF(e3, e5));
  END_ENTITY;
END_SCHEMA;
```

Note that when a supertype tree is pruned, the supertype constraints, if any, are also effectively pruned to eliminate reference to those subtypes which have been lopped off.

6.4.2 Specialization

A model may be specialized from a more general model by:

- Adding global rules to constrain entities (but this should only be done in exceptional circumstances as it violates the nym principle);
- Creating new Subtypes of (**Reference** or **Use**) imported entities to:
  - Add attributes;
  - Add constraint rules. In this context these may be:
    * all types of attribute specializations
    * new cardinality constraints
    * new uniqueness constraints
    * new local rules
    * new global rules

Note that creating new definitions does not result in a specialization but rather in a different model.

6.4.3 ASIM structure

In an ASIM it is typical that many of the items are only there to support the major items in the model. That is, they are second-class items. Note that this may also apply in an IIM but is usually much more noticeable in an ASIM. The reason for this is that an IIM is developed as a consistent whole, whereas an ASIM relies on an pre-existing IIM and therefore, unlike those producing an IIM, the developers of the ASIM do not have complete control.

In general, we can consider an ASIM to consist of the following components

1. The base IIM;

2. Specification of the IIM items of interest to the ASIM;

3. Possibly, additional ASIM specific items.

In EXPRESS terms, component 1 is represented by one or more schemas, component 2 by one or more schemas that import from the IIM, and component 3 by additional items within the schemas from component 2 and/or by other additional schemas.

There arises the question of how to document an ASIM, particularly if the IIM is large and the ASIM only represents a small portion of the IIM. We suggest that the IIM be contained in one report and the ASIM in a separate report that references the IIM. The ASIM should be a complete document in itself, containing the scope statement, model representation and other supporting material necessary to completely document the information model. The representations in the ASIM report may take two forms:

1. The primary, and required form, being component 2 together with, if necessary, component 3. We will call this the *short form* of the model. The purpose of this is to document the items of interest from the IIM,

together with any additional constructs necessary for completion or specialization.

2. A secondary form, which we will call the *long form*, which is a complete expansion of the short form which makes no reference to the IIM. It is this representation that enables the ASIM report to be read in isolation from the possibly voluminous IIM. It should therefore include all the relevant descriptive material from the IIM report.

The long form is derived from the IIM and the short form. Both the short and long forms are information models, and should abide by the information modeling principles described earlier.

As a guide to developing the short form, we suggest the following:

- By definition, the scope of the ASIM will be different from the scope of the IIM — a new scope statement is required. Almost by definition the viewpoint of the ASIM developers will be different from that of the IIM developers. The short form should be constructed to reflect the specific viewpoint. This implies that it will be partitioned and grouped differently from that of the IIM. Items in several IIM schemas may be put into a single ASIM schema, and conversely items in a single IIM schema may require separation into differing ASIM schemas.

- Utilize the EXPRESS schema interfacing capabilities to distinguish between first- and second-class items (i.e., utilize the Use import for first-class and the Reference import for second-class items).

- Utilize the schema interfacing capabilities to prune subtype trees, if required (i.e., only import those things that are required).

- If additional constructs are required, place them in the appropriate short form schema (and interface between the short form schemas as necessary).

As we said earlier, the long form representation is derived from the short form and the IIM. This is done by expanding out the short form schemas.

- For each short form schema that Use imports from the IIM, create a long form schema that includes the expansion of these imports, together with any additional ASIM specific constructs within the schema.

- The expansion of items that are Reference imported from the IIM should be placed in a separate long form schema(s), and Reference import these into the schemas that refer to them (this preserves the first- and second-class distinctions).

- In the expansion of entities, prune subtype trees and supertype constraints as appropriate.

We have observed that some ASIM developers like to represent the model by a single schema (one short form and one long form). This is bad practice as it contradicts the grouping principle and leads into modeling contortions.

For example, there may well be a desire in an ASIM to constrain many of the items that were first-class in the IIM to be second-class in the ASIM. We have seen models that use a global rule for this purpose. For instance:

```
SCHEMA poor_asim;
  USE FROM iim (first_class);

  ENTITY thing;
    attr : first_class;
  END_ENTITY;

  RULE second_class FOR (first_class);
  LOCAL
    s : BAG [0:?] OF first_class;
  END_LOCAL;
    s := QUERY(t <* first_class | SIZEOF(ROLESOF(t) = 0);
  WHERE
    r1 : SIZEOF(s) = 0;
  END_RULE;
END_SCHEMA;
```

The rule named **second_class** examines every instance of the entity called **first_class** in an information base and determines whether or not the instance is referenced by any other entity instance in the information base. The rule is violated if any instance is not so referenced.

This is extremely bad practice! Among other things it violates the principle of structural constraints. We repeat: an ASIM is an information model and it should be constructed according to the well founded principles of information modeling.

6.5 Exercises

6.1 Evaluate the allowable instance combinations in the following supertype tree.

```
SCHEMA super;
  ENTITY a SUPERTYPE OF (ONEOF(b, c) AND
                         ONEOF(d, e));
  END_ENTITY;

  ENTITY b SUBTYPE OF (a);
  END_ENTITY;

  ENTITY c SUBTYPE OF (a);
  END_ENTITY;

  ENTITY d SUBTYPE OF (a);
  END_ENTITY;
```

```
ENTITY e ABSTRACT SUPERTYPE OF
        (ONEOF(g, h))
        SUBTYPE OF (a);
END_ENTITY;

ENTITY f SUBTYPE OF (a);
END_ENTITY;

ENTITY g SUBTYPE OF (e);
END_ENTITY;

ENTITY h SUBTYPE OF (e);
END_ENTITY;
END_SCHEMA;
```

6.2 Section 6.4.1 shows examples of expanding a short from model into
an equivalent long form model. The third example has two dissimiliar
looking expansions. Explain why both the long forms have the same
affect.

6.3 Given the following schema

```
SCHEMA sub;
    USE FROM super (b, f, h);
END_SCHEMA;
```

where the schema **super** is as specified in Exercise 6.1, then:

1. Expand schema **sub** into a long form.
2. What are the allowable instance combinations in a model composed of schema **sub** or, equivalently, its long form?

6.4 In order to respond to increasing budget deficits and voter antipathy
to increased taxes, it has been decided to combine the Car Registration Authority (see Appendix A) and the BDM Authority (see
Exercise 5.5). Integrate the two information models to represent the
combined Authority.

6.5 Because of the rising unemployment rate, the government of Fluidistan is planning to increase the number of bureaucrats it employs by
splitting its postal service into three parts. One will be responsible
for setting the rules and regulations, another will be responsible for
delivering cards and letters, while the third will be responsible for
parcel delivery.

1. Starting with the model resulting from Exercise 4.4, produce two
   ASIMs, one for the letter and card·branch and the other for the
   parcel branch. These models should be presented in both short
   and long forms.
2. What happens to the ASIMs if the governemnt decide to alter
   the postal regulations and charges? What combination of IIM,
   short form ASIM and long form ASIM best meets the need to
   cater for change?

6.6 Further reading

For those coming from an OO programming background, the EXPRESS supertype constraints seem to pose a problem. Most OO programming languages, such as C++ [Str86] and Smalltalk [GR89], only support OneOf between sub-classes. Translating from EXPRESS entities to OO classes can then be tedious, but certainly not difficult.

Many of the modeling languages provide similar facilities to the EXPRESS supertype constraints. Examples include the extended entity relationship languages EER [BCN92, EN89] and XER [MVL92], NIAM [NH89], OMT [RBP+91], and the OSAM* language developed by Stanley Su and his co-workers [SKL89]. Even more complicated constraints are described in [Len90]. Kung [Kun90], on the other hand, puts forward a scheme whereby the simpler contraints can be added to SQL.

Batini, Ceri and Navathe [BCN92] provide some useful insights into the technical aspects schema integration in the EER modeling environment. The report by Winnie Lew and Patricia Machmiller [LM85], on the other hand, provides a look at some of the more human and managerial problems that can occur during a large integration project.

Chapter 7

Model documentation

> The historian, essentially, wants more
> documents than he can really use; the
> dramatist only wants more liberties than he
> can really take.

Prefaces: The Aspen Papers
Henry James

As is noted throughout this book, an information model does not merely consist of the formal model but also includes supporting editorial and technical material. Reading an uncommented EXPRESS model is like trying to decipher undocumented program code — possible, but error prone. Further, there are many things that cannot be expressed in EXPRESS — diagrams, for example, or references to the general literature, and so on.

Two forms of documentation appear to be prevelant: the *embedded* and the *partitioned* style. We discuss both of these, although we prefer the former of the two. The model developer, though, should decide on a style that suits the purposes at hand. We also indicate how versions of a document could be produced in either style. This is based on the fact that an information model can be stored electronically (i.e., as computer files), and printed versions produced via a wordprocessor or other kind of desktop publishing system.

7.1 General

The document style for an information model is typically much more detailed than is found for computer programs. On the other hand, it is usually less complex in its ordering than in the program documentation style known as *literate programming*.

In addition to documenting the overall scope and purpose of the model, the content and relationship of the schemas in the model should be described in broad terms. A diagrammatic sketch of the major elements and relationships in the model is also useful. This overview material should also

104

```
SCHEMA embedded_style;
  REFERENCE (embedded_style_support);

  ENTITY model_document
    introductory : description;
    schemas      : LIST [1:?] OF schema_document;
    finishing    : description;
  END_ENTITY;

END_SCHEMA; -- end of embedded_style
```

Figure 7.1: Main schema for a simple model of the embedded document style.

contain the definitions of terms that are used in the model. A section could also be included on the usage of the model, as seen by the authors.

Each aspect of a model (i.e., schema, entity, attribute, function, rule, etc.) should have a related description.

Each schema requires a description of its scope and its relationship, if any, to other schemas in the model. This sets the context for the entities and other constructs that form the schema content.

The semantics of each type should be described. In particular, the meanings of enuneration items require a description — the meaning of a name may be obvious to the author, but not necessarily to the reader.

Each entity should have an associated description of its meaning, and possibly its intended usage. This is meant to be a general description. Details are added to this by describing each attribute. All constraints on an entity should be precisely described, particularly if they take the form of a complex logical expression or function.

Functions, procedures and rules also require documentation. The input and output parameters should be specified and described, and the algorithm embodied within should be explained.

7.2 Embedded style

In the embedded documentation style each formal model construct is represented together with its appropriate text description and diagrams. In effect, the model is documented in the form of a report with 'code chunks' embedded in the general run of the text. An example of this style can be seen in Appendix A.

A very simple **EXPRESS** model of the embedded documentation style is shown in Figure 7.1 and 7.2. Note that the model is not documented in order to save space; typically, a fully documented model is several times

```
SCHEMA embedded_style_support;

  TYPE express_code = LIST [1:?] OF STRING; END_TYPE;
  TYPE description = LIST [1:?] OF STRING; END_TYPE;

  ENTITY document
    ABSTRACT SUPERTYPE OF (ONEOF(schema_document,internal_document));
    introductory : description;
  END_ENTITY;

  ENTITY schema_document
    SUBTYPE OF (document);
    schema_heading : express_code;
    constants      : LIST [0:?] OF internal_document;
    types          : LIST [0:?] OF internal_document;
    entities       : LIST [0:?] OF internal_document;
    algorithms     : LIST [0:?] OF internal_document;
    schema_ending  : express_code;
    finishing      : description;
  END_ENTITY;

  ENTITY internal_document
    SUBTYPE OF (document);
    specification : express_code;
    finishing     : description;
  END_ENTITY;

END_SCHEMA;  -- end of embedded_style_support
```

Figure 7.2: Support schema for a simple model of the embedded document style.

longer than the formal code portion of the specification.

From the **embedded_style** schema it can be seen that a complete model document consists of introductory material, then one or more documented schemas, and completed by some finishing material. The details of schema documentation are specified in the **embedded_style_support** schema.

A schema is documented using some introductory material, EXPRESS code for the start of the schema, documentation of the definitions within the schema, the EXPRESS code that ends the schema, and finally some finishing statements. Each definition within a schema is documented in a similar manner; that is, there is some introductory material, the relevent EXPRESS code, and some finishing material. We suggest that the ordering of definitions within a schema should be maintained throughout the document.

7.3 Partitioned style

In the partitioned style of model documentation, the formal specification and the descriptive part of the specification are seperated. Typically, the first part of the documentation will contain all the descriptive material, on the lines that this is of general interest. The formal specification is normally given at the end of the document because this is likely only to be of interest to a fewer number of readers (e.g., those who may have to implement the model in some manner). The formal specification portion has little or, more likely, no documentation in addition to the previous narrative material.

7.4 Putting it together

The model documentation styles noted in Section 7.2 and 7.3 have their pluses and minuses. Fortunately, with a little bit of work, and the right computer tools, there is a way of getting the best of both worlds.

First, note that EXPRESS has two forms of comments. An EXPRESS compiler should ignore any characters that occur between the symbol -- and the end of the line, as well as ignoring the symbol itself. The other form of comment is an *embedded remark*. In this case the characters between an initial (* symbol and a final matching *) symbol are treated as whitespace; the two symbols are also ignored. An embedded remark can consist of many lines of characters and other symbols. Given the availabilty of the embedded remark, the textual and graphical documentation may be represented as remarks within the source code. For an example of this, note that the model in Appendix A starts each EXPRESS construct with a *) symbol, indicating the end of a remark, and that there is a (* symbol at the end of each construct, denoting the start of a remark. If the source for Appendix A was in a single computer file, the first characters of which were (*, then the complete documented model could be submitted to an EXPRESS compiler for syntax checking, etc.

If, however, the file did not begin with the start of remark characters, the compiler would complain. The function given in Figure 7.3 takes an EXPRESS model documented in the above manner and delivers EXPRESS source stripped of all embedded remarks, independently of how the file started.

The function takes two inputs: a list of **String** where it is assumed that each string corresponds to a line in the source file, and a boolean value that indicates whether or not the file begins with a start of remark symbol. It returns a list of **String**, one **String** for each non-remark source line. After setting the local variables, it loops over the list of source lines. It checks each source line for the presence of (* and *) symbols. If either of these are found, it alters the comment symbol counter **numcom** appropriately and increments the loop counter. It is an error if the number of closing symbols

```
FUNCTION remcom(input : LIST OF STRING;
                in_comment : BOOLEAN) : LIST OF STRING;
LOCAL
  result  : LIST [0:?] OF STRING := [];
  numcom  : INTEGER := 0;
  line    : STRING;
  outline : STRING;
END_LOCAL;
  IF (in_comment) THEN numcom := 1; END_IF;
  REPEAT i := 1 TO SIZEOF(input);
    line := input[i] + '\\';
    outline := '';
    REPEAT k := 1 TO (LENGTH(line) - 2);
      IF (line[k:k+1] = '(*') THEN
        numcom := numcom+1; k := k+1;
        SKIP;
      ELSE
        IF (line[k:k+1] = '*)') THEN
          numcom := numcom-1; k := k+1;
          IF (numcom < 0 ) THEN error; END_IF;
          SKIP;
        END_IF;
      END_IF;
      IF (numcom = 0) THEN
        outline := outline + line[k];
      END_IF;
    END_REPEAT;
    result := result + outline;
  END_REPEAT;
  RETURN(result);
END_FUNCTION;
```

Figure 7.3: Algorithm to strip remarks from EXPRESS source.

is ever more than the (implied) number of opening symbols (the error procedure is assumed to be defined elsewhere). Input source characters that
do not form remarks are added to the output string list.

A simple program, such as an extension of the algorithm outlined in
Figure 7.3, could be used to seperate a file containing a model written in
the embedded style, into two files, one containing the documentation and
diagrams only, and the other consisting of the formal specification. These
could then be concatenated to give a model documented in the partitioned
style.

If the model document is created using a wordprocessing or typesetting
sytem that utilises tagging, then more sophisticated manipulations are possible. Tagging is also refered to in the literature as document markup. Two

```
\subsubsection{Entity VECTOR}
\begin{Mnamedesc}{VECTOR}
  \begin{Mdesctext}
    A vector is defined in terms of the direction cosines
with respect to the three cartesian axes.
  \end{Mdesctext}
  \begin{Mexp}
  \begin{verbatm}
*)
ENTITY vector;
  xd, yd, zd : REAL;
WHERE
  unit : xd**2 + yd**2 + zd**2 = 1.0;
END_ENTITY;
(*
  \end{verbatm}
  \end{Mexp}

  \begin{Matts}
  \item[xd:] Direction cosine with respect to the X axis.
  \item[yd:] Direction cosine with respect to the Y axis.
  \item[zd:] Direction cosine with respect to the Z axis.
  \end{Matts}

  \begin{Mprops}
  \item[unit:] The sum of the squares of the
                direction cosines shall be equal to unity.
  \end{Mprops}

\end{Mnamedesc}
```

Figure 7.4: Sample LaTeX source.

such systems are LaTeX and SGML. The original manuscript for this book was created using LaTeX. Figure 7.4 shows a short example of the kind of source used in Appendix A, while the result of processing this through the LaTeX system is shown in Figure 7.5.

In the LaTeX source the tags (or commands) all begin with a backslash (\). The tag \subsubsection{...} has the effect of creating a new section of a document. Other tags have different effects. LaTeX enables the user to create new tags (i.e., commands) to extend the processing capability of the system above the baseline set. In the sample source, the tags with an upper-case letter (e.g., \begin{Mexp}) are user-defined macros. Most of their effects can be seen by looking at the result; typically those shown create additional headings in the output text. The point to note, though, is

Entity VECTOR

A vector is defined in terms of the direction cosines with respect to the three cartesian axes.

EXPRESS specification:

```
*)
ENTITY vector;
  xd, yd, zd : REAL;
WHERE
  unit : xd**2 + yd**2 + zd**2 = 1.0;
END_ENTITY;
(*
```

Attribute definitions:

xd: Direction cosine with respect to the X axis.

yd: Direction cosine with respect to the Y axis.

zd: Direction cosine with respect to the Z axis.

Propositions:

unit: The sum of the squares of the direction cosines shall be equal to unity.

Figure 7.5: Processed sample LATEX source.

that each kind of model description is enclosed within a pair of \begin{...} and \end{...} tags.

It requires little imagination to see that if each kind of description within the documented model is bounded by some readily identifiable symbols, then it is possible to write programs to manipulate a document structured in a particular descriptive order into one that is structured in another order.

In effect, the combination of EXPRESS remarks and document tagging provide the basis for presenting an information model in a variety of styles from a single source. As to why this may be important, consider what it is necessary to do if one wants to create a model that is a subset of an existing model and document this as a stand-alone report. EXPRESS provides the capability to define the elements to be extracted from the original model, by using the Use and Reference constructs. It is possible to conceive of a processor that could read both the subset model (defined as schemas that import from the original model) and the original model, extract the original EXPRESS constructs, and output a file containing the

EXPRESS declarations necessary for the subset model. Such a processor is similar to, but somewhat simpler than, Knuth's `WEB` program.

However, if the subset model is to be placed in a self-contained document, then a subset of the original documentation also needs to be copied and placed in the subset report. Using the appropriate tags, this could be accomplished by an extension of the processor suggested previously for extracting EXPRESS source.

Information models of any significant application area tend to be complex. The methods described above for reconfiguring the presentation of a model are a step forward from a single paper document. The advent of documentation in a Hypertext form will provide additional benefits to the readers in that they will be able to navigate around the models in a way that suits their needs. Hypermedia documentation will add a further dimension, increasing the understandability of the model but also increasing the authorship time involved.

7.5 Exercises

7.1 Create an information model of the partitioned document style.

7.2 Document the model given in Figure 7.1 and 7.2 in the embedded style.

7.3 Repeat Exercise 7.2 using the partitioned style.

7.4 Extend the partitioned document style model to cater for diagrams as well as text descriptions. (Hint — don't forget that that there is a `Binary` type in EXPRESS.)

7.5 Write an information model for the style of documentation shown in Appendix A.

7.6 Explain why the `remcom` algorithm (Figure 7.3) includes the line:
`line := input[i] + '\\';`

7.7 Write a program in your favourite language to strip remarks from EXPRESS source code according to the algorithm outlined in Figure 7.3.

7.8 Extend the function in Figure 7.3 to:
1. Strip comments as well as remarks from the source file.
2. Return the remark text as well as the source code.
3. Generate and return line numbers, based on the original source, for both the text and source code. (Hint — functions can return an entity.)

7.6 Further reading

LaTeX is a public domain typesetting program developed by Leslie Lamport [Lam86]. It is based on the TeX program, which is also public domain, developed by Donald Knuth [Knu84b]. When using either LaTeX or TeX the text is tagged with control commands that specify both the logical structure of the document, and some of its typographical appearance. Both of these programs are very popular among the academic community.

More recently the Standard Generalized Markup Language (SGML) tagging system has become an ISO standard for document markup [ISO86]. A gentle introduction to SGML is provided by Bryan [Bry88], while Goldfarb provides an annotated and more user-friendly description of the ISO standard [Gol90]. A new standard called HyTime, based on SGML, is being developed that caters for hypermedia documents [NKN91].

The concept of literate programming was introduced by Donald Knuth in [Knu84a] and a very extended example of this programming style is in [Knu86] which describes the actual TeX program. Jon Bentley, in collaboration with Knuth, devoted two of his *Programming Pearls* column to the topic [Ben86b, Ben86a]. An occasional column on the topic appeared for some time in the Cummunications of the ACM, moderated by Christopher Van Wyk starting in 1987 [Van87a]. These showed various styles of literate programming, and were coupled with reviews of the resulting work. In his last column, however, he did not appear to be too optimistic about the future [Van90]. Smith [SS91b] has provided a bibliography on literate programming which gives many more references than those cited here.

The WEB program was written by Knuth [Knu83, Knu84a] to support his concept of literate programming. It was explicitly developed for programs written in Pascal but later authors have revised it to cater for other programming languages [Van89b].

James Bigelow [Big88] discusses the application of hypertext systems to Computer Aided Software Engineering (CASE) tools, while Garg and Scacchi [GS90] describe a hypertext system called DIF which is designed to facilitate information management during the software process life cycle.

Chapter 8

EXPRESS information bases

> Errors using inadequate data are much less than those using no data at all.

The Exposition of 1851
Charles Babbage

One of the assumptions underlying EXPRESS is that there is, somewhere, going to be an *information base* that contains instances of data corresponding to the information model. In this Chapter we examine aspects of this hypothetical information base. We also briefly note some of the software tools that could be useful when you are modeling using EXPRESS.

8.1 Information bases

We use the term information base in a very general sense; it is any repository that contains data corresponding to an EXPRESS (or EXPRESS-G) information model. The idea that probably comes to mind when hearing the term is that 'an information base is a fancy name for a database.' In our sense, an information base may be a database, but it may also be more than or less than a database. In fact, it may not even be computer-based at all! Some examples of information bases are:

- Intelligent Knowledgebases
- Knowledgebases
- Databases
- Computer files
- Printed documents

These examples are listed in approximately decreasing order of technical complexity and increasing order of technology age. Thus, intelligent knowledgebases are at, or even beyond, the leading edge of technology, while printed documents have been available for some centuries, although the technology for producing these has made dramatic strides over the last decade.

Below we briefly describe various types of information bases, starting with databases. Knowledgebases are at the leading edge of the technology and are not treated; we merely note that there appears to be no fundamental reason why EXPRESS models should not be stored and instanced using this advanced technology.

Databases provide a structured means of both storing data in a computer system and of querying the data in an efficient manner. Internally, the data may be structured in the form of a network, a hierarchy, or in tables following the relational model. Most new databases are relational, while older ones may be hierarchical or network based. Object-Oriented databases have recently appeared, but as yet there appears to be no consensus on exactly what an OODB is.

Databases are designed so that they can be modified and queried by mutiple users. However, in order to maintain the database in a consistent state, various stratagems are resorted to so that two users cannot simultaneously change the data in an inconsistent manner. For example, in an airline seating reservation system, it is undesireable (from the passenger's view) to sell the same seat to two different passengers. The database management system (DBMS) is a software suite that is intended to take care of such problems. It typically does this by 'locking' a portion of the data so that only one user can update it at any one time. The process of locking, updating, and unlocking is called a *transaction* (there is actually more to a transaction than this, but the details are not relevent). The database must be in a consistent state both before and after each transaction.

Internally, the data in a database may be stored in many computer files. A file, though, may be used to store data independently of an overlying database. Many computer programs read in and write out data to files. Sometimes these are only meant to be manipulated and seen by the program; other times they are meant to be human readable. The original source for this book was maintained as a set of computer files.

Computer programs typically manipulate data in one form or another. The data internal to a program is non-persistent. That is, when the program ends, its internal stores of data are lost, unless they have been written to some permanent storage system, like a file or a database. We consider programs also to be information bases, at least while they are active.

Much data is stored in printed documents, this book being an example. Reports, international and national standards, memoranda and so on are all examples of information bases in our sense of the term. They all contain data which is representative of some set of information. A particular example can be found within this book. Appendix E contains a meta-model of EXPRESS written in EXPRESS. The EXPRESS Language Reference Manual is one information base for this meta-model. This book itself is another information base of the meta-model.

The mind is also an information base and is arguably the most sophisticated of all the different kinds.

8.2 The EXPRESS connection

The data corresponding to an information model may be stored in a wide variety of information bases. For discussion purposes we will assume that the information base is akin to a database. That is, there is some means of putting data into the information base, and there is some means of querying the information base to ascertain its contents. In our hypothetical system, these functions are carried out by programs. If the information base was paper-based, then the input and output 'programs' are the human writers and readers.

EXPRESS makes certain assumptions about the information base. In a nutshell these are:

- Exactly one schema defines the contents of the information base. That is, even when several schemas contribute to the information model, only one schema assembles the bits and pieces into the final product.

- Every entity value in the information base will have a unique identifier, but the form or structure of the identifier is not important to EXPRESS.

- The uniqueness of identifiers does not extend beyond the information base.

- The population of values is not ordered and there is no restriction against having duplicate values. In other words, an entity population is treated as a bag.

- Only datatype values that are associated with an entity value are of interest.

- There is no restriction on the number of things held by an information base, or its size, or the magnitude or resolution of numbers.

- Anything is legal in the information base unless it is explicitly forbidden.

- Instances within the information base either do or do not conform to the model that defines it. If queried, the information base will be able to report the state of instances.

- The information base will do nothing to keep the information system from creating an illegal state or, once having become illegal, doing anything to correct itself.

Obviously, these properties ignore certain functions and limits within a practical computing environment, but these functions are not interesting when performing information modeling; they are, however, very important when doing data modeling.

EXPRESS tries hard to avoid implementation issues. One example of this concerns the constraints which, as we have tried to emphasize, form a significant part of an information model. The question is, when are the constraints checked within the information base? The EXPRESS answer is that it does not care — it is up to the user of the information base to decide when it is appropriate.

Consider an information base that stores geometric lines where there is an EXPRESS definition for a line which says that every line shall have a start and an end point (the line being the shortest distance between these points). The information base may also support some geometry application which is satisfied if a line has zero, one, or two points. This application understands that a line instance with no points is the set of all lines, and a line instance with one point is the set of all lines that pass through that point. In this case, the time when the EXPRESS constraints needs to be checked is when an application that only understands the EXPRESS line accesses the data.

8.3   The computer connection

EXPRESS is designed to be computer-processible. You can use EXPRESS without computer support, but you will be missing a lot. If you use it without intending to develop an information base managed by computer resources, you may not be wasting your time as there is much to be gained by a formal modeling exercise. Nevertheless, EXPRESS is aimed directly at the world of computing.

What you need to support the development of information models in EXPRESS is listed next. This discussion centers on functionality, not the way functionality is packaged into a product. That is, two or more of the functions might appear in a single application.

8.3.1   Environment

EXPRESS does not define the environment within which projects are developed. Even so, when more than one schema is involved, some kind of environment will be needed. Here are some thoughts about what that environment should be.

The easiest approach is to simply put the different source files in the same directory. That should work well for a single project. However, when several projects are underway, contention, confusion and conflict are sure to plague you. A more thoughtful environment should do these things:

- Provide for several concurrent projects.

- Provide for several resource libraries.

- Have a mechanism for locating the various schemas needed for a project, even when they are distributed across several projects and libraries.

- Automatically compile schemas that have changed (a make utility should work.)

- Lock schemas which are proven, i.e., configuration management.

- Protect certain work from prying eyes.

8.3.2   Editor

Almost any kind of text editor or word processor can be used to create and edit EXPRESS source. A language sensitive editor offers certain advantages, but is not essential. A robust language sensitive editor might incorporate layout and capitalization management. If so, you should be able to make your own rules. Do not be content with an editor that fixes the layout or enforces rules you do not like.

8.3.3   Capitalizer and pretty printer

If you adopt a style of capitalization (which you should) it helps to use software to maintain uniformity throughout the source.

Consistent layout (i.e., the use of whitespace for indentation, tabulation, breaks between declarations, etc.) is an essential aspect of model development. And, like capitalization, this is a job that software can do faster, cheaper and better than people.

8.3.4   Parser

A parser (or compiler) is the most important tool in the toolkit. It should detect every syntax error, and most of the semantic errors, in the source. It should not falsely report errors where the source is correct. Accurate and meaningful reporting of errors is essential. It should produce compiled output (the analog of object files in the computer programming world) which can be bound together when schemas are interfaced. It should produce a variety of outputs to help with project documentation.

8.3.5   Semantic analyzer

Some aspects of EXPRESS, like the restriction against contradicting rules, requires deep and elaborate semantic analysis and probably some reasoning too. This kind of analysis is probably not required of the parser, but an occasional and final check for conflicts and contradictions is necessary.

8.3.6 Visualizer

EXPRESS-G is a graphical subset of the full language. Many people find it useful to see (and work with) graphics rather than text. If you are one of those people, a visualizer will be essential.

A dedicated product which imports and exports the written language is the ideal solution. Some alternatives are hand-drawn sketches and CAD systems. Neither of those alternatives will be very effective in the long run, but one can make do in a pinch.

A visualizer product should be able to import and export EXPRESS source. It should be possible to edit the graphics model, both in terms of layout and content. A really good product will take care of page splitting and off-page connectors. Needless to say, any such product should conform to the standard.

8.3.7 Compiler

If you are going to generate computer-based information bases corresponding to EXPRESS models, then some sort of compiler is essential. The compiler should transform the EXPRESS source into the native language of the information base. This could be done manually, but usually with many errors; any change to the EXPRESS model will require a further round of translation and yet more errors.

8.3.8 Documenter

A computer-based documentation system is highly desireable. Chapter 7 discusses some of the aspects of such a system. It is most important that the formal model description and the ancilliary documentation be kept synchronized.

8.4   Further reading

Knowledgebase and knowledge representation research is described in the collection of research papers edited by Cercone and McCalla [CM87], while a more general discussion of knowledge- and object-bases can be found in [PCKW89]. The integration of rule-bases, databases and the OO paradigm within the Tanguy knowledge-base system is described by Czejdo and his co-workers [CET93]. Other research in this area is described, for example, by Higa *et al* [HMMS92], Risch [RRHD88], and by Su and his co-workers [SLH+92]. In a slightly different vein, Gadia [Gad93] is researching methods to integrate spatial, temporal and belief data together with the more usual kinds of data contained in databases. Eick and Werstein [EW93] discuss the timing of constraint checking within information bases in general and the DALI system in particular.

Traditional databases are described by many authors, for example Date [Dat90], and Elmasri and Navathe [EN89]. Other books on the topic may be found in the Bibliography. Recent descriptions of some typical databases are: GemStone by Butterworth, Otis and Stein [BOS91], ObjectStore by Lamb *et al* [LLOW91] O_2 by Deux *et al* [D$^+$91], POSTGRES by Stonebraker and Kemnitz [SK91], ROSE by Hardwick and Spooner [HS89], and Starburst by Lohman *et al* [LLPS91].

The relational database community is trying to decide what it should be doing in advancing the technology [S$^+$90] while the OO database community is also trying to reach a consensus [A$^+$90]. Alvi Silberschatz and a distinguished group of database researchers have provided one view of the challenges facing database technology [SSU91].

Even though EXPRESS is a new language, there are many software tools that support a modeling environment and enable compilation into other languages. Some of these have been described at the annual EXPRESS User Group conferences [Wil91a, Wil92a, Wil92b].

Modeling environments and storage sytstems have been developed by, for example, Phil Spiby and his co-workers [Spi91, Ash91] and by Dahl [Dah92].

The interaction between EXPRESS and Object-Oriented databases has been treated by, among others, Martin Hardwick [H$^+$91, Har92] and by Sian Hope [Hop92]. Clements [Cle92] uses an EXPRESS to SQL compiler.

Several compilers have been developed for converting EXPRESS into C++. Examples are given by Steve Clark and Don Libes [Cla91, LC92], by Hardwick [Har92] and by Lutz Blencke [BP92]. EXPRESS has also been compiled into other languages like Smalltalk [Yin91] and Prolog [LM91]. Pravir Chawdhry [Cha92] describes a different kind of compiler that converts NIAM to EXPRESS.

Several groups have developed EXPRESS-G visualizer and compiler tools. Among these are Uwe Jasnoch and his colleagues [JvLN$^+$91], Peter Roesch [Roe91], and Wolfgang Mueller and Bernd Kleinjohann [MK92].

These, and many other tools, for example Emacs-based editors, are described in the software tool directory that is maintained by the EXPRESS Committee[Wil92d]. This is updated on roughly an annual basis.

Part II

The EXPRESS Language

Now we turn our attention to the EXPRESS language itself. First we explain the lexical language, followed in turn by its graphical and instance representation cousins.

For EXPRESS we start with the basics in Chapter 9 and then cover increasingly complex subjects: datatypes, declarations, references to named things, executable statements, expressions, interfacing, and finally a comprehensive presentation of the syntax. The coverage of EXPRESS-G begins with Chapter 17 and covers the graphic symbols that correspond to the written language. EXPRESS-I, which begins with Chapter 21, shows how values can be associated with EXPRESS declarations as an aid to understanding.

Two appendices will be of particular interest. Appendix C explains how to interpret complex supertype structures. Appendix F explains the standard resources (functions, procedures and constants) that can be used by EXPRESS and EXPRESS-I.

Examples are used to illustrate the way the language is written and what is meant by certain features. For the most part they are trivial and we caution you not to use these examples as a model for work you might do later (at any rate, the coverage of methodology and modelling issues in Part I should have prepared you to look past these examples). For now, concentrate on the features of the language and the mechanics of writing EXPRESS correctly.

Exercises are given to stimulate interest. Try to work out your own answer before looking at the answers we give, and note that the answers given here are not necessarily the only ones possible.

Overview

The main elements of EXPRESS are the schema, the type, the entity and the rule.

The schema is a container for the work you do. Much like canisters for flour, sugar and so forth you should plan to use as many different containers (schemas) as you have different kinds of work. Interfacing can be used to import whole schemas or just parts of them into another schema.

Types (or datatypes) are used to represent value domains. EXPRESS offers the usual assortment of built-in datatypes such as real and integer numbers, character strings and so on. These datatypes, however, are unusual because they are not in general bounded. For example, integer numbers in EXPRESS represent a vast domain, which includes minus and plus infinity, and real numbers are considered to have infinite resolution. Fortunately, you can build your own datatypes on top of the built-in ones and put constraints on the domain as necessary.

Entities are the real meat of EXPRESS. They are the things (concepts, etc.) that you really care about. EXPRESS entities have a lot of the characteristics common to Object Oriented Programming (OOP) languages, but strictly speaking it is not one. The general methods found in OOP languages have been specialized by EXPRESS to deal specifically with derived (calculated) values and constraint management, but EXPRESS does not offer a generalized method capability otherwise.

Rules allow you to deal with a variety of constraints that are difficult to handle without this special facility. Rules can describe the interaction of different sets of entity values and situations where only partial coverage of a set of values is involved in a constraint.

There are other aspects of EXPRESS to learn such as constants, functions and procedures and a fairly complete collection of executable statements. However, EXPRESS is not a programming language as it does not deal with input and output, exception handling and other features necessary for that purpose.

> *That is so important it is worth saying again.* EXPRESS *is not a programming language!*

EXPRESS is a complex language when taken as a whole. But, a lot of it is simple and once the fundamentals have been mastered the difficult aspects will fall into place.

EXPRESS divides the information modeling problem into parts. It provides a wrapper for collections of related definitions, a way to express a definition of an information unit and a way to represent value domains. The wrapper is called a *schema*, an information unit is called an *entity* and a value domain is called a *datatype*. It turns out that an entity can also be a datatype when we want it to be.

The entity is the focal point of information modeling. To describe its characteristics in enough detail to be meaningful and useful you need to talk about the facts known about it, how those facts are realized and the rules that regulate its behavior. We call the facts known about an entity *attributes* and in EXPRESS, attributes are always have a value domain representation.

Rules of behavior are explained by various kinds of constraints that apply to attributes, populations of entities or the interaction between them. A constraint could be as simple as saying that a numeric value must be greater than zero. They can also be enormously complicated. It is worth noting that EXPRESS is permissive when it comes to rules. That is, if you do not explicitly say that something is impossible, then it is possible.

Supertypes, Inheritance and Such

You will probably find that a lot of the things you model are related to each other in the same way that apples are related to fruit: i.e., an apple is a kind of fruit. In EXPRESS, that kind of relationship is called a supertype/subtype relationship. In the case of fruit and apples, fruit is the supertype because it is more general and apple is the subtype because it is more specific.

It is possible to create many levels of subtypes. When an entity has no subtypes, it is as specific as it can get. A subtype inherits everything from all of its supertypes. For example, fruit might have weight — so apple has weight too. You do not put a specific declaration in apple that it has weight because that attribute is inherited. In fact, making a specific declaration of it would be an error.

Rules are inherited also, so if we say that fruit can only be sold in army surplus stores, then the same rule applies to apples too. Remember that once you put a constraint on a supertype, all of its subtypes inherit it and you cannot contradict it. Subtypes are more specific than their supertypes so they have attributes or rules or other behavior the supertype doesn't.

A value of a subtype is also a value of its supertypes, but not necessarily vice versa; EXPRESS allows you to define a supertype that does not have to have subtype values. Once you say that something is a subtype you can never think of it as an independent thing. That idea is a little hard to get used to, but it is fundamental to EXPRESS.

Identity

When you model an entity you may be tempted to include an attribute which is used to *identify* a value. In other words, an *access key*.

Don't do it.

One of the goals of information modeling is to keep the information content separate from the environment in which values will eventually live.

The EXPRESS viewpoint is that keys are not part of the natural information content. They are artifacts of the implementation (after all, what is the natural key of apple?) That idea can be tested by thinking about all of the forms an access key can take for a variety of database, file or other storage forms. Generally speaking, you cannot speak of access keys in general.

EXPRESS asks you think along these lines: *Every value of every entity type will have a unique identity, but the form of it is not important to the information modeling process.*

Sometime in the future you will wish to build an implementation from your EXPRESS information model. At that time you need to think about the number and form of the access keys needed for your purposes and permitted by your host environment. Creating those access keys is part of the art of implementation building.

Having said that, it is worth noting that some attributes — those with a uniqueness constraint on them — may be natural candidates for keys. For example, the name of a person. Having attributes that are candidate keys is not the same as introducing keys just for the sake of key-ness.

Chapter 9

Basic elements

> "Where shall I begin, please Your Majesty?"
> he asked. "Begin at the beginning," the
> King said very gravely, "and go on till you
> come to the end—then stop."

> *Alice in Wonderland*
> *Lewis Carroll*

We start with the basic stuff used to build EXPRESS: the characters you use to build 'words' and the different kinds of words that may appear in the source. Computer languages call these words tokens.

You compose characters according to syntax rules to form different kinds of tokens. In turn, tokens are composed into statements and statements are composed into blocks (we will get to statements and blocks directly).

The syntax alone does not define the language however — we also need to be concerned with semantics. Semantics deals with the meaning of well formed syntax. As an example, EXPRESS has tokens for identifiers and reserved words. Although they both look like 'words' they are different; an identifier cannot be the same as a keyword. EXPRESS expects to see identifiers and reserved words in specific places within statements. It is an error to put an identifier where a reserved word is expected and vice versa. EXPRESS is correctly written only when both the syntactic and semantical rules are observed.

9.1 Composing the source

EXPRESS source is composed as a stream of characters. The source stream is decoded into tokens, statements and blocks according to the syntax rules. The source is typically broken into a number of physical lines, which is any number (including zero) of characters ended by a 'newline.' The source will be more attractive and easier to read when statements are broken into lines and whitespace is used to set off different constructs. The following declarations are the same to an EXPRESS parser, but give different impressions to human readers.

127

Table 9.1: The EXPRESS character set

	0	1	2	3	4	5	6	7	8	9	A	B	C	D	E	F
2x	␣	!	"	#	$	%	&	'	(	)	*	+	,	−	.	/
3x	0	1	2	3	4	5	6	7	8	9	:	;	<	=	>	?
4x	@	A	B	C	D	E	F	G	H	I	J	K	L	M	N	O
5x	P	Q	R	S	T	U	V	W	X	Y	Z	[	\	]	^	_
6x	`	a	b	c	d	e	f	g	h	i	j	k	l	m	n	o
7x	p	q	r	s	t	u	v	w	x	y	z	{	|	}	~	■

```
entity foo;x,y,z:real;end_entity;

ENTITY foo;
  x,
  y,
  z : REAL;
END_ENTITY;
```

9.2   The character set

The EXPRESS character set is easy to explain — just look at your computer keyboard. Most of the characters you see there are used to write EXPRESS.

However, there is a more complicated explanation which follows: the EXPRESS character set is defined as cells 00–7F of plane 00 of group 00 of ISO 10646. Of those characters, cells 20–7E as shown in Table 9.1 are actually used to write EXPRESS. Any other character (cells 00–1F, 7F) is called a 'rogue' character, and if used is treated as a space unless it appears within a string literal or a remark.

Characters or groups of characters that are commonly used within the syntax rules are named as shown in Table 9.2. The odd looking symbols (\a, etc.) stand for character classes recognized by the syntax definition language. Therefore, if you see \a in a syntax rule it means that any 'displayable' character can be used there.

EXPRESS may be written in upper, lower or mixed case letters of the alphabet. The case of letters is significant only within quoted strings and within remarks (where they are insignificant anyway).

Note: *This only refers to the characters used to specify the source, and does not specify the domain of characters allowed within a string value.*

Note: *The newline character is [computer] system dependent.*

Note: *Implementations of EXPRESS are free to display rogue characters in any manner they wish.*

Table 9.2: EXPRESS character classes

Name		Cell	Display
Letter		41–5A, 61–7A	A–Z, a–z
Digit		30–39	0–9
Display	\a	21–7E	! – ~
Newline	\n	*System dependent*	*Invisible*
Rogue	\o	00–1F, 7F	*Implementation dependent*
Quote	\q	27	'
Space	\s	20	⊔

Table 9.3: Whitespace Characters

Character	Description
Space Character	A character that produces no visible display. One or more blank spaces can appear between two tokens. The notation \s is used to represent a blank space character in the meta-language.
Newline	A character (or characters) used to mark the end of a source line. Newline is normally treated as a space but is significant when it terminates a tail remark or abnormally terminates a string literal. A newline is represented by the notation \n in the meta-language.
Rogue Characters	Characters not defined as a digit, letter, special character, space or newline are treated as whitespace, unless within a string literal or remark. The notation \o is used to represent these rogue characters in the meta-language. *Although rogue characters are ignored by EXPRESS, thoughtful parsers should issue a warning when they are detected.*

Whitespace

Whitespace is any character (space, newline, etc.) that does not 'display.' It is required between two word-like tokens and can optionally be used to separate any other tokens. It is used to improve the structure and readability of the source, i.e., to indent sections or leave blank lines. The liberal and consistent use of whitespace is a good practice to follow. The whitespace characters are shown in Table 9.3.

Example 9.1

This shows how whitespace is and is not used.

```
2+2                     -- this can also
2 + 2                   -- be written
SCHEMA Widget;          -- but these "words"
SCHEMAWidget;           -- cannot be written without whitespace
```

```
IF a THEN              -- a newline helps to give a
   dothis;             -- structured look to the source
ELSE
   dothat;
ENDIF;
```

9.3   Remark

A remark is used for documentation and is invisible as far as EXPRESS is concerned. There are two forms of a remark. The embedded remark may be placed between any two tokens. The tail remark appears at the end of a physical line and is equivalent to a line terminator.

Remark

EmbeddedRemark
TailRemark

9.3.1   Embedded remark

EmbeddedRemark

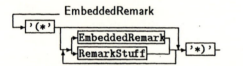

'(*'   EmbeddedRemark   '*)'
        RemarkStuff

An embedded remark may appear anywhere whitespace is allowed. The character pair (* marks the start of an embedded remark and *) ends it. Anything (as RemarkStuff suggests) can be written between the start and end of an embedded remark, including the newline character — therefore embedded remarks can span several physical lines.

Embedded remarks may be nested. However, care must be taken when nesting remarks to ensure that each (* has a matching *). So, the claim made earlier about allowing any characters inside an embedded remark is not quite true: (* is forbidden unless it starts a nested embedded remark and *) is only used to terminate one.

Example 9.2

Here is a nested embedded remark:

```
(* The
  '(*' symbol starts a remark and the
  '*)' symbol ends it
*)
```

9.3.2   Tail remark

TailRemark

'--'   RemarkStuff   NewLineChar

Table 9.4: EXPRESS Symbols

.	,	;	:	*	+	-	=	\	/	<
>	[	]	{	}	|	(	)	**	<=	<>
>=	<*	:=	||	:=:	:<>:	%	'	(*	*)	--

The tail remark is written at the end of a physical line. Two consecutive hyphens (--) start the tail remark and a newline terminates it. Anything, including nothing, can be written between -- and newline.

Example 9.3

> Here is a tail remark.

> `-- this is a remark that ends with a newline`

Exercise 9.1 *Is a remark a token or a statement?*

9.4 Symbols

Symbols are groups of non-letter characters that have a special meaning in EXPRESS. Symbols are used as punctuation or operators. Punctuation is used to separate adjacent lexical elements. Operators denote that actions are to be performed on the operands associated with them (Chapter 14 explains how operators are used). The EXPRESS symbols are shown in Table 9.4.

9.5 Reserved words

The reserved words of EXPRESS include keywords, some operators and the names of standard constants, functions and procedures. They are called reserved words because EXPRESS got there first and you cannot create identifiers that have the same spelling.

Note: *A few of the reserved words have been set aside for use by* EXPRESS-I: `Context`, `End_Context`, `Model` *and* `End_Model`. *They are not used by* EXPRESS *itself.*

Note: *It is important to remember that* EXPRESS, *unlike many programming languages, does not allow you to redeclare its standard functions. For example, it is possible in some languages to declare your own SQRT function, which might not even compute the square root of a number.* EXPRESS *forbids this to safeguard uniformity of meaning. See scope rule 3 on page 180.*

Reserved words may be written using upper, lower or mixed case (and the underscore character where needed). The keywords and reserved words of EXPRESS are shown in Table 9.5.

Table 9.5: EXPRESS Keywords

Abs	Abstract	ACos	Aggregate	Alias
And	AndOr	Array	As	ASin
ATan	Bag	Begin	Binary	BLength
Boolean	By	Case	Constant	Const_E
Context	Cos	Derive	Div	Else
End	End_Alias	End_Case	End_Constant	End_Context
End_Entity	End_Function	End_If	End_Local	End_Model
End_Procedure	End_Repeat	End_Rule	End_Schema	End_Type
Entity	Enumeration	Escape	Exists	Exp
False	Fixed	For	Format	From
Function	Generic	HiBound	HiIndex	If
In	Insert	Integer	Inverse	Length
Like	List	LoBound	Local	Log
Log10	Log2	Logical	LoIndex	Mod
Model	Not	Number	NVL	Odd
Of	OneOf	Optional	Or	Otherwise
Pi	Procedure	Query	Real	Reference
Remove	Repeat	Return	RolesOf	Rule
Schema	Select	Self	Set	Sin
SizeOf	Skip	Sqrt	String	Subtype
Supertype	Tan	Then	To	True
Type	TypeOf	Unique	Unknown	Until
Use	UsedIn	Value	Var	Where
While	XOr			

9.6 Identifiers

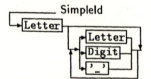

Identifiers are names you give to the things you declare. The first character of an identifier is a letter The remaining characters, if any, may be any combination of letters, digits or the underscore character. The letters used to form identifiers are *not* case sensitive as upper and lower case letters are treated as equal. However, an identifier cannot be the same as one of the EXPRESS reserved words shown in Table 9.5.

Identifiers are created within a region of the source called a 'scope.' When a reference is made to an identifier, it must be visible at the place from which the reference is made and furthermore it may be necessary to 'qualify' it. Scope, references and qualification are covered in Chapter 12.

Example 9.4

These are valid identifiers:

```
Widget                    wiDget                        WIDGET
accounts_payable          AccountsPayable
withholding_tax           withholdingTax
employee__name            EMPLOYEEname
```

. . . but these are not valid.

```
1Widget                   -- first character not a letter
_accounts_payable         -- underscore can't be first
with holding_tax          -- no spaces allowed
```

9.7   Literals

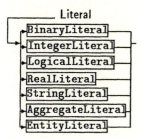

A literal is a constant value whose data type interpretation depends on how characters are composed. Chapter 10 explains datatypes.

9.7.1   Binary literal

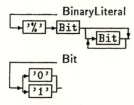

A binary literal is a token that represents a value of a binary datatype and is written as a % followed by one or more binary digits (0 or 1).

Example 9.5

This are some valid and invalid binary literals:

```
%0101001100       -- Ok
%00000101         -- Ok
%0102001100       -- 2 is not a valid binary digit
%010 1001100      -- no spaces allowed
```

9.7.2   Integer literal

```
_____ IntegerLiteral
  [Digits]
```

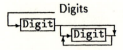

Digits

An integer literal is a token that represents a value of an integer datatype and is written as a string of digits.

Example 9.6

> Here are some integer literals:
>
> 4016
> 38

Exercise 9.2 *Is -21 an integer literal?*

9.7.3   Real literal

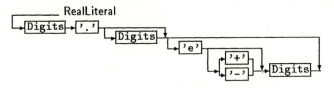

RealLiteral

A real literal is a token that represents a value of a real datatype and is written as a mantissa with a decimal point and an optional exponent.

Example 9.7

> Some real literals are:
>
> ```
> 1.E6        "E" may be written in upper or lower case
> 3.5e-5
> 359.62
> ```

Exercise 9.3 *Why are these real literals invalid?*

> a)   .001
> b)   1e10

9.7.4   String literal

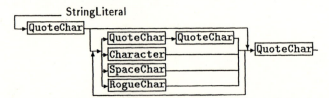

StringLiteral

A string literal is a token that represents a value of a string datatype and is written as a string of characters enclosed by quote marks (apostrophes). If a quote mark is itself part of the string, then two consecutive quote marks are written. A newline character is not legal within a string literal and therefore never spans a physical line boundary.

Example 9.8

Valid string literals:

```
'Baby needs a new pair of shoes!'      'Baby needs a new pair of shoes!'
'Ed''s Computer Store'                         'Ed's Computer Store'
```

... and some invalid ones:

```
'Ed's Computer Store'   There are always an even number of quote marks.
'Ed''s Computer
Store'                                        Spans a physical line
```

9.7.5 Logical literal

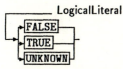

A logical literal is a token that represents a value of a logical or boolean datatype and is written literally as `True`, `False` or `Unknown`. Note that `Unknown` is not a legal value of a boolean datatype.

9.7.6 Aggregate literal

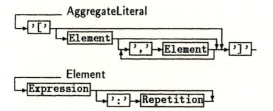

An aggregate literal is a value of an aggregation datatype (array, bag, list or set) and is written as zero or more comma separated expressions that evaluate to values compatible with the base type of the aggregation. All of this is enclosed within square brackets. Empty positions are denoted by ? to represent a 'null.' The number of expression values that appear between the brackets have to agree with the bound specification given for the aggregation.

Example 9.9

Given the declaration:

```
a : SET OF INTEGER;
```

a value can be assigned as:

```
a := [ 1, 3, 6, 9*8, -12 ] ; -- 9*8 is an expression = 72
```

A repetition factor may be used when several consecutive values are the same. This is represented by two expressions separated by a colon (:). The expression on the left of the colon is the value to be repeated; the integer valued expression on the right of the colon gives the number of times the value is repeated.

Example 9.10

Given the declaration:

```
a : BAG OF BOOLEAN ;
```

These statements are equivalent

```
a := [ TRUE:5 ] ;
a := [ TRUE, TRUE, TRUE, TRUE, TRUE ];
```

Exercise 9.4 *Think of a situation where ? can be used in an aggregate literal.*

Exercise 9.5 *Did you notice that the aggregate literal was not called a token? Can you explain why?*

9.7.7   Entity literal

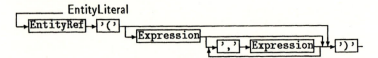

An entity literal is a value of a given entity type and is written as the entity name followed by a comma separated list of expressions enclosed by parentheses. Each value represents an explicit attribute value given in the same order in which they were declared. Explicit attributes declared to allow optional values may be given a 'null' value by using ?.

The entity literal is treated as a function that is implicitly declared (see 11.4.5) when the entity is declared.

Example 9.11

Given the declaration:

```
ENTITY foo;
    x, y, z : NUMBER;
END_ENTITY;

ENTITY goo;
    f0, f1 : foo;
END_ENTITY;
```

```
LOCAL
  a : LIST[0:?] OF foo;
  b : goo;
END_LOCAL;
```

values may be assigned as:

```
a := [ foo(1, 2, 3), foo(2, 3, 4), foo(3, 4, 5) ];
  (* a is a list containing 3 foo's *)
b := goo( foo(4, 5, 6), a[3] );
  (* b is a goo with f0 equal to an embedded foo and
     f1 equal to the third foo in the a list *)
```

Individual entity literals are concatenated to create a complex entity literal, i.e., a value of a supertype/subtype lattice. Concatenation is indicated by the (| |) operator.

Example 9.12

This shows entity concatenation.

```
ENTITY a SUPERTYPE OF (ONEOF(b, c));
  a1 : INTEGER;
END_ENTITY;
ENTITY b SUBTYPE OF (a);
  b1 : STRING;
END_ENTITY;
ENTITY c SUBTYPE OF (a);
  c1 : REAL;
END_ENTITY;
```

Here then are two complex values:

```
LOCAL
  v1 : a ;
  v2 : c ;
END_LOCAL;
v1 := a(1) || b('abc');
v2 := a(2) || c(7.998e-5);
```

Exercise 9.6 *Why is the following not a valid entity literal given the example just above?*

```
v1 := b('abc');
```

Answers to Exercises

Answer 9.1 *Oddly enough, remarks are defined in the language syntax but are never referenced by it — they are neither. In effect, the machine that reads and parses* EXPRESS *needs to look for remarks so that it can treat embedded remarks as a space and tail remarks as a newline.*

Answer 9.2 *No, this is a trick question. It is an expression made up of a unary minus and an integer literal. See Chapter 14 for more about expressions.*

Answer 9.3

  a)   `.001`   `No digit before the decimal point.`
  b)   `1e10`   `Don't forget to include a decimal point`

Answer 9.4 *It turns out that* ? *is legal in an aggregate initializer when the aggregate is an array, and the elements are declared as optional. The* ? *is nonsense in a bag, list or set.*

Answer 9.5 *Tokens do not allow embedded whitespace. The aggregate literal, and the ones following, can use whitespace between the elements; e.g.,*

  `... [ 1, 2, 3] ...`

Answer 9.6 *A subtype cannot exist without a supertype. Therefore,* b *cannot exist apart from* a. *It must be coupled with an* a.

Chapter 10

Datatypes

This chapter explains the **EXPRESS** pseudotypes and datatypes. You will also want to read about defined types and entity types, both of which are covered in Chapter 11.

Datatypes represent domains of values. A domain is the set of possible values associated with an attribute, local variable or formal parameter. Datatype values can be operated upon as explained in Chapter 14.

EXPRESS is fussy about the way datatypes are used. The datatypes are grouped this way:

- Pseudo (Generic and Aggregate — see 10.1)

- Simple (Integer, String, etc. — see 10.2)

- Collection (Array, List, etc. — see 10.3)

- Enumeration and Select (see 10.4 and 10.5).

- Named (entities and defined types — Chapter 11)

Then, the context in which a reference to a datatype is made will be

- as the type of an attribute,

- as the type of a local variable,

- as the type of a formal parameter, or

- as the underlying type of a *defined type.*

At last, a summary of the datatypes that can be used in the different contexts is given in Table 10.1. Notice that pseudotypes can only be used as formal parameter types and, the enumeration and select types can only be used as the underlying types of defined types.

139

Table 10.1: Datatype context usage.

	Attribute	Variable	Parameter	Underlying
Pseudo			Yes	
Simple	Yes	Yes	Yes	Yes
Collection	Yes	Yes	Yes	Yes
Enumeration/Select				Yes
Named	Yes	Yes	Yes	Yes

10.1   Pseudotypes

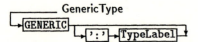

Pseudotypes are used only as the types of the formal parameters of functions and procedures. They can be regarded as templates into which various specific types can be placed. See 11.5.1 for more about formal parameters.

10.1.1   Generic pseudotype

GenericType

The domain of a generic pseudotype is every conceivable value. When a procedure or function that has a generic type parameter is invoked it will accept any kind of actual parameter. No questions asked! Functions or procedures that use formal parameters typed as generic must be prepared to deal with whatever actual stuff is tossed its way and any operations performed on them will depend on the specific type of the actual parameter.

Generic parameters should never be used when a more specific type can be used instead. In any event, the mechanics involved in writing an algorithm that is capable of handling every possible input value are tricky. The message is: *Don't use generic parameters unless you simply have to.*

10.1.2   Aggregate pseudotype

AggregateType

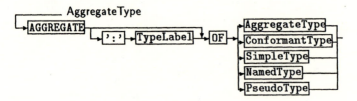

The domain of an aggregate pseudotype includes any kind of aggregate value. When a procedure or function that has an aggregate datatype parameter is invoked it will expect an actual parameter that is an array, bag, list or set. Functions or procedures that use formal parameters typed as aggregate must be prepared to deal with their actual bounds (by using the LoBound, LoIndex, etc. functions probably).

Example 10.1

This is a function that accepts an aggregate of numbers. It returns the same type of aggregate input with scaled values.

```
FUNCTION scale(in:AGGREGATE:intype OF NUMBER;
   scalar:NUMBER) : AGGREGATE:intype OF NUMBER;
LOCAL
   result : AGGREGATE:intype OF NUMBER := [];
END_LOCAL;

REPEAT i := LoIndex(in) TO HiIndex(in);
   result[i] := scalar * in[i];
END_REPEAT;

RETURN(result);

END_FUNCTION;
```

10.2 Simple datatypes

The simple datatypes represent *atomic* units of data. They cannot be further subdivided into elements that EXPRESS recognizes. All representations of data will eventually wind up being one of these simple datatypes (they could therefore be called terminal datatypes).

10.2.1 Number datatype

A number datatype is supertype of the real and integer datatypes. Its domain is all numbers and is used when you don't care whether the actual representation type is an integer or real.

Exercise 10.1 *Think of a situation where number types would be useful.*

10.2.2   Real datatype

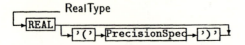

A real datatype is a subtype of the number datatype that represents rational and irrational numbers. Its domain is all real numbers,

$$-\infty \le Real \le \infty$$

A real number is represented by a mantissa with an exponent. The number of significant digits in the mantissa is optionally given by `PrecisionSpec`. There is no limit on the number of digits in the mantissa unless a precision specification is given. A constraint on the precision does not constrain the magnitude.

When a precision constraint is given, it should be based on the number required by your application (if you know it), not on limits presumed to exist in some computer architecture.

Example 10.2

Here we give a precision specification that affects the number of digits kept when a computation is assigned to the variable.

```
LOCAL
  a : REAL;
  b : REAL(4);
  ...
  a := 1/3;      -- 0.333333333333333333333333...
  b := 1/3;      -- 0.3333
```

The value of a has an arbitrarily large number of digits since no precision specification was given; b on the other hand has four significant digits because of the way it was declared.

10.2.3   Integer datatype

```
_____ IntegerType
   └→INTEGER├
```

The integer datatype is a subtype of the number datatype that represents a value of an integer number. Its domain is all whole numbers,

$$-\infty \le Integer \le \infty$$

You cannot constrain the number of digits in a integer datatype in the same manner as a real. However, you can constrain the domain either by creating a type with a constraint or by adding a local rule to an entity declaration. Example 10.3 shows how this is done.

Example 10.3

> Here are two ways to constrain an integer domain. The first one puts the constraint in a type declaration. The second uses a local rule. We suggest that the first way is the better practice, especially when the same constraint is used several times. In general, the same techniques can be used for any type.

```
TYPE MyInteger : INTEGER;        -- the constraint is
WHERE                            -- put in a type declaration
  {0 <= Self <= 100};
END_TYPE;
ENTITY foo;
  goo : MyInteger;
  ...
END_ENTITY;

ENTITY foo;
  goo : INTEGER;
  ...
WHERE
  {0 <= goo <= 100};             -- the constraint is put
END_ENTITY;                      -- in a local rule
```

10.2.4 Logical datatype

```
_____ LogicalType
 └─►│LOGICAL│─
```

A logical datatype represents the domain values false, unknown and true, where:

$$False < Unknown < True$$

Logical datatypes are compatible with boolean datatypes, except that unknown cannot be assigned to a boolean variable.

10.2.5 Boolean datatype

```
_____ BooleanType
 └─►│BOOLEAN│─
```

A boolean datatype represents the domain values false and true, where:

$$False < True$$

10.2.6 String datatype

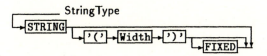

Table 10.2: String definition formats

Specification	Description
`string1 : STRING;`	Defines a varying string that has no defined maximum length.
`string2 : STRING(10);`	Defines a string that is a maximum of ten characters in length, but which can vary in actual length from zero to ten characters.
`string3 : STRING(10) FIXED;`	Defines a string that is exactly ten characters in length; it cannot vary in actual length.

A string datatype represents a sequence of zero or more characters. The domain of a string is every permutation of characters, where character is defined by the EXPRESS character set (for all practical purposes, the ASCII character set will do). The case (upper or lower) of letters within a string is significant. EXPRESS expects implementations built around it to produce the same comparison and ordering results regardless of the peccadillos of the implementation platform. For example, implementations based on ASCII and EBCDIC should give the same comparison results.

A string may be defined as either fixed or varying length. If a string is not specifically declared as fixed length (using the `Fixed` reserved word in the declaration) the string is has varying length. The varying property indicates that the string is allowed to grow and shrink in apparent size.

The optional `Width` specification gives the maximum number of characters a string value can hold. This must be an integer result that is positive. When no `Width` specification is given, the length of the string is unlimited. You cannot make the length fixed unless it has a width. The effect of different specification forms is shown in Table 10.2.

Substrings and individual characters may be addressed using subscripts as described in 14.3.

Exercise 10.2 *Let's assume that* EXPRESS *did not provide a built-in string type, but did give you a character type. How would you make a string type of your own?*

10.2.7 Binary datatype

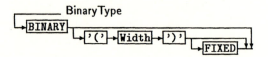

A binary datatype represents a sequence of bits (0 or 1's). The domain of a binary is every permutation of bits, where:

$$0 < 1$$

A binary may be defined as either fixed or varying length. If a binary is not specifically declared as fixed length (using the `Fixed` reserved word in the declaration) the binary has varying length. The varying property indicates that the binary is allowed to grow and shrink in apparent size.

The optional `Width` specification gives the maximum number of bits that a binary value can hold. This must be an integer result that is positive. When no `Width` specification is given, the number of bits in the binary values is unconstrained.

The binary will have a varying length unless you declare it as fixed by including the `Fixed` keyword. You cannot make the length fixed unless it has a width.

Parts of a binary and individual bits may be addressed using subscripts as described in 14.3.

Warning: *A binary value has no defined meaning. For example, it is wrong to assume that %0101 is the binary representation of the number five. However, it can be useful to represent things such as graphic image data. Just be sure to carefully document what is going on.*

Example 10.4

The following may be used to hold character encoding data.

```
ENTITY character;
  representation : ARRAY [0:255] OF BINARY (8) FIXED;
END_ENTITY;
```

10.3   Collection datatypes

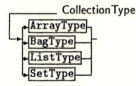
CollectionType

Collection types are used to represent ordered or unordered collections. These collections can have fixed or varying sizes depending on which specific collection type being considered. Each collection datatype has different behavior that suits it to different purposes.

- An array datatype is a fixed-size structure where the position of a given element has a specific meaning.

  Note: EXPRESS *does not allow you to say explicitly why a given position is important so be sure to cover that subject in the supporting documentation!*

  A *transformation matrix* (for geometry) may be defined as an array of arrays (of numbers).

- A bag datatype is a collection of elements in which order is not relevant and duplication is allowed. The number of elements in a bag may vary, depending on the limit specification.

  Fasteners (where nuts, bolts, screws, rivets, etc. are subtypes of fastener) could be treated as a bag in an assembly problem. That is, there may be a number of values of the same bolt, but which one is used in a particular hole is unimportant.

- A list datatype is used to represent a sequence of things. The number of elements in a list may vary, depending on the limit specification.

  The *operations* of a *process plan* might be represented as a list. One property of a list is that items can be inserted and removed. It is up to you to decide where elements are inserted if you wish to preserve some kind of collating sequence. Therefore, *operations* can be added to or removed from a *process plan* if it is represented this way.

- A set datatype is a collection of elements in which order is not relevant and where duplicate elements are not allowed. The number of elements in a set may vary, dependent on the limit specification.

  The population of people in this world is a set.

Collection types have but one *dimension*. Things that have multiple-dimensions (such as a mathematical array) may be represented by an collection whose base type is another collection type. Collection types can be nested that way to an arbitrary depth, allowing the representation of any number of dimensions. You could define:

```
... LIST[1:3] OF
      ARRAY[5:10] OF
         INTEGER ...
```

which would, in effect, have two dimensions.

10.3.1 Array datatype

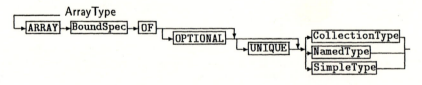

An array datatype represents an ordered, fixed-size collection of elements of a given type. The number of elements in an array is fixed by its lower and upper bound.

Both the lower (Bound1) and upper (Bound2) bounds are integer valued expressions that may be negative, zero or positive, where $Bound1 \leq Bound2$.

There are exactly $Bound2 - Bound1 + 1$ array elements that can be addressed by a subscript.

You can indicate that elements of an array type are allowed to have a missing (or null) value by using the **Optional** keyword in the declaration. Otherwise, every array element is required to be not-null.

You can also indicate that each element of an array must be different from every other element in the same array value by using the **Unique** keyword.

10.3.2 Bag datatype

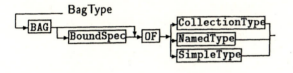

A bag datatype represents an unordered collection of like element types within which duplicate element values are permitted. The number of bag elements can be specified if needed. Otherwise, the bag can hold any number of elements.

Although the position of an element in a bag is not significant, every element will be at some position (which can be accessed by a subscript). A bag value is guaranteed to be stable until an operation either inserts or removes an element. After such an operation there is no guarantee that any element will be in the same position as before.

A **BoundSpec** is not required. If it is omitted, the specification [0:?] is assumed. **Bound1** is an integer valued expression ≥ 0. **Bound2** is an integer valued expression $\geq Bound1$, or ? to indicate the upper bound is unlimited. **Bound1** gives the minimum number of elements required by the collection and **Bound2** gives the maximum number of elements allowed in it (remember that the upper bound is unlimited when ? is used.)

Note: *The bag type is similar to the set type.*

10.3.3 List datatype

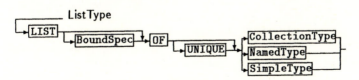

```
        ┌────── BoundSpec
        └→['']→Bound1→[':']→Bound2→[']']
```

A list datatype represents an ordered collection of like element types. The number of list elements can be specified if needed. Otherwise, the list can hold any number of elements. Duplicate elements are allowed in a list unless it is declared as unique.

A BoundSpec is not required. If it is omitted, the specification [0:?] is assumed. Bound1 is an integer valued expression ≥ 0. Bound2 is an integer valued expression $\geq Bound1$, or ? to indicate the upper bound is unlimited. Bound1 gives the minimum number of elements required by the collection and Bound2 gives the maximum number of elements allowed in it (remember that the upper bound is unlimited when ? is used.)

The Unique keyword may optionally be used to indicate that each element of a list is different from every other element in the same list value.

Example 10.5

This example defines a list of arrays. The list can contain zero to ten arrays. Each array is different from all other arrays in the list.

```
ComplexList : LIST[0:10] OF
                  UNIQUE ARRAY[1:10] OF
                  INTEGER;
```

There are zero, 10, 20, ..., 90, 100 integer values associated with the attribute named ComplexList depending on the number of list elements. Each array is different than every other array as specified by the Unique keyword.

10.3.4 Set datatype

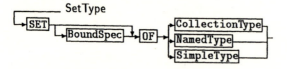

```
        ┌────── BoundSpec
        └→['']→Bound1→[':']→Bound2→[']']
```

A set datatype represents an unordered collection of like element types. No two elements of a set can have the same value. The number of set elements can be specified if needed. Otherwise, the set can hold any number of elements.

Although the position of an element in a set is not significant, every element will be at some position (which can be accessed by a subscript). A set value is guaranteed to be stable until an operation either inserts or removes an element. After such an operation there is no guarantee that any element will be in the same position as before.

A BoundSpec is not required. If it is omitted, the specification [0:?] is assumed. Bound1 is an integer valued expression ≥ 0. Bound2 is an integer valued expression $\geq$ *Bound*1, or ? to indicate the upper bound is unlimited. Bound1 gives the minimum number of elements required by the collection and Bound2 gives the maximum number of elements allowed in it (remember that the upper bound is unlimited when ? is used.)

Note: *The set type is similar to the bag type.*

10.4   Enumeration type

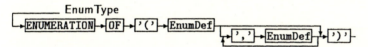

An enumeration type is an ordered list of values represented by names. The values of the enumeration type are designated by enumeration items. An enumeration item belongs only to the type that defines it and must be unique within that type definition.

The order of the values of an enumeration type is determined by their relative position in the enumeration item list: the first occurring item is less than the second, the second is less than the third, etc. Comparison between values in different enumeration types is undefined even if the item names are the same.

Two different defined types may have the same enumeration item. In this case, to ensure that a reference to the enumeration item is unambiguous, the reference must be qualified with its type name this way:

TypeRef.EnumRef

However, It never hurts to qualify even when there is no need to do it.

It is not possible to use an enumeration type directly. You must first create a defined type with the enumeration type as its base.

Example 10.6

Here we create some enumeration types to represent color values. Note that this kind of modeling is not always good practice.

```
TYPE StopOrStart = ENUMERATION OF (Red, Amber, Green);
END_TYPE;
TYPE AlertStatus = ENUMERATION OF (Green, Yellow, Red);
END_TYPE;
```

The type identifiers StopOrStart and AlertStatus each have an enumerated item called Red. There is no connection between these two definitions. A reference to Red by itself is ambiguous. To resolve the ambiguity, a reference to either of these values is qualified by the type name, e.g., AlertStatus.Red.

Warning: *Enumerated lists can disguise true information content. They should only be used when the item names truly represent a finite number of discrete values — Green, Amber, Red for traffic signal colors as an example. But, are you modeling traffic signal colors or what they mean — Go, Caution, Stop? Think about it.*

When an enumeration represents selected values from a continuum — per-haps the colors of the spectrum — another modeling approach might be better. In the later case, Red has no real meaning since it is really a contin-uum of colors. Would it be better then to model an entity called color *with a color* name? *Then values of it can accommodate red, scarlet, pink, etc. Other attributes might define the color wave length, or chemical makeup, or whatever.*

10.5   Select type

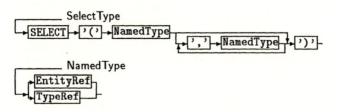

A select type defines a named collection of other types called a select list. A value of a select type is a value of *one* of the types specified in the select list where each item is an entity type or a defined types. This allows an attribute or variable to be one of several possible types. Therefore, the domain of values for such a type is the union of the domains of the types in its select list.

It is not possible to use a select type directly. You must first create a defined type with the select type as its base.

Note: *This is a way to create a heterogeneous type if you need such a thing.*

Warning: *A select type is an implicit supertype that is disguised and stripped of its power to bequeath to its offspring. Whenever you think of creating a select type, consider the merits of using supertypes and subtypes instead. After all, collecting several disjoint things together suggests some amount of likeness or commonality. In other words, those things apparently are not quite as disjoint as once thought.*

Example 10.7

Here a choice must be made among several otherwise unrelated things in a given context.

```
TYPE SnackFood = SELECT(Apple, Orange);
END_TYPE
...
snack : SnackFood;
```

A snack can be any of the things named Apple or Orange. Who says you can't mix apples and oranges?

Answers to Exercises

Answer 10.1 *Number types are useful in a supertype declaration. This allows the subtypes to refine the number type as needed. For example:*

```
ENTITY Money;
   MonetaryUnit : NUMBER;
END_ENTITY;
ENTITY AmericanMoney SUBTYPE OF(Money);
   Self\Money.MonetaryUnit : REAL;   -- this is a redeclaration
END_ENTITY;
ENTITY JapaneseMoney SUBTYPE OF(Money);
   Self\Money.MonetaryUnit : INTEGER;
END_ENTITY;
```

Answer 10.2 *These declarations are one way to do the trick. First the varying string.*

```
TYPE String = LIST OF CHARACTER;
END_TYPE;
```

The fixed length string needs a little more work.

```
ENTITY FixedString;
   Width : INTEGER;
   Chars : LIST[Width:Width] OF CHARACTER;
END_ENTITY;
```

Can you explain the peculiar looking declaration for the type of the Chars *attribute? The list sets the minimum and maximum to the same value, which makes it fixed length.*

Answer 10.3 *The first array has 10 elements of datatype* ARRAY[11:14] OF *a, which has four elements. Therefore,* sectors *has 40 elements in all.*

Chapter 11

Declarations

I have nothing to declare except my genius.

Oscar Wilde

This Chapter explains the objects that you create to represent information of interest to you. The purpose of EXPRESS, and the information modeling process in general, centers on these declarations.

The main object you declare is a schema. Within a schema you might declare constants, types, entities, functions, procedures and rules. Within those things are sub-objects such as attributes, local variables and parameters.

The structure of EXPRESS source defines the scope of declarations. The statements Schema...End_Schema mark the boundaries for a group of declarations. In a like manner an entity or function declaration bounds the declarations made within them and so forth. This process of declaring things inside other things indicates the way one declaration 'owns' other things.

In the case of an entity declaration, the attributes and local rules represent the properties that define it. So, an attribute is owned by a particular entity and also is a property of it.

The rule is an exception to the way the structure of the source shows ownership and property definition. Rules are structurally subordinate to a schema, but they are logically subordinate to the entities to which they apply. Unlike an attribute that is owned by exactly one entity, a rule can be owned by more than one of them and conversely, a rule can be a property of several entities. This exception to an otherwise orderly correlation between the source structure and the way ownership and property definition is shown is a potential cause of confusion. Keep this special situation in mind as you build information models with EXPRESS.

Exercise 11.1 *Why do you think the authors of* EXPRESS *treated the rule differently?*

152

11.1 Schema

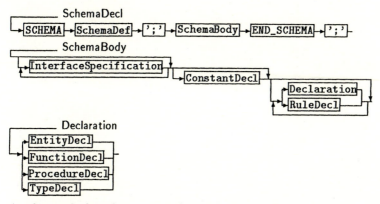

A schema declaration surrounds every other thing you declare. Therefore,

```
SCHEMA YourSchemaName;
END_SCHEMA;
```

is the smallest possible EXPRESS legal source. Normally, however, a schema declaration contains declarations of constants, entities, functions, procedures, rules and types.

A schema defines a collection of objects that have a related meaning and purpose. For example, geometry might be the name of a schema that collects declarations of points, curves, surfaces and other related objects. The order in which objects are declared is never relevant to the meaning of a schema as a whole or to the individual things declared in it.

A schema can stand alone or it can draw from declarations made in other schemas. See Chapter 15 for more about interfacing.

11.2 Constant

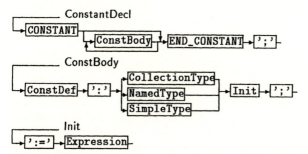

A constant declaration is used to create values that never change. You cannot use a constant in any situation that possibly could change its value. In other words, constants cannot appear as the target of an assignment statement and may not be used as an actual parameter when the corresponding formal parameter is Var.

A constant may appear in the declaration of another constant but circular definitions are not allowed.

EXPRESS forces you to declare all constants (in a schema) in the same 'block' before any other declarations are made.

Example 11.1

Here are a few legal constants:

```
CONSTANT
   thousand : NUMBER := 1000;
   million  : NUMBER := thousand**2;
   origin   : point := point(0.0, 0.0, 0.0);
END_CONSTANT;
```

... and some illegal ones:

```
CONSTANT
   a : NUMBER := b;
   b : NUMBER := a;
END_CONSTANT;
```

11.3   Type

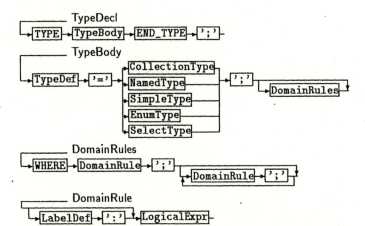

EXPRESS offers a good assortment of built-in datatypes (see Chapter 10), but you probably do not want to use them directly. Instead, you should create your own types using the facilities explained here or in Section 11.4.

The problem with using the built-in datatypes directly is that they carry little semantic weight. Although they do provide the ability to represent data values and operate upon them in the expected ways, a declaration that something is (represented as) a real number says nothing about the specific role it plays. The defined type is used to distinguish conceptually different collections of values that happen to have similar representations.

This helps you (and others) to understand the intent (or context) of the use of the underlying type.

Example 11.2 shows two defined types — `money` and `distance`. Each has an underlying datatype which is a real number. Clearly these things can be added, multiplied or whatever, but not with each other! The use of these defined types helps to distinguish one from another.

This is where human intuition and deduction become a problem to the information modeling process. Most of us will be able to figure out the context of use for a type most of the time — even when no one bothers to give us explicit clues. Therefore, we might say "Why bother to go to the trouble of defining those 'extra' types when we can figure out what is going on. Thank you very much!" The answer is that none of us can come to the right answer, all of the time, without help. These defined types are part of that help.

Example 11.2

Defined Types Help to Reveal Meaning

```
TYPE money = REAL;
END_TYPE;


TYPE distance = REAL;
END_TYPE;
```

A type declaration creates a new type (a 'defined type') based on another type (the 'underlying type'). The new type has the same domain of values as the underlying type (unless a constraint is put on it) and the operations that can be performed on the new type are the same as those applicable to the underlying type.

Type and **End_Type** bound the declaration of a type. `TypeDef` is the name you give to the defined type that is based on the given underlying type. The where clause, which is optional, is used to place constraints on the domain of the underlying type.

Example 11.3

A new type based on integers is created with a constraint that the allowed values are never less than zero.

```
TYPE positive = INTEGER;
WHERE NotNegative : SELF >= 0;
END_TYPE;
```

Then, every use of `positive` carries the constraints given in the type declaration.

Here are the rules that govern the constraint:

1. The keyword **Self** will appear at least once in the where clause. It is considered to be a value of the base type.

2. A `Boolean` or `Logical` result is produced by the expressions that appear within the where clause.

3. Every 'variable' appearing in the constraint expression must be `Self`, or a constant or function visible to the declaration being made.

Any constraint put on a type declaration applies to every value of that type. That is, the value is tested against the where rules to find out if it falls in the required domain. The result of the logical expression determines the outcome.

1. The value is acceptable when the logical expression gives a true or unknown answer.

2. The value is not acceptable when the logical expression gives a false answer.

When there is more than one where rule, if any of them gives a false answer the value is unacceptable.

Exercise 11.2 *Define a type whose domain is just the prime numbers.*

11.4   Entity

```
_____ EntityDecl
  └→EntityHead→EntityBody→END_ENTITY→';'┤

_____ EntityHead
  └→ENTITY→EntityDef→SubSuper→';'┤

_____ EntityBody
  └→Attributes→LocalRules┤
```

An entity declaration creates a type that defines the properties of real-world or conceptual objects.

An entity is said to be either 'simple' or 'complex'. A simple entity is one that is neither a subtype or a supertype. A complex entity is part of a system (a lattice) of supertypes and subtypes. A subtype entity inherits the properties of its supertypes and probably has additional ones.

Even though the properties of a complex entity are distributed over several entity declarations, an instance of the thing must be thought of as a whole. For example, you might declare fruit as a supertype and apple and pear as subtypes of it. A pear is also a fruit and a fruit is also an apple or pear. This example is somewhat of a simplification as we will see later. However, for the example given the statement is reasonable enough.

The properties of an entity are defined in terms of attributes and constraints. Attributes define the material properties of an entity and always have a value domain. Attributes may have values that are explicit or derived.

Constraints are static (meaning once they are made they never change) and may govern any of the following properties.

- Required relationships between a value of an entity itself and some other entity that uses it as a type through one of its attributes. These are given as inverse attributes and are referred to as 'cardinality constraints.'

- Limits on the uniqueness of attribute values applied across the population of entity values. These appear in the unique clause and are referred to as 'uniqueness rules.'

- Limits on the domain of attribute values applied to individual entity values. These appear in the where clause and are referred to as 'domain rules.'

- Other constraints that cannot be given in the local context of an entity declaration. These do not appear in the entity declaration itself, but as 'global rules' (see 11.6).

Of course, the domain of an attribute can also be viewed as a constraint. The domain is given in the attribute declarations.

The scope of an entity declaration is the entity itself plus all of its supertypes (if any). Every identifier created in the entity declaration is unique within the current scope. This includes all attribute names and rule labels appearing within the entity declaration itself and all those inherited from any of its supertypes (see 11.4.3).

It is possible to refine the declaration of an attribute of one of its supertypes by giving it a different type in the subtype declaration. This is not an exception to the rules of scope (see page 169).

11.4.1 Attribute

The explicit and derived attributes of an entity represent its material properties. Inverse attributes represent existential dependency (independent existence is another term for this). Attributes are explicit (the values are static), derived (the values are calculated in some manner) or inverse (defines existential dependency). In all cases, attributes have a domain of values that is defined by its type.

Explicit attribute

ExplicitClause
ExplDef
ExplRedef

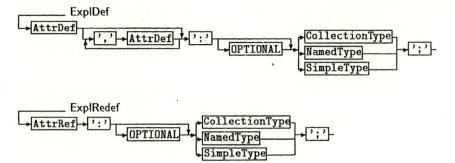

An explicit attribute is a property of an entity whose value is static and independent. Once a value is given to an explicit attribute, it does not change until another value is substituted for it — and when other attribute values change, its value is not influenced. Probably the easiest way to think of an explicit attribute (value) is what you would find in a database or written on a piece of paper.

An explicit attribute declaration gives a list of role names and a type, plus the keyword **Optional** if you want to allow it to have a null value. Unless an explicit attribute is declared as optional valued, a legal value is mandatory.

The effect of allowing an optional valued attribute is that null is added to the value domain defined by its type. Saying that an attribute is allowed to have an optional value *absolutely does not mean that the entity has an optional attribute!* The distinction is important. When you say that an entity has several attributes (properties) it always has them. When you say that a given attribute may have an optional value you are saying that a value for it is not always needed.

Here is a guideline for deciding whether optional valued attributes should be used or not: *When your interpretation of the entity in question changes depending on the presence or absence of a value, optional valued attributes should not be used. By interpretation we mean: Is the behavior of the thing different? Is it used in a different context? Would you rather pretend that the attribute itself can be ignored? The recommended practice is to use supertypes and subtypes instead. On the other hand, when the interpretation does not change, it is probably safe to use them.*

Warning: *Optional valued attributes offer considerable potential for abuse and misuse. Always think carefully about what your goals are when you are tempted to use them.*

Warning: *Pay close attention to optional valued attributes, especially in rules. Look at Example 11.8 for a way to handle optional valued attributes.*

Exercise 11.3 *Try to think of a good reason to use optional valued attributes.*

Note: *It is possible to 'redeclare' explicit attributes in a subtype. See page 169.*

One or more attributes can be declared in the same statement when everything to the right of the colon is identical for all of them. Therefore,

```
ENTITY widget;
  p, i, g : real;
END_ENTITY;
```

is equivalent to:

```
ENTITY widget;
  p : real;
  i : real;
  g : real;
END_ENTITY;
```

Derived attribute

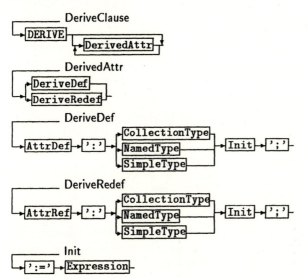

A derived attribute is a property of an entity whose value changes in response to changes to other attribute values.

A derived attribute declaration gives a role name, a type and an expression that defines how its value is derived. The expression must be assignment compatible with the declared type of the attribute (see 13.3). The expression can operate on any attribute value known to the entity scope (which of course includes those from supertypes) and any constants or functions in scope. The keyword **Self** refers to a value of the entity being declared.

Note: *It is possible to 'redeclare' derived attributes in a subtype. See page 169.*

A derived attribute can be based on another derived attribute, but you should be careful to avoid circular references.

Example 11.4

Derive a bank balance.

```
ENTITY BankBook;
  Deposits     : REAL;
  Withdrawals : REAL;
DERIVE
  Balance      : REAL := Deposits - Withdrawals;
END_ENTITY;
```

Inverse attribute

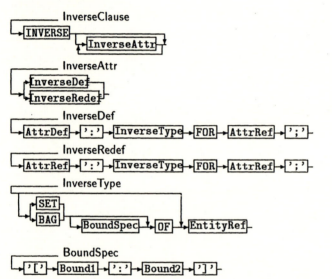

An inverse attribute is a property of an entity whose value represents the coupling between a value of the 'subject' entity (the one in which the inverse attribute is declared) and values of the 'user' entity that refers the subject entity as a type. The value of an inverse attribute is dynamic as it changes in response to changes that occur elsewhere in the information base.

An inverse attribute declaration gives a role name, the user entity type and the attribute of the user that refers to the subject entity. Only one inverse attribute can be declared in the same statement.

The user entity must have an explicit attribute whose type is the subject entity (or one of its supertypes if any).

Note: *It is possible to 'redeclare' inverse attributes in a subtype. See page 169.*

This is as good a time as any to discuss the way EXPRESS views relationships and relationship types. There are many distinctions that can be made about relationships, but EXPRESS boils them down to three: 'is-a', 'is-defined-by' and 'is-represented-as'. Each relationship goes in both directions, with a corresponding symmetry of terminology ('defines' corresponds to 'is-defined-by'). Let's forget 'is-a' for the moment as it has to do with supertypes and subtypes.

The relationship between an entity and an attribute is 'is-defined-by;' the relationship between an attribute and a type is 'is-represented-as'. The inverse attribute is an anomaly, however, since its role is to show existential dependence instead of definition. Every entity (that has an attribute) does depend on the existence of attribute values. But, that is not what is meant by existential dependence! Consider this simple declaration:

```
ENTITY PersonName;
   LastName  : STRING;
   FirstName : STRING;
END_ENTITY;
```

A value of `PersonName` depends on values of strings since they are required as representations of attributes, which in turn define the properties of the entity. Existential dependence means that a value of an entity must exist based on a relationship that neither defines or represents as in:

```
ENTITY Employee;
   Name : PersonName;
   ...
END_ENTITY;
ENTITY PersonName;
   LastName  : STRING;
   FirstName : STRING;
INVERSE
   Link       : Employee AS Name;
END_ENTITY;
```

The `Link` attribute does not contribute to the definition of `PersonName`, but it does stipulate that a value of `PersonName` cannot exist unless there is exactly one value of `Employee` that has an attribute named `Name` whose value is `Self`. In fact, the value of `Link` is exactly the value of `Employee` that does that.

Example 11.5

These declarations say that `Point` cannot exist without `Line` also.

```
ENTITY Line;
   StartsIt,
   EndsIt    : Point;
END_ENTITY;
```

we constrain the declaration of `Point` such that points can only exist if they are used in the role of `StartsIt` in exactly one value of `Line`.

```
ENTITY Point;
   ...
INVERSE
   StartsLine : Line FOR StartsIt;
END_ENTITY;
```

Notice that the representation of EndsIt is also Point. Therefore, Point plays two different roles in the definition of Line. However, the existence of a value of Point depends on one of those roles, namely StartsIt.

Warning: *The use of inverse attributes limits the use of an entity declaration as a general resource. Taking* PersonName *as an example, it would be inconvenient to use it in the context of members of a social club. Why? Because the social club probably does not have any interest in employees and all the representations needed to define and represent it. The interface specification offers a way to preserve entity declarations as a resource while allowing control over existential dependence.*

11.4.2   Local rule

> When you have eliminated the impossible,
> whatever remains, *however improbable,* must
> be the truth.
> _____
> *The Sign of Four — Sir Arthur Conan Doyle*

```
_____ LocalRules
 ┌──→UniqueRules──┐
 │                └→DomainRules─→
```

In EXPRESS, rules are written to identify all of the situations that are illegal in the context of the problem being modeled. Anything not explicitly forbidden is legal. Local rules are given in the local context of an entity declaration. The local rules are assertions on the validity of entity values and apply to all values of that entity type. There are two kinds of local rules. Uniqueness rules govern the sameness of attribute values across the information base. Domain rules describe other constraints on or among attribute values for each value of a entity type taken individually.

Note: *They are called local because of where they are declared, not because of the scope of application.*

Local rules may optionally be given a label. Labels are used to identify rules in documentation, in error reports and in enforcement specifications. Putting labels on rules is always a good idea even though EXPRESS does not force you to do it.

A local rule has one of three states for a population of entity values: true, false or unknown. The information base conforms to the information model when the state is true or unknown; otherwise it does not conform.

Unique rule

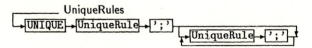

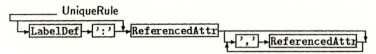

A uniqueness constraint can be given for individual explicit attributes or combinations of them by means of a unique rule. These rules follow the **Unique** keyword. A unique rule specifies either a single attribute name or a list of two or more of them. A rule that gives a single attribute name is a 'simple uniqueness constraint.' A rule that gives two or more attribute names is a 'joint uniqueness constraint,' requiring that a tuple of values, one from each of the attributes named, will be unique.

Uniqueness spans the collection of entity values known as the 'information base'. Within a given information base, the attribute (or combination of attributes) are required to be unique.

An explicit attribute can be both optional valued and unique. When an attribute that is allowed to have optional values appears in a uniqueness constraint the uniqueness constraint evaluates to 'unknown' when there is a missing value.

Example 11.6

> If an entity had three attributes called A, B and C, we could have:
>
> ```
> UNIQUE
>     A;
>     B;
>     C;
> ```
>
> which means that the uniqueness constraint applies to each of the attributes individually. Or we could have:
>
> ```
> UNIQUE
>     A, B;
>     C;
> ```
>
> This means that the uniqueness constraint applies jointly to A and B together and also to C individually.

Exercise 11.4 *Would the uniqueness rule above be any different if it was written* B,A *instead of* A,B*?*

Exercise 11.5 *How would you guarantee uniqueness of the entire entity value?*

Domain rule

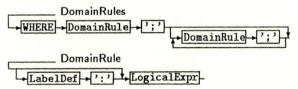

Domain rules are used to specify constraints on the value of individual attributes or a combinations of attributes in an entity value. Domain rules follow the `Where` keyword.

The domain rule is given by a sequence of logical valued expression. When all of those expressions evaluate to true or unknown, the domain rule is asserted. Otherwise, it is violated.

The ingredients in the expression must come from a single entity value taken in isolation. That is, it must be possible to evaluate the expression even if every other entity declaration (except for the ones needed to support the one in question) did not exist. However, the expression can reference constants and functions as long as those things do not refer to other entity declarations. The keyword `Self` refers to a value of the entity being declared.

Example 11.7 shows a fairly simple domain constraint.

Example 11.7

> Constraining a unit vector.
>
> ```
> ENTITY UnitVector;
>   a, b, c : REAL;
> WHERE
>   LengthIsOne :
>     a**2 + b**2 + c**2 = 1.0;
> END_ENTITY;
> ```

Domain rules sometimes have to deal with optional valued attributes. A domain rule that contains an optional valued attribute is treated this way:

- When the expression evaluates to null, the rule is treated as unknown (which is just as good as true as far as EXPRESS is concerned).

- Otherwise, the expression will evaluate to true or false, meaning asserted or violated respectively.

Example 11.8

> Here is a variation of Example 11.7 in which an optional valued attribute is used.
>
> ```
> ENTITY UnitVector;
>   a, b : REAL;
>   c    : OPTIONAL REAL;
> WHERE
>   LengthIsOne :
>     a**2 + b**2 + c**2 = 1.0;
> END_ENTITY;
> ```
>
> The intent of the domain rule is to ensure that a `UnitVector` is unitized. However, when c has a null value the domain rule will always yield unknown no matter what the values of a and b are.

A correct approach for dealing with domain rules that contain optional valued attributes is to use the NVL standard function (Appendix F.2) to supply a substitute value when the attribute value is null. When the attribute does have a value, the NVL function returns it; otherwise the substitute value is returned. This is one correct approach to the declaration given above.

```
ENTITY UnitVector;
   a, b : REAL;
   c    : OPTIONAL REAL;
WHERE
   LengthIsOne :
      a**2 + b**2 + NVL(c, 0.0)**2 = 1.0;
END_ENTITY;
```

Remember the warnings given earlier about the use, or probable abuse, of optional valued attributes. They offer abundant opportunities for trouble, and the handling of them in domain rules is just one of them. Think about using supertypes and subtypes as another solution to the problem you are modelling. Luckily, we discuss supertypes next.

11.4.3 Supertypes and subtypes

> Oh, what a tangled web we weave, When
> first we practice to deceive.
>
> *Sir Walter Scott*

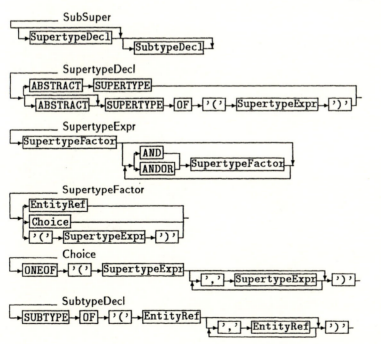

Subtypes and supertypes are used to build a classification structure. In that structure, subtypes are more specific than supertypes and supertypes are more general than subtypes. Since the subtype is a more specific kind of its supertype, every value of a subtype is a value of its supertypes.

The following facts pertain to subtype/supertype relationships. These facts refer to a 'subtype/supertype lattice' — a directed graph where the nodes are the entity types and the links represent the subtype to supertype relationships. Following the `subtype of` links leads to more general types while following the `supertype of` links leads to more specific types.

1. A subtype may have more than one supertype.

2. A supertype may have more than one subtype.

3. A supertype may itself be a subtype.

4. The subtype/supertype relationship is transitive. If A is a subtype of B and B is a subtype of C, then A is a subtype of C. The entities that are supertypes of a particular entity type are those entities to which it is possible to traverse, starting at the entity type and following the subtype of links.

5. A subtype cannot directly or indirectly be the supertype of itself nor may a supertype be a subtype of itself (directly or indirectly). Another way to state this is that the lattice is acyclic — loops are illegal.

An entity is a subtype only when it contains a `subtype of` clause that gives the names of its supertypes. However, a supertype entity does not have to make an explicit declaration that it is a supertype. It is a supertype if it is mentioned in the subtype clause of any other entity declaration. Of course, it is possible (and sometimes necessary) to include an explicit `supertype of` clause. When an explicit supertype of clause is given, there must be a correspondence between the two statements.

Abstract supertypes

Every value of a subtype is also a value of its supertypes. The opposite may or may not be true, however.

When you say that a supertype is abstract, you are saying that every value of a supertype is also a value of one (or more) of its subtypes. Abstract is supposed to evoke a feeling that the entity in question is incomplete without more information to make it complete and useful.

When you do not say that a supertype is abstract, you are saying that a value of a supertype does not have to be coupled with a value of any of its subtypes — that it can be complete and useful without more information.

For instance, mammal (in an animal classification schema) is an abstract supertype because whatever we know about mammal by itself is insufficient. It must have more information about what kind of mammal it is: human or dog or whatever.

Subtype constraints

When a supertype has more than one subtype (which it usually will) then a value of the supertype may involve zero or more of its subtypes. Since the relationship spans all the known subtypes of the supertype the supertype constraint is specified in the supertype definition if needed. If no relationship constraints are given, a default constraint is used (see page 167).

Given a supertype S and two subtypes s_1 and s_2 the following couplings are allowed depending on the supertype expression:

$$S$$
$$Ss_1$$
$$Ss_2$$
$$Ss_1s_2$$

The first case is only possible when S is an abstract supertype. We will ignore that possibility for the moment. Now let's see how the other cases can arise.

The relationship between s_1 and s_2 can be OneOf, And and AndOr. OneOf, as the name suggests, says that only s_1 or s_2 can exist (along with S) at the same time; And says that both s_1 and s_2 must exist at the same time; AndOr says that either or both of s_1 and s_2 can exist at the same time. Additional subtypes are handled in the same manner.

Exercise 11.6 *What are the declarations that make the examples shown above legal? Hint: there are more than one in some cases.*

OneOf If the subtypes are mutually exclusive, then the relationship between the subtypes is specified using the OneOf constraint.

AndOr If the subtypes are not mutually exclusive or mutually inclusive, then the relationship between the subtypes is specified using the AndOr constraint.

And If the subtypes are mutually inclusive, then the relationship between the subtypes is specified using the And constraint. The And constraint should only used to relate groupings of other constraints.

Default subtype constraint

If no supertype constraint is given in the declaration of an entity, then the subtypes are mutually inclusive, i.e., as if all subtypes were explicitly mentioned in an AndOr construct.

When the supertype clause defines the constraint among some, but not all, of its subtypes, then the constraint is as specified for those subtypes mentioned and AndOr for the other subtypes. The relationship between the subtypes specified in the supertype clause and those subtypes that are not specified in the supertype clause is AndOr.

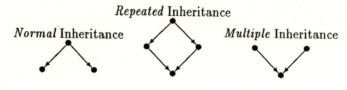

Figure 11.1: Inheritance alternatives

Inheritance

A subtype inherits all the properties of its supertypes — the attributes, labels and rules. Do not forget that subtypes also inherit all the global rules written against its supertypes. That is, subtypes inherit all the constraints.

Attribute inheritance   The names of attributes in a supertype are visible within the scope of its subtypes.   A subtype 'inherits' all of those supertype attributes. When a subtype has more than one supertype, it inherits all supertype attributes. This is sometimes called multiple inheritance. When a subtype inherits attributes from two supertypes that are themselves disjoint, it is possible that they will have attributes that have the same name. The naming ambiguity is resolved by prefixing the name with the name of the supertype entity. These inheritance alternatives are shown in Figure 11.1.

Example 11.9

Here we show a multiply inherited attribute and a qualified reference to resolve confusion about which one is of interest.

```
ENTITY e1;
  attr : REAL;
  ...
END_ENTITY;

ENTITY e2;
  attr : BINARY;
  ...
END_ENTITY;

ENTITY e12
  SUBTYPE OF (e1, e2);
  ...
WHERE
  positive :
    SELF\e1.attr > 0.0 ; -- attr as declared in e1
END_ENTITY;
```

A subtype may inherit the same attribute from different supertypes that in turn have inherited it from a common ancestor. This is called repeated inheritance. In this case the subtype only inherits the attribute once.

Attribute redeclaration An attribute declared in a supertype can be redeclared in its subtypes.

- The domain of the representation of an inherited attribute can be restricted (it cannot be expanded). For example, you can change a number type given in the supertype to a real type in the subtype, or restrict the elements of an aggregate to be unique.

- An explicit attribute from the supertype can be changed to a derived attribute in a subtype. However, optional valued attributes in the original declaration cannot be optional in a derived attribute. Therefore, the `Optional` keyword is omitted in the redeclaration.

- An optional valued attribute in the supertype can be changed to a mandatory attribute in the subtype. However, a mandatory attribute in the supertype cannot be changed to an optional valued attribute in the subtype.

- The bound specification of bag, list or set datatypes can be changed if the new bounds constrain the original declaration (e.g., change from `[0:?]` to `[0:10]`). You are not allowed to change the bounds of an array type however.

Example 11.10

It may be important to know that all closed planar curves have an area associated with them, in which case they could be modeled this way.

```
ENTITY ClosedPlanarCurve
    ABSTRACT SUPERTYPE;
   area : REAL;
END_ENTITY;
```

For a particular type of closed planer curve, in this case a circle, the derivation of the area could be given this way:

```
ENTITY circle
    SUBTYPE OF (ClosedPlanarCurve);
   center : point;
   radius : REAL;
DERIVE
   SELF\ClosedPlanarCurve.area : REAL := PI * radius ** 2;
END_ENTITY;
```

Rule inheritance Every rule (either local or global) that applies to a supertype is inherited by its subtypes. If a subtype has more than one supertype, then it inherits all the rules constraining the behavior of those supertypes.

It is not possible to change the rules that are associated with a subtype through inheritance, but it is possible to add rules that constrain the behavior of the subtype further.

11.4.4   Interpreting supertype relationships

EXPRESS allows you to create supertype relationships that are quite complex, thereby creating two problems:

1. The writer of the schema may have a problem trying to say what they mean to say.

2. The reader of the schema may not be able to figure out what the writer had in mind to say (or in fact, did say whether it was right or wrong).

These problems can be solved to some extent by subjecting these relationships to formal analysis. Turn to Appendix C for a discussion about how to do that.

Exercise 11.7 *Read Appendix C and list out all the valid possibilities for this declaration:*

```
ENTITY a SUPERTYPE OF ( (b AND c) AndOr OneOf(d, e, f));
```

11.4.5   Implicit declarations

When an entity is declared, a constructor function is implicitly declared. The function identifier is the same as the entity name and the visibility of the function declaration is the same as the entity declaration.

The constructor function has one formal parameter for each explicit attribute. The parameter names and types are identical to the corresponding attribute names and types with the same order. When the constructor function is invoked (as a function call) it returns a value of the entity type with the explicit attributes initialized to the values given by the actual parameters.

Note: *Order of declaration is never significant except in this context!*

When a complex entity value is constructed, individual constructors for each component entity are concatenated using the || operator (see 9.7.7).

Example 11.11

Assuming the following entity declaration:

```
ENTITY Gnome;
  Gname : STRING;
END_ENTITY;
```

the implicitly declared constructor function for it is:

```
FUNCTION Gnome(Gname:STRING;):Gnome;
```

the constructor then may be used when assigning values to an object of this type.

```
CONSTANT
  Gnu : Gnome := Gnome('Gnorbert');
END_CONSTANT;
```

11.5 Algorithm

An algorithm is a sequence of statements that do something. Two kinds of algorithms that can be specified in EXPRESS: functions and procedures. It is also possible to consider the rule an algorithm, but we discuss it separately.

Formal parameters define the input to an algorithm. When an algorithm is called, actual parameters supply values upon which the algorithm will presumably operate. The actual parameters must agree with the formal parameters in number, order and type. Declarations local to the algorithm are given following the header as needed. These declarations can be types, local variables, other algorithms, etc. The scope of formal parameters and local declarations is the same. The body of the algorithm follows local declarations.

11.5.1 Formal parameter

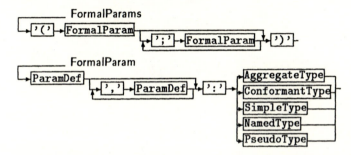

Formal parameters tell functions and procedures what kind of input is required, and in the case of procedures, what kind of output can be produced. Each formal parameter has a name and a type. The name is an identifier within the scope of the function or procedure. A formal parameter to a procedure may be declared as **Var** (variable), which means that if its actual value is changed within the procedure the change is apparent to the point of invocation. Function parameters cannot be variable (thereby avoiding side effects). Parameters not declared as **Var** are treated within the function or procedure as constants and they follow the same rules (see 11.2).

Example 11.12

> The parameters named p1 and p2 are constant parameters and cannot be assigned a value by the algorithm. The one called result, on the other hand, is a variable and can have a value assigned to it.
>
> ```
> FUNCTION dist(p1, p2 : point) : REAL;
> PROCEDURE midpt(p1, p2 : point; VAR result : point);
> ```

Pseudotypes (**Aggregate** or **Generic**) or conformant types can be used to generalize the kind of actual values that may be passed to functions and procedures. The `Aggregate` pseudotype stands for any kind of aggregate (array, bag, list or set). The `Generic` pseudotype stands for anything.

When it is necessary to ensure that two (or more) of those general parameters have the same actual type or that the result type of a function agrees with one of its actual parameters, use a type label. Examples of type label usage can be seen in Appendix F.2.

Conformant aggregate

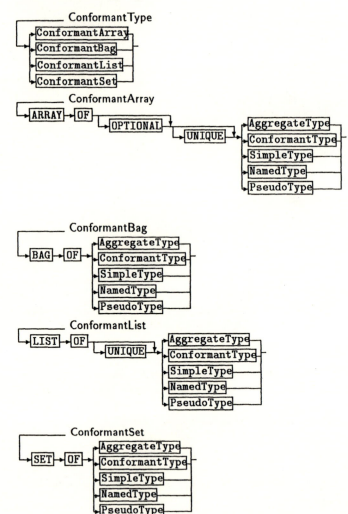

A conformant aggregate is a form of aggregation that does not specify its bounds. The function or procedure is required to detect the actual bounds and act accordingly. The `HiIndex` and `LoIndex` functions can be used to determine the actual indexing system of the aggregate value.

11.5.2 Local variable

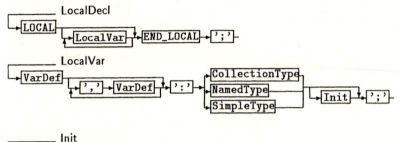

LocalDecl

LocalVar

Init

Local variables of an algorithm are declared inside a local block; between `Local` and `End_Local`. However, the scope of the local variable spans the algorithm.

Local variables are not static (i.e., values do not persist from one invocation to another). A value is assigned to a local variable upon entry to the algorithm either implicitly or explicitly. The implicit value is null unless a an explicit initialization is given. It is a good practice to supply an explicit initialization for every local variable you declare.

```
LOCAL
  r : REAL := 0.0;
  i : INTEGER;
END_LOCAl;
  ...
  EXISTS(r) -- TRUE
  EXISTS(i) -- FALSE assuming no value has ever been assigned
```

11.5.3 Function

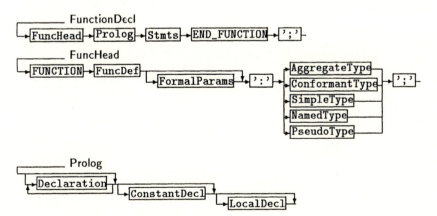

FunctionDecl

FuncHead

Prolog

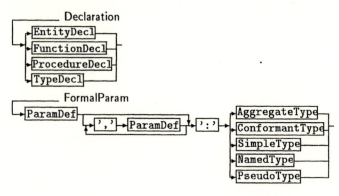

A function is an algorithm that operates on its input parameters and returns a single value of the specified type to the point of invocation (see 14.5). However, note that the 'single' value that is returned can be composite.

A function is terminated by execution of a **Return** statement. If the return statement does not get executed, then the function simply does not return. The function head defines the type of the value required by the **Return** statement.

Note: *Part 11 does not say what happens when return is not executed so the statement made above is speculative.*

The actual parameters supplied to a function are treated locally as constants. Therefore, they cannot appear as the target of an assignment statement or be passed as **Var** parameters to a procedure within a function.

11.5.4   Procedure

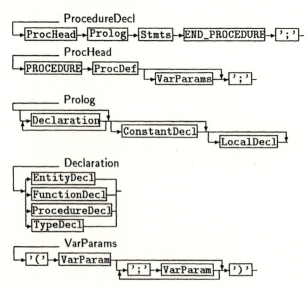

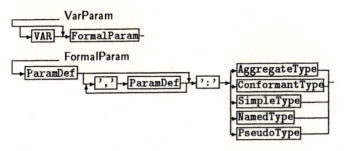

A procedure is an algorithm that receives parameters from the point of invocation and operates on them in some manner to produce the desired goal.

The actual parameters supplied to a procedure are treated locally as constants unless they are declared as variables. Therefore, any constant parameters cannot appear as the target of an assignment statement or be passed as `Var` parameters to a procedure within a function.

A procedure terminates either when a return statement is executed or when `End_Procedure` is encountered.

Note: *Part 11 is vague about this.*

11.6 Rule

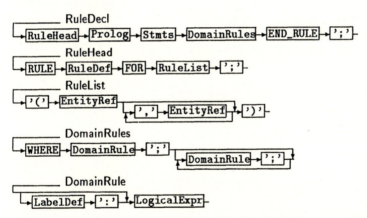

Let's say we need to write a constraint that applies to only part of a population of entities, or to more than one population. The 'local rules' we learned about earlier will not do the job because they apply to whole populations.

This is where the 'global rule' comes into play.

The rule header names the rule and specifies the entities affected by it. The list of affected entities is similar in appearance to a formal parameter list but they are not parameters in the usual sense. What we have to do is pretend that these 'rule parameters' give us access to the mythical information base and the entity populations in it. Those populations are treated as constants, and therefore the rule is not allowed to alter entity values (i.e., a rule cannot be used to repair a bad information base).

Within a rule we treat a reference to one of these entity names as a bag where each element in the bag is an instance of the named entity type. Therefore, we could operate on a single instance by a subscript, or we could use a query expression to test the whole bag (which is what often happens).

The body of the rule is much like the body of a function or procedure. The chief difference is that the 'goal' of a rule indicates whether or not some constraint is satisfied. In many cases it is possible to express this 'goal' without resorting to any procedural code at all.

Each of the expressions following 'where' evaluates to true, unknown or false. The rule is asserted (meaning the information base conforms) when every expression evaluates to true or unknown; otherwise, the information base does not conform.

Example 11.13

> This rule coordinates debits and credits. (Use your imagination about how these things are declared.) Procedural code is needed to sum up the debits and credits for the goal test.

```
RULE balance FOR (credit, debit);
  LOCAL
    CreditSum : REAL := 0.0;
    DebitSum  : REAL := 0.0;
  END_LOCAL;
  REPEAT C := 1 TO HiBound(Credit);
    CreditSum := CreditSum + Credit.Entry;
  END_REPEAT;
  REPEAT D := 1 TO HiBound(Debit);
    DebitSum := DebitSum + Debit.Entry;
  END_REPEAT;
WHERE
  BalanceOk :
    CreditSum = DebitSum;
END_RULE;
```

Example 11.14

> This rule ensures that exactly one employee is the president. We don't need any procedural code to do this one.

```
RULE chief FOR (employee);
WHERE
  IsThereOne:
    SizeOf(Query(E <* employee | E.Title = 'President')) = 1;
END_RULE;
```

Answers to Exercises

Answer 11.1 *Global rules sometimes regulate the behavior of two or more entity types. The rule declaration is made apart from the entities to avoid a duplication of the rule and the potential for missed coordination that could cause.*

Answer 11.2 *Try this:*

```
FUNCTION Prime(I:INTEGER):LOGICAL;
   (* you figure this part out *)
END_FUNCTION;

TYPE PrimeNumber = INTEGER;
WHERE Prime(Self);
END_ENTITY;
```

Answer 11.3 *Optional valued attributes should not be used when the interpretation or meaning of an entity changes depending on the presence or absence of a value. There are surprisingly few cases when that test can be met, and even then other modeling practices can be used. But, here is a case that can be rationalized: A person's name (in most of western civilization anyway) consists of a surname, a given name and often a middle name. People can also have a nickname. We could make the middle name and the nickname optional valued attributes because the interpretation of name is not affected one way or the other by having or not having values.*

Actually, the question of modeling a person's name is quite interesting and complex. Too complex to elaborate upon here. It is a good subject for practice modeling, however, and one you might try on your own.

Answer 11.4 *The three redeclared attributes would, of course, be inherited. But, it does not matter what values we give to center (for example) since the true center point is derived from p1, p2 and p3. The redeclaration makes certain that everything will be coordinated.*

Area does not require redeclaration because its value is inherited and no change has been made to its derivation.

Answer 11.5 *No. The order of values is not important to the uniqueness test.*

Answer 11.6 *You would list every explicit attribute. It would seem easier to use* Self *here, but* EXPRESS *does not allow that.*

Answer 11.7 *S is legal by itself only when it is declared without saying it is abstract.*

```
ENTITY S SUPERTYPE OF ...
ENTITY S ...
```

Ss₁ and Ss₂ are legal when it is declared either of these ways.

```
ENTITY S SUPERTYPE OF (OneOf( s1, s2 ));
ENTITY S SUPERTYPE OF ( s1 AndOr s2 );
```

Ss_1s_2 is legal when it is declared either of these ways.

```
ENTITY S SUPERTYPE OF ( s1 And s2 );
ENTITY S SUPERTYPE OF ( s1 AndOr s2 );
```

Answer 11.8 *A, ABC, ABCD, ABCE and ABCF are all valid combinations.*

Chapter 12

References

I have called you by name; You are Mine.

Isaiah 43:1

Identifiers (or names) are created by a declaration. They are referenced by various statements. EXPRESS does not require declaration before reference, therefore the reference can come after or before the place where the declaration is given. The usual way of referring to a thing is to simply write its name. However, there are situations where a more elaborate reference — called a qualified reference — is needed.

Some qualified names can be quite long. The `Alias` statement (13.2) can be used to simplify matters when the qualified name gets too clumsy to work with conveniently.

12.1 Names, scope and visibility

A scope is a region of the source within which a name is visible. References to a name are legal in its scope but are illegal outside it. Scopes can be thought of as boxes nested within other boxes as illustrated by Figure 12.1. EXPRESS assumes that there is a giant box called the 'universe' which surrounds every other scope. All of the standard identifiers (`Integer`, `Real`...`Abs`, `UsedIn`...) and all schemas are in the scope of the universe. As an example Figure 12.2 gives an inventory of the full names of the things shown in Figure 12.1 (but note that 'universe' is never specifically written).

Although it may seem that some of the 'given' names are duplicates (`AnAttribute` for instance), when the full name is written out every name is unique. Name uniqueness is a requirement of EXPRESS.

Peer names are visible to one another. The picture shows peer names as the ones inside the same box. The same effect is shown in the inventory by tracing common name elements from left to right until a name difference is found. Peer names are the ones at the level where the difference occurs. Visibility to other names starts at some point in the name chain. Every name along the path (reading from right to left) and their

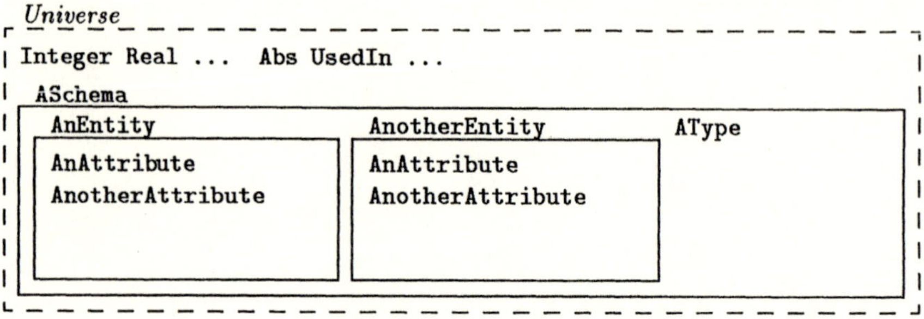

Figure 12.1: Scope

Universe
Universe.Integer
Universe.Real
Universe.Abs
Universe.UsedIn
Universe.ASchema
Universe.ASchema.AnEntity
Universe.ASchema.AnEntity.AnAttribute
Universe.ASchema.AnEntity.AnotherAttribute
Universe.ASchema.AnotherEntity
Universe.ASchema.AnotherEntity.AnAttribute
Universe.ASchema.AnotherEntity.AnotherAttribute
Universe.ASchema.AType

Figure 12.2: An inventory of full names

peers are visible. In the picture, start inside some box and jump outside. The names in that outer box are visible. Then jump to the next
outer box, etc., until there are no more outer boxes. As an example,
ASchema.AnotherEntity.AnotherAttribute ('Universe' will no longer be
used) can 'see' the things shown in Figure 12.3. In fact, references can to
their simple names can be used.

Some important exceptions should be kept in mind.

1. The contents of one schema are ordinarily invisible to others. However, the interface specification can be used to expose declarations
   made in one schema to another one.

2. Entities that are part of a supertype/subtype lattice share the same
   scope even though the declarations are made piecemeal.

3. EXPRESS prohibits the redeclaration of standard constants, functions
   and procedures.

```
Integer
Real
Abs
UsedIn
ASchema
ASchema.AnEntity ................................................. AnEntity
ASchema.AnotherEntity ...................................... AnotherEntity
ASchema.AnotherEntity.AnAttribute .......................... AnAttribute
ASchema.AType ....................................................... AType
```

Figure 12.3: Full names and simple names

Exercise 12.1 *Why do you think* EXPRESS *does this?*

4. Sometimes when a reference to a name is made, the rules of scope and visibility are modified.

   - The type of an attribute must not be resolved in the scope where the reference is made. This has the interesting effect that

     ```
     ENTITY a;
       b : b;
     END_ENTITY;
     ```

     is legal since the type b cannot be resolved by the attribute of the same name.

   - The references made in a uniqueness rule must be resolved in the current scope, and those made from a where rule must be resolved in the current scope unless the reference is to a visible constant or function.

   - *An apparent exception to this rule is when an attribute is redeclared in a complex entity,* i.e., an entity subtype. This is not really a redeclaration at all, but is a specialization of the type (see 11.4.3).

12.2 The anatomy of a name

Every identifier is created within a scope. An alias can be given to an identifier by an interface specification. In that case, the alias is a name in the scope of the importing schema.

An attribute name is appended to the entity name in which it is declared to get its full name; e.g., `EntityName.AttributeName`.

An attribute which is part of a complex entity type is declared within one of the 'chunks' which make up the whole definition. The name of that chunk is part of the attribute name; e.g., `EntityName\AttributeName`. Chunk qualification is needed when several attributes in a complex entity have the same name.

When a name represents an aggregate, one or more subscripts (depending on the depth of the aggregate) are part of the full name; e.g., `A[1]`. Subscripts are used to reference pieces of the aggregate value instead of the whole thing.

Enumeration items are associated with a single enumeration type and you need to give the name of the enumeration type as part of the enumeration item name; e.g., `TypeName.ItemName`.

12.3   References in general

A simple reference is made by writing a name as given in a declaration. Simple references are legal unless the simple name is not unique to the scope from which the reference takes place. When a simple reference is not unique, some form of qualification is needed. The exact kind of qualification depends upon the kind of thing that name represents.

You may need to refer to pieces of a composite (entity or aggregate including string and binary) value instead of the whole value. Subscripts are used to refer to elements of an aggregate value, attribute names are used to refer to pieces of an entity value and chunk references give access to individual entities that make up a supertype instance.

12.4   Entity references

Entities are referenced by writing the entity name. The reserved word `Self` is used when the reference comes from inside the entity declaration as when writing rules.

Here a self reference is used in a local rule:

```
ENTITY foo;
   ...
WHERE
   Ok(Self);
END_ENTITY;
```

The function `Ok` accepts an actual parameter whose type is `foo`, presumably checks for validity, and returns a logical value to the local rule.

Warning: *This kind of global validity checking is very much frowned upon! The recommended practice is to check for each constraint individually. This is true even when there is only one constraint because more may be added in the future.*

Exercise 12.2 *Can you explain how the syntax allows you to write* `Self` *in local rules?*

12.5   Type references

```
_____ TypeRef
└→│TypeDef│─
```

Types are referenced by writing the type name. The reserved word **Self** is used when the reference comes from inside the type declaration as when writing rules.

A type self reference looks like this:

```
TYPE foopaux = INTEGER;
WHERE
    Self > 42;
END_TYPE;
```

Self implies that any value of type **foopaux** will be greater than **42**.

12.6   Attribute references

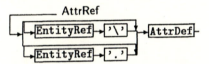

Attribute references can be simple or can be qualified with an entity name. A simple reference is made from within the entity scope in which the attribute is declared. Remember that the entity scope includes supertype entities if there are any.

Dot qualification connects an entity variable with an attribute name, like this: **EntityName.AttributeName** where **EntityName** is an entity whose scope includes **AttributeName**. On the other hand, chunk qualification also connects an entity name with an attribute name: **EntityName\AttributeName** where **EntityName** is the name of a chunk in which **AttributeName** is declared. This is needed only when two or more attributes in the same complex entity have the same (local) name.

When an attribute has a composite value, individual components can be referred to with subscripts or attribute names as required. See 12.9.

Exercise 12.3 *If attribute names are unique in the scope of an entity declaration (including complex entities), how is it possible to have duplicate names?*

12.7   Enumeration item references

```
_____ EnumRef
└→│TypeRef│→│'.'│┘→│EnumDef│─
```

An enumeration item can be a simple reference unless the same name appears in another enumeration type. In that case it is necessary to qualify the enumeration item with the type to which it belongs, like this:

TypeName.ItemName

where TypeName is the name of the type and ItemName is the name of an enumeration item in TypeName.

12.8   Function references

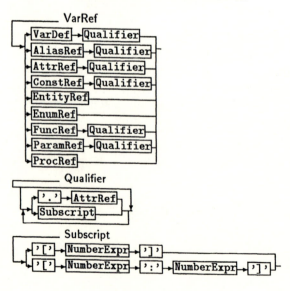

A function reference invokes the algorithm and returns a value to the place where the reference is made. You can think of a function reference as a value of the type returned by it. That is, if F is a function that returns the integer value one:

```
A := A + F;
```

has the same effect as:

```
A := A + 1;
```

When a function returns a composite type, qualification can be used to access pieces of the returned value. Let's say for example that a function F returns an array. You could refer to an element of that returned value this way:

```
IF F[22] = 5 THEN ...
```

12.9   Variable references

A variable represents (or holds) a value of a particular type. A reference to the variable name by itself accesses the whole value (whether something simple such as an integer or something very complex such as an array of entities). When the value is composite, pieces of the whole can be referenced by subscripts or attribute names as appropriate.

Subscripts reference specific elements in an aggregate value. If the aggregate value is a string or binary, ranges (or substrings) can be referenced. Given:

```
A : STRING := 'QWERTY';
B : LIST OF STRING := [ 'ABC', 'DEF', 'GHIJ' ] ;
Function F:SET OF INTEGER; -- [3,2,4,1]
```

the following references produce:

```
A[3:4] → 'ER'
B[1][1:2] → 'AB'
F[3] → 4
```

Entity attributes are referenced this way:

```
ENTITY E;
  a : INTEGER;
END_ENTITY;
...
IF E(17).a = 17 THEN ...
```

which would evaluate to true. Did you notice the use of the constructor function which initializes the attribute values?

Example 12.1

Here is a case that uses a lot of qualification.

```
ENTITY a;
  b : ARRAY[2:10] OF INTEGER;
END_ENTITY;
ENTITY c;
  d : ARRAY[200:1000] OF a;
END_ENTITY;
ENTITY e;
  f : ARRAY[0:8] OF c;
WHERE
  f[0].d[500].b[2] = 0;
END_ENTITY;
```

Answers to Exercises

Answer 12.1 *Since* EXPRESS *is the standard used to write other standards the requirement is to enforce uniformity as much as possible. In the case of the built-in constants, functions and procedures it is considered dangerous to allow a redeclaration of something like SQRT because of the confusion it could cause.*

Answer 12.2 *The expression in a local rule can refer to constants, and* Self *is defined as one of them. In the context of use,* Self *means a value of the type being declared which can be operated upon in some way.*

Answer 12.3 *There are two cases. One of them suggests a modeling problem.*

The first case stems from multiple inheritance. That is, when a subtype has two (or more) disjoint supertypes. The same attribute (name) can appear in each of the supertypes, and of course, those attributes are inherited. Now, there is no guarantee that the attributes are (mean) the same thing even though they have the same name. Quite possibly the conflict, if there is one, is a product of evolution; the subtype attached itself to two supertypes that were at one time completely unrelated. Chunk qualification allows you to avoid going back to the supertypes to reconcile the difference.

```
ENTITY OldOne;          ENTITY OldAnotherOne;
   A : AType;              A : AnotherType;


ENTITY NewSub SUBTYPE OF (OldOne, OldAnotherOne);
   -- inherits two different A's from two places.
END_ENTITY;
```

The second case has duplicate attribute names in different subtypes of the same supertype. In this case, very probably the duplicate attributes are (mean) the same thing, and if they are, they positively should be migrated into the supertype. Why? Otherwise, EXPRESS *and everyone who looks at your model has to conclude that the attributes are different because, by definition, they are not the same.*

```
ENTITY TopOne;
END_ENTITY;


ENTITY SubOne SUBTYPE OF (TopOne);
   A : AType; -- this should migrate up
END_ENTITY;


ENTITY SubTwo SUBTYPE OF (TopOne);
   A : AType; -- this should migrate up
END_ENTITY;
```

Chapter 13

Executable statements

Execute their aery purposes.

Paradise Lost
John Milton

Executable statements define the actions of functions, procedures and rules. They define the logic and actions needed to support the definition of constraints by acting on parameters, local variables and constants.

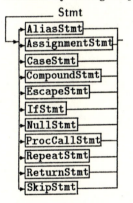

13.1   Null (statement)

NullStmt

The shortest possible 'executable' statement is just a semicolon. It is called a null statement because it does nothing. Such a statement is not useless, however, as you can use a null statement to stake out territory for future use, or perhaps to make the absence of a statement stand out more clearly as in the example following.

187

```
IF a = 13 THEN
  ;                -- do nothing
ELSE
  b := 5 ;         -- otherwise give b a value
END_IF ;
```

13.2   Alias statement

```
         ____ AliasStmt
```

ALIAS → AliasDef → FOR → VarRef → ';' → Stmts → END_ALIAS → ';'

The **Alias** statement gives a short name (alias) to an identifier that might be long or clumsy to write. The alias exists only in the scope of the alias statement and references to the alias is the same as writing out the identifier out in full.

Example 13.1

Some longish identifiers are given aliases both to shorten the code and to make it more readable.

```
ENTITY Line;
StartPoint,
EndPoint : Point;
END_ENTITY;

LOCAL
  ThisLine : Line;
END_LOCAL;

ALIAS Start FOR ThisLine.StartPoint;
  DistToOrigin := SQRT(Start.X**2 + Start.Y**2 + Start.Z**2);
END_ALIAS;
```

13.3   Assignment statement

```
         ____ AssignmentStmt
```

VarRef → ':=' → Expression → ';'

The assignment statement is used to give a value to a local variable or parameter. The type of the expression assigned to the variable must be compatible with the variable or parameter. Some assignments are shown below.

```
LOCAL
  a, b : REAL ;
  p    : point;
END_LOCAL ;
  ...
  a := 1.1 ;
```

```
b := 2.5 * a;
p.x = b ;
```

Assignment Compatibility

The target variable and the expression being assigned to it are assignment compatible if any of the following hold true:

- The types are the same.
- The expression results in a type which is a subtype of the type declared for the variable being assigned to.
- The type of the variable being assigned to is a select type and the expression results in a type which is a member of that select type.

13.4 Case statement

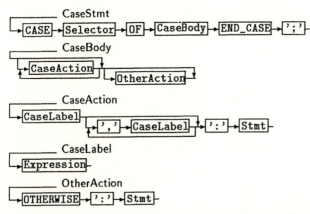

The `Case` statement executes one (or perhaps zero) statement based on the value of an expression. The statement executed is chosen depending on the value of the `Selector`. The case statement consists of an expression, which is the case selector and a list of alternative actions, each one preceded by a case label. Agreement between the type of the case label and the case selector is required. The first occurring statement having a case label that evaluates to the same value of the case selector is executed. At most, one case-action is executed. If none of the case labels evaluates to the same value as the case selector then:

- if the `Otherwise` phrase is present the statement associated with otherwise is executed,
- if the `Otherwise` phrase is not present no statement associated with a case action is executed.

Example 13.2

This case statement executes one of several statements depending on the value of a selector.

```
LOCAL
   a : INTEGER ;
   x : REAL ;
END_LOCAL ;
   ...
a := 3 ;
x := 34.97 ;
CASE a OF
   1    : x := SIN(x) ;
   2    : x := EXP(x) ;
   3    : x := SQRT(x) ;   -- This is executed!
   4, 5 : x := LOG(x) ;
   OTHERWISE : x := 0.0 ;
END_CASE ;
```

13.5   Compound statement

```
          CompoundStmt
→BEGIN→Stmts→END→';'

          Stmts
→Stmt
    →Stmt→
```

The compound statement is a sequence of statements delimited by Begin and End. A compound statement behaves as a single statement.

```
BEGIN
   a = a+1 ;
   IF a > 100 THEN
     a := 0 ;
   END_IF;
END ;
```

13.6   If ... Then ... Else Statement

```
          IfStmt
→IF→Expression→THEN→Stmts
                         →ELSE→Stmts→END_IF→';'
```

The If...Then...Else statement allows the conditional execution of statements based on the value of a logical expression. When the logical expression evaluates to true the statement after Then is executed. When the logical expression evaluates to false or unknown the statement after Else is executed if the Else phrase is present. If the expression evaluates to false or unknown and the Else phrase is omitted, then control is passed to the next statement.

```
IF a < 10 THEN
  c := c + 1;
ELSE
  c := c - 1;
END_IF;
```

13.7   Procedure call statement

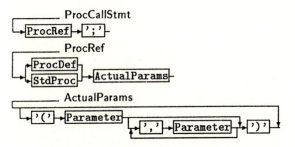

The procedure call statement invokes a procedure. Agreement between the actual parameters (in number, order and type) and the formal parameters defined for that procedure is required.

Note: *The standard procedures are described in Appendix F.*

```
INSERT (PointList, ThisPoint, Here );
```

13.8   Repeat statement

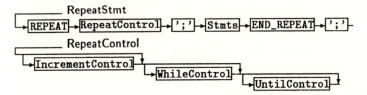

The **Repeat** statement is used to execute a sequence of statements a number of times based on the outcome of various control conditions. Those control conditions are: finite iteration, while a condition is true and until a condition is true. These controls can be used in combination to specify the conditions that terminate the repetition.

The control conditions are evaluated this way to control the iterations:

1. When the repeat statement omits all control conditions, execution of the body continue forever or until an escape statement is executed.

2. When the repeat statement is entered the increment control statement is evaluated as described in 13.8.1 if it is given.

3. The while control expression is evaluated. If the result is true (or no while control exists), then the body of the repeat statement is executed; otherwise, the execution of the repeat statement is terminated.

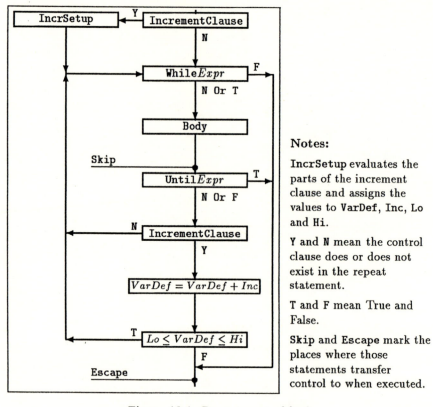

Notes:

IncrSetup evaluates the parts of the increment clause and assigns the values to VarDef, Inc, Lo and Hi.

Y and N mean the control clause does or does not exist in the repeat statement.

T and F mean True and False.

Skip and Escape mark the places where those statements transfer control to when executed.

Figure 13.1: Repeat control logic

4. When the execution of the body of the repeat statement is complete, the until control expression is evaluated if there is one. If the resulting value is true, then the execution of the repeat statement is complete; otherwise, the increment control is evaluated.

5. The value of the increment control variable (if iteration control is present) is incremented by Incr. If the iteration control variable is between Lo and Hi, then control passes to step 3; otherwise the execution of the repeat statement is terminated.

This logic is diagrammed in Figure 13.1.

Example 13.3

This fragment of source shows how more than one controlling condition can be used in a repeat statement. The statement iterates until the desired tolerance is achieved or one hundred cycles are executed, whichever occurs first.

```
REPEAT i:=1 TO 100 UNTIL epsilon<1.E-6;
   ...
   epsilon := ...;
END_REPEAT;
```

13.8.1 Increment control

```
           IncrementControl
  ┌──────────
  └→│VarDef│→│':='│→│Bound1│→│TO│→│Bound2│────────────────┐
                                         └→│BY│→│Incr│─┘
```

The increment control initiates and continues the execution of the body of the repeat statement while the value of VarDef is between the specified bounds.

When the repeat statement is entered Bound1, Bound2 and Incr (if present) are evaluated and assigned to the private variables Lo, Hi and Inc respectively. (These variables are encapsulated within the repeat statement and are not separately declared.) When Incr is not present, Inc is set to one. Then Lo is assigned to VarDef, which is also a private variable.

If any of the expressions representing Bound1, Bound2 and Incr in the increment control produce a null then the repeat statement is not executed. Furthermore, the repeat statement will not be executed when:

$$((Incr > 0) \, And \, (Bound1 > Bound2)) \, Or \, ((Incr < 0) \, And \, (Bound1 < Bound2))$$

If Incr is zero, the repeat statement is executed forever unless a While or Until control causes termination, or an Escape statement is executed. When Incr is non-zero, if $Bound1 = Bound2$ then the repeat statement is executed once.

EXPRESS does not allow changes to any of the variables given in any of the iteration control expressions within the body of the repeat statement. The repeat statement creates a temporary scope within which those variables are treated as constants.

After each iteration, the value of VarDef is incremented:

$$VarDef \leftarrow VarDef + Inc$$

Then execution continues when

$$Lo \leq VarDef \leq Hi$$

13.8.2 While control

```
           WhileControl
  ┌──────────
  └→│WHILE│→│LogicalExpr│─
```

The While control continues the execution of the body of the repeat statement while the control expression is true. The expression is evaluated before each iteration. If the While control expression evaluates to false initially, the body will not be executed.

13.8.3   Until control

```
_____ UntilControl
└→│UNTIL│→│LogicalExpr│─
```

The **Until** control continues the execution of the body of the repeat statement until the control expression evaluates to true. The expression is evaluated after each iteration. If the **Until** control is the only control present, at least one iteration will always be executed.

13.8.4   Escape statement

```
_____ EscapeStmt
└→│ESCAPE│→│';'│─
```

An **Escape** statement causes an immediate transfer to the statement after the end of the repeat statement in which it appears.

```
REPEAT UNTIL (a=1);
  ...
  IF (a<0) THEN
    ESCAPE; (* When executed, control passes to
               the statement after END_REPEAT *)
  END_IF;
  ...
END_REPEAT;
-- control transferred to here
```

13.8.5   Skip statement

```
_____ SkipStmt
└→│SKIP│→│';'│─
```

A **Skip** statement causes an immediate transfer to the end of the repeat statement in which it appears. The control conditions are then evaluated as described in 13.8.

```
REPEAT UNTIL (a=1);
  ...
  IF (a<0) THEN
    SKIP; (* When executed, control passes to the
             END_REPEAT statement where the UNTIL
             condition is evaluated. *)
  END_IF;
  ...
END_REPEAT;
```

Exercise 13.1 *What happens when none of the controls are given?*

13.9 Return statement

```
_____ ReturnStmt
→RETURN┬──────────────────────────────────────┬→
       └→'('→Expression→')'┬→';'┘
```

The `Return` statement terminates the execution of a function or procedure. A function return includes an expression that is the value returned to the point of invocation. A procedure return does not include an expression.

```
RETURN(50) ;          (* from a function *)
RETURN(WorkPoint) ;   (* from a function *)
RETURN ;              (* from a procedure *)
```

Answers to Exercises

Answer 13.1 *The* Repeat *statement continues forever unless an* Escape *statement inside it is executed.*

Chapter 14

Expressions

> The tenuity and paleness of a symbolic expression.
>
> *James Clerk Maxwell*

Expressions are combinations of operators and operands which are evaluated to produce a value of a specific type. Infix operators require two operands with an operator written between them. A prefix operator requires one operand with an operator written before it. (The expression syntax starts on page 208.)

Evaluation proceeds from left to right, governed by the precedence of the operators. The lowest numbered precedence as shown in Table 14.1 is evaluated first. Operators in the same row have the same precedence. Expressions enclosed by parentheses are evaluated before being treated as a single operand. An operand between two operators of different precedence is bound to the operator with the higher one; e.g., $-10*20$ means $(-10)*20$. An operand between two operators of the same precedence is bound to the one on the left; e.g., $10/20 * 30$ means $(10/20) * 30$.

Exercise 14.1 *Work out the intermediate steps for this expression:*

$$-2/(4+4)*5+6$$

When a null value is encountered in an expression where a non-null is expected, evaluation is short circuited and a null answer is produced. Oth-

Table 14.1: Operator Precedence

Precedence	Description	Operators
1	Component references	[ ] . \
2	Prefix operators	+ - Not
3	Exponentiation	**
4	Multiplication/Division	* / Div Mod And
5	Addition/Subtraction	- + Or XOr
6	Relational	= <> <= >= < > :=: :<>: In Like

erwise, all expressions are fully evaluated even when the outcome is known after partial evaluation.

Exercise 14.2 *Can you think of an expression that does not require complete evaluation to get the correct answer?*

The operands of an operator must be compatible with the operator and with each other. Operands can be compatible without having identical types and are compatible when any of these conditions are satisfied:

- The types are the same.
- One type is a subtype of the other (e.g., one is a number and the other is an integer).
- Both types are strings.
- Both types are binaries.
- Both types are arrays which have compatible base types and identical bounds.
- Both types are bags which have compatible base types.
- Both types are lists which have compatible base types.
- Both types are sets which have compatible base types.

Operations are organized by the kind of result they produce, namely: numeric, boolean or logical, string or binary, or aggregate.

14.1 Numeric valued operations

The prefix arithmetic operators are identity (+) and negation (-). Each accepts a single numeric (number, integer or real) operand and produces a value of the same type. In the case of + the result is equal to the operand and in the case of - the result is the negation of the operand.

The infix arithmetic operators are addition (+), subtraction (-), multiplication (*), division (/), exponentiation (**), integer division (Div) and modulo (Mod). They produce these result types:

- Addition, subtraction, multiplication, exponentiation and division perform the expected mathematical operation and produce an integer result if both operands have integer datatypes and a real result otherwise.
- Modulo and integer division always produce an integer result. If either operand has a real datatype, then it is truncated to an integer before the operation takes place. Given two integer values a and b, it is always true that (a Div b)*b+(a Mod b) = a, the absolute value of a Mod b is less than the absolute value of b and the sign of a Mod b is the same as the sign of b.

Arithmetic operations retain all digits of resolution. There is no rounding or truncation (at least until the value is assigned to a variable). This has the unexpected effect that

$$(1/3) * 3 \rightarrow 1.0000000\ldots$$

even though you might be used to this answer

$$(1/3) * 3 \rightarrow 0.9999999\ldots$$

Of course, when the answer is assigned to a variable, rounding is required when the variable has fewer digits of precision than the expression.

Rounding and truncation

When necessary, rounding is performed when an (evaluated) expression is assigned to a variable. Given P, which is the precision, the digit at $P+1$ is examined. If that digit is five or greater, a carry over of one is added to the digit P and all digits beyond P are discarded; otherwise all digits beyond P are discarded.

Example 14.1

> This example shows the effect of defining the number of decimal digits in the fraction part of a real number; i.e, its precision.

```
LOCAL
   distance   : REAL(6);
   x1, y1, z1 : REAL;
   x2, y2, z2 : REAL;
END_LOCAL;
   ...
   x1 := 0; y1 := 0; z1 := 0;
   x2 := 10; y2 := 11; z2 := 12;
   ...
   distance := SQRT((x2-x1)**2 + (y2-y1)**2 + (z2-z1)**2);
```

> distance is computed to a value of 1.9104973...e+1 but has an actual value of 1.91050e+1 since the specification calls for six digits of precision; thus, only six significant digits are retained.

Truncation drops all digits to the right of the decimal point, producing an integer value.

14.2   Logical and boolean valued operations

The following operators produce logical or boolean values: Not, And, Or and XOr, comparison, interval, In, Like, subset (<=) and superset (>=).

14.2.1 NOT operator

Not is a prefix operator which returns a logical value given a logical or boolean operand.

$$Not \begin{cases} True & \to & False \\ Unknown & \to & Unknown \\ False & \to & True \end{cases}$$

14.2.2 AND operator

And is an infix operator which returns a logical value given two logical or boolean operands.

$$\left. \begin{array}{l} True \\ True \\ True \\ Unknown \\ Unknown \\ Unknown \\ False \\ False \\ False \end{array} \right\} And \begin{cases} True & \to & True \\ Unknown & \to & Unknown \\ False & \to & False \\ True & \to & Unknown \\ Unknown & \to & Unknown \\ False & \to & False \\ True & \to & False \\ Unknown & \to & False \\ False & \to & False \end{cases}$$

14.2.3 OR operator

Or is an infix operator which returns a logical value given two logical or boolean operands.

$$\left. \begin{array}{l} True \\ True \\ True \\ Unknown \\ Unknown \\ Unknown \\ False \\ False \\ False \end{array} \right\} Or \begin{cases} True & \to & True \\ Unknown & \to & True \\ False & \to & True \\ True & \to & True \\ Unknown & \to & Unknown \\ False & \to & Unknown \\ True & \to & True \\ Unknown & \to & Unknown \\ False & \to & False \end{cases}$$

14.2.4 XOR operator

XOr is an infix operator which returns a logical value given two logical or boolean operands.

$$
\left.\begin{array}{c}
True \\
True \\
True \\
Unknown \\
Unknown \\
Unknown \\
False \\
False \\
False
\end{array}\right\} XOr \left\{\begin{array}{ccc}
True & \rightarrow & False \\
Unknown & \rightarrow & Unknown \\
False & \rightarrow & True \\
True & \rightarrow & Unknown \\
Unknown & \rightarrow & Unknown \\
False & \rightarrow & Unknown \\
True & \rightarrow & True \\
Unknown & \rightarrow & Unknown \\
False & \rightarrow & False
\end{array}\right.
$$

14.2.5   Comparison

The basic comparison operators are less than (<), equal (=) and instance equality (:=:). The other comparison operators are derived from them this way:

$$
\begin{aligned}
a <= b \quad &\equiv \quad (a < b)\,Or\,(a = b) \\
a <> b \quad &\equiv \quad Not\,(a = b) \\
a >= b \quad &\equiv \quad Not\,(a < b) \\
a > b \quad &\equiv \quad (Not\,(a < b))\,And\,(Not\,(a = b)) \\
a :<>: b \quad &\equiv \quad Not\,(a :=: b)
\end{aligned}
$$

Comparison for equal and not equal (= and <>) can be used with all operand types. Comparison for less than, less than or equal, greater than and greater than or equal (<, <=, > and >=) requires operands with a defined order; namely: number, string, binary, boolean, logical and enumeration. Instance comparison (:=: and :<>:) requires entity operands.

Numeric values

The expected ordering of numbers is used when two numeric values are compared. If one operand is an integer and the other is a real, the integer is promoted to a real before comparison.

String and binary values

String and binary values use the same procedure for comparison, but use different character sets. The character set and collating order for string values is defined by the ordering of the EXPRESS character set; the character set for binary values is 0 and 1 where 0 < 1.

To compare two values, compare the first (leftmost) pair of characters, then the pair at the second position, etc., until an unequal pair is found or until all pairs have been examined in the following order:

1. If an unequal pair is found, the one containing the lesser character is less than the other and no additional comparison is needed.

2. If one value has fewer characters than the other, then it is the lesser, assuming condition 1.

3. If both values have the same length and all pairs are equal, the two are equal.

Logical and boolean values

Comparisons of two logical or boolean values observe the following ordering:
$$False < Unknown < True$$

Exercise 14.3 *What do you think the answer to this is?*
$$Unknown = Unknown$$

Enumeration values

The order of the values of an enumeration type is determined by their relative position in the declaration of the defined type (see 10.4): the first occurring item is less than the second; the second is less than the third; etc.

Aggregate values

Aggregate values can be compared for equal (=) and not equal (<>). Two aggregate values can be compared only if their types are compatible, which is to say that they are both the same kind of aggregate (array, bag, list or set), have the same declared bounds in the case of an array or same actual size in the case of a bag, list or set and have compatible base types. The precise definition of equality depends on the kind of aggregate being compared:

- Two arrays a and b are equal if and only if each element of a is equal to the element of b at the same position.
- Two bags a and b are equal if and only if each element which occurs in a occurs the same number of times in b and each element which occurs in b also occurs in a.
- Two lists a and b are equal if and only if each element of a is equal to the element of b at the same position.
- Two sets a and b are equal if and only if each element found in a is equal to an element in b and each element found in b is likewise equal to an element in a.

Those conditions are, of course, recursively applied as necessary.

Entity instance values

The instance equal (:=:) and instance not equal (:<>:) operators produce a logical result. They operate only on compatible entity values. a :=: b is true if the identifier of a is the same as b. It is false otherwise.

Note: *Remember that all values have a unique identifier even though we do not care about its form.*

Example 14.2

If a `line` is defined by two points the two points cannot be the same. The instance not equal operator can be used in a where rule to assert that constraint (although this particular test does not guarantee that the values are not the same, i.e., p0 = p1 may still be true).

```
ENTITY line;
  p0, p1 : point;
WHERE
  NotTheSame : p0 :<>: p1;
END_ENTITY;
```

Entity values

For two compatible entity values a and b, a = b is true when a :=: b or both of these conditions hold:

1. `TypeOf(a) = TypeOf(b)`

2. For each explicit attribute c which is declared in a, `a.c = b.c` (this implies that neither `a.c` nor `b.c` is null).

Entire entity values or just chunks (page 183) can be compared. In the former case, all explicit attributes of all supertypes and subtypes of the values under consideration are compared. In the latter case, only the explicit attributes in the chunks are compared.

Note: *Unless otherwise noted, entity value comparison is used when two entity values are to be compared (e.g., during aggregate operations).*

14.2.6   Interval

An interval expression tests whether or not a value falls within a given interval. It contains three compatible operands and two operators. The operands must have a defined ordering.

The interval expression evaluates to true if both relational operations are true, false if either relational operation is false, and unknown if either operand has a missing value.

The interval expression:

$$\{X < Y < Z\}$$

is equivalent to

$$(X < Y)\ AND\ (Y < Z)$$

Table 14.2: Pattern matching characters

Wild	Meaning
@	Matches any letter
^	Matches any upper case letter
?	Matches any character
&	Matches remainder of string
#	Matches any digit
$	Matches any substring terminated by a blank or end-of-string
*	Matches any number of characters
\	Begins a pattern escape sequence

Exercise 14.4 *However, note that*

$$X < Y < Z$$

won't work. Do you know why?

14.2.7   IN operator

The **In** operator tests an item for membership in some aggregate. The right operand is a value of an aggregate type and the left operand is compatible with the base type of the aggregate value. The expression a **IN** b is true when there exists any element b[i] such that a = b[i]. Otherwise, it is false.

14.2.8   LIKE operator

The **Like** operator is a string matching operator. It examines a target string using a pattern string as a control. The left operand is the target string. The right operand is the pattern string. The result is true if the pattern string matches the target string and false if the match fails.

The pattern matching algorithm works this way: Characters in the target string are compared to the corresponding character(s) of the pattern string. The result is true when all characters in the target match those in the pattern string (either exactly or as a wildcard). If any comparison does not match, then the match fails and the answer is false.

Certain characters (called *wildcards*) in the pattern string may match more than one character in the target string. The wildcard characters are shown in Table 14.2.

When any of the special pattern matching characters is itself to be matched, an escape sequence must be used. An escape sequence is a backslash (\) immediately followed by the wildcard character you wish to match. For example, to match @, the escape sequence \@ is used.

Example 14.3

Here are several examples to illustrate how these pattern matching characters might be used.

```
a := '\AAAA';
a LIKE '\\AAAA'        --> TRUE
a LIKE '\AAAA'         --> FALSE
a LIKE '\\A?AA'        --> TRUE
a LIKE '\\&'           --> TRUE
a LIKE '\$'            --> FALSE


a := 'The quick red fox';
a LIKE '$$$$'          --> TRUE


a := 'Page 407';
a LIKE '$*'            --> TRUE
```

14.2.9   Subset operator

The subset operator (<=) accepts two compatible bags or sets and evaluates to true if the first operand is a (not necessarily proper) subset of the second. If the first operand is not a subset of the second, then false is returned.

- A set a is a subset of another set b if and only if every element in a occurs in b.

- A bag a is a subset of another bag b if and only if, for any element e which occurs n times in a, e occurs at least n times in b.

- If a <= b then b >= a.

14.2.10   Superset operator

The superset operator (>=) accepts two compatible bags or sets and evaluates to true if the first operand is a (not necessarily proper) superset of the second. If the first operand is not a superset of the second, then false is returned.

- A set a is a superset of another set b if and only if every element in b occurs in a.

- A bag a is a superset of another bag b if and only if, for any element e which occurs n times in a, e occurs at most n times (possibly not at all) in b.

- If b >= a then a <= b.

14.3   String and binary valued operations

The concatenation operator (+) is an infix operator which combines two string or binary values.

```
AString := 'ABC' + ' ' + 'DEF';        -- 'ABC DEF'
ABinary := %010 + %111;                -- %010111
```

Table 14.3: Union operation results

Bag	Bag	⇒	Bag
Bag	element	⇒	Bag
Bag	Set	⇒	Bag
Bag	List	⇒	Bag
Set	Set	⇒	Set
Set	element	⇒	Set
Set	Bag	⇒	Set
Set	List	⇒	Set
List	List	⇒	List
element	List	⇒	List
List	element	⇒	List

14.4 Aggregate valued operations

The aggregate valued operators are intersection (*), union (+), difference (-) and Query.

14.4.1 Intersection operator

The intersection operator (*) accepts either two sets or two bags and evaluates to a set or bag containing the elements which are common to both operands. The operands must have compatible base types.

The lower index of the returned type is one and the upper index will match the size of the returned value.

If the operands are sets then the result will contain every element that appears in both of the operand sets.

If the operands are bags and a particular element e occurs m times in one bag and n times in the other (where m is less than n), then the result will contain m occurrences of e.

14.4.2 Union operator

The union operator (+) evaluates to an aggregate value which is the combination of the elements in the first operand and those in the second. Various combinations of operand types may be used as shown below. The lower bound of the returned type will be one and the upper bound will be the size of the returned aggregate (not greater than the sum of the upper bounds of the operands).

If the first operand is a set, then the second operand is converted to a set if necessary before the union operation is performed. This has the effect of removing duplicate elements from the second operand before performing the operation.

If the first operand is a bag and a particular element e occurs m times in one operand and n times in the other, then the result will contain m+n

Table 14.4: Difference operator results

Bag	Bag	$\Rightarrow$	Bag
Bag	Set	$\Rightarrow$	Bag
Bag	element	$\Rightarrow$	Bag
Set	Set	$\Rightarrow$	Set
Set	Bag	$\Rightarrow$	Set
Set	element	$\Rightarrow$	Set

occurrences of **e**.

If the first operand is a list, then the second operand is appended to produce the result. If the first operand is an element and the second operand is a list, the element is prepended to the list giving the result.

14.4.3   Difference operator

The difference operator (-) evaluates to an aggregate containing the elements in the second operand removed from the first. Various combinations of operand may be used as shown below. The lower bound of the returned type will be one and the upper bound will be the size of the returned aggregate (not greater than the larger of the upper bounds of the operands).

The type of the result will be the same as the first operand. If the first operand is a bag which contains duplicate elements, only one of those elements is removed for each matching element in the second operand.

Example 14.4

If A is a bag of integers [1, 2, 1, 3] then

A - 1

evaluates to [1, 2, 3] (or [2, 1, 3], [2, 3, 1], etc.)

14.4.4   Query expression

QueryExpr

QUERY → '(' → QueryAssignment → '|' → QueryScan → ')'

QueryAssignment

VarDef → '<*' → AggregateExpr

QueryScan

LogicalExpr

The query expression evaluates a logical expression against each element of an aggregation, returning an aggregate containing only those elements for which the logical expression evaluates to true. This has the effect of returning a subset of the original aggregation where all of the elements of the subset satisfy the given condition.

The first operand (`VarDef`) is implicitly declared as a local variable which exists only within the scope of this expression. This variable does not have to be declared elsewhere and does not persist outside the expression. This temporary variable is used in the `LogicalExpr` to hold the value being operated upon. The second operand (`AggregateExpr`) is an aggregate (array, bag, list or set) value. The third operand (`LogicalExpr`) is an expression which produces a logical result. Ordinarily, `VarRef` is used in this expression.

Elements are taken from the source aggregate and placed in `VarDef` one by one. Then, the logical expression is evaluated. When the logical expression evaluates to true, the value held by `VarDef` is added to the result; otherwise, it is not. The result aggregation is populated according to the specific kind of aggregation:

- **Array:** The result array has the same base type and bounds as the source array. The array elements are treated as optional valued and each element is initially null. Any element in the source for which `expression` yields true is then placed at the corresponding index position in the result.

- **Bag:** The result bag has the same base type and upper bound as the source bag. The lower bound is zero. The result bag is initially empty. Any element in the source for which `expression` yields true is then added to the result.

- **List:** The result list has the same base type and upper bound as the source list. The lower bound is zero. The result list is initially empty. Any element in the source for which `expression` yields true is then added to the end of the result. The order of the list is preserved.

- **Set:** The result set has the same base type and upper bound as the source set. The lower bound is zero. The result set is initially empty. Any element in the source for which `expression` yields true is then added to the result.

Example 14.5

This rule uses a query expression to examine all values of entity type point. The resulting set contains all of the values located at the origin. The rule is violated when the resulting set is empty, meaning that no point lies at the origin.

```
RULE PointAtOrigin FOR (point);
WHERE
  SizeOf(Query(temp <* point | temp = point(0, 0, 0))) <> 0;
END_RULE;
```

14.5 Function call

```
_____ FuncRef
  ┌─►┌FuncDef┐
──┤  └───────┘├──►┌ActualParams┐──
  └─►└StdFunc─┘   └────────────┘
```

The function call activates a function which returns a value to the point of invocation. Write the name of the function followed by actual parameters (if there are any). Actual parameters are required to agree with formal parameters in number, order and type. Qualification can be used when the result is an aggregate or an entity type.

Note: *The standard functions are described in Appendix F.*

Example 14.6

> The function call shown here returns a value of a Point type and qualifies that value to 'look at' just the x component.

```
ENTITY Point;
   x, y, z : NUMBER;
END_ENTITY;

FUNCTION MidpointOfLine(l:Line):Point;
   ...
END_FUNCTION;

IF (MidpointOfLine(l506).x = 9.0) THEN
   ...
END_IF;
```

Expression syntax

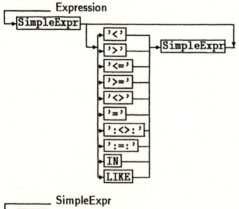

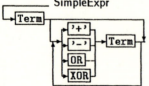

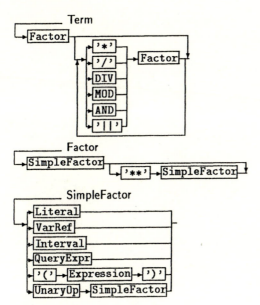

Answers to Exercises

Answer 14.1 *This expression:*

$$-2/(4+4)*5+6$$

takes these steps:

$$-2/\underline{8}*5+6$$

$$\underline{-2/8}*5+6$$

$$\underline{-0.25}*5+6$$

$$\underline{-1.25}+6$$

$$\underline{4.75}$$

Answer 14.2 *Here is one:*

```
X := True;
Y := False;
Z := X Or Y;
```

The outcome does not depend on the value of Y *when* X *is True.*

Answer 14.3 *Oddly enough,*

$$Unknown = Unknown \rightarrow True$$

However, the same cannot be said of

$$? =?$$

since ? (or null if you prefer) does not represent a known value. My col-league Bernd Wenzel explains it this way: If you have something in both pockets, but don't know what, you cannot conclude that the contents are equal or unequal, or that one is less than the other. In the same manner, we cannot conclude that one unknown is equal to (or different from or less than) the other.

Answer 14.4 *When* X < Y < Z *is evaluated the subexpression* X < Y *is done first producing a logical result we will call* R. *Then* R *is used to evaluate* R < Y *which mixes a logical with a number (or whatever).*

Chapter 15

Interfacing

> All animals are equal but some animals are
> more equal than others.
>
> *Animal Farm* — *George Orwell*

Interfacing allows you to define a schema and then use some or all of the material in it to build other ones.

The basic idea is simple, and common in the programming world. However, the EXPRESS rendition of the interface has some twists and turns that go beyond the simple mechanics involved of importing declarations.

Note: *Ada, Modula-2 and some variants of Pascal to mention a few offer similar capabilities.*

The introduction of the schema earlier characterized it as a container for the work you do. But, no distinctions about the kind of work was ever made. That is because EXPRESS makes no such distinction. A schema can represent a library of basic definitions, a collection gathered in preparation for assembly into a final product or the description of the information base you eventually wish to build.

There is a strong connection between the properties of the information base and interfacing. Specific interface specifications are used to define those properties. EXPRESS takes the view that, in the information base, certain objects will be more important than others. Values of datatypes (an integer for example) are always seen as 'less important.' Values of specific entity types can be seen as 'more important' or 'less important' as need dictates. This is where the twists and turns enter the picture. In EXPRESS, the interface does more than assemble diverse objects into a whole — it also defines certain properties of them for a given context.

Let's return to the subject of less or more important objects. On one hand it is reasonable to regard an integer and an entity (no matter how complex it is) on the same level. After all, both can exist, both have well defined behavior, etc. On the other hand, we do not attach the same importance to those things as they exist in the information base. This premise can be tested by asking the questions: *Will I ask for a list of all*

211

the integer values independent of how they are used? (never) versus *Will I ask for a list of all the values of some entity?* (sometimes yes, sometimes no). By extension, it might be possible that certain entity types should be treated in the same manner as integers while others are not. Consider this scenario:

> We have an entity called PersonName and two contexts for its use: a mailing label application and an employee information application. In the first case it is reasonable to ask for a list of all PersonNames. In the other case, it is only reasonable to ask for the PersonNames associated with an Employee. Going further, it is not reasonable to have any PersonName which is not associated with an *Employee.*

How then, can the person who modeled PersonName anticipate both eventual uses? The answer (in general) is that they cannot. Therefore, EXPRESS postpones the decision until the context schemas are being constructed.

The key distinction is whether or not an entity is owned by the context schema (remember that EXPRESS does not have an explicit thing called a context schema. However, the context schema is the one from which the information base is manufactured). Entities owned by the context schema are allowed to have *independent existence;* entities not owned by the context schema are *not* allowed to have independent existence. When the Use specification imports an entity it is treated as if it is owned; when the Reference specification imports an entity it is treated as if it is not owned; when an entity is imported implicitly it is treated as if it is not owned and furthermore, it cannot even be mentioned by name.

15.1   The interface specification

Interface specifications are given immediately after the schema declaration. Two different kinds of specifications are used to effect an interface: Reference and Use. They may be repeated any number of times without regard to order as long as other declarations do not intervene (i.e., you cannot write a few interface specifications, then some entity declarations, then some more interface specifications). Both Use and Reference give access to declarations made in other schemas.

In either case, foreign declarations can be given another name (an alias) to avoid clashes, or just to put the declaration in a familiar context. When an alias is given, the original name is never used in the importing schema.

15.1.1 Use

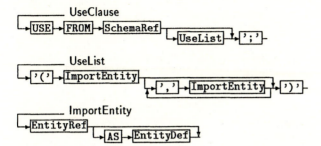

A foreign entity declaration is treated as a local declaration by importing it with a **Use** specification. The **Use** specification gives the name of a schema and optionally names of entities declared in it. When no entity names are specified, all entities within the foreign schema are treated as if they were declared locally.

Here we import a single entity:

```
SCHEMA importer;
USE FROM exporter (contraband);
...
```

...but we can also import everything simply by specifying only the schema name, like this:

```
SCHEMA importer;
USE FROM exporter;
...
```

15.1.2 Reference

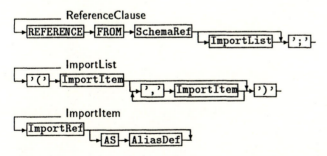

When a foreign declaration is imported with a reference specification, it may be used to resolve references made within the importing schema. However, that thing is not owned by the importing schema. The reference specification gives the name of a foreign schema and optionally the names of objects declared in it. The entire foreign schema is referenced by omitting the resource list and the enclosing parentheses.

The foreign declarations which may be specified in a reference specification are constants, entities, functions, procedures and types. There is no need to specifically import rules because they are implicitly imported.

15.2   Multiple specifications

You might ask 'What happens when the same foreign declaration appears in both a use and a reference specification?' The Use specification takes precedence. That is, the entity is treated as owned. The order in which the Use and Reference specifications are given does not matter.

This sequence:

```
REFERENCE FROM s1 (a1);
USE FROM s1 (a1);
```

treats a1 as a local declaration.

15.3   Chaining

When an entity has been imported into a schema with a use specification, it becomes virtually part of that importing schema. Therefore, it may be mentioned in the use phrase of yet another schema; i.e., use specifications may be chained like this:

```
SCHEMA s1;
  ENTITY e1;
  END_ENTITY;
END_SCHEMA;

SCHEMA s2;
  USE FROM s1 (e1 AS e2);
END_SCHEMA;
```

Now the following specifications are equivalent.

```
SCHEMA s3;                    SCHEMA s4;
  USE FROM s1 (e1 AS e2);       USE FROM s2 (e2);
END_SCHEMA;                    END_SCHEMA;
```

However, since reference does not treat its objects as local it is not possible to chain references.

15.4   Implicit references

A foreign declaration may rely on other declarations that are not visible to the importing schema. Those indirect references may in turn rely on other things. Indirect references implicitly become part of the importing schema, but they cannot be mentioned.

Example 15.1

> The entity e2 is the type of the attribute a3. Since e2 requires e1 in its
> definition, e1 is implicitly required by schema s2. However, e1 cannot be
> specifically mentioned within s2. Similarly e1 requires t1 in its definition, t1
> is therefore implicitly required by schema s2.

```
SCHEMA s1;
  TYPE t1 = REAL;
  END_TYPE;

  ENTITY e1;
    a  : t1;
  END_ENTITY;

  ENTITY e2;
    a1 : e1;
  END_ENTITY;
END_SCHEMA:

SCHEMA s2;
  REFERENCE FROM s1 (e2);

  ENTITY e3;
    a3: e2;
  END_ENTITY;
END_SCHEMA;
```

Everything imported will bring along with it every declaration needed
to support its definition. When an entity is imported, it is important to
remember that the following things implicitly become part of the importing
schema:

- All entities which are supertypes of the foreign entity.
- All rules that apply to the foreign entity under the following conditions:
    - The rule applies to a single foreign entity.
    - The rule applies to several foreign entities, all of which are explicitly or implicitly imported.

15.5 Subtype pruning

By mentioning only those entities which are required in the current schema
(either with a use or a reference), a lattice of entity types may be pruned
for use within the current schema. Pruning chops off branches but never
the root.

The resultant lattice must allow only a subset of the complex values
that were allowed in the foreign lattice, i.e., the process of pruning cannot
violate the integrity of the original lattice.

Example 15.2

Suppose we have the following entities:

```
SCHEMA s1;
  ENTITY e1 SUPERTYPE OF ( ONEOF( e2, e3) );
  END_ENTITY;

  ENTITY e2 SUBTYPE OF (e1);
  END_ENTITY;

  ENTITY e3 SUBTYPE OF (e1);
  END_ENTITY;

  ENTITY e4 SUBTYPE OF (e1);
  END_ENTITY;

END_SCHEMA;
```

The possible values are:

$$e1, e1e2, e1e3, e1e4, e1e2e4, e1e3e4$$

Then we could do this:

```
SCHEMA s2;
  USE FROM s1 (e1);
END_SCHEMA;
```

which prunes everything giving only $e1$. That is, only $e1$ can exist in the importing schema.

We can bring in $e1$'s subtypes this way:

```
SCHEMA s3;
  USE FROM s1 (e2, e4);
END_SCHEMA;
```

which gives $e1e2, e1e4, e1e2e4$. Note that $e1$ cannot exist alone because it is implicitly referenced. This is a way of simulating an abstract supertype without making the declaration in the source schema.

15.6   Independent existence

Every entity (the ones that have attributes anyway) will depend on the existence of values of some kind. Those values might be integers, strings or other so-called simple things, or they might be entity values — something perceived as more complex. In either case, those values are representations of the attributes used to define the properties of an entity, so the existence of an entity is seldom completely independent. The term independent existence does not mean independent of the values needed for an entity definition. It does mean independent of its use as a value by other entities.

Note: *You may be more familiar to terms such as functional dependence or existence dependence.*

Independent existence reflects the viewpoint that, in a given implementation of an information base, certain things will be more important than others. In EXPRESS, all entities are equal but some entities are more equal than others and no type (unless it is an entity) is equal to an entity.

In a practical sense, all this means is that the unequal things owe their existence to entities that can have an independent existence. As an example consider a date. It could be defined as a entity with attributes such as month, day and year, or it could be defined as a type based on an integer number (representing the count of days from some arbitrary date in history). Either way, we might insist that the information base should never have values of date unless they are used in some context by some entity — the birth date of a person for example. Therefore, date would not have an independent existence and could only be accessed through some entity value; in this case, a person.

There is no hard and fast rule that we can use when resource schemas are being developed that will tell us whether an entity should have independent existence or not. The needs of the application will be the determining factor, mainly on the grounds that questions about a certain entity are asked at the level of the information base.

15.7 Putting it all together

Now we present a fairly large example to illustrate how interfacing can be used to build a project. Four schemas are used here: Library which gives us some general reference material, Resource which gives specialized information about materials we will use, and ProjectResource and Project which are about the project itself. To save space, only the entity headers are displayed.

```
(* This schema contains the reference materials we will need
   to tell us how to do the project. *)
SCHEMA Library;
  ENTITY Book;
  ENTITY HowTo SUBTYPE OF (Book);
  ENTITY Fiction SUBTYPE OF (Book);
  ENTITY Magazine;
  ENTITY ComicBook SUBTYPE OF (Magazine);
  ENTITY Crafts SUBTYPE OF (Magazine);
END_SCHEMA;

(* This schema is the source of information about building
   supplies we will use *)
SCHEMA Resource;
  ENTITY Catalog;
```

```
   ENTITY Flooring SUBTYPE OF (Catalog);
   ENTITY Cabinet SUBTYPE OF (Catalog);
   ENTITY Appliance SUBTYPE OF (Catalog);
   ENTITY DoorPull SUBTYPE OF (Catalog);
END_SCHEMA;

(* This schema collects all the things needed by the project
   and adds some constraints *)
SCHEMA ProjectResource;
   USE FROM Library (HowTo, Crafts);
   USE FROM Resource (Flooring, Cabinet, Appliance, DoorPull);
   RULE ColorsWeLike FOR (Appliance);
END_SCHEMA;

(* This is the project, which simply enumerates the things of
   primary and secondary interest *)
SCHEMA Project;
   USE FROM ProjectResource (HowTo, Crafts, Flooring, Cabinet,
        Appliance);
   REFERENCE FROM ProjectResource (DoorPull);
END_SCHEMA;
```

Building an inventory of each schema is a good way to understand how interfacing works. Table 15.1 shows the things owned, which can be referenced and which are implicitly part of (but cannot be referenced) each of our four schemas.

Note: *We could have pruned some of the uninteresting book subtypes, which would remove them from our inventory. However, there is no real need to do that for this example.*

The Library and Resource schemas are easy since each is complete, self contained and owns everything declared in them (remember that when something is declared within something else, it is owned).

Although the Project schema is the one in which our interest lies, we create an intermediate — ProjectResource. Why? The answer has two parts. First, the intermediate schema is a convenient place to gather together everything we will eventually need; call it an index or table of contents. Second, we want to explicitly control what we perceive as owned versus what we are able to reference.

Specifically, we have an interest in door pulls because they are needed for our cabinets. That interest is secondary, however, since door pulls are never interesting except as they relate to cabinets. Still, we may need to reference door pulls — perhaps to coordinate colors or the way they mount.

A few things are part of the Project schema, but cannot be mentioned. Namely: Book, Magazine and ColorsWeLike. Keep in mind that one of our HowTo resources is a Book, but in the context of this example we never care about books in general, just specific kinds of books. The rule we added in

Table 15.1: An inventory of schema resources

Library Schema	
Owned:	Book, HowTo, Fiction, Magazine, ComicBook, Crafts
Can Reference:	
Implicit:	
Resource Schema	
Owned:	Catalog, Flooring, Cabinet, Appliance, DoorPull
Can Reference:	
Implicit:	
ProjectResource Schema	
Owned:	HowTo, Crafts, Flooring, Cabinet, Appliance, DoorPull
Can Reference:	
Implicit:	Book, Magazine, ColorsWeLike
Project Schema	
Owned:	HowTo, Crafts, Flooring, Cabinet, Appliance
Can Reference:	DoorPull
Implicit:	ColorsWeLike, Book, Magazine

`ProjectResource` is there too, but there is never a need to make reference to rules.

Other situations may want to treat `DoorPull` as owned. What if we were a wholesaler of door pulls? In that context, `DoorPull` is of primary interest. The proper application of use and reference allows you to put emphasis where it is needed without restricting the base definition.

Chapter 16

EXPRESS Syntax

> If language is not correct, then what is said
> is not what is meant; if what is said is not
> what is meant, then what ought to be done
> remains undone.

Confucius

Here is the entire syntax except for constant tokens (i.e., reserved words and such), character sets, standard constants, functions and procedures, and simple equates to tokens that create or reference identifiers.

The following conventions will help to interpret the syntax presentation:

- Identifiers written in upper case letters are keywords of the language. For example, when you see **SCHEMA** this means that the word 'schema' must be written at this place (using mixed case if you wish.) The names of these syntax productions are identical to the keywords of the language.

- Elements that follow the pattern *xxxDef* represent an identifier declaration. For example, *VarDef* shows where a variable declaration takes place. This also implies that the name created at this place is subject to the scoping rules that apply to the object in question.

- Elements that follow the pattern *xxxRef* represent a reference to some explicit definition. For example, a *VarRef* requires a *VarDef*.

Syntax

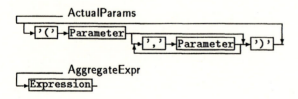

220

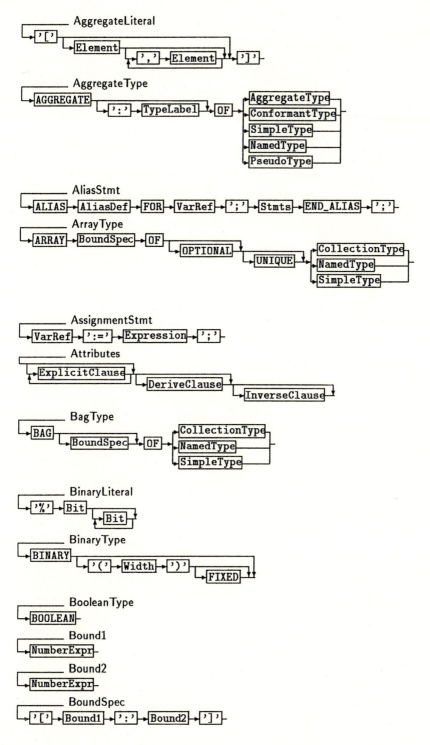

AggregateLiteral

AggregateType

AliasStmt

ArrayType

AssignmentStmt

Attributes

BagType

BinaryLiteral

BinaryType

BooleanType

Bound1

Bound2

BoundSpec

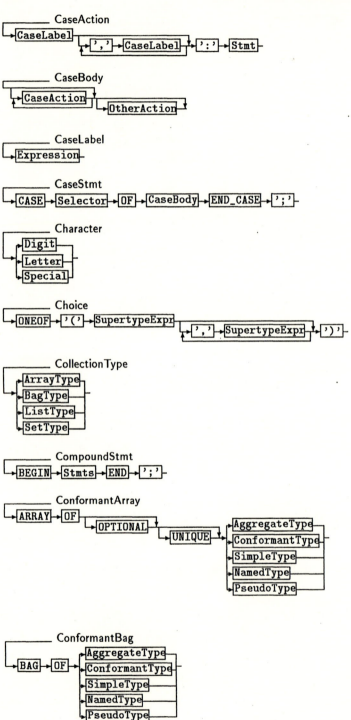

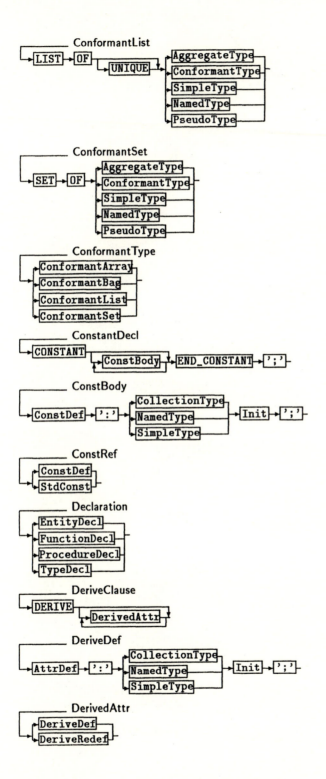

ConformantList

LIST → OF → UNIQUE → AggregateType / ConformantType / SimpleType / NamedType / PseudoType

ConformantSet

SET → OF → AggregateType / ConformantType / SimpleType / NamedType / PseudoType

ConformantType

ConformantArray / ConformantBag / ConformantList / ConformantSet

ConstantDecl

CONSTANT → ConstBody → END_CONSTANT → ';'

ConstBody

ConstDef → ':' → CollectionType / NamedType / SimpleType → Init → ';'

ConstRef

ConstDef / StdConst

Declaration

EntityDecl / FunctionDecl / ProcedureDecl / TypeDecl

DeriveClause

DERIVE → DerivedAttr

DeriveDef

AttrDef → ':' → CollectionType / NamedType / SimpleType → Init → ';'

DerivedAttr

DeriveDef / DeriveRedef

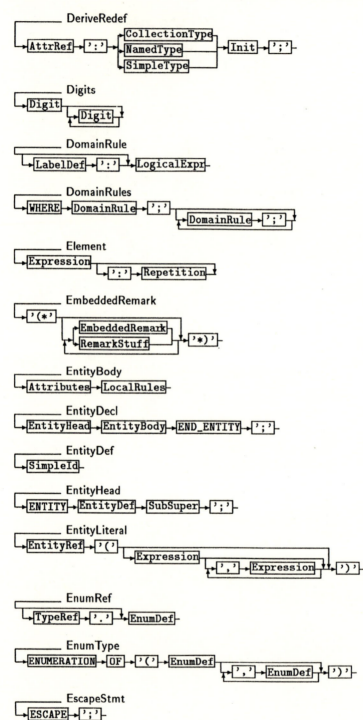

DeriveRedef

AttrRef → ':' → CollectionType / NamedType / SimpleType → Init → ';'

Digits

Digit → Digit

DomainRule

LabelDef → ':' → LogicalExpr

DomainRules

WHERE → DomainRule → ';' → DomainRule → ';'

Element

Expression → ':' → Repetition

EmbeddedRemark

'(*' → EmbeddedRemark / RemarkStuff → '*)'

EntityBody

Attributes → LocalRules

EntityDecl

EntityHead → EntityBody → END_ENTITY → ';'

EntityDef

SimpleId

EntityHead

ENTITY → EntityDef → SubSuper → ';'

EntityLiteral

EntityRef → '(' → Expression → ',' → Expression → ')'

EnumRef

TypeRef → '.' → EnumDef

EnumType

ENUMERATION → OF → '(' → EnumDef → ',' → EnumDef → ')'

EscapeStmt

ESCAPE → ';'

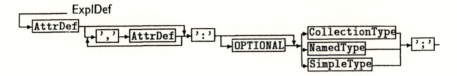

ExplDef

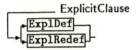

ExplicitClause

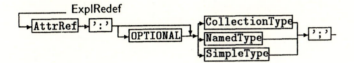

ExplRedef

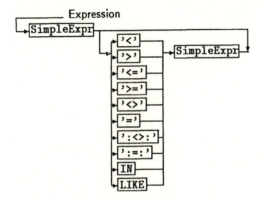

Expression

Factor

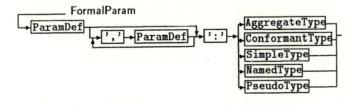

FormalParam

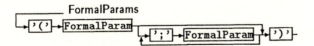

FormalParams

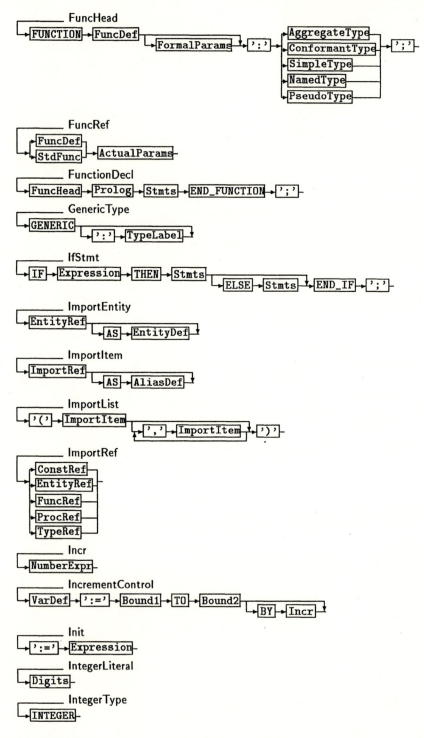

FuncHead

FUNCTION → FuncDef → FormalParams → ':' → AggregateType / ConformantType / SimpleType / NamedType / PseudoType → ';'

FuncRef

FuncDef / StdFunc → ActualParams

FunctionDecl

FuncHead → Prolog → Stmts → END_FUNCTION → ';'

GenericType

GENERIC → ':' → TypeLabel

IfStmt

IF → Expression → THEN → Stmts → ELSE → Stmts → END_IF → ';'

ImportEntity

EntityRef → AS → EntityDef

ImportItem

ImportRef → AS → AliasDef

ImportList

'(' → ImportItem → ',' → ImportItem → ')'

ImportRef

ConstRef / EntityRef / FuncRef / ProcRef / TypeRef

Incr

NumberExpr

IncrementControl

VarDef → ':=' → Bound1 → TO → Bound2 → BY → Incr

Init

':=' → Expression

IntegerLiteral

Digits

IntegerType

INTEGER

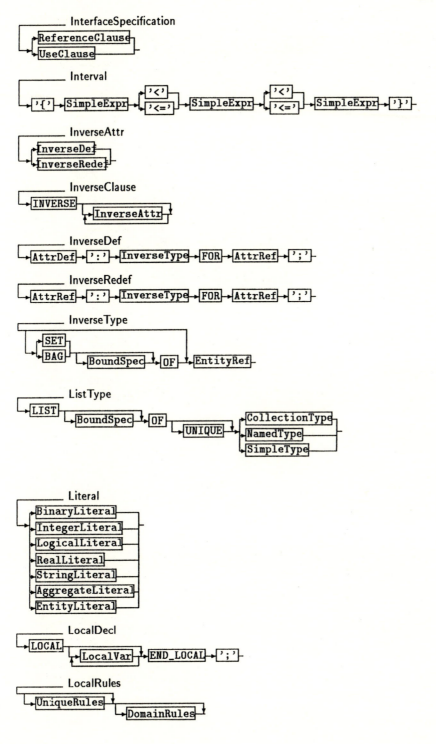

InterfaceSpecification
ReferenceClause
UseClause

Interval
'{' → SimpleExpr → '<' / '<=' → SimpleExpr → '<' / '<=' → SimpleExpr → '}'

InverseAttr
InverseDef
InverseRedef

InverseClause
INVERSE → InverseAttr

InverseDef
AttrDef → ':' → InverseType → FOR → AttrRef → ';'

InverseRedef
AttrRef → ':' → InverseType → FOR → AttrRef → ';'

InverseType
SET / BAG → BoundSpec → OF → EntityRef

ListType
LIST → BoundSpec → OF → UNIQUE → CollectionType / NamedType / SimpleType

Literal
BinaryLiteral
IntegerLiteral
LogicalLiteral
RealLiteral
StringLiteral
AggregateLiteral
EntityLiteral

LocalDecl
LOCAL → LocalVar → END_LOCAL → ';'

LocalRules
UniqueRules → DomainRules

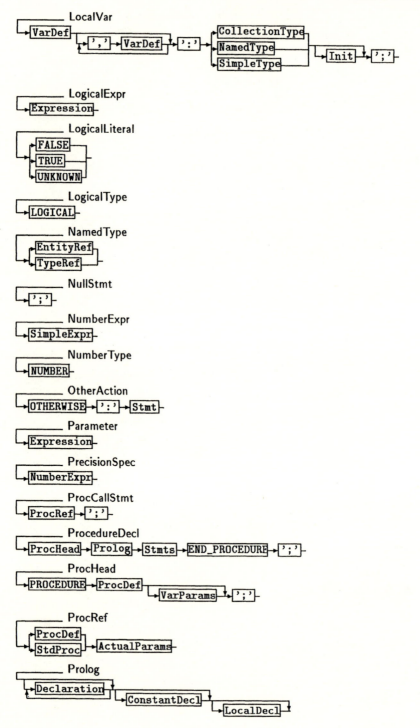

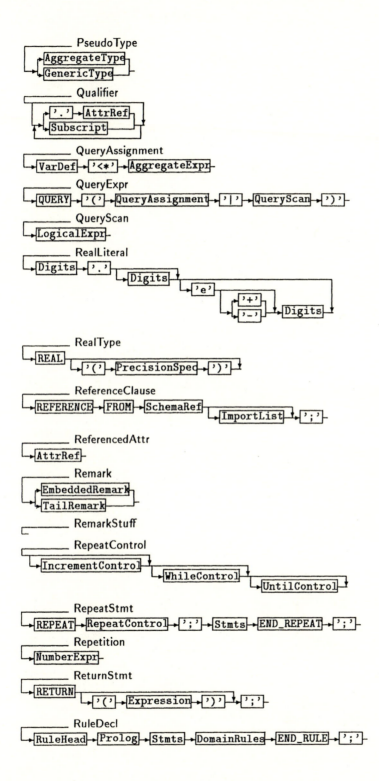

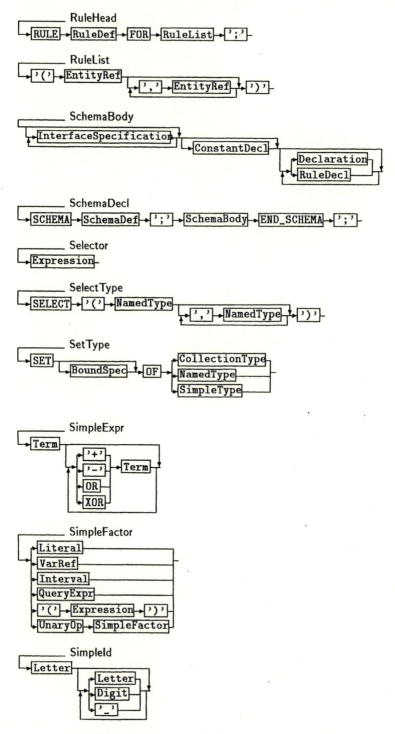

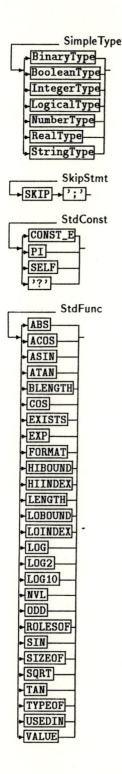

SimpleType

BinaryType
BooleanType
IntegerType
LogicalType
NumberType
RealType
StringType

SkipStmt

SKIP `';'`

StdConst

CONST_E
PI
SELF
`'?'`

StdFunc

ABS
ACOS
ASIN
ATAN
BLENGTH
COS
EXISTS
EXP
FORMAT
HIBOUND
HIINDEX
LENGTH
LOBOUND
LOINDEX
LOG
LOG2
LOG10
NVL
ODD
ROLESOF
SIN
SIZEOF
SQRT
TAN
TYPEOF
USEDIN
VALUE

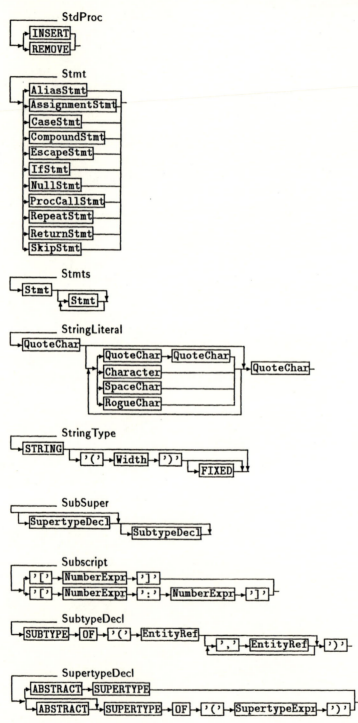

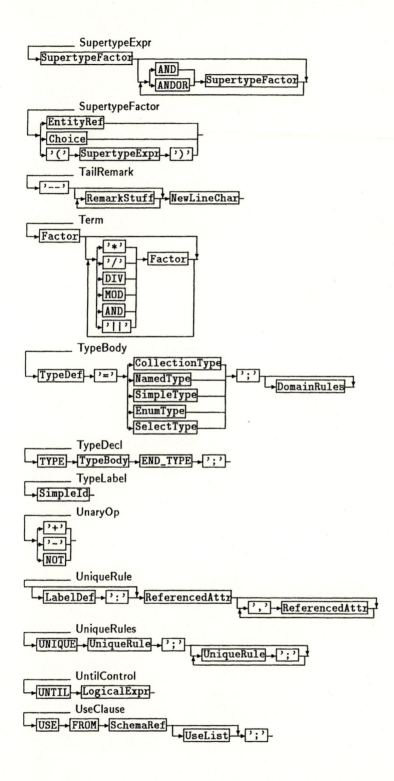

UseList

VarParam

VarParams

VarRef

WhileControl

Width

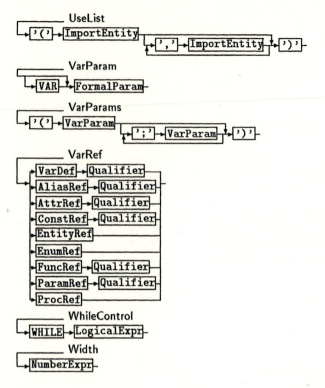

Chapter 17

A graphical form of EXPRESS

> Or if by some chance our minds do muse on aught,
> It is some picture on the margin wrought.

The World. Flowers of Sion
William Drummond

EXPRESS-G is a graphical notation for the display of information models. Using the EXPRESS language, an information model is represented by *sentences* in the language. In EXPRESS-G, an information model is represented by graphic symbols forming a diagram. Although EXPRESS-G has been specifically developed for the graphical rendition of information models defined in the EXPRESS language, it may be used as a modeling technology in its own right.

EXPRESS-G supports the notions of entity, type, relationship and cardinality. It also separately supports the notion of schema. The notation only supports a subset of the EXPRESS language as it does not provide any support for the complex constraints which can be represented in the EXPRESS lexical language.

The design goals for the notation are:

- The diagrams should be intuitively understandable.

- The diagrams should support levels of model abstraction.

- A diagram must be able to span more than one sheet of paper.

- The pictures should be definable using minimal computer graphics capabilities. Further, it should be possible to print the diagrams using only non-graphic symbols, for example on a line printer.

- It should be possible to develop a processor that automatically converts from EXPRESS source to the graphical description.

17.1   Graphics requirements

EXPRESS-G requires almost minimal graphical capabilities, namely the ability to draw straight lines of three kinds, to draw rectangular and rounded boxes, to draw small circles, and to put text onto a drawing.

Two kinds of boxes are used as symbols:

Definition These symbols denote the things (i.e., concepts, ideas, etc.) which form the basis of the information model. Rectangular boxes are used for these symbols.

Composition These symbols enable a model diagram to be displayed on more than one sheet of paper. Boxes with rounded corners are used for these.

Three styles of lines are used by EXPRESS-G — a thin solid line, a thick solid line, and a dashed line — each of which should be readily distinguishable. For computer displays that support graphics there should be no problems in choosing suitable line styles. For displays that only support a single line width, thick lines can be drawn as two closely spaced parallel lines. For line printer type displays, the lines have to be drawn using characters rather than graphics.

There is also a third kind of symbol:

Relationship These are lines which connect the definition and composition symbols denoting relationships between the defined items.

17.2   Model forms

An EXPRESS-G model can take one of several forms depending on whether a single schema or multiple schemas are being represented, and on the amount of detail being displayed. These will be discussed in more detail later but for now it is noted that an EXPRESS-G model is either

1. A single schema with only the definitions and relations within the schema being displayed (an entity-level model), or

2. Multiple schemas, where only the schemas and schema-schema relations are displayed (a schema-level model).

17.3   Example model

Before going into the details of the EXPRESS-G notation, Figure 17.1 and Figure 17.2 show an entity level EXPRESS-G model for the single EXPRESS schema given in Example 20.1 (see Chapter 20).

For illustrative purposes, the graphical model has been spread over two 'pages' to show cross-page referencing. The EXPRESS-G model contains most of the notational symbols described later and is intended to provide a sample context for the more detailed exposition.

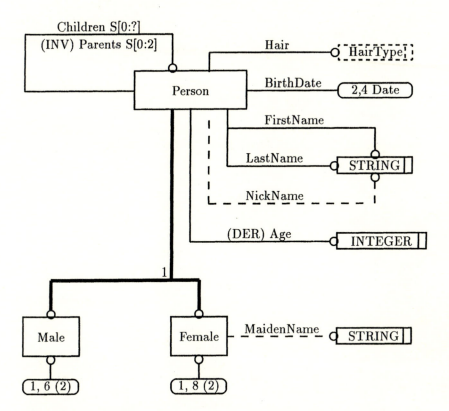

Figure 17.1: Complete entity-level model of Example 20.1 (Page 1 of 2).

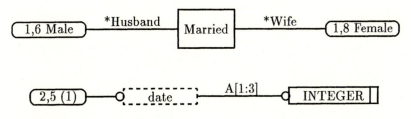

Figure 17.2: Complete entity-level model of Example 20.1 (Page 2 of 2).

The model is about the concept of person. A `Person` has certain defining characteristics, such as first and last names (and maybe a nickname), date of birth, and some description of their hair. A `Person` is either `Male` or `Female`. A `Female` may have a maiden name. A `Person` may have `Children`, who, of course, are also people. Two people may be `Married`, and there are some constraints on the people involved in this relationship.

The definitions of things within the model are denoted by the boxes, and relationships among the definitions are denoted by the lines joining the boxes. Cross-page referencing is accomplished via the oval boxes; matches between boxes whose first pair of numbers are the same constitute the connectivity across pages. The idea lying behind the differing line styles displayed is that the weight of the line gives an indication of the *strength* of the relationship.

17.4   Further reading

The manual layout of complex diagrams is an art form. It is desireable that things that are related to each other are located near each other in a diagram. Also, it is undesireable that lines should cross each other. Changing the location of elements in a diagram, particularly on one that spreads across several pages, can have a significant effect on what the viewer perceives to be the relative importance of the differing elements.

It is a difficult task to develop computer based automatic tools to even produce a half-way decent initial layout of a diagram. For example, Moen [Moe90] describes a tree-drawing algorithm and Kamada describes a more general layout system [KK91]. It is likely that, even if an EXPRESS-G processor does lay out a diagram for you, you will probably want to edit the layout to improve both the aesthetics and to change the visual emphasis of your model.

Processors for EXPRESS-G are described by Jasnoch and his co-workers [JvLN+91], by Mueller and Kleinjohann [MK92], and by Roesch [Roe91].

Chapter 18

Symbols

> In a symbol there is concealment and yet revelation.

Sartor Resartus
Thomas Carlyle

EXPRESS-G has three basic kinds of symbol; defintion, relation, and composition. Definition and relation symbols are used to define the contents and structure of an information model. Composition symbols enable the diagrams to be spread across many physical pages.

18.1 Definition symbols

A definition symbol is a rectangle enclosing the name of the thing being defined. The type of the definition is denoted by the style of the box. Symbols are provided for EXPRESS simple types, defined types, entity types and schemas.

18.1.1 Simple type symbols

The EXPRESS language offers a number of predefined simple types, namely Binary, Boolean, Integer, Logical, Number, Real and String. These are the terminal types of the language. The symbol for them is a solid rectangle with a double vertical line at its right end. The name of the type is enclosed within the box, as shown in Figure 18.1. The EXPRESS Generic pseudotype is not represented in EXPRESS-G as it is only used as a formal parameter to a function or procedure, and EXPRESS-G does not have these.

18.1.2 Type symbols

The symbols for the select, enumeration and defined data type are dashed boxes as shown in Figure 18.2.

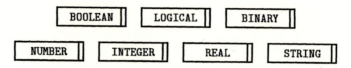

Figure 18.1: Simple type symbols.

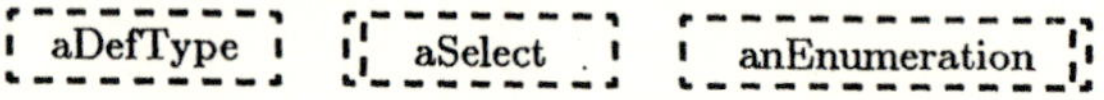

Figure 18.2: Type definition symbols.

- The symbol for a defined data type is a dashed box enclosing the name of the type.
- The symbol for a select type is a dashed box with a double vertical line at the left end, enclosing the name of the select.
- The symbol for an enumeration type is a dashed box with a double vertical line at the right end, enclosing the name of the enumeration. Although an enumeration is not a terminal of the EXPRESS language (because its definition includes the enumerated things), it is a terminal of the EXPRESS-G language.

18.1.3 Entity symbol

Figure 18.3 shows the symbol for an entity, which is a solid rectangle enclosing the name of the entity.

18.1.4 Schema symbol

The symbol for a schema is shown in Figure 18.3. It is a solid rectangle divided in half by a horizontal line. The name of the schema is written in the upper half of the rectangle. The lower half of the symbol is empty.

18.1.5 Algorithm symbols

EXPRESS-G does not support any notation for either function or procedure definitions. Neither does it support notation for a rule definition. However, as discussed in 19.2.2, the names of entities that are governed by a global

Figure 18.3: Entity and schema definition symbols.

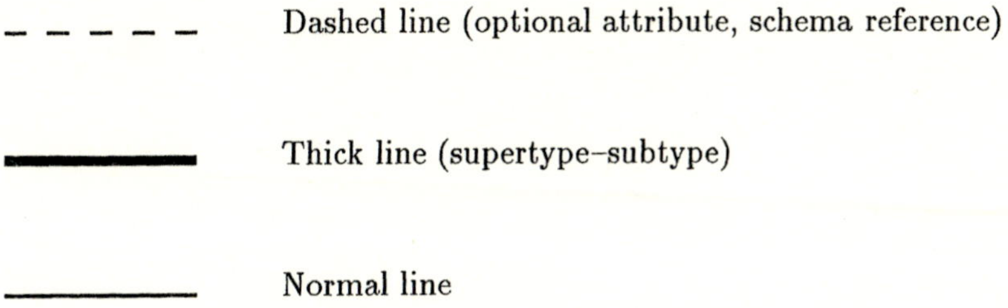

_ _ _ _ _   Dashed line (optional attribute, schema reference)

██████████   Thick line (supertype–subtype)

_____   Normal line

Figure 18.4: Relationship Line Styles

rule may be flagged with an asterisk to show that a constraint applies to them.

18.2 Relationship symbols

Related definition symbols are connected via lines of different types as shown in Figure 18.4. There are three different line styles — dashed, thick, and normal.

A relationship for an optional valued attribute of an entity is displayed as a dashed line, as is a schema–schema reference. A supertype–subtype relation is displayed as a thick solid line. All other relationships are displayed as normal width solid lines.

Relationships are bi-directional, but, following the EXPRESS style, one of the directions is emphasized. For example, if entity E has an explicit attribute whose type is T, then the emphasized direction is from E to T. Similarly, when schema S refers to a schema R for importing definitions, the emphasized direction is from S to R. As anothe example, when a Select type S makes a selection among types Ts the emphasized direct is from S to Ts. In EXPRESS-G, the *to* end of a relationship is marked with an open circle.

Relationship directions are illustrated in Figure 18.5, which is a partial diagram of the EXPRESS source given in Example 20.2. The model consists of six entities, one select type, two defined types, and three simple types. Starting at the top left hand corner the entity Root has two subtypes, Leaf1 and Leaf2. The leaf entities are subtypes because they are at the circled end of a supertype-subtype relationship line, while Root is a supertype as it is at a non-circled end of a supertype-subtype relationship line.

The entity Leaf2 has two attributes, one of simple type Binary and the other being a Select type called Pick. These are attributes of Leaf2 because they are at the circled end of a relationship line.

Pick is a selection between the entity called AnEnt and the defined type called Name. Again, the circles indicate that they are at the to end of the relationship with Pick. In turn, the defined type Name is composed of the

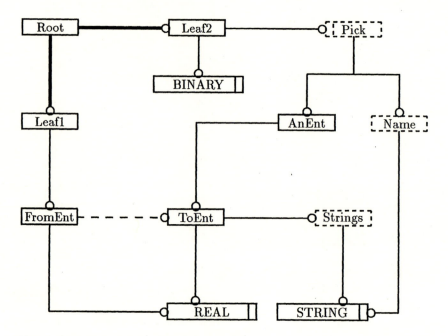

Figure 18.5: Partial entity-level model showing relationship directions from Example 20.2. (Page 1 of 1)

String simple type.

The remainder of the diagram can be read in a similar manner, the only other point to note being that the dashed relationship line from **FromEnt** to **ToEnt** indicates that **FromEnt** has an optional valued attribute whose representation is **ToEnt**.

18.3   Composition symbols

Graphical model representations often span many pages. Each page in a model must be numbered. This is partly so that you can keep track of where you are in the model, but primarily to enable inter-page referencing. The symbols for inter-page references are shown in Figure 18.6.

Likewise, a schema may utilize definitions from another schema. The symbols for inter-schema references are also shown in Figure 18.6.

18.3.1   Page references

Conceptually, an **EXPRESS-G** model resides on a single logical sheet of paper. However, typically any non-trivial model will not fit onto a single physical sheet of paper. Therefore a facility is provided to split the single virtual

Page references

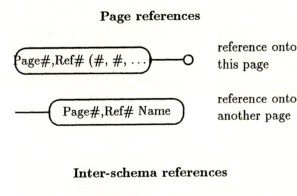

reference onto
this page

reference onto
another page

Inter-schema references

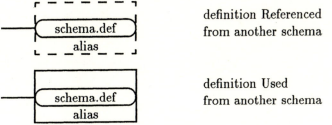

definition Referenced
from another schema

definition Used
from another schema

Figure 18.6: The composition symbols.

page into several physical pages. This is done by breaking the relationship lines at the boundaries of the physical pages.

Where there is a relationship between definitions on separate pages, the relationship line on the two pages is terminated by an oval (rounded) box that contains a page number and a reference number as shown in Figure 18.6. The page number is the number of the page where the *to definition* resides. The page number is the first of the numbers in the box. The second number is a reference number. The reference number is used to distinguish between multiple references onto a page.

The composition box on the *from page* additionally contains the name of the *to definition*. The reference oval on the *to page* additionally contains a list of the page numbers, enclosed within parentheses, of the *from pages* which refer to this reference.

The EXPRESS-G model in Figure 17.1 and 17.2 shows some examples of page referencing. For instance, look at the Married entity in Figure 17.2. The oval labelled 1,6 indicates that the Husband attribute type is defined on page 1 of the model as reference 6; also, the attribute is type is called Male. On page 1 of the model (Figure 17.1) the oval box labelled 1,6 indicates that there is a reference to the entity Male from page 2 of the model. Other page references in the model occur between the Female and Married entities, and between Person and date.

18.3.2   Inter-schema references

Some definitions needed by a schema may actually be defined in another one. Inter-schema references are indicated by a rounded box enclosing the name of the definition qualified by the schema name as shown in Figure 18.6.

Definitions that are taken from another schema by a `Use` statement are enclosed by a solid rectangle. If the definition is aliased, then the alias name is placed within the box below the oval.

Definitions that are taken from another schema by a `Reference` statement are enclosed by a dashed rectangle. If the definition is aliased, then the alias name is placed within the box below the oval.

Figure 19.5 shows an example of the use of inter-schema references. This model is described later.

Chapter 19

EXPRESS-G models

> No two motions can be less like each other
> than that of meandering level and that of
> mounting upwards.
>
> *Literary Essays*
> *Thomas Babington Macaulay*

EXPRESS-G provides for two levels of modeling — a *schema-level* model and
an *entity-level* model. Further, either of these may be *complete* or *partial*.
This Chapter describes these various kinds of model.

19.1   Schema level model

A schema-level model is one which displays the schemas, and the relationships between these schemas, that comprise an information model. The
contents of the schemas (i.e., the entities, types, etc.) are not displayed. A
schema level model, then, consists of:

- The schemas that another schema Uses.
- The schemas that another schema References.
- The names of the things used and referenced.

An example schema level model is shown in Figure 19.1. The Use relation
is shown by a normal width relation line *from* the using schema *to* the
used schema, with an open circle denoting the used schema end of the
relationship line. The Reference relation is shown by a dashed relation
line *from* the referencing schema *to* the referenced schema, with an open
circle denoting the referenced schema end of the relationship line.

The definitions used or referenced are shown as a list of names adjacent
to the relevant relationship line, and connected to the relationship line by
an arrowheaded line. If a definition is aliased, then this is indicated by
following the original name of the definition by a 'greater than' (>) sign
and the alias name.

The model in Figure 19.1 consists of three schemas called fem, geom and
mat. The fem schema Uses the property entity from the mat schema. It

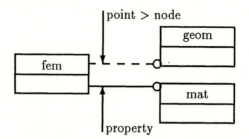

Figure 19.1: Complete schema-level model of Example 20.5. (Page 1 of 1)

also **References** the **point** entity from the **geom** schema, and gives it the **node** alias.

Schema-level models may be too large to fit on a single physical page. If this is the case then the page referencing symbols can be used to split the schema-schema relationship lines. The names of imported definitions should be on the same page as the importing schema symbol.

19.2   Entity level model

An entity-level model is an EXPRESS-G model that represents the definitions and relationships that comprise a single schema. Thus, the components of such a model consist of type, entity and relationship symbols, together with role and cardinality information as appropriate. Note that schema symbols do not appear in an entity-level diagram.

19.2.1   Role names and cardinalities

In EXPRESS the attributes of an entity are role named. The text string representing the role name is placed on the relationship line connecting an entity symbol to its attribute representation.

Similarly, if an attribute is an aggregation, this is indicated after the role name on the relationship line. EXPRESS-G supports array, bag, list and set aggregation types, just as does EXPRESS. However, whereas EXPRESS denotes an aggregation with a phrase like LIST [1:?] OF ..., EXPRESS-G only uses the first letter of the aggregation and omits the word OF. This is done in order to save space on the diagram. The aggregations also denote cardinality. Note that no aggregation specification is required for a cardinality of exactly one (a required relation) or a cardinality of zero or one (use a dashed relationship line).

As an illustration, the EXPRESS model given in Example 20.2 is fully displayed in EXPRESS-G in Figure 19.2. Compare this with Figure 18.5 which shows the same EXPRESS model but without the role names and aggregations.

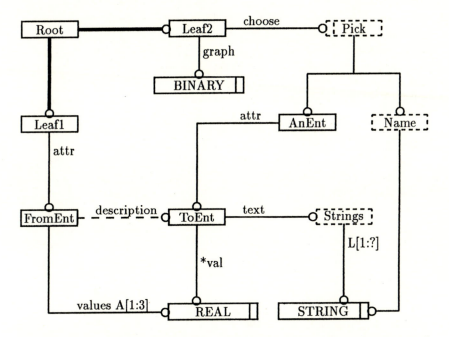

Figure 19.2: Complete entity-level model of Example 20.2. (Page 1 of 1)

Two aggregations are shown. The attribute called **values** of the entity
FromEnt is represented as an **Array** of **Real**. The defined type **strings** is
represented as a **List** of **String**.

19.2.2 Constraints

EXPRESS-G provides no methods for defining constraints, other than cardinalities. However, the fact that something is constrained is indicated by
preceding the name of the thing with an asterisk (*) symbol.

- Mark each entity governed by a rule with an asterisk.
- Mark each attribute with an asterisk if it is constrained by a unique
  or where clause within the entity.

The additional documentation accompanying the EXPRESS-G model should
specify exactly what the indicated constraints are.

The models in Figure 17.2 and in Figure 19.2 both show some constrained
attributes. The exact nature of the constraints is given in the accompanying
EXPRESS code in Chapter 20.

19.2.3 Type modeling

EXPRESS-G uses dashed box symbols (Figure 18.2) for type definitions. The name of the definition is enclosed by the box.

A defined data type is modeled by the type definition symbol, the representation type definition, and the relationship line from the type definition to its representation definition; the cardinality of the attribute may be placed on the relation. Note that there is no role name to be placed on the relationship line.

An example of defined data type modeling can be seen in the **strings** type in Figure 19.2.

A **Select** type is modeled in a similar fashion to the defined data type, except that there is one relationship and representation definition for each of the items that can be selected. There are no role names or cardinalities that can be placed on the relationship lines. The type named **Pick** in Figure 19.2 is an example of a select type which selects between the entity **AnEnt** and the defined type **Name**.

An **Enumeration** type is modeled solely by its symbol. EXPRESS-G does not provide a mechanism for noting the enumerated items. The **HairType** in Figure 17.1 is an example of an enumeration type.

19.2.4 Entity modeling

EXPRESS-G uses a solid box symbol (Figure 18.3) for entity definitions. The name of the entity is enclosed by the box.

In EXPRESS, an entity may be part of a Supertype Tree, it may have explicit attributes, it may have derived attributes, it may have inverse attributes, and attribute values may be constrained via unique and/or where clauses.

EXPRESS-G supports Supertyping and explicit, derived, and inverse attributes only. Attributes are represented by relationships in EXPRESS-G. The role name of the attribute is placed on the relationship line followed, if necessary, by a cardinality specification. A derived attribute is distinguished from an explicit attribute by preceding the name of the attribute by (DER). In the case where there is an inverse attribute defined for an entity-entity relationship, the name and cardinality of the attribute is placed on the other side of the relationship line from the *forward* attribute, and the name is preceded by (INV). Typical entity models can be seen in Figure 17.1 and Figure 19.2.

Supertypes and subtypes

The entities forming a Supertype Tree are connected by thick solid lines. The circled end of the relationship line denotes the Subtype end of the relationship. An **Abstract** Supertype is indicated by putting the characters (ABS) before the name of the entity within the entity symbol box.

EXPRESS enables very complex constraints to be specified regarding the allowable combinations of subtype instances for a given supertype instance.

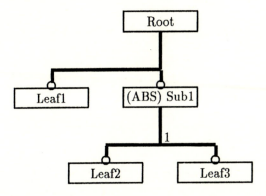

Figure 19.3: Complete entity-level model of the Supertype tree from Example 20.3. (Page 1 of 1)

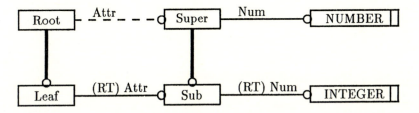

Figure 19.4: Complete entity-level model of Example 20.4 showing attribute redeclarations in subtypes. (Page 1 of 1)

EXPRESS-G is much more limited in this respect. The OneOf relation may be indicated by a *T branching* relationship line from the Supertype to each of its Subtypes that are in a OneOf relation to each other, together with the digit 1 being placed at the T junction. No implications about the logical structure can be drawn from a T junction that is not marked by the digit 1.

Figure 19.3 shows an example model of a supertype tree. The entity Sub1 is an abstract supertype that is a subtype of Root. Entities Leaf2 and Leaf3 are both subtypes of Sub1 and are in a OneOf relationship to each other. Entities Leaf1 and Sub1 are both subtypes of Root. We cannot identify the relationship between these two subtypes.

EXPRESS-G also supports the EXPRESS capability of a subtype redeclaring inherited attributes. Figure 19.4 gives an example of this.

When an inherited attribute is redeclared in a subtype, then a relationship line is drawn from the subtype to the new attribute representation. The line is role-named with the name of the inherited attribute (and the new cardinality if necessary); the role name is preceded by (RT).

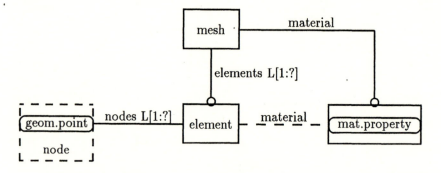

Figure 19.5: Complete entity-level model of the fem schema of Example 20.5 illustrating inter-schema references. (Page 1 of 1).

In the example, the entity **Leaf** redeclares the inherited attribute **Attr** to be represented by a subtype of the original attribute representation. It also declares that the value is mandatory rather than optional. The subtype **Sub** redeclares the representation of the inherited attribute **Num** to be an integer rather than a number (which could be either integer or real).

19.2.5 Inter-schema references

When a definition in one schema is utilized as part of a definition in another schema, this is represented by the oval box containing the qualified name of the definition.

Figure 19.5 is the entity-level model for the **fem** schema that was illustrated in the schema-level model displayed in Figure 19.1. Remember that a **Used** definition is surrounded by a solid box and a **Referenced** definition is surrounded by a dashed box. It can be seen that that the entity **element** has two attributes. The **nodes** attribute representation has been **Referenced** from the **geom** schema and has been aliased as **node** instead of its original name **point**. The **material** attribute representation is **property** which has been **Used** from the **mat** schema.

19.3 Complete and partial models

In EXPRESS-G a *complete model* is one that, within the limits of the EX-PRESS-G notation, accurately represents all the relationships and constraints pertinent to a model — either an entity-level model or a schema-level model. A *partial model* is one that is not complete.

This Section provides check lists for both kinds of model. Note that model completeness and model level are orthogonal concepts; either kind of model level can be complete or partial. Remember also that an entity-

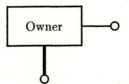

Figure 19.6: Partial entity-level model showing an abstraction of an Owner entity. (Page 1 of 1)

level model contains only the contents of a single schema, and that schema symbols cannot appear (although inter-schema refrences can). Similarly, the entity and type symbols cannot appear in a schema-level model.

Each page in a model must be titled and numbered. Use the form *Page* X *of* N, where N is the total number of pages in the model and X is the particular page number.

19.3.1 Complete models

In addition to the above general requirements, here is a check list for complete models.

- Titles for entity-level models start with the words *Complete entity-level model* ..., while those for schema-level models start with *Complete schema-level model* ....
- All elements of the model are displayed.
- All relationships are displayed.
- All constraints are marked (entity-level model only).
- All elements imported from other schemas are displayed.

19.3.2 Partial models

When developing a model, or sometimes when viewing a model, it is useful to be able to display a model at varying levels of abstraction. The foregoing discussion was concerned with the representation of fully detailed models. EXPRESS-G provides some capabilities for the representation of an abstraction of an information model.

We can usefully note that an EXPRESS-G model is an abstraction of an EXPRESS model as the graphics notation only provides a subset of the semantic modeling capabilities of the EXPRESS language. Further, EXPRESS-G naturally provides two levels of abstraction in that a schema-level model displays none of the internal details of the schemas, which, if required, have to be displayed via individual entity-level models.

For a complete EXPRESS-G model, every definition must be related to its components (i.e., an EXPRESS-G terminal or another definition). Depending on either the state of a model or a desire to eliminate minor details from a model, it is permissible in a partial model to indicate the existence of a relationship from a definition yet not define the thing being related to. A relation line may end in a circle with no adjoining definition symbol box. The meaning of such a relation is unspecified (except insofar that it indicates that the model is incomplete), but it can be taken to imply one of the following:

- Further details are known to the producer of the diagram but are not exhibited.

- Further details are required but these were unknown at the time the diagram was produced.

Figure 19.6 shows an abstraction of an `Owner` entity. The abstraction basically says that there is a thing called `Owner` which has some (undefined or undisplayed) attributes and which has some (undefined or undisplayed) subtypes.

Depending on the information modeling being performed, this abstraction could be the first attempt at a definition of a `Owner`, in which case the details will have to be developed. Alternately, it could appear in a much larger model where the concept of owner was necessary, but of minor importance, to the overall model concept, and hence the `Owner` details were available but not displayed.

Just as with entities, schemas may also be abstracted using the same mechanism.

There is really only one requirement that has to be met by a partial model, in addition to the general requirements of numbering pages, etc. The requirement is that the titles on the pages do not start with the word 'Complete'. Instead, we suggest that titles start with the words *Partial entity-level model . . .* or *Partial schema-level model . . .*, as appropriate.

It should be emphasised that in a partial model the absence of something in a model (perhaps the fact that a supertype is not marked as abstract) does not mean that the thing would still be absent in a complete model. Effectively, the difference between a complete model and a partial model is that in the former case the modeler has put down all that he can and knows, whereas a partial model has things missing but you cannot tell what they are — the model might be one percent or ninety-nine percent of a complete rendition.

Chapter 20

Sample Models

> 'Twill be recorded for a precedent,
> And many an error by the same example
> Will rush into the state.

The Merchant of Venice
William Shakespeare

This Chapter contains a sampler of EXPRESS models, each of which has been used as the basis for the earlier EXPRESS-G model illustrations. No claim is made that the models are either realistic or good — the models have been constructed to show certain aspects of EXPRESS-G rather than to illustrate information modeling in general.

Here is a summary of what the model in Example 20.1 says: a person must be either a male or a female. Every person has some defining characteristics, such as first and last names, date of birth, type of hair, and may also have zero or more children (which are, of course, also people). A male may be married to a female, and vice-versa. The partners in a marriage must be unique — this model is only appropriate for monogamous societies. There is one particular piece of information about females that does not apply to males; a female may have a maiden name.

The **Age** of a person is a derived attribute that is calculated through the function **years**, which determines the number of years between the date input as a parameter and the current date.

A **Person** has an inverse attribute which relates people who are children to their parents.

Example 20.1

A Single Schema EXPRESS Model

```
SCHEMA Example;

TYPE Date = ARRAY [1:3] OF INTEGER;
END_TYPE;
```

253

```
TYPE HairType = ENUMERATION OF
    (bald, dyed, natural, wig);
END_TYPE;

ENTITY Person
  SUPERTYPE OF (ONEOF(Female, Male));
  FirstName : STRING;
  LastName  : STRING;
  NickName  : OPTIONAL STRING;
  BirthDate : Date;
  Children  : SET [0:?] OF Person;  .
  Hair      : HairType;
DERIVE
  Age : INTEGER := years(BirthDate);
INVERSE
  parents : SET [0:2] OF Person FOR Children;
END_ENTITY;

ENTITY Female
  SUBTYPE OF (Person);
  MaidenName : OPTIONAL STRING;
END_ENTITY;

ENTITY Male
  SUBTYPE OF (Person);
END_ENTITY;

ENTITY Married;
  Husband : Male;
  Wife    : Female;
UNIQUE
  no_polyandry : Husband;
  no_polygamy  : Wife;
END_ENTITY;

FUNCTION years(past : date): INTEGER;
  (* This function calculates the number of years
     between the past date and the current date *)
END_FUNCTION;

END_SCHEMA; -- end of Example
```

Example 20.2 is a simple single schema model that shows some of the kinds of relationships that can be specified in an **EXPRESS** model. The model has no intrinsic meaning — it is merely a collection of arbitrarily named types and entities. It includes entities, both simple and complex (i.e., supertypes and subtypes), defined types and a select type.

Example 20.2

A Simple EXPRESS Entity and Type Relationship Model

```
SCHEMA EntitiesAndTypes;

ENTITY Root;
END_ENTITY;

ENTITY Leaf1
  SUBTYPE OF (Root);
  attr : FromEnt;
END_ENTITY;

ENTITY Leaf2
  SUBTYPE OF (Root);
  graph  : BINARY;
  choose : Pic1;
END_ENTITY;

TYPE Pick = SELECT (AnEnt, Name);
END_TYPE;

ENTITY An Ent;
  attr : ToEnt;
END_ENTITY;

TYPE Name = STRING;
END_TYPE;

ENTITY FromEnt;
  description : OPTIONAL ToEnt;
  values      : ARRAY [1:3] OF REAL;
END_ENTITY;

ENTITY ToEnt;
  text : strings;
  val  : REAL;
WHERE
  positive : val >= 0.0;
END_ENTITY;

TYPE Strings = LIST [1:?] OF STRING;
END_TYPE;

END_SCHEMA; -- end of EntitiesAndTypes
```

EXPRESS allows you to define very complex supertype trees (and networks). The tree shown in Example 20.3 is relatively simple. No attributes have been shown for the entities as they are not relevant to the tree structure.

Example 20.3

Supertype and Subtype Tree in EXPRESS

```
SCHEMA SimpleTrees;

ENTITY Root;
END_ENTITY;

ENTITY Leaf1
  SUBTYPE OF (Root);
END_ENTITY;

ENTITY Sub1
  ABSTRACT SUPERTYPE OF (ONEOF(Leaf2, leaf3))
  SUBTYPE OF (Root);
END_ENTITY;

ENTITY Leaf2
  SUBTYPE OF (Sub1);
END_ENTITY;

ENTITY Leaf3
  SUBTYPE OF (Sub1);
END_ENTITY;

END_SCHEMA; -- end of SimpleTrees
```

Subtypes may redeclare inherited attributes. Example 20.4 is a simple model where the redeclared attributes are specialisations of the inherited value representations, and one attribute representation has been made mandatory rather than optional.

Example 20.4

Attribute redeclaration

```
SCHEMA Retype;

  ENTITY Root;
    Attr : OPTIONAL Super;
  END_ENTITY;

  ENTITY Super;
    Num : NUMBER;
  END_ENTITY;

  ENTITY Leaf
    SUBTYPE OF (Root);
    SELF\Root.Attr : Sub;
```

```
   END_ENTITY;

   ENTITY Sub
     SUYBTYPE OF (Super);
     SELF\Super.Num : INTEGER;
   END_ENTITY;

   END_SCHEMA;  -- end of Retype
```

EXPRESS models consist of at least one schema. Example 20.5 shows a model that consists of three schemas. The primary schema is called **fem** and is illustrative of an initial model that might support Finite Element Modeling. A **mesh** is composed of a list of **elements** and information about the material of the real life object that the mesh represents. An **element** is defined in terms of a list of **nodes**. An element may have material information. A **node** in finite element modeling terms is equivalent to a geometric point.

The schemas **mat** and **geom** are support schemas in this model. They contain models of material properties and geometric constructs. The **fem** schema imports definitions from these schemas.

This model is also illustrative of a modeling technique that we deplore as it is contrary to the principle of implementation independence (see 5.5). The intent of the **mesh** is that each element has material information, but the material need not be the same for each element in a mesh. By having material associated with both the **mesh** and optionally with an **element** the idea is that all elements in a mesh have the same material information, except for those elements which have material values which differ from the (default) value for the mesh. In information modeling terms, if one of the defining characteristics of an **element** is that it always has a value for material properties, then the value should be mandatory, not optional.

Example 20.5

A Three Schema EXPRESS Model

```
SCHEMA fem;
   REFERENCE FROM geom (point AS node);
   USE FROM mat (property);

   ENTITY mesh;
     material : property;
     elements : LIST [1:?] OF element;
   END_ENTITY;

   ENTITY element;
     nodes    : LIST [1:?] OF node;
     material : OPTIONAL property;
   END_ENTITY;
```

```
END_SCHEMA; -- end of fem schema

SCHEMA geom;

  ENTITY point;
    -- attributes of point;
  END_ENTITY;

  -- other definitions

END_SCHEMA; -- end of geom schema

SCHEMA mat;

  ENTITY property;
    -- attributes of property
  END_ENTITY;

  -- other definitions

END_SCHEMA; -- end of mat schema
```

Chapter 21

The EXPRESS-I
Language

Now for something completely different.

Monty Python

Now we turn to the question: 'Once I have created an abstract declaration in EXPRESS, what would an instance of that thing look like?' EXPRESS-I allows you to create instances of EXPRESS things that have values in place of references to datatypes. The main reason for doing this is to study some realistic examples of things that otherwise might be difficult to understand. After all, it is one thing to describe a tree and quite another to actually see one.

Some of the design goals of EXPRESS-I are based on these requirements:

- Major information modeling projects are large and complex. Managing them without appropriate tools based on formal languages and methods is a risky proposition. Informal specification techniques eliminate the possibility of employing computer automation in checking for inconsistencies in presentation or specification.

- The language should focus on the display of the realization of the properties of *entities*, which are the things of interest. The definition of entities is in terms of data and behavior. Data represents the properties by which an entity is realized and behavior is represented by constraints.

- The language should seek to avoid, as far as possible, specific implementation views. That is, EXPRESS-I models do not suggest the structure of databases, object bases, or of information bases in general.

- The language should provide a means for displaying small populated models of EXPRESS schemas as examples for design reviews.

- The language should provide a means for supporting the specification of test suites for information model processors.

259

EXPRESS-I represents entity instances in terms of the values of its attributes (attributes are the traits or characteristics considered important for use and understanding). These values have a representation which might be considered simple (an integer value) or something more complex (an entity value). A geometric point might be defined in terms of three real numbers named x, y and z, and the actual values associated with those attributes might be 1.0, 2.5 and 7.9.

The EXPRESS-I instance language provides a means of displaying instantiations of EXPRESS data elements. The language is designed principally for human readability and for ease of generating EXPRESS-I element instances from definitions in an EXPRESS schema.

The language has two major parts. The first part is used to display data instances. You can display the data on an entity by entity basis, on a schema basis or as a collection of schema instances which are taken to be a display of some model of a *universe of discourse*. Within the language these are called *object instances, schema instances* and a *model*. In Figure 21.1 the model of the *universe of discourse* is assumed to have been defined using EXPRESS.

The second part of the language is for the specification of abstract test cases for the purposes of formally describing tests to be performed against an implementation of an information model that was defined using EXPRESS. The language constructs provided for this purpose are the *test case* and the *context*. This portion of the language also utilizes the procedural aspects of the EXPRESS language. Instances of data may be parameterized and stored in a context. Many different test cases may assign values for the parameterized data in a context and use that data as part of their test specification. The data instances resulting from the application of a test case may be displayed via the model portion of the language.

The major elements of the language are shown in Figure 21.1.

Note: *We will discuss only schema instances in this book. To be specific, we do not explore context or abstract test cases here.*

21.1   Governing principles

The value instances put on display in an EXPRESS-I model may or may not be governed by an EXPRESS schema. Without trying to be comprehensive, here are some of the connections between EXPRESS and EXPRESS-I.

- The value type of an EXPRESS-I attribute must agree with the EXPRESS datatype.

- If you use a Nil attribute value where EXPRESS expects an attribute value, then the entity instance is non-conforming. That is, Nil attribute values are only conforming for `Optional` valued attributes.

- The number of EXPRESS-I attributes must agree with the EXPRESS declaration.

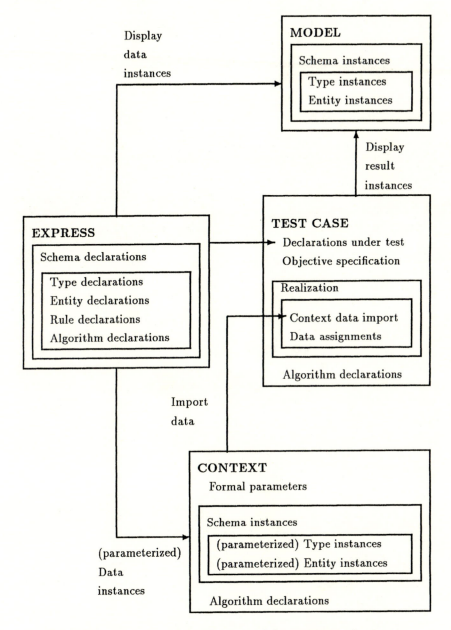

Figure 21.1: The major elements of the EXPRESS-I language.

- Subtype instances must list every direct legal supertype instance.

- Supertype instances must list every direct legal subtype instance.

When there is no EXPRESS schema, every effort should be made to preserve consistency.

- The corresponding attributes in all instances of the same entity type should have compatible representation types. That is, one should not be a number and another a string.

- Supertype and subtype instances should be uniform. That is, one instance should not be a simple instance and another a subtype.

- A particular attribute should not be explicit in one instance and derived in another.

Keep in mind that it will be very difficult to 'reverse engineer' the meaning of EXPRESS-I instances. This is especially true for supertype lattices, the coverage of enumeration items, the allowable choices of select items, the bounds of arrays, lists, etc. and the nature of constraints. This does not make the use of ungoverned instances useless, but it is dangerous when used on a large scale.

21.2   Basic values

The representation of basic values — numbers, strings, etc. — follow the pattern set by the EXPRESS literals. However, there are a few important differences that we will cover here. The value representations that are the same as EXPRESS are mentioned, but you will have to refer to EXPRESS for their definitions.

21.2.1   Numbers

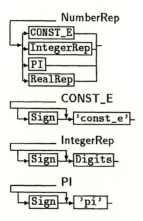

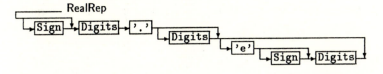

RealRep

EXPRESS-I allows you to use a preceding sign with these numeric literals or either of the math constants (`Pi` and `Const_E`). Otherwise, expressions are not allowed in value representations.

21.2.2 Strings

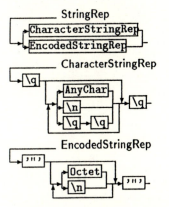

StringRep

CharacterStringRep

EncodedStringRep

Unlike their EXPRESS counterparts, these literals are allowed to span physical lines.

Example 21.1

These strings span physical source lines.

```
'This is
    a string value
        that spans lines'

"0000000000000751
0000006500000088"
```

21.3 Enumeration items

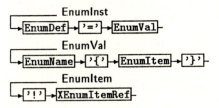

EnumInst

EnumVal

EnumItem

EXPRESS-I precedes the name of an enumeration item with an exclamation mark (!).

EXPRESS	EXPRESS-I

`TYPE Color = ENUMERATION OF`
`  (Red, Blue, Purple);`
`END_TYPE;`
	`The --> Color{!Purple};`

21.4   Select values

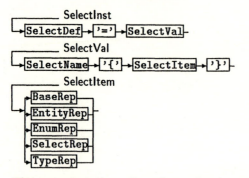

The representation of a select value starts with the name of the EXPRESS type (which of course has to be a select type) followed by a reference to the object selected.

EXPRESS	EXPRESS-I

`TYPE Pastime = SELECT`
`  (Munch,Fish);`
`END_TYPE;`
	`Entertainment = Pastime{@HotDog};`
	`Entertainment = Pastime{@FlyCast};`

21.5   Aggregate values

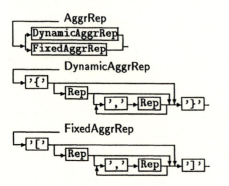

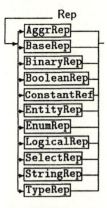

Rep
- AggrRep
- BaseRep
- BinaryRep
- BooleanRep
- ConstantRef
- EntityRep
- EnumRep
- LogicalRep
- SelectRep
- StringRep
- TypeRep

EXPRESS-I offers two forms of aggregate values: dynamic and fixed. The fixed aggregate represents EXPRESS array values. The dynamic aggregate represents bag, list and set values. When you look at a dynamic aggregate there is no way (other than referring to the EXPRESS declarations) to know which type it really is.

```
EXPRESS                          EXPRESS-I

TYPE Matrix = ARRAY[0:5] OF      M --> Matrix[0,1,2,3,4,5];
  INTEGER;
END_TYPE;
TYPE Sparse = ARRAY[0:5] OF      S --> Sparse[0,?,2,?,4,5];
  OPTIONAL INTEGER;
END_TYPE;
TYPE Lotto  = SET[6:6] OF        L --> Lotto{32,10,7,54,19,41};
  INTEGER;
END_TYPE;
```

21.6 Entity values and representations

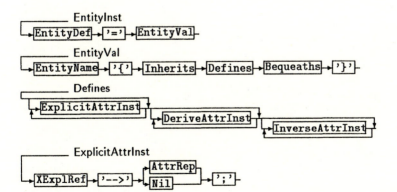

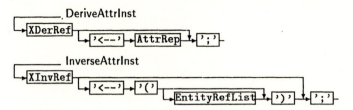

An entity representation starts with the name **EXPRESS** gave it (possibly qualified with its schema name). Its value includes any supertypes, its explicit, derived and inverse attributes, and any subtypes. All of this is enclosed within curly braces.

EXPRESS	EXPRESS-I	
SCHEMA Tools;	Sam = Widget{};	Not qualified
ENTITY Widget;	Joe = Tools.Widget{};	Qualified
END_ENTITY;	A --> @Joe;	Reference
END_SCHEMA;	B --> Tools.Widget{};	Anonymous

21.6.1   Attribute values

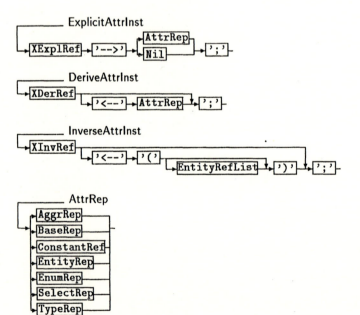

Attribute values follow any supertype entities which are direct ancestors (we will cover supertypes and subtypes directly). As with **EXPRESS**, explicit attributes are given first followed in order by derived and inverse attributes.

EXPRESS	EXPRESS-I
| ```
ENTITY Widget;
  E : INTEGER;
DERIVE
  D : INTEGER = E+6;
INVERSE
  I : SomeEntity FOR SomeAttr;
END_ENTITY;
``` | ```
Joe = Widget{
  E --> 27;
  D <-- 33;
  I <-- (@Sam);
  } ;
``` |

You do not have to give a value for derived or inverse attributes (but we assume that the value can be derived when we want it!).

EXPRESS	EXPRESS-I
| ```
ENTITY Widget;
  E : INTEGER;
DERIVE
  D : INTEGER = E+6;
INVERSE
  I : SomeEntity FOR SomeAttr;
END_ENTITY;
``` | ```
Joe = Widget{
  E --> 27;
  D;          Ok to leave this out
  I;          and this
  } ;
``` |

21.6.2 Supertypes and subtypes

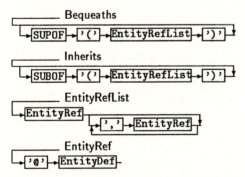

When the entity is a subtype it needs to list its ancestors and when it is a supertype it needs to list its descendants. In other words, the entity *inherits from* and *bequeaths to* other entities.

EXPRESS	EXPRESS-I
| ```
ENTITY Top;
  A : INTEGER;
END_ENTITY;
ENTITY Middle SUBTYPE OF (Top);
  B : INTEGER;
END_ENTITY;
``` | ```
T = Top{99;
        SUPOF(M);};};

M = Middle{SUBOF(@T);
           66;
           SUPOF(@B);};};
``` |

```
ENTITY Bottom SUBTYPE OF (Middle);    B = Bottom{SUBOF(@M);
  C : INTEGER;                             33}};
END_ENTITY;
```

21.7   Constant values

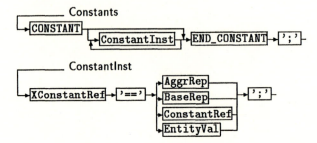

Constant values are put inside a block. The value given for these constants is fully evaluated (and in the case of numeric constants shown at the resolution required by the application).

EXPRESS

```
CONSTANT
  Thousand : INTEGER := 100*10;
  AThird   : REAL    := 1/3;
  Version  : STRING  := '1.00';
END_CONSTANT;
```

EXPRESS-I

```
CONSTANT
  Thousand == 1000;
  AThird == 0.3333333333333333;
  Version == '1.00',
END_CONSTANT;
```

21.8   Schema data instance

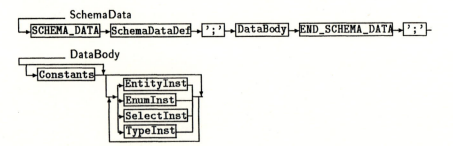

Usually entity instance values will be wrapped by a schema data value. Constants, if needed, appear immediately after the start of the schema data block. After that, you may write entity, enumeration, select and type values in any order you wish.

The name you give to these objects (including constants) must be unique within the schema data block.

EXPRESS

```
SCHEMA Example;
CONSTANT
  Thousand : INTEGER := 100*10;
  Million  : INTEGER := 1000000;
END_CONSTANT;

TYPE Money = REAL;
END_TYPE;

TYPE Color = ENUMERATION OF
  (Red, Green, Blue);
END_TYPE;

ENTITY BalanceSheet;
  In  : Money;
  Out : Money;
DERIVE
  Position : Money := In - Out;
END_ENTITY;

ENTITY Fruit;
  Weight : REAL;
END_ENTITY;

ENTITY Apple SUBTYPE OF(Fruit);
  Hue : Color;
END_ENTITY;

END_SCHEMA;
```

EXPRESS-I

```
SCHEMA_DATA Example;
CONSTANT
  Thousand == 1000;
  Million  == 1000000;
END_CONSTANT;

Income = Money{100.00};
Expenses = Money{300.00};

Go = Color{!Green};
Stop = Color{!Red};

Balance = BalanceSheet{
  In  --> @Income;
  Out --> @Expenses;
  Position <-- -200.00;
  };

Snack = Fruit{
  Weight --> 6.0;
  SupOf(@Noon)
  };

Noon = Apple{
  SubOf(@Snack)
  Hue --> Color{!Red};
  };
END_SCHEMA_DATA;
```

Chapter 22

Usage notes

> Mr. Gladstone: 'But, after all, what use is it?'
>
> Michael Faraday: 'One day, Sir, you may tax it.'
>
> *Discussion between the politician and the scientist on electricity*

Now we discuss some of the potential uses of the EXPRESS-I language.

In Object-Oriented terms, an EXPRESS entity would be called a class, and an instance of a class is termed an object. One object may reference another object. EXPRESS, though, distinguishes between entities and types (i.e., the enumeration, select and the defined data type) as entities may be subtyped whereas types cannot be. EXPRESS-I treats entity instances as objects in the OO sense. It also allows types to be treated as objects in that they can be instantiated and referenced. Alternatively, type values may be embedded in entity instances.

22.1   EXPRESS data examples

The simplest use of EXPRESS-I is as a paper exercise in displaying examples of EXPRESS declarations that are populated with data. The language allows the display of entity instances as referenceable objects. Types instances may also be displayed as referenceable objects, or they may appear as unreferenceable values within other objects' values. Examples in this book show both forms of type instantiation.

Values of explicit entity attributes are required. The values of derived or inverse attributes need not be displayed, except as exemplars, because as noted, these are essentially calculable from the values of the explicit attributes.

Examples of EXPRESS schemas can also be displayed, as well as individual objects.

The EXPRESS-I model construct is provided to enable the display of multiple schemas. Typically, a model would be used when two or more EXPRESS schemas interact with each other. Note that EXPRESS itself does not support such a construct.

Note: *We do not discuss models in this book.*

22.2 Abstract test cases

The test case construct is provided to assist in the formal specification of test cases against the implementation of an EXPRESS schema. EXPRESS itself does not provide an equivalent construct.

For a test case, a base set of EXPRESS-I objects must be defined which will be the objects (and their supporting data) to be tested. The values of these objects may be in the form of parameters, whose formal definition are given in an enclosing context. A series of test cases may then be defined on the context, by providing actual parameter values. Thus, a single 'parameterized' context may support many different tests. The test case documentation will also have to include the test purposes and expected results.

Note: *We do not discuss test cases in this book.*

22.3 Object bases

Here, we assume the availability of some object base that stores objects according to EXPRESS defined schemas. That is, the object base has the capability of maintaining a partitioning of the objects according to the EXPRESS schemas in which their definitions are declared. An object base, in the sense used here, is an information base that is computer supported. The design and implementation of such an object base is left as an exercise for the reader.

22.3.1 Input

Given an object base, EXPRESS-I could be used as one means of inputting objects into the object base. This process could be either a batch process, where a previously prepared EXPRESS-I file was read into the object processor, or it could be an interactive process, where the user incrementally added EXPRESS-I objects.

Depending on the sophistication of the object base, the user may or may not need to explicitly provide values for derived and inverse attributes.

22.3.2   Output

Given a populated object base, EXPRESS-I could be used as a data output language for displaying some or all of the contents of the object base to a human reader.

Depending on the sophistication of the object base, the displayed entity objects may or may not include values for derived and inverse attributes. Note, though, that at least the role names of these attributes are required.

The EXPRESS-I model construct is designed for the display of the population of an object base.

22.3.3   Code testing

An implementation of an object base should provide all of the functionality needed to evaluate all the constraints on EXPRESS entities and types that may occur as objects or values within the object base. For instance, a schema may contain an entity definition that includes a derived attribute and a constraint on the derived value. An object base should be able to evaluate the derived attribute and also reject any object of that entity class whose attribute values do not satisfy the constraints. This requires code. EXPRESS-I could be used as data input for testing such code.

Other code examples include:

- Determination of the values of inverse attributes.

- Checking uniqueness constraints across an object population.

- Code to implement EXPRESS defined rules.

Note that these types of functions are also required for physical file test systems and other forms of exchange data processors.

22.4   Non-EXPRESS data examples

As EXPRESS-I entity instances are in the form of named tuples it may also be used to display objects or records from languages other than EXPRESS. For example, instances of C **structs** or the state of objects representing instances of classes from Object Oriented languages such as C^{++} or Eiffel. Similarly for languages that support Frames.

It may even be used to represent tabular data from relational databases, where the entity name is equivalent to a table name, and each instance is a (identified) line in the table, or network or Object Oriented type databases.

Chapter 23

EXPRESS-I Syntax

Proper words in proper places.

Jonathon Swift

Here is the whole syntax of EXPRESS-I except for constant tokens (i.e., reserved words and such), character sets, standard constants, functions and procedures, and simple equates to tokens that create or reference identifiers.

Conventions

The conventions we use to name the syntax rules are explained below. The *xxx* referred to means *Entity, Type* or one of the other objects that might appear in a schema data block.

xxxDef	– represents the identifier given to a schema data object. It is a simple identifier that is unique in the scope of the schema data block.
xxxRef	– represents a reference to a *xxxDef* which must exist somewhere in the scope of the schema data block.
xxxRep	– represents the representation of a *xxx*, usually a *xxxRef* or a *xxxVal*.
xxxVal	– represents a particular value (an anonymous instance) of a *xxx*.
xxxName	– represents the name of a *xxx* as given in an EXPRESS schema.
xxxInst	– represents a particular value of a *xxx* which can be refered to within the scope of a schema data block.
XxxxRef	– represents a reference to the name of a *xxx* as given in an EXPRESS schema.

Syntax

Schema data block

_____ SchemaData

→ SCHEMA_DATA → SchemaDataDef → ';' → DataBody → END_SCHEMA_DATA → ';' ⊢

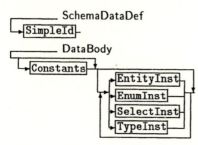

Constant

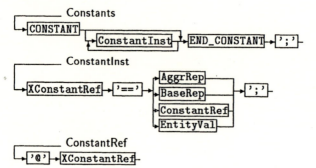

Entity

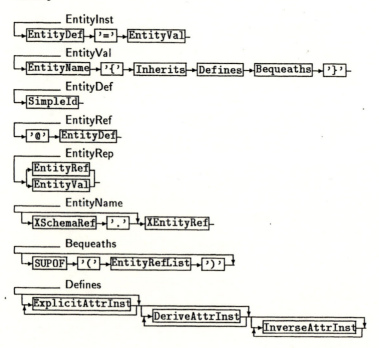

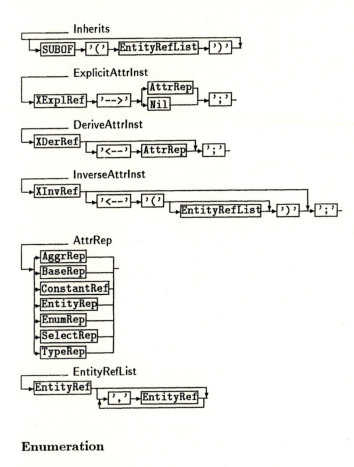

Enumeration

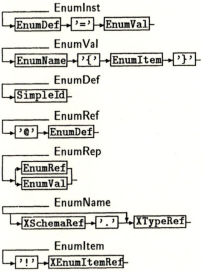

Select

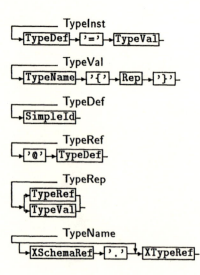

```
_____ SelectInst
└▸ SelectDef ▸ '=' ▸ SelectVal ┘

_____ SelectVal
└▸ SelectName ▸ '{' ▸ SelectItem ▸ '}' ┘

_____ SelectName
└▸ XSchemaRef ▸ '.' ┴▸ XTypeRef ┘

_____ SelectDef
└▸ SimpleId ┘

_____ SelectRef
└▸ '@' ▸ SelectDef ┘

_____ SelectRep
├▸ SelectRef ┐
└▸ SelectVal ┘

_____ SelectItem
├▸ BaseRep ┐
├▸ EntityRep ┤
├▸ EnumRep ┤
├▸ SelectRep ┤
└▸ TypeRep ┘
```

Type

```
_____ TypeInst
└▸ TypeDef ▸ '=' ▸ TypeVal ┘

_____ TypeVal
└▸ TypeName ▸ '{' ▸ Rep ▸ '}' ┘

_____ TypeDef
└▸ SimpleId ┘

_____ TypeRef
└▸ '@' ▸ TypeDef ┘

_____ TypeRep
├▸ TypeRef ┐
└▸ TypeVal ┘

_____ TypeName
└▸ XSchemaRef ▸ '.' ┴▸ XTypeRef ┘
```

Supporting constructs

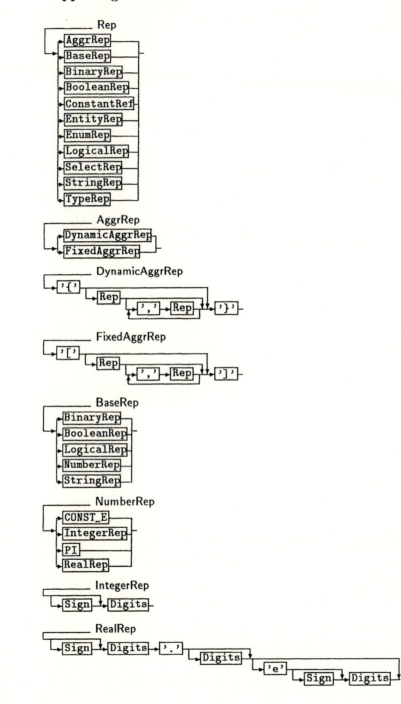

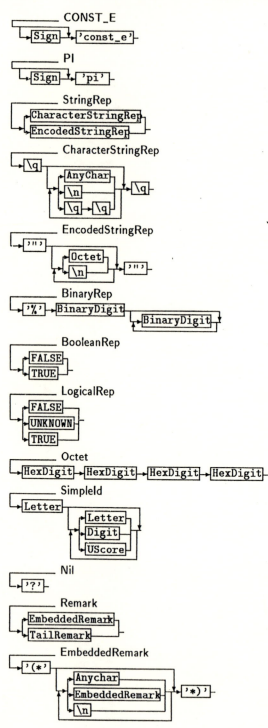

279

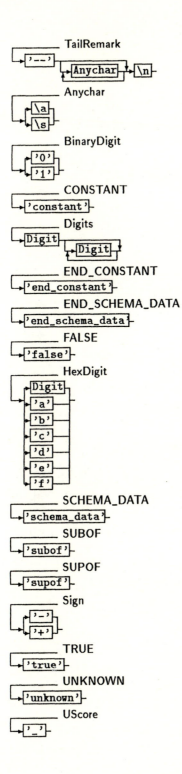

TailRemark

Anychar

BinaryDigit

CONSTANT

Digits

END_CONSTANT

END_SCHEMA_DATA

FALSE

HexDigit

SCHEMA_DATA

SUBOF

SUPOF

Sign

TRUE

UNKNOWN

UScore

Appendix A

EXPRESS example model

Example is the school of mankind, and they will learn at no other.

Letters on a Regicide Peace
Edmund Burke

This Appendix contains a complete and documented EXPRESS model for the worked example whose starting point was described in Chapter 4.1. An EXPRESS-G version of the model is also included. The model is documented using the embedded style described in Chapter 7.

A.1 Scope

The model has to do with the registration of cars and is limited to the scope of interest of the Registration Authority. This Authority exists for the purpose of:

- Knowing who is or was the registered owner of a car at any time from construction to destruction of the car;
- To monitor laws regarding the transfer of ownership of cars;
- To monitor laws regarding the fuel consumption of cars;
- To monitor laws regarding manufacturers of cars.

A.2 Model overview

The model is described using both EXPRESS and EXPRESS-G. The EXPRESS definitions are primary and the EXPRESS-G diagrams are to assist in understanding the primary model. If there is any conflict between the EXPRESS and EXPRESS-G, then the EXPRESS takes precedence.

The model consists of three schemas, as shown in Figure A.1. The schema **authority** is the primary schema. It references items from the two

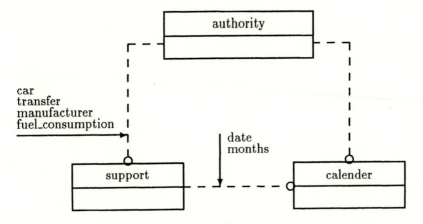

Figure A.1: Complete schema-level model for Registration Authority example (Page 1 of 1).

ancilliary schemas, namely **support** and **calendar**. The **support** schema also references items from the **calendar** schema.

A.3   Authority schema

This schema is the primary one in the model and is principally concerned with the main functions of the Registration Authority.

The schema imports definitions from two sources, namely the **support** and the **calendar** schemas.

Figure A.2 is an EXPRESS-G complete entity-level model for this schema.

EXPRESS specification:

```
*)
SCHEMA authority;
  REFERENCE FROM support (car,
  transfer,
  manufacturer,
  fuel_consumption,
  mnfg_average_consumption);
  REFERENCE FROM calendar (current_date);
(*
```

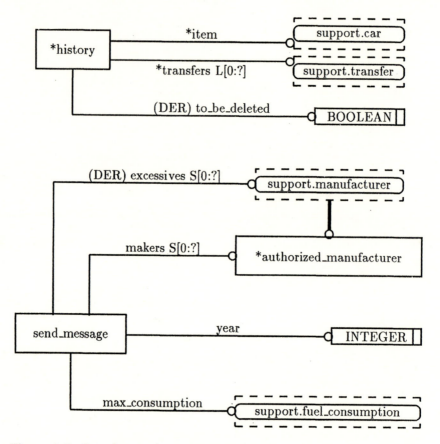

Figure A.2: Complete entity-level model of the Authority schema (Page 1 of 1).

A.3.1 Entity definitions

Entity HISTORY

A history records the transfers of ownership of a car over its lifetime. A history must be kept for a certain period after the car is destroyed, after which the ownership records may be destroyed.

EXPRESS specification:

```
*)
ENTITY history;
  item : car;
  transfers : LIST [0:?] OF UNIQUE transfer;
DERIVE
  to_be_deleted : BOOLEAN := too_old(SELF);
```

```
UNIQUE
  un1 : item;
WHERE
  one_car  : single_car(SELF);
  ordering : exchange_ok(transfers);
END_ENTITY;
(*
```

Attribute definitions:

item: The `car` whose ownership history is being tracked.

transfers: The ownership `transfer` records of the `item`.

to_be_deleted: A flag which indicates that this `history` record may be deleted because the `item` has been destroyed (TRUE), or that the record shall not be deleted (FALSE).

Propositions:

un1: The value of `item` shall be unique across all instances of `history`.

one_car: Each `transfer` collected in a `history` shall be of the same `car`.

ordering: The list of `transfer` shall be in increasing historical order.

Entity AUTHORIZED MANUFACTURER

An **authorized manufacturer** is a **manufacturer** who has been given permission by the Registration Authority to make cars.

EXPRESS specification:

```
*)
ENTITY authorized_manufacturer
  SUBTYPE OF (manufacturer);
END_ENTITY;
(*
```

Rule MAX NUMBER

No more than five **authorized manufacturers** are permitted at any one time.

EXPRESS specification:

```
*)
RULE max_number FOR (authorized_manufacturer);
WHERE
```

```
    max_of_5 : SIZEOF(authorized_manufacturer) <= 5;
END_RULE;
(*
```

Propositions:

max_of_5: The rule is violated if there are more than five **authorized manufacturers** at any time.

Entity SEND MESSAGE

In January each year the Registration Authority shall send a message to each **manufacturer** whose cars' average fuel consumption exceeds a certain limit, which may vary from year to year.

EXPRESS specification:

```
    *)
ENTITY send_message;
   max_consumption : fuel_consumption;
   year            : INTEGER;
   makers          : SET [0:?] OF authorized_manufacturer;
DERIVE
   excessives : SET [0:?] OF manufacturer := guzzlers(SELF);
END_ENTITY;
(*
```

Attribute definitions:

max_consumption: The legal maximum average fuel consumption.
year: The year for which the **max consumption** value applies.
makers: The **authorized manufacturers** operating during the **year**.
excessives: The **manufacturers** whose cars exceed the consumption limit.

A.3.2   Function and procedure definitions

Function GUZZLERS

This function returns the set of **manufacturers** whose cars exceed an average fuel consumption limit.

Parameters:

par: An instance of a **send message** entity.
RESULT: A set of instances of **manufacturer** whose cars' average fuel consumption is excessive.

EXPRESS specification:

```
    *)
    FUNCTION guzzlers(par : send_message) : SET OF manufacturer;
    LOCAL
       result : SET OF manufacturer := [];
       mnfs   : SET OF manufacturer := par.makers;
       limit  : fuel_consumption := par.max_consumption;
       time   : INTEGER := par.year;
    END_LOCAL;
      REPEAT i := 1 TO SIZEOF(mnfs);
        IF (mnfg_average_consumption(mnfs[i],time)> limit) THEN
          result := result + mnfs[i];
        END_IF;
      END_REPEAT;
    RETURN(result);
    END_FUNCTION;
    (*
```

Function TOO OLD

This function calculates whether the car in a history was destroyed more than two years ago.

Parameters:

par: An instance of a history.

RESULT: A Boolean value. TRUE if the car in the input history was destroyed two or more years ago; otherwise FALSE.

EXPRESS specification:

```
    *)
    FUNCTION too_old(par : history) : BOOLEAN;
      (* The function returns TRUE if the input history is
        outdated. That is, if it is of an item that was destroyed
        more than 2 years ago. *)
      IF ('SUPPORT.DESTROYED_CAR' IN par.item) THEN
        IF (current_date.year-par.item.destroyed_on.year >= 2) THEN
          RETURN(TRUE);
        END_IF;
      END_IF;
      RETURN(FALSE);
    END_FUNCTION;
    (*
```

Function EXCHANGE OK

This function checks whether or not the **transfers** in a list are ordered.

Parameters:

par A list of **transfer** instances.

RESULT A Boolean value. TRUE if the recipient in the Nth transfer is the same as the giver in the $(N + 1)^{th}$ transfer.

EXPRESS specification:

```
*)
FUNCTION exchange_ok(par : LIST OF transfer) : BOOLEAN;
  (* returns TRUE if the "to owner" in the N'th transfer of a
     car is the "from owner" in the N+1'th transfer *)
  REPEAT i := 1 TO (SIZEOF(par) - 1);
    IF (par[i].new :<>: par[i+1].prior) THEN
      RETURN (FALSE);
    END_IF;
  END_REPEAT;
  RETURN (TRUE);
END_FUNCTION;
(*
```

Function SINGLE CAR

This function checks whether or not the **car** in a transfer **history** is the same **car** specified in each individual **transfer**.

Parameters:

par: A **history** instance.

RESULT: A Boolean value. TRUE if the **history** and all its **transfers** are of the same **car**, otherwise FALSE.

EXPRESS specification:

```
*)
FUNCTION single_car(par : history) : BOOLEAN;
  (* returns TRUE if a history is of a single car *)
  REPEAT i := 1 TO SIZEOF(par.transfers);
    IF (par.item :<>: par.transfers[i].item) THEN
      RETURN (FALSE);
    END_IF;
  END_REPEAT;
  RETURN (TRUE);
```

```
END_FUNCTION;
(*
```

A.3.3 Entity classification structure

The following indented listing shows the entity classification structure. Entities in upper case characters are defined in this schema. Entities in lower case characters are defined in other schemas.

```
HISTORY
manufacturer (in schema support)
   AUTHORIZED_MANUFACTURER
SEND_MESSAGE


*)
END_SCHEMA;  -- end of authority schema
(*
```

A.4 Support schema

This schema contains supporting definitions for the primary authority schema.

An EXPRESS-G model of the contents of this schema is given in Figure A.3 and in Figure A.4.

The schema imports definitions from the calendar schema.

EXPRESS specification:

```
*)
SCHEMA support;
   REFERENCE FROM calendar (date, months, days_between);
(*
```

A.4.1 Type definitions

Type NAME

The 'name' of something. A human interpretable name which may identify some object, thing or person, etc. For example, Widget Company, Inc..

EXPRESS specification:

```
*)
TYPE name = STRING;
END_TYPE;
(*
```

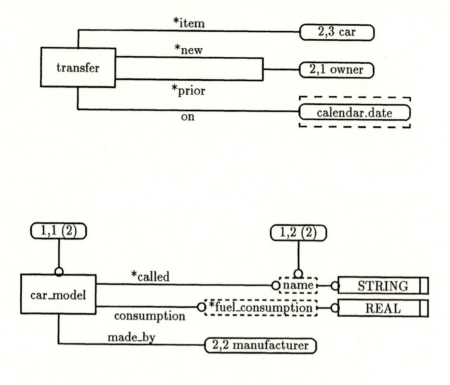

Figure A.3: Complete entity-level model of the Support schema (Page 1 of 2).

Type IDENTIFICATION NO

A character string which may be used as the 'identification number' for a particular instance of some object. This is typically a mixture of alphanumeric characters and other symbols. For example, D20-736597WP23.

EXPRESS specification:

```
*)
TYPE identification_no = STRING;
END_TYPE;
(*
```

Type FUEL CONSUMPTION

A measure of the fuel consumption of some powered device.

EXPRESS specification:

```
*)
TYPE fuel_consumption = REAL;
WHERE
  range : {4.0 <= SELF <= 25.0};
END_TYPE;
(*
```

Propositions:

range: The value is limited to lie in the range 4 to 25 inclusive.

A.4.2   Entity definitions

Entity TRANSFER

A record of a transfer of a car from one owner to a new owner.

EXPRESS specification:

```
*)
ENTITY transfer;
  item  : car;
  prior : owner;
  new   : owner;
  on    : date;
WHERE
  wr1 : NOT ('SUPPORT.MANUFACTURER' IN TYPEOF(new));
  wr2 : (NOT ('SUPPORT.MANUFACTURER' IN TYPEOF(prior))) XOR
      (('SUPPORT.MANUFACTURER' IN TYPEOF(prior)) AND
      ('SUPPORT.GARAGE' IN TYPEOF (new)));
  wr3 : (NOT ('SUPPORT.GARAGE' IN TYPEOF(prior))) XOR
      (('SUPPORT.GARAGE' IN TYPEOF(prior)) AND
      (('SUPPORT.PERSON' IN TYPEOF(new)) XOR
      ('SUPPORT.GROUP' IN TYPEOF(new))));
  wr4 : (NOT ('SUPPORT.DESTROYED_CAR' IN TYPEOF(item)) XOR
      (('SUPPORT.DESTROYED_CAR' IN TYPEOF(item)) AND
      (days_between(on, item\destroyed_car.destroyed_on) > 0)));
END_ENTITY;
(*
```

Attribute definitions:

item: The car being transferred.

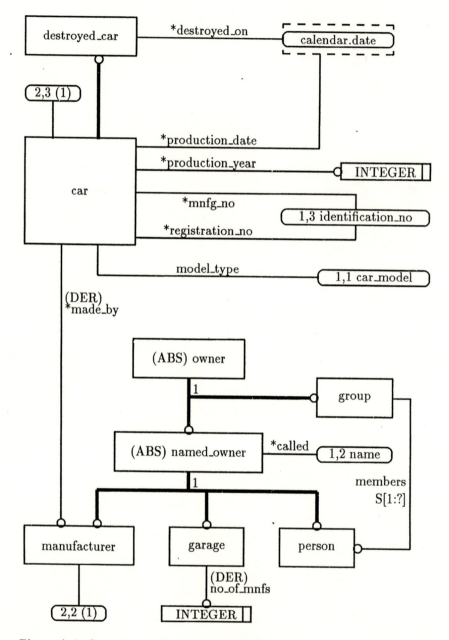

Figure A.4: Complete entity-level model of the Support schema (Page 2 of 2).

prior: The prior owner of the `item`.

new: The new owner of the `item`.

on: The `date` of the `transfer`.

Propositions:

wr1: A `car` cannot be transferred to a `manufacturer`.

wr2: A `manufacturer` can only transfer a `car` to a `garage`.

wr3: A `garage` can only transfer a `car` to either a `person` of a group of people.

wr4: A `car` which has been destroyed cannot be transferred.

Entity CAR

A `car`.

EXPRESS specification:

```
*)
ENTITY car;
   model_type       : car_model;
   mnfg_no          : identification_no;
   registration_no  : identification_no;
   production_date  : date;
   production_year  : INTEGER;
DERIVE
   made_by : manufacturer := model_type.made_by;
UNIQUE
   joint  : made_by, mnfg_no;
   single : registration_no;
WHERE
   jan_prod : (production_year = production_date.year) XOR
             ((production_date.month = months.January) AND
              (production_year = production_date.year - 1));
END_ENTITY;
(*
```

Attribute definitions:

model_type: The `car model`.

mnfg_no: An identification number of the `car` assigned by the car's manufacturer.

registration_no: An identification number for the `car` assigned by the Registration Authority.

production_date: The date on which the car was produced.

production_year: The registered year of production of the `car`.

made_by: The `manufacturer` of the `car`.

Propositions:

joint: The `mnfg no` given to a `car` is unique for the given car manufacturer.

single: Each car is given a unique `registration no` by the Registration Authority.

jan_prod: The registered `production year` is the same as the year in which the car was produced, except that cars produced in January may be registered as having been produced in the previous year.

Entity DESTROYED CAR

A `car` may be destroyed, in which case its date of destruction is recorded.

EXPRESS specification:

```
*)
ENTITY destroyed_car
  SUBTYPE OF (car);
  destroyed_on : date;
WHERE
  dates_ok : days_between(production_date, destroyed_on) >= 0;
END_ENTITY;
(*
```

Attribute definitions:

destroyed_on: The date on which the `car` was destroyed.

Propositions:

dates_ok: A `car` cannot be destroyed before it has been made.

Entity CAR MODEL

A particular type of `car`.

EXPRESS specification:

```
*)
ENTITY car_model;
  called      : name;
  made_by     : manufacturer;
  consumption : fuel_consumption;
UNIQUE
  un1 : called;
END_ENTITY;
(*
```

Attribute definitions:

called: The name of the model.
made_by: The manufacturer of the model.
consumption: The average fuel consumption of all cars of this model type.

Propositions:

un1: Each car model has a distinct name.

Entity OWNER

An owner of a car. Owners are categorized into named owner and group.

EXPRESS specification:

```
*)
ENTITY owner
  ABSTRACT SUPERTYPE OF (ONEOF(named_owner,
                               group));
END_ENTITY;
(*
```

Entity NAMED OWNER

An owner who has a name. These are categorized into manufacturer, garage and person.

EXPRESS specification:

```
*)
ENTITY named_owner
  ABSTRACT SUPERTYPE OF (ONEOF(manufacturer,
                               garage,
                               person))
  SUBTYPE OF (owner);
  called : name;
UNIQUE
  un1 : called;
END_ENTITY;
(*
```

Attribute definitions:

called: The name of the owner.

Propositions:

un1: Owner's names are unique.

Entity MANUFACTURER

A type of named car owner. Manufacturers may also manufacture cars.

EXPRESS specification:

```
*)
ENTITY manufacturer
  SUBTYPE OF (named_owner);
END_ENTITY;
(*
```

Entity GARAGE

A type of named car owner.

EXPRESS specification:

```
*)
ENTITY garage
  SUBTYPE OF (named_owner);
DERIVE
  no_of_mnfs : INTEGER := dealer_for_mnfs(SELF);
WHERE
  wr1 : {1 <= no_of_mnfs <= 3};
END_ENTITY;
(*
```

Attribute definitions:

no_of_mnfs: The number of different manufacturers of the cars owned by
the **garage**.

Propositions:

wr1: At any particular time, a **garage** shall not own cars made by more
than three manufacturers.

Entity PERSON

A type of named car owner.

EXPRESS specification:

```
*)
ENTITY person
  SUBTYPE OF (named_owner);
END_ENTITY;
(*
```

Entity GROUP

A type of car owner consisting of a group of people.

EXPRESS specification:

```
*)
ENTITY group
  SUBTYPE OF (owner);
  members : SET [1:?] OF person;
END_ENTITY;
(*
```

Attribute definitions:

members: The people who form the **group**.

A.4.3   Function and procedure definitions

Function DEALER FOR MNFS

This function calculates the total number of distinct manufacturers of cars owned by a **garage**.

Parameters:

dealer: An instance of a **garage**.

RESULT: The number of distinct manufacturers of the cars owned by the **garage**.

EXPRESS specification:

```
*)
FUNCTION dealer_for_mnfs(dealer : garage) : INTEGER;
  LOCAL
    cars : SET OF car := [];
    transfers : SET OF transfer := [];
    makers : SET OF manufacturer := [];
  END_LOCAL;
  transfers := USEDIN(dealer, 'TRANSFER.NEW');
  REPEAT i := 1 TO SIZEOF(transfers);
    cars := cars + transfers[i].item;
  END_REPEAT;
  transfers := USEDIN(dealer, 'TRANSFER.PRIOR');
  REPEAT i := 1 TO SIZEOF(transfers);
    cars := cars - transfers[i].item;
  END_REPEAT;
  REPEAT i := 1 TO SIZEOF(cars);
```

```
      makers := makers + cars[i].model_type.made_by;
    END_REPEAT;
    RETURN (SIZEOF(makers));
  END_FUNCTION;
  (*
```

Function MNFG AVERAGE CONSUMPTION

This function calculates the average fuel consumption in a given year of all
the cars made by a particular manufacturer.

Parameters:

mnfg: A manufacturer.

when: An INTEGER representing a particular year.

RESULT: A REAL giving the average fuel consumption of the manufacturer's cars during a particular year.

EXPRESS specification:

```
  *)
  FUNCTION mnfg_average_consumption(mnfg : manufacturer;
                                    when : INTEGER) : REAL;
    (* returns the average fuel consumption of the given
       manufacturer's cars produced in the given year *)
    LOCAL
      models : SET OF car_model := [];
      cars   : SET OF car := [];
      num    : INTEGER := 0;
      tot    : INTEGER := 0;
      fuel   : REAL := 0;
      result : REAL := 0.0;
    END_LOCAL;
      -- set of mnfg's models
    models := USEDIN(mnfg, 'MODEL.MADE_BY');
    REPEAT i := 1 TO SIZEOF(models);
      -- cars of particular model year
      cars := QUERY(temp <* USEDIN(models[i], 'CAR.MODEL_TYPE')
            | temp.production_year = when);
      num := SIZEOF(cars);
      fuel := fuel + num*models[i].consumption;
      tot := tot + num;
    END_REPEAT;
    IF tot > 0.0 THEN
      result := fuel/tot;
    END_IF;
    RETURN (result);
  END_FUNCTION;
```

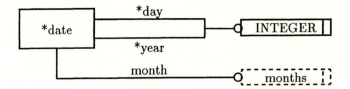
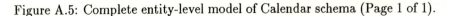

Figure A.5: Complete entity-level model of Calendar schema (Page 1 of 1).

```
(*
```

A.4.4 Entity classification structure

The following indented listing shows the entity classification structure. Entities in upper case characters are defined in this schema. Entities in lower case characters are defined in other schemas.

```
CAR
     DESTROYED_CAR
CAR_MODEL
OWNER
     GROUP
     NAMED_OWNER
          GARAGE
          MANUFACTURER
          PERSON
TRANSFER

*)
END_SCHEMA;  -- end of support schema
(*
```

A.5 Calendar schema

This schema contains definitions related to dates and other calendrical items.

Figure A.5 is an EXPRESS-G model showing the contents of this schema.

EXPRESS specification:

```
*)
SCHEMA calendar;
(*
```

A.5.1   Type definitions

Type MONTHS

An enumeration of the months of the year. **January** is the first month in a year and **December** is the last month in a year.

EXPRESS specification:

```
*)
TYPE months = ENUMERATION OF
    (January,  February,  March,
     April,    May,       June,
     July,     August,    September,
     October,  November,  December);
END_TYPE;
(*
```

A.5.2   Entity definitions

Entity DATE

A date AD in the Gregorian calendar.

EXPRESS specification:

```
*)
ENTITY date;
   day   : INTEGER;
   month : months;
   year  : INTEGER;
WHERE
   days_ok : {1 <= day <= 31};
   year_ok : year > 0;
   date_ok : valid_date(SELF);
END_ENTITY;
(*
```

Attribute definitions:

day: The day of the month.

month: The month of the year

year: The year.

Propositions:

days_ok: The day shall be numbered between 1 and 31 inclusive.

year_ok: The year shall be greater than zero.

date_ok: The combination of **day**, **month** and **year** shall form a valid date, taking into account the differing numbers of days in particular months, and also the effect of leap years.

A.5.3 Function and procedure definitions

Function VALID DATE

This function checks a **date** for valid day, month, year combinations.

Parameters:

par: A **date**.

RESULT: A Boolean. TRUE if the **date** has a valid day, month, year combination, FALSE otherwise.

EXPRESS specification:

```
*)
FUNCTION valid_date (par : date) : BOOLEAN;
   (* returns FALSE if its input is not a valid date *)
   CASE par.month OF
      April     : RETURN (par.day <= 30);
      June      : RETURN (par.day <= 30);
      September : RETURN (par.day <= 30);
      November  : RETURN (par.day <= 30);
      February  : IF (leap_year(par.year)) THEN
                     RETURN (par.day <= 29);
                  ELSE
                     RETURN (par.day <= 28);
                  END_IF;
      OTHERWISE : RETURN (TRUE);
   END_CASE;
END_FUNCTION;
(*
```

Function LEAP YEAR

This function checks whether a given integer could represent a leap year.

Parameters:

year: An INTEGER.

RESULT: A Boolean. TRUE if **year** is a leap year, otherwise FALSE.

EXPRESS specification:

```
*)
```

```
FUNCTION leap_year(year : INTEGER) : BOOLEAN;
  (* returns TRUE if its input is a leap year *)
  IF ((((year MOD 4) = 0) AND ((year MOD 100) <> 0)) OR
      ((year MOD 400) = 0)) THEN
    RETURN (TRUE);
  ELSE
    RETURN (FALSE);
  END_IF;
END_FUNCTION;
(*
```

Function CURRENT DATE

This function returns the current date.

Parameters:

RESULT: The current date.

EXPRESS specification:

```
*)
FUNCTION current_date : date;
  (* This function returns the date when it is called.
     Typically, it will be implemented via a system provided
     procedure within the information base *)
END_FUNCTION;
(*
```

Function DAYS BETWEEN

This function returns the number of days between any two dates.

Parameters:

d1: A date.
d2: A date.
RESULT: An Integer. The number of days between the two input dates.
  If d1 is earlier than d2 a positive integer is returned; if d1 is later than
  d2 a negative integer is returned; otherwise zero is returned.

EXPRESS specification:

```
*)
FUNCTION days_between(d1, d2 : date) : INTEGER;
  (* returns the number of days between two input dates. If d1
     is earlier than d2, a positive number is returned. *)
END_FUNCTION;
(*
```

A.5.4 Entity classification structure

The following indented listing shows the entity classification structure. Entities in upper case characters are defined in this schema. Entities in lower case characters are defined in other schemas.

```
DATE

*)
END_SCHEMA; -- end of calendar schema
(*
```

Appendix B

Example model instance

Full of wise saws and modern instances.

As You Like It
William Shakespeare

This Appendix provides an example of an instance of the EXPRESS model in Appendix A. The EXPRESS-I model below represents the data of interest to the Registration Authority corresponding to the following facts.

Some of the car manufacturers with permission to operate are Ford, General Motors, Honda, and Volkswagen. The models made by Ford include the Escort, the Mustang and the Sierra. The Escort has a fuel consumption of 10 litres per 100 kilometres. Among others, Honda makes the Accord, Civic and CRX models. The fuel consumption of the CRX is 9 litres per 100 kilometres. GM constructs the Cavalier and the Impala models, as well as some others. Volkswagen makes the Rabbit which has a fuel consumption of 12 litres per 100 kilometres.

The history of a Rabbit, serial number 334482WX85, is as follows. It was constructed in 1985 and registered on 25 January 1985 with registration number NBG 341. On the same day it was supplied to Jones and Son garage. They sold it on 1 April 1985 to Mrs. Brown. On 5 May 1985 it was stolen by the Fox gang from outside her house and was wrecked.

The Ford Escort, serial number 85GPSE2710, was also built in 1985 and registered the same day as the Rabbit. It was given the registration number APU 231 and was transferred to Smith's garage who sold it to Mr. White on 17 April. Mr. White kept the car until 15 May 1988 when he sold it to Mr. Black. Unfortunately, Mr. Black's son wrecked the car on 27 June 1991.

Honda made a CRX, serial number 87BUB89163 in 1987 and registered it on 9 December 1987, at which time it was sent to Smith's garage. The registration number was 2BW 477. The car was sold on 20 December 1987 to Miss Green, who eventually sold it on 27 June 1991 to her neighbor Mr. Black.

Another CRX, serial number 88BUB31412, was made in 1988 and registered on 15 May 1988 with registration number MNS 478. It was transferred the same day to Jones and Son garage. They immediately sold it on the same day to Mr. White.

For 1990 the average fuel consumption was established as a maximum of 12 liters per 100 kilometers, while it has been changed to a maximum of 10 litres per 100 kilometers for 1991.

Given the above information, then the state of the model in December 1991 is given below.

B.1   The authority schema instance

The instances in this schema instance consist of the transfer `history` of those cars which are still relevent. Although four cars are described in the preamble above, only three are relevent, as Mrs. Brown's Rabbit was destroyed more than two years prior to the date of this snapshot of the information base. Also included are the authorized manufacturers and an instance of the `send_message` entity.

```
*)
MODEL dec_1991;

SCHEMA_DATA authority;

rapu231 = history{item --> @esc1;
            transfers --> (@tesc1_1, @tesc1_2, @tesc1_3);
            to_be_deleted; };

r2bw477 = history{item --> @crx1;
            transfers --> (@tcrx1_1, @tcex1_2, @tcrx1_3);
            to_be_deleted; };

rmns478 = history{item --> @crx2;
            transfers --> (@tcrx2_1, @tcrx2_2);
            to_be_deleted; };

ford_am  = authorized_manufacturer{SUBOF(@ford); };
gm_am    = authorized_manufacturer{SUBOF(@gm); };
honda_am = authorized_manufacturer{SUBOF(@honda); };
vw_am    = authorized_manufacturer{SUBOF(@vw); };

message_90 = send_message{max_consumption --> 12.0;
            year --> 1990;
            makers --> (@ford_am, @gm_am, @honda_am, @vw_am);
            excessives; };

END_SCHEMA_DATA;   -- end of authority data
(*
```

B.2   The support schema instance

The data in this schema instance is purely in support of the main `authority` schema instance.

The first set of instances are for the individual `transfers` which are used in the `history` records.

```
*)
SCHEMA_DATA support;

tesc1_1 = transfer{item --> @esc1;
            prior --> @ford;
            new --> @g_jones;
            on --> @d250185; };

tesc1_2 = transfer{item --> @esc1;
            prior --> @g_jones;
            new --> @p_white;
            on --> @d170485; };

tesc1_3 = transfer{item --> @esc1;
            prior --> @p_white;
            new --> @p_black;
            on --> @d150588; };

tcrx1_1 = transfer{item --> @crx1;
            prior --> @honda;
            new --> @g_smith;
            on --> @d091287; };

tcrx1_2 = transfer{item --> @crx1;
            prior --> @g_smith;
            new --> @p_green;
            on --> @d201287; };

tcrx1_3 = transfer{item --> @crx1;
            prior --> @p_green;
            new --> @p_black;
            on --> @d270691; };

tcrx2_1 = transfer{item --> @crx2;
            prior --> @honda;
            new --> @g_jones;
            on --> @d150588; };

tcrx2_2 = transfer{item --> @crx2;
            prior --> @g_jones;
            new --> @p_white;
            on --> @d150588; };
```

```
*)
```

The next set of instances are of the **cars** and **car_models** which are of
interest.

```
*)
esc1 = car{model_type --> @escort;
            mnfg_no --> '85GPSE2710';
            registration_no --> 'APU 231';
            production_date --> @d290185;
            production_year --> 1985;
            made_by;
            SUPOF(@dest_esc1); };

dest_esc1 = destroyed_car{SUBOF(@esc1);
            destroyed_on --> @d270691; };

crx1 = car{model_type --> @crx;
            mnfg_no --> '87BUB89163';
            registration_no --> '2BW 477';
            production_date --> @d091287;
            production_year --> 1987;
            made_by; };

crx2 = car{model_type --> @crx;
            mnfg_no --> '88BUB31412';
            registration_no --> 'MNS 478';
            production_date --> @d150588;
            production_year --> 1988;
            made_by; };

escort = car_model{called --> 'Escort';
            made_by --> @ford;
            consumption --> 10.0; };

crx = car_model{called --> 'CRX';
            made_by --> @honda;
            consumption --> 9.0; };
(*
```

The next set of instances are of the **owners** that are relevent to the
Registration Authority.

```
*)
owner0 = owner{SUPOF(@n_owner0);};
owner1 = owner{SUPOF(@n_owner1);};
owner2 = owner{SUPOF(@n_owner2);};
owner3 = owner{SUPOF(@n_owner3);};
owner4 = owner{SUPOF(@n_owner4);};
owner5 = owner{SUPOF(@n_owner5);};
owner6 = owner{SUPOF(@n_owner6);};
```

```
owner7 = owner{SUPOF(@n_owner7);};
owner8 = owner{SUPOF(@n_owner8);};

n_owner0 = named_owner{SUBOF(@owner0);
           called --> 'Volkswagen';
           SUPOF(@vw);};

n_owner1 = named_owner{SUBOF(@owner1);
           called --> 'Ford';
           SUPOF(@ford); };

n_owner2 = named_owner{SUBOF(@owner2);
           called --> 'General Motors';
           SUPOF(@gm); };

n_owner3 = named_owner{SUBOF(@owner3);
           called --> 'Honda';
           SUPOF(@honda); };

n_owner4 = named_owner{SUBOF(@owner4);
           called --> 'Jones and Son';
           SUPOF(@g_jones); };

n_owner5 = named_owner{SUBOF(@owner5);
           called --> 'Smith''s Garage';
           SUPOF(@g_smith); };

n_owner6 = named_owner{SUBOF(@owner6);
           called --> 'Mr. White';
           SUPOF(@p_white); };

n_owner7 = named_owner{SUBOF(@owner7);
           called --> 'Mr. Black';
           SUPOF(@p_black); };

n_owner8 = named_owner{SUBOF(@owner8);
           called --> 'Miss Green';
           SUPOF(@p_green); };

vw = manufacturer{SUBOF(@n_owner0);
           SUPOF(@vw_am); };

ford = manufacturer{SUBOF(@n_owner1);
           SUPOF(@ford_am); };

gm = manufacturer{SUBOF(@n_owner2);
           SUPOF(@gm_am); };

honda = manufacturer{SUBOF(@n_owner3);
```

```
                    SUPOF(@honda_am); };

g_jones = garage{SUBOF(@n_owner4);
            no_of_mnfs; };

g_smith = garage{SUBOF(@n_owner5);
            no_of_mnfs; };

p_white = person{SUBOF(@n_owner6); };

p_black = person{SUBOF(@n_owner7); };

p_green = person{SUBOF(@n_owner8); };

END_SCHEMA_DATA; -- end of support data
(*
```

B.3 The calendar schema instance

The entity instances in the `calendar` schema instance are limited to those dates which appear in the records of transfers maintained by the Registration Authority.

```
*)
SCHEMA_DATA calendar;

d250185 = date{day --> 25;
                month --> !January;
                year --> 1985; };

d170485 = date{day --> 17;
                month --> !April;
                year --> 1985; };

d091287 = date{day --> 9;
                month --> !December;
                year --> 1987; };

d201287 = date{day --> 20;
                month --> !December;
                year --> 1987; };

d150588 = date{day --> 15;
                month --> !May;
                year --> 1988; };

dd270691 = date{day --> 27;
                month --> !June;
```

```
          year --> 1991; };

END_SCHEMA_DATA;  -- end calendar data

END_MODEL;   -- end dec_1991 data
(*
```

Appendix C

Interpreting supertype relationships

> The whole is more than the sum of the parts.
>
> *Metaphysica*
> *Aristotle*

EXPRESS allows you to create relationships between supertypes and subtypes that are not possible with the run of the mill Object Oriented language which typically only provides for simple hierchies with a single root. EXPRESS allows multiple roots (inheritance) and overlap of the nodes in the lattice. These enhancements give you considerable power to model reality, and also to confuse yourself and others. The main questions that arise when these powerful features are used are:

1. Are the relationships well formed?

2. What are the permissible combinations of entity instance values?

To a large degree the first question is answered when we know the answer to the second one. However, even fairly simple situations can produce scores of legal combinations. Therefore, it is important to understand the concepts behind these relationships to avoid the rather tedious job of manually checking all possibilities.

Relationships between supertypes and subtypes are defined in terms of these four operators: `Abstract`, `AndOr`, `And` and `OneOf`. The `Abstract` operator acts upon a supertype and its subtypes as a group. The other three operators act on combinations of subtypes as a group.

Review

Remember that EXPRESS does not force a complete specification of subtypes in a supertype entity, but that if an entity is a subtype it has to mention all of its supertypes. Therefore, you can write something like this:

```
ENTITY super; ...
ENTITY sub1 SUBTYPE OF (super); ...
ENTITY sub2 SUBTYPE OF (super); ...
```

When nothing explicit is said in the supertype entity the meaning is that there is an **AndOr** relationship between its subtypes. Therefore, saying nothing is the same as saying:

```
ENTITY super SUPERTYPE OF (sub1 ANDOR sub2); ...
ENTITY sub1 SUBTYPE OF (super); ...
ENTITY sub2 SUBTYPE OF (super); ...
```

This 'defaulting' of the supertype expression is a handy way of allowing growth of the information models. For example, one schema might consist of 'stub' supertype entity declarations and others might contain the specific subtype declarations (this is, in fact, the way the STEP standard is put together). However, it is easy for people to overlook the fact that these relationships exist. But, as supertypes are being interpreted it is a serious mistake to forget about this kind of defaulting.

Notation

We will use the following notation to explain how these operators are used to construct valid relationships and to interpret permissible instance combinations. First, here is the syntax of the supertype expression, where the operators mentioned in the syntax are explained in Table C.1.

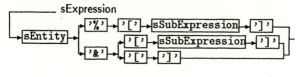

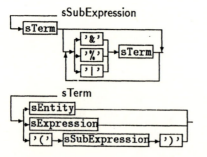

Upper case letters are used to represent an entity type. The subtypes of a supertype are represented as a list of entities enclosed by square brackets. Parentheses are used to factor sub-expressions where needed. Therefore, we might write

$$A \% [B|C|(D \% E)]$$

Table C.1: Supertype operators

&	**And** — the result is a combination of both operands. Given $A \& B$ the result is AB. The **And** relationship is commutative $(A \& B \equiv B \& A)$ and associative $(A \& (B \& C) \equiv (A \& B) \& C \equiv A \& B \& C)$.
%	**AndOr** — the result is one operand, or the other, or a combination of both. Given $A \% B$ the result is A, B or AB. The **AndOr** relationship is commutative $(A \% B \equiv B \% A)$ and associative $(A \% (B \% C) \equiv (A \% B) \% C \equiv A \% B \% C)$.
|	**OneOf** — the result is a selection, or choice, between the operands. When several operands are written in series, exactly one from that series is selected. Given $A|B|C$ the result is A, B or C.

Evaluating the supertype expression

The supertype expression is similar in appearance to a mathematical expression. The method of evaluation and the result produced is quite different however. The result is the expansion of the expression to an evaluated set $\{\ldots\}$ that contains all of the permutations possible for a given subexpression. To illustrate,

$$A \% (B|C)$$

produces this evaluated set:

$$\{A, B, C, AB, AC\}$$

It is often necessary during intermediate expansion to apply an operator to two evaluated sets or to an entity and an evaluated set as in

$$\{A, B\} \& \{C, D\}$$

in which case a cross product is produced (discarding any like combinations where $AC \equiv CA$). The case given earlier yields

$$\{AC, AD, BC, BD\}$$

Interpreting relationships

The relationship between a supertype and its subtypes (as a group) is abstract when the keyword **Abstract** appears in the supertype expression. Otherwise, this relationship is not abstract. The abstract relationship is written

$$A \& [\ldots]$$

because an abstract supertype is bound to its subtypes.

The non-abstract relationship is written

$$A \& [\ldots] + A$$

because a non-abstract supertype may or may not be bound to its subtypes.

Here are some simple illustrations of these cases:

$$A \& [B] \quad \rightarrow \quad \{AB\}$$
$$A \& [B] + A \quad \rightarrow \quad \{A, AB\}$$

The 'Supertype Of' phrase written as part of an entity declaration translates to the notation we use in a fairly straightforward way.

$$(\text{OneOf}(A,B,C)) \quad \rightarrow \quad [A, B, C]$$
$$(A \text{ AndOr } B \text{ AndOr } C) \quad \rightarrow \quad [A \% B \% C]$$
$$(A \text{ And } B \text{ And } C) \quad \rightarrow \quad [A \& B \& C]$$
$$(A \text{ And } B \text{ AndOr } C) \quad \rightarrow \quad [A \& B \% C]$$

Sometimes, however, this phrase is not complete or is missing entirely. In that case, the unannounced subtype entities are AndOr'ed to whatever expression is present as in:

```
ENTITY a SUPERTYPE OF (ONEOF(b,c)); ...
ENTITY b SUBTYPE OF (a); ...
ENTITY c SUBTYPE OF (a); ...
ENTITY x SUBTYPE OF (a); ...
ENTITY y SUBTYPE OF (a); ...
ENTITY z SUBTYPE OF (a); ...
```

This gives:

$$\ldots [(B|C) \% (X \% Y \% Z \% \ldots)]$$

since the default relationship is AndOr between the specified and unspecified parts as a group and between each entity within the unspecified part.

The process to evaluate the allowable combination of supertype and subtype instances is reasonably simple in most cases. It helps if the supertype tree is drawn out graphically, although this is not strictly necessary.

1. Construct the supertype expression for each supertype in the tree.

2. Starting at the root supertype, recursively replace each supertype appearing in the expression by its supertype expression.

3. Evaluate the resulting expression. Call this the result set.

4. As a final check, delete from the result set any combination of elements that includes entities that are in a OneOf relationship to each other.

Multiple roots

So far we have not touched on the problem of multiple roots (inheritance). When a subtype has two or more supertypes, the relationship is And (i.e., between the subtype and its supertypes). The following trickery is needed to deal with this condition. First of all, though, note that if there are multiply inheriting subtypes, then there may be multiple roots of the supertype tree.

In this case, apply steps 1 through 3 above to each root, and then add the resulting sets together to produce a combined result set.

For each multiply inheriting subtype in the result set, do the following:

1. For each of its immediate supertypes form the set of entity combinations from the result set that include the subtype and the supertype. Call these sets the supertype sets.

   For example, if M is a multiply inheriting subtype and the result set is

   $$\{AB, AM, CD, CM\}$$

   then the two supertype sets are: $\{AM\}$ and $\{CM\}$.

2. Combine the supertype sets using the & operator.

   Continuing the example, we get

   $$\{AM\} \& \{CM\} = \{ACM\}$$

3. Delete the supertype sets from the result set and add the combined supertype set to the result set.

   Completing the example, the result set finally is:

   $$\{AB, AM, CD, CM\} - \{AM, CM\} + \{ACM\} = \{AB, ACM, CD\}$$

After all the multiply inheriting subtypes have been processed, then perform the last step (4) of the original algorithm to eliminate any disallowed OneOf combinations from the result set.

Here is a case study to illustrate how this works. Let's start with an EXPRESS-G-like representation (except here we underline the abstract supertypes to save space) of a dual rooted system.

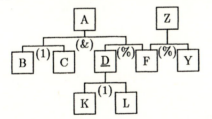

This corresponds to the following EXPRESS code:

```
ENTITY A SUPERTYPE OF (ONEOF(B,C) AND (D ANDOR F)); ...
ENTITY B SUBTYPE OF (A); ...
ENTITY C SUBTYPE OF (A); ...
ENTITY D ABSTRACT SUPERTYPE OF (ONEOF(K,L))
         SUBTYPE OF (A); ...
ENTITY F SUBTYPE OF (A,Z); ...
ENTITY K SUBTYPE OF (D); ...
ENTITY L SUBTYPE OF (D); ...
```

```
ENTITY Y SUBTYPE OF (Z); ...
ENTITY Z; ...
```

Here is a view from the other perspective (this is not official EXPRESS-G) to show how multiple supertype relationships are handled.

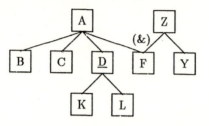

Starting with A we form the expressions:

$$A' = A \& [(B|C) \& (D \& [K|L] \% F)] + A$$
$$Z' = Z \& [F \% Y] + Z$$

(Z' is needed because F has multiple supertypes). The evaluated sets produced by these expressions are:

$$A'' = \{A, ABDFK, ABDFL, ABDK, ABDL,$$
$$ABF, ACDFK, ACDFL, ACDK, ACDL, ACF\}$$
$$Z'' = \{FYZ, FZ, YZ, Z\}$$

From these two sets we extract the elements that have the subtype F in common and $\&$ them together, giving

$$\{ABDFK, ABDFL, ABF, ACDFK, ACDFL, ACF\} \& \{FYZ, FZ\}$$
$$= \{ABDFKYZ, ABDFKZ, ABDFLYZ, ABDFLZ,$$
$$ABFYZ, ABFZ, ACDFKYZ, ACDFKZ,$$
$$ACDFLYZ, ACDFLZ, ACFYZ, ACFZ\}$$

We then subtract the supertype sets from the result set and add the combined supertype set to give a result set of 19 instance values:

$$R = \{A, ABDFKYZ, ABDFKZ, ABDFLYZ,$$
$$ABDFLZ, ABDK, ABDL, ABFYZ,$$
$$ABFZ, ACDFKYZ, ACDFKZ, ACDFLYZ,$$
$$ACDFLZ, ACDK, ACDL, ACFYZ,$$
$$ACFZ, YZ, Z\}$$

In this case there are no disallowed **OneOf** combinations in the result set, so we are finished.

However there are cases when the result set includes disallowed combinations as the next example shows. We start with the following EXPRESS code.

```
ENTITY A SUPERTYPE OF (ONEOF (B, C)); ....
ENTITY B SUBTYPE OF (A); ....
ENTITY C SUBTYPE OF (A); ....
ENTITY D SUBTYPE OF (B, C); ....
```

Starting with A we form the supertype expressions:

$$\begin{aligned} R &= A \,\&\, [(B \,\&\, [D] + B)|(C \,\&\, [D] + C)] + A \\ &= \{A, AB, AC, ABD, ACD\} \end{aligned}$$

For the multiply inheriting subtype D, the combined supertype set is

$$\{ABD\} \,\&\, \{ACD\} = \{ABCD\}$$

and hence the result set R becomes

$$\begin{aligned} R &= R - \{ABD, ACD\} + \{ABCD\} \\ &= \{A, AB, AC, ABCD\} \end{aligned}$$

As the final step we check whether any of the OneOf constraints have been violated. In this case B and C are in a OneOf relationship to each other, and hence any combination involving these must be deleted from the result set. Thus, we end up with only three legal instance values:

$$R = \{A, AB, AC\}$$

In other words, there can never be an instance of this complex entity which involves the D subtype.

Appendix D

Relationships and cardinality

> [Turgenieff] saw them subject to the chances, the complications of existence, and saw them vividly, but then had to find for them the right relations, those that would bring them out.

Prefaces. Portrait of a Lady
Henry James

The EXPRESS language does not support relationships in the same manner as, say an Entity-Relationship (ER) model, where entities and relationships are modeled by different constructs. In EXPRESS the declaration of an attribute in one entity whose domain is another entity explicitly defines a relationship between the two.

```
ENTITY first;
   ref  : second;
   attr : STRING;
END_ENTITY;

ENTITY second;
   sec_att : STRING;
END_ENTITY;
```

Thus, entities **first** and **second** are related through the role **ref**. The cardinality of **first** with respect to **second** in this case is [1:1] (i.e., every instance of **first** requires one instance of **second**). The default cardinality of **second** with respect to **first** is [0:?] (i.e., one instance of **second** may be used by zero or more instances of **first**).

The following is a set of recommendations for modeling relationships under various cardinality constraints in EXPRESS. The main rationale for these recommendations is to lead to stable information models and to support model integration. There may, of course, be very valid reasons for not

316

Table D.1: Cardinality constraint matrix

one two	[1 : 1]	[0 : 1]	[1 :?]	[0 :?]
[1 : 1]	1	5	9	13
[0 : 1]	2	6	10	14
[1 :?]	3	7	11	15
[0 :?]	4	8	12	16

following the recommendations; in this case, it is advisable to document them clearly as comments in the information model.

EXPRESS explicitly supports cardinalities of the form $[m : n]$, where $0 \leq m \leq n \leq \infty$. The ones of principal concern here are where m and n have the values 0, 1 and ∞ (which can be considered to be represented by the ? symbol in EXPRESS). Thus, altogether there are 16 cases to consider. These are detailed below. In each case described, an initial model is presented. This is created by firstly defining the entity called **one** with its cardinality defined with respect to the entity called **two**. Then the **two** entity is defined, using an `Inverse` attribute to represent its cardinality with respect to the entity **one**. In some cases the result could be better modeled, and this is also presented.

Table D.1 shows the cases considered below. The general principles underlying the recommendations are:

1. When the cardinality pairs are identical (i.e., along the matrix diagonal), the model should be symmetric.

2. If an entity has a [1:1] cardinality with respect to another (i.e., the first row and column of the matrix), then the other entity should be an attribute value of the first entity.

3. A cardinality that requires another entity takes precedence over one that does not (i.e., the third row and column).

4. The default inverse cardinality constraint (i.e., the last row and column of the matrix) should not be made explicit.

As a general remark, a reference between entities in EXPRESS is not a pointer (although in a information base it could be implemented as one). In particular, *an inverse attribute is not a pointer*; it is a cardinality constraint. Its presence in an entity, though, does have the side-effect of enabling access to the other entity.

D.1 Forward cardinality of [1:1]

In this section we consider the representation of the cardinality of an entity called **one** of [1:1] with respect to an entity called **two**. Figure D.1 shows the representations in EXPRESS-G. Representations in EXPRESS are given below.

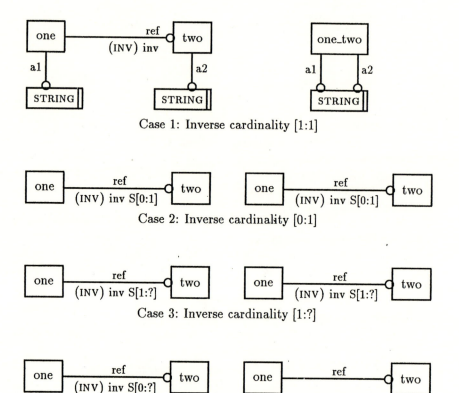

Case 1: Inverse cardinality [1:1]

Case 2: Inverse cardinality [0:1]

Case 3: Inverse cardinality [1:?]

Case 4: Inverse cardinality [0:?]

Figure D.1: EXPRESS-G representation of [1:1] cardinalities.

D.1.1   Inverse cardinality of [1:1]

This is Case 1 in Table D.1 where the cardinality of **two** with respect to **one** is [1:1].

Here an instance of one of the entities requires an instance of the other — they are in one-to-one correspondance. Merge the two entities into a single entity.

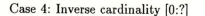

INITIAL

```
ENTITY one;
  ref : two;
  a1  : STRING;
END_ENTITY;
```

SUGGESTED

```
ENTITY one_two;
  a1 : STRING;
  a2 : STRING;
END_ENTITY;
```

```
ENTITY two;
  a2 : STRING;
INVERSE
  inv : one FOR ref;
END_ENTITY;
```

D.1.2   Inverse cardinality of [0:1]

This is Case 2 in Table D.1 where the cardinality of **two** with respect to
one is [0:1].

According to criteria 1 above, the entity that has a [1:1] cardinality with
respect to the other, takes the other as one of its explict attributes. In this
instance, nothing needs altering in the original model.

```
ENTITY one;
  ref : two;
  -- other attributes
END_ENTITY;

ENTITY two;
  -- other attributes
INVERSE
  inv : SET [0:1] OF one FOR ref;
END_ENTITY;
```

Note that this can also be modeled in the form below as a single uniqueness constraint has the effect of defining a [0:1] inverse cardinality constraint. For the sake of consistency in the general modeling style we prefer
the first model, although there is little to choose between them.

```
ENTITY one;
  ref : two;
  -- other attributes
UNIQUE
  un1 : ref;
END_ENTITY;

ENTITY two;
  -- other attributes
END_ENTITY;
```

D.1.3   Inverse cardinality of [1:?]

This is Case 3 in Table D.1 where the cardinality of **two** with respect to **one** is [1:?]. No alteration needs to be made to the original model.

```
ENTITY one;
  ref : two;
  -- other attributes
END_ENTITY;

ENTITY two;
  -- other attributes
INVERSE
  inv : SET [1:?] OF one FOR ref;
END_ENTITY;
```

D.1.4   Inverse cardinality of [0:?]

This is Case 4 in Table D.1 where the cardinality of **two** with respect to **one** is [0:?].

Here there is no need for specifying the [0:?] cardinality as this is the default constraint.

```
INITIAL                      SUGGESTED

ENTITY one;                  ENTITY one;
  ref : two;                   ref : two;
  -- other attributes          -- other attributes
END_ENTITY;                  END_ENTITY;

ENTITY two;                  ENTITY two;
  -- other attributes          -- other attributes
INVERSE                      END_ENTITY;
  inv : SET [0:?] OF
        one FOR ref;
END_ENTITY;
```

Specifying the inverse attribute within the entity **two** merely repeats the default cardinality constraint. However, it can be read as documenting an access need to all referencing instances of **one** from the referenced instances of **two**, although this is perilously close to violating the principle of implementation independence.

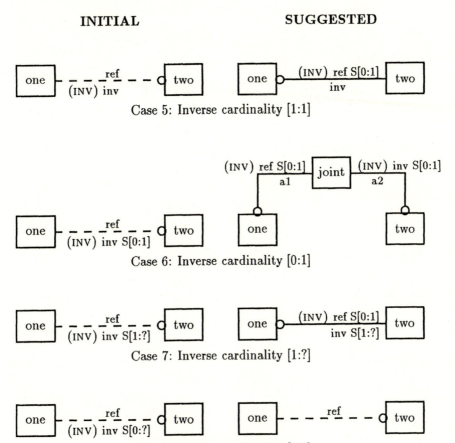

Figure D.2: EXPRESS-G representation of [0:1] cardinalities.

D.2 Forward cardinality of [0:1]

In this section we examine the cases where entity **two** is an optional valued attribute of entity **one**. Figure D.2 shows the EXPRESS-G representations of the four cases.

D.2.1 Inverse cardinality of [1:1]

This is Case 5 of Table D.1 where the cardinality of **two** with respect to **one** is [1:1]. It is the reverse of Case 2.

```
INITIAL                          SUGGESTED

ENTITY one;                      ENTITY one;
  ref : OPTIONAL two;              -- other attributes
  -- other attributes            INVERSE
END_ENTITY;                        ref : SET [0:1] OF two FOR inv;
                                 END_ENTITY;
ENTITY two;
  -- other attributes;           ENTITY two;
INVERSE                            -- other attributes
  inv : one FOR ref;               inv : one;
END_ENTITY;                      END_ENTITY;
```

D.2.2   Inverse cardinality of [0:1]

This is Case 6 of Table D.1 where the cardinality of two with respect to one is [0:1].

Neither of the entities is existence dependent on the other. The relationship is symmetrical and there is no reason to prefer one entity to another. A new entity should be created to preserve the symmetry. This also enables an easy check to be made to determine if an instance of the relationship exists in an information base.

```
INITIAL                          SUGGESTED

ENTITY one;                      ENTITY one;
  ref : OPTIONAL two;              -- other attributes
  -- other attributes            INVERSE
END_ENTITY;                        ref : SET [0:1] OF joint FOR a1;
                                 END_ENTITY;
ENTITY two;
  -- other attributes            ENTITY two;
INVERSE                            -- other attributes
  inv : SET [0:1] OF             INVERSE
        one FOR ref;               inv : SET [0:1] OF joint FOR a2;
END_ENTITY;                      END_ENTITY;

                                 ENTITY joint;
                                   a1 : one;
                                   a2 : two;
                                 END_ENTITY;
```

D.2.3 Inverse cardinality of [1:?]

This is Case 7 of Table D.1 where the cardinality of **two** with respect to **one** is [1:?].

According to the principle given in 3 above, an entity that requires another entity for its completion takes precedence over one that does not.

```
INITIAL                        SUGGESTED

ENTITY one;                    ENTITY one;
  ref : OPTIONAL two;            -- other attributes
  -- other attributes          INVERSE
END_ENTITY;                      ref : SET [0:?] OF two FOR inv;
                               END_ENTITY;

ENTITY two;
  -- other attributes
INVERSE                        ENTITY two
  inv : SET [1:?] OF             -- other attributes
        one FOR ref;            inv : SET [1:?] OF one;
END_ENTITY;                    END_ENTITY;
```

D.2.4 Inverse cardinality of [0:?]

This is Case 8 in Table D.1 where the cardinality of **two** with respect to **one** is [0:?].

```
INITIAL                        SUGGESTED

ENTITY one;                    ENTITY one;
  ref : OPTIONAL two;            ref : OPTIONAL two;
  -- other attributes;          -- other attributes
END_ENTITY;                    END_ENTITY;

ENTITY two;                    ENTITY two;
  -- other attributes            -- other attributes
INVERSE                        END_ENTITY;
  inv : SET [0:?] OF
        one FOR ref;
END_ENTITY;
```

The situation here is akin to that in Case 6 as neither **one** nor **two** are existence dependent on each other. Consequently, like Case 6, the relationship could be modeled as an entity on its own, to allow an easy check on whether a (instance) relationship exists or not.

INITIAL   **SUGGESTED**

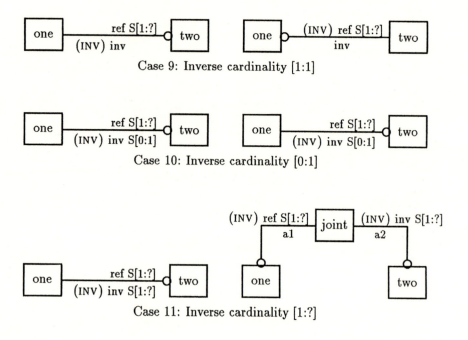

Case 9: Inverse cardinality [1:1]

Case 10: Inverse cardinality [0:1]

Case 11: Inverse cardinality [1:?]

Case 12: Inverse cardinality [0:?]

Figure D.3: EXPRESS-G representation of [1:?] cardinalities.

D.3   Forward cardinality of [1:?]

This Section discusses the cases where the cardinality of **one** with respect to **two** is [1:?]. EXPRESS-G representations are given in Figure D.3.

D.3.1   Inverse cardinality of [1:1]

This is Case 9 of Table D.1 where the cardinality of **two** with respect to **one** is [1:1] and is the reverse of Case 3.

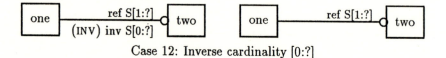

INITIAL   SUGGESTED

ENTITY one;   ENTITY one;
  ref : SET [1:?] OF two;   -- other attributes

```
   -- other attributes            INVERSE
END_ENTITY;                          ref : SET [1:?] OF two FOR inv;
                                  END_ENTITY;
ENTITY two;
   -- other attributes            ENTITY two;
INVERSE                              -- other attributes
   inv : one FOR ref;                inv : one;
END_ENTITY;                       END_ENTITY;
```

D.3.2 Inverse cardinality of [0:1]

This is Case 10 in Table D.1 where the cardinality of **two** with respect to **one** is [0:1]. It is the reverse of Case 7. The original model needs no alteration.

```
ENTITY one;
   ref : SET [1:?] OF two;
   -- other attributes
END_ENTITY;

ENTITY two;
   -- other attributes
INVERSE
   inv : SET [0:1] OF one FOR ref;
END_ENTITY;
```

D.3.3 Inverse cardinality of [1:?]

This is Case 11 in Table D.1 where the cardinality of **two** with respect to **one** is [1:?]. This is another example of symmetry between the participating entities.

```
INITIAL                            SUGGESTED

ENTITY one;                        ENTITY one;
   ref : SET [1:?] OF two;            -- other attributes
   -- other attributes            INVERSE
END_ENTITY;                          inv : SET [1:?] OF joint FOR a1;
                                  END_ENTITY;
ENTITY two;
   -- other attributes            ENTITY two;
INVERSE                              -- other attributes
   inv : SET [1:?] OF one FOR ref; INVERSE
         one FOR ref;                inv : SET [1:?] OF joint FOR a2;
END_ENTITY;                       END_ENTITY;
```

```
ENTITY joint;
  a1 : one;
  a2 : two;
END_ENTITY;
```

D.3.4   Inverse cardinality of [0:?]

This is Case 12 in Table D.1 where the cardinality of **two** with respect to
one is [0:?].

INITIAL	SUGGESTED
| ```
ENTITY one;
  ref : SET [1:?] OF two;
  -- other attributes
END_ENTITY;

ENTITY two;
  -- other attributes
INVERSE
  inv : SET [0:?] OF
        one FOR ref;
END_ENTITY;
``` | ```
ENTITY one;
  ref : SET [1:?] OF two;
  -- other attributes
END_ENTITY;;

ENTITY two;
  -- other attributes
END_ENTITY;
``` |

D.4   Forward cardinality of [[0:?]

This Section describes the cases where the cardinality of **one** with respect
to **two** is [0:?]. EXPRESS-G representations are displayed in Figure D.4.

D.4.1   Inverse cardinality of [1:1]

This is Case 13 in Table D.1 where the cardinality of **two** with respect to
one is [1:1]. This is the reverse of Case 4.

INITIAL	SUGGESTED
| ```
ENTITY one;
  ref : SET [0:?] OF two;
  -- other attributes
END_ENTITY;

ENTITY two;
  -- other attributes
``` | ```
ENTITY one;
  -- other attributes
END_ENTITY;

ENTITY two;
  -- other attributes
``` |

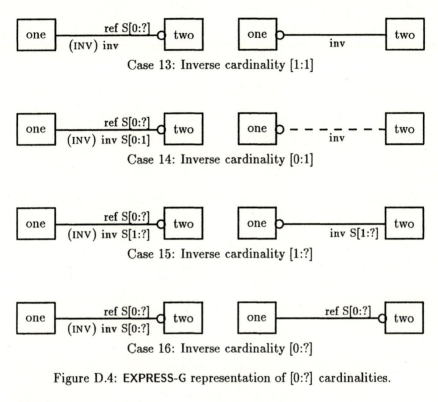

INITIAL   **SUGGESTED**

Case 13: Inverse cardinality [1:1]

Case 14: Inverse cardinality [0:1]

Case 15: Inverse cardinality [1:?]

Case 16: Inverse cardinality [0:?]

Figure D.4: EXPRESS-G representation of [0:?] cardinalities.

```
INVERSE                         inv : one;
  inv : one FOR ref;            END_ENTITY;
END_ENTITY;
```

D.4.2   Inverse cardinality of [0:1]

This is Case 14 in Table D.1 where the cardinality of **two** with respect to
one is [0:1]. This is the reverse to Case 8.

INITIAL   SUGGESTED

```
ENTITY one;                     ENTITY one;
  ref : SET [0:?] OF two;          -- other attributes
  -- other attributes          END_ENTITY;
END_ENTITY;
```

```
ENTITY two;                      ENTITY two;
  -- other attributes              -- other attributes
INVERSE                            inv : OPTIONAL one;
  inv : SET [0:1] OF             END_ENTITY
        one FOR ref;
END_ENTITY;
```

D.4.3   Inverse cardinality of [1:?]

This is Case 15 in Table D.1 where the cardinality of **two** with respect to **one** is [1:?]. This is the reverse to Case 12.

INITIAL   SUGGESTED

```
ENTITY one;                      ENTITY one;
  ref : SET [0:?] OF two;          -- other attributes
  -- other attributes            END_ENTITY;
END_ENTITY;

ENTITY two;                      ENTITY two;
  -- other attributes              -- other attributes
INVERSE                            inv : SET [1:?] OF one;
  inv : SET [1:?] OF             END_ENTITY;
        one FOR ref;
END_ENTITY;
```

D.4.4   Inverse cardinality of [0:?]

This is Case 16 in Table D.1 where the cardinality of **two** with respect to **one** is [0:?].

Although this is a further example of a symmetric relationship, we do not treat it as such. Applying the principle that [0:?] inverse cardinalities are not indicated within an EXPRESS model, then utilising an extra entity to hold the relationship, like Cases 6 and 11, adds nothing to the EXPRESS reader. We therefore leave it up to the modeler as to how he wishes to represent this relationship, although we prefer the following (or its reverse).

INITIAL   SUGGESTED

```
ENTITY one;                      ENTITY one;
  ref : SET [0:?] OF two;          ref : SET [0:?] OF two;
  -- other attributes              -- other attributes
END_ENTITY;                      END_ENTITY;
```

```
ENTITY two;                          ENTITY two;
  -- other attributes                  -- other attributes
INVERSE                              END_ENTITY;
  inv : SET [0:?] OF
        one FOR ref;
END_ENTITY;
```

Appendix E

An EXPRESS Meta-model

Look to the essence of a thing, whether it be a point of doctrine, of practice, or of interpretation.

Meditations
Marcus Aurelius Antonius

This Appendix describes a meta-model of the EXPRESS language defined using EXPRESS itself. It is intended to give a different view of the language than that which is provided by the formal specification and to act as an extended example of an EXPRESS rendition of a universe of discourse. Note that the model is documented using an embedded style, but the style differs a little from that presented in Appendix A.

The names used in this presentation are similar to the syntax productions of the language, but sameness is not possible since EXPRESS names cannot be used as declaration names. The language constructs do not have a one-to-one correspondence to the meta-model, but the accompanying narrative should help to sort things out.

The meta-model has two pieces. The metaEXPRESS schema is the focal point. It references materials declared within the Support schema. The hierarchy of existence dependence (i.e., nothing in the support schema can exist except in support of the main schema) is established by referencing (as opposed to using) those supporting declarations.

E.1 Scope

EXPRESS can be considered to consist of two language subsets. One of these describes the structure of an information model. The other is a procedural language that may be used to define complex constraints. The scope of this meta-model is limited to the structural aspects of the language. Since the procedural aspects of the language are out of scope, expressions and statements have entity representations, but they are empty.

The type system is not fully elaborated in this meta-model. In particular, the way in which numbers, strings and so forth are represented is left out. It is possible to do such a thing, but it is a lot of work and all that extra work adds nothing to what this meta-model is intended to convey.

E.2   The metaEXPRESS Schema

The entire `metaEXPRESS` schema is shown below. It has one explicit declaration, `MetaSCHEMA`, and references to things declared in the support schema. All of the other material needed for the meta-model is obtained via implicit references.

```
*)
SCHEMA metaEXPRESS;

    REFERENCE FROM Support
      (Import,
      Declaration,
      NamesUnique,
      NameList);

    ENTITY metaSCHEMA;
      References : SET OF Import;
      Uses       : SET OF Import;
      Owns       : SET OF Declaration;
    WHERE
    InScope : NamesUnique(NameList(Owns)
      + NameList(Uses)
      + NameList(References));
    END_ENTITY;

    END_SCHEMA; -- end of metaEXPRESS
    (*
```

The metaSCHEMA Entity

The `metaSCHEMA` entity assembles a collection of declarations, including any imported via a use or reference interface. Each of the declarations in the schema will have a unique identification, or name.

The things declared within the schema (i.e., `Owns`) plus the things imported via a use interface (i.e., `Uses`) are owned by the schema. Things imported vis a reference interface may be mentioned, but they are not owned. In effect, things not owned cannot exist independently. That is, they cannot exist unless they are used to support one of the owned things.

```
ENTITY metaSCHEMA;
  References : SET OF Import;
  Uses      : SET OF Import;
  Owns      : SET OF Declaration;
WHERE
  InScope : NamesUnique(NameList(Owns)
    + NameList(Uses)
    + NameList(References));
END_ENTITY;
```

Attributes:

References : SET OF Import (Explicit)

This is the collection of declarations taken from another schema. These declarations may be mentioned by name, but they are not considered part of the schema into which they are imported.

Uses : SET OF Import (Explicit)

This is the collection of declarations taken from another schema. These declarations may be mentioned by name, and they are considered part of the schema into which they are imported.

Owns : SET OF Declaration (Explicit)

These are the declarations made directly within the schema.

Propositions:

InScope : The names of the declaration made in this schema, plus any declarations imported via use or reference interfaces, will be unique.

E.3 Support Schema

The Support schema contains everything needed to flesh out the meta-model of EXPRESS.

```
*)
SCHEMA Support;

  REFERENCE FROM metaEXPRESS
    (metaSCHEMA);
(*
```

The GlueItem Type

A GlueItem type selects between a Glue and a metaENTITY.

```
*)
TYPE GlueItem = SELECT(Glue, metaENTITY);
END_TYPE;
(*
```

The ListOfNames Type

A `ListOfNames` type represents a list of names.

```
*)
TYPE ListOfNames = LIST OF ExpressName;
END_TYPE;
(*
```

The ExpressName Type

An `ExpressName` is a character string which conforms to the EXPRESS rules for forming an identifier.

```
*)
TYPE ExpressName = STRING;
WHERE
  Conforms : ParseOK(SELF);
END_TYPE;
(*
```

The CharSet Type

The `CharSet` is the set of characters that can be used in forming an EXPRESS string value.

```
*)
TYPE CharSet = SET OF STRING (1) FIXED;
END_TYPE;
(*
```

The Declaration Entity

A `Declaration` is one of the things created directly within a schema, namely a constant, type, entity, rule, function or procedure. Each declaration has a name which conforms to the EXPRESS rules.

```
*)
ENTITY Declaration
    ABSTRACT SUPERTYPE OF (OneOf(
        metaCONSTANT,
        metaTYPE,
        metaENTITY,
        metaRULE,
        metaFUNCTION,
        metaPROCEDURE));
  Name : ExpressName;
END_ENTITY;
(*
```

Attributes:

Name : ExpressName (Explicit)
    This is the name given to a declaration.

The metaCONSTANT Entity

A `metaCONSTANT` is a (named) value which never changes.

```
*)
ENTITY metaCONSTANT
    SUBTYPE OF (Declaration);
  Representation : Expression;
END_ENTITY;
(*
```

Attributes:

Representation : Expression (Explicit)
    A constant has a value given by this expression.

Propositions:

(Informal) Once a constant has been given a value, it is illegal to use it
    in any situation that will, or has the potential to, alter that initial
    value.

The metaTYPE Entity

A `metaTYPE` defines the characteristics and domain of values. There are two
main subtypes: standard types and author created types. The standard
types are predeclared by EXPRESS. Author created types are built on top
of standard types.

```
*)
ENTITY metaTYPE
    ABSTRACT SUPERTYPE OF (OneOf(
        AuthorType,
        StandardType))
    SUBTYPE OF (Declaration);
END_ENTITY;
(*
```

The AuthorTYPE Entity

An `AuthorTYPE` is one created by the author of a schema, not a type predeclared by EXPRESS.

```
*)
ENTITY AuthorTYPE
    SUBTYPE OF (metaTYPE);
  Representation : metaType;
  Constraint     : SET OF DomainRule;
END_ENTITY;
(*
```

Attributes:

Representation : metaType (Explicit)
  The underlying representation of an author defined type is a `metaTYPE`.

Constraint : SET OF DomainRule (Explicit)
  These are any constraints on the domain of the underlying type.

The StandardType Entity

A `StandardType` is one of the types predeclared by EXPRESS.

```
*)
ENTITY StandardType
    ABSTRACT SUPERTYPE OF (OneOf(
      SimpleType,
      AggregateType,
      PseudoType,
      EnumerationType,
      SelectType))
    SUBTYPE OF (metaTYPE);
END_ENTITY;
(*
```

The SimpleType Entity

A `SimpleType` covers the most fundamental[1] data representations: numbers, strings and logicals. The underlying means of representation of these datatypes is considered *axiomatic*.

```
*)
ENTITY SimpleType
    ABSTRACT SUPERTYPE OF (OneOf(
      NumberType,
      StringType,
      LogicalType))
    SUBTYPE OF (StandardType);
END_ENTITY;
(*
```

---

[1] At least as fundamental as we care about. Bits are, indeed, more fundamental than these.

The NumberType Entity

A NumberType represents the set of all natural decimal numbers (negative, zero and positive; rational, irrational and whole). It does not include complex numbers.

```
*)
ENTITY NumberType
    SUPERTYPE OF (RealType)
    SUBTYPE OF (simpletype);
END_ENTITY;
(*
```

The RealType Entity

A RealType represents the subset of all natural decimal numbers which are rational or irrational numbers.

```
*)
ENTITY RealType
    SUPERTYPE OF (IntegerType)
    SUBTYPE OF (numbertype);
END_ENTITY;
(*
```

The IntegerType Entity

An IntegerType represents the subset of natural decimal numbers which are whole numbers.

```
*)
ENTITY IntegerType
    SUBTYPE OF (RealType);
END_ENTITY;
(*
```

The StringType Entity

A StringType represents a list of characters.

```
*)
ENTITY StringType
    SUPERTYPE OF (BinaryType)
    SUBTYPE OF (simpletype);
  Representation : LIST OF CharSet;
END_ENTITY;
(*
```

The BinaryType Entity

A BinaryType is a specialized string type which restricts the domain of characters to zero's and one's.

```
*)
ENTITY BinaryType
    SUBTYPE OF (StringType);
WHERE
  OnlyTwo : BinaryChars(SELF\StringType.Representation);
END_ENTITY;
(*
```

Propositions:

OnlyTwo : The domain of the character set is '0' and '1'.

The LogicalType Entity

A `LogicalType` represents these three logic states: **False, Unknown** and **True**.

```
*)
ENTITY LogicalType
    SUPERTYPE OF (BooleanType)
    SUBTYPE OF (simpletype);
END_ENTITY;
(*
```

The BooleanType Entity

A `BooleanType` is a specialization of logical type which excludes `Unknown` from its domain.

```
*)
ENTITY BooleanType
    SUBTYPE OF (LogicalType);
WHERE
  ExcludeUnknown : SELF <> Unknown;
END_ENTITY;
(*
```

Propositions:

ExcludeUnknown : Boolean excludes `Unknown` from its domain.

The AggregateType Entity

All `AggregateTypes` represent collections of values represented by its underlying type. The bounds (and therefore the size) is established by its bounds. Its subtypes have different behavior as explained in the following sections.

```
     *)
     ENTITY AggregateType
        ABSTRACT SUPERTYPE OF (OneOf(
          FixedAggregate,
          DynamicAggregate))
        SUBTYPE OF (StandardType);
      MinBound    : INTEGER;
      MaxBound    : INTEGER;
      Underneath : metaTYPE;
     END_ENTITY;
     (*
```

Attributes:

MinBound : INTEGER (Explicit)

　　The minimum, or lower, bound of an aggregate is given by this integer.

MaxBound : INTEGER (Explicit)

　　The maximum, or upper, bound of a aggregate is given by this integer.

Underneath : metaTYPE (Explicit)

　　The underlying type of the aggregate is this metaTYPE.

The FixedAggregate Entity

`FixedAggregates` have fixed lower and upper bounds. Each element in the aggregate has a value (null or otherwise) and the position occupied by a value presumably has meaning (although that meaning is not explicitly stated).

```
     *)
     ENTITY FixedAggregate
        ABSTRACT SUPERTYPE OF (ArrayType)
        SUBTYPE OF (AggregateType);
     WHERE
       BoundsNeeded  :
         Exists(MinBound) And Exists(MaxBound);
       BoundsOrdered :
         MinBound <= MaxBound;
     END_ENTITY;
     (*
```

Propositions:

BoundsNeeded : Fixed aggregates are required to give both bounds.

BoundsOrdered : The lower bound must not be greater than the upper bound.

The ArrayType Entity

An `ArrayType` is the only kind of fixed aggregate available in EXPRESS.

```
*)
ENTITY ArrayType
    SUBTYPE OF (FixedAggregate);
END_ENTITY;
(*
```

The DynamicAggregate Entity

DynamicAggregates have a fixed lower bound and a possibly open upper bound. The lower bound establishes the minimum number of values populating the aggregate; the upper bound establishes the maximum number of values populating the aggregate. There is no constraint on the size of the population when no upper bound is given. Each element in a dynamic aggregate has a non-null value. The position occupied by a value may or may not have meaning depending on the specific subtype (bag, list or set).

```
*)
ENTITY DynamicAggregate
    ABSTRACT SUPERTYPE OF (OneOf(
      BagType,
      ListType,
      SetType))
    SUBTYPE OF (AggregateType);
WHERE
  LoBoundNeeded : Exists(MinBound);
  LoBoundLimit  : MinBound >= 0;
  BoundsOrdered :
    (Exists(MaxBound)
      And
    (MinBound <= MaxBound))
      Or
    (Not Exists(MaxBound));
END_ENTITY;
(*
```

Propositions:

LoBoundNeeded : Dynamic aggregates require a lower bound. (The upper bound may be specified, but is not required.)

LoBoundLimit : The lower bound must be greater than or equal to zero.

BoundsOrdered : The lower bound must not be greater than the upper bound if an upper bound is given.

The BagType Entity

A BagType is a dynamic aggregate which allows duplicate value entries. The position of a particular value entry has no meaning, and when values are added to or removed from the aggregate, any given value might move anywhere (just like shaking marbles in a sack).

```
*)
ENTITY BagType
    SUBTYPE OF (DynamicAggregate);
END_ENTITY;
(*
```

The ListType Entity

A ListType is a dynamic aggregate. The position of every value entry is ordered (i.e., one value goes before or after another one). Values are inserted at a specific position and everything after it moves up one position. When values are removed the stuff after closes the gap.

```
*)
ENTITY ListType
    SUBTYPE OF (DynamicAggregate);
END_ENTITY;
(*
```

The SetType Entity

A SetType is a dynamic aggregate which does not allow duplicate value entries. The position of a particular value entry has no meaning, and when values are added to or removed from the aggregate, any given value might move anywhere (just like shaking marbles in a sack).

```
*)
ENTITY SetType
    SUBTYPE OF (DynamicAggregate);
END_ENTITY;
(*
```

The PseudoType Entity

A PseudoType is not really a type, but rather a template which accepts one of several specific types. Pseudotypes are only used in the context of the type of a formal parameter (of a function of procedure).

```
*)
ENTITY PseudoType
    ABSTRACT SUPERTYPE OF (OneOf(
      GenericType,
      AggregationType))
    SUBTYPE OF (StandardType);
  Label : OPTIONAL ExpressName;
END_ENTITY;
(*
```

Attributes:

Label : OPTIONAL ExpressName (Explicit)

Labels may be associated with pseudotypes to coordinate the types of actual parameters passed to a function or procedure. That is, when two formal parameters have the same label, then when one actual parameter is $TYPE_x$ the other one must be $TYPE_x$ also.

The GenericType Entity

A GenericType is a pseudotype used to indicate that any datatype will be acceptable as an actual parameter of a function or procedure.

```
*)
ENTITY GenericType
    SUBTYPE OF (pseudotype);
END_ENTITY;
(*
```

The AggregationType Entity

An AggregationType is a pseudotype used to indicate that any aggregate datatype is acceptable as an actual parameter of a function or procedure.

```
*)
ENTITY AggregationType
    SUBTYPE OF (pseudotype);
END_ENTITY;
(*
```

The EnumerationType Entity

An EnumerationType is a list of names which is its domain.

```
*)
ENTITY EnumerationType
    SUBTYPE OF (StandardType);
  Domain : LIST[1:?] OF UNIQUE STRING;
END_ENTITY;
(*
```

The SelectType Entity

A SelectType is an implicit supertype which allows a choice from a list of candidate types.

```
*)
ENTITY SelectType
    SUBTYPE OF (StandardType);
END_ENTITY;
(*
```

The metaENTITY Entity

A `metaENTITY` is a declaration which describes an object in terms of properties: attributes and constraints.

```
*)
ENTITY metaENTITY
    SUBTYPE OF (Declaration);
  Ancestors  : SET OF metaENTITY;
  Definition : SET OF Property;
  Offspring  : SET OF Glue;
WHERE
  InScope : NamesUnique(NameList(Definition));
END_ENTITY;
(*
```

Attributes:

Ancestors : SET OF metaENTITY (Explicit)
These are the ancestors, or supertypes, of this entity. Properties are inherited from these ancestors.

Definition : SET OF Property (Explicit)
These are the properties, attributes and constraints, used to define this entity.

Offspring : SET OF Glue (Explicit)
These are (indirectly) the subtypes of this entity. Glue shows how the subtypes are bound together.

Propositions:

InScope : All of the names known to an entity declaration must be unique.

The metaRULE Entity

A `metaRULE` defines a constraint on one or more populations of entities.

```
*)
ENTITY metaRULE
    SUBTYPE OF (Declaration);
  AppliesTo : SET OF metaENTITY;
  Variables : SET OF LocalVariable;
  Code      : LIST OF Statement;
  Goal      : SET OF DomainRule;
END_ENTITY;
(*
```

Attributes:

AppliesTo : SET OF metaENTITY (Explicit)
These are the entity populations this rule governs.

Variables : SET OF LocalVariable (Explicit)
These local variables may be used to reach the rule's goal.

Code : LIST OF Statement (Explicit)
These are any executable statements needed to reach the goal.

Goal : SET OF DomainRule (Explicit)
The goal of the rule is defined by these domain rules.

The metaFUNCTION Entity

A metaFUNCTION is an algorithm which returns a result value of a given type.

```
*)
ENTITY metaFUNCTION
    SUBTYPE OF (Declaration);
  ReturnType : metaTYPE;
  Variables  : SET OF Variable;
  Code       : LIST OF Statement;
  Returns    : Expression;
END_ENTITY;
(*
```

Attributes:

ReturnType : metaTYPE (Explicit)
This is the type returned by the function.

Variables : SET OF Variable (Explicit)
These local variables may be used to reach the rule's goal.

Code : LIST OF Statement (Explicit)
These are any executable statements needed to reach the goal.

Returns : Expression (Explicit)
This is the value returned by the function. It must be compatible with ReturnType.

The metaPROCEDURE Entity

A metaPROCEDURE is an algorithm which acts on its input parameters.

```
*)
ENTITY metaPROCEDURE
    SUBTYPE OF (Declaration);
  Variables : SET OF Variable;
  Code      : LIST OF Statement;
END_ENTITY;
(*
```

Attributes:

Variables : SET OF Variable (Explicit)
    These local variables may be used by the procedure.

Code : LIST OF Statement (Explicit)
    These are any executable statements needed by the procedure.

The Variable Entity

A Variable is a typed value which exists within the scope of a rule, function or procedure. Variables are parameters or local variables.

```
*)
ENTITY Variable
    ABSTRACT SUPERTYPE OF (OneOf(
        Parameter,
        LocalVariable));
    Name           : ExpressName;
    Representation : metaTYPE;
END_ENTITY;
(*
```

Attributes:

Name : ExpressName (Explicit)
    This is the name of the variable.

Representation : metaTYPE (Explicit)
    This is the type used to represent the value of the attribute.

The Parameter Entity

A Parameter is used to link an algorithm to potential callers.

```
*)
ENTITY Parameter
    ABSTRACT SUPERTYPE OF (OneOf(
        ConstantParameter,
        VariableParameter))
    SUBTYPE OF (Variable);
END_ENTITY;
(*
```

The ConstantParameter Entity

A ConstantParameter is a parameter which is treated by its function or procedure as a constant. That is, it will not tolerate attempts to change its value.

```
*)
ENTITY ConstantParameter
    SUBTYPE OF (Parameter);
END_ENTITY;
(*
```

The VariableParameter Entity

A `VariableParameter` is a parameter which is treated by its function or procedure as a variable.

```
*)
ENTITY VariableParameter
    SUBTYPE OF (Parameter);
END_ENTITY;
(*
```

The LocalVariable Entity

A `LocalVariable` is a variable of a function or procedure.

```
*)
ENTITY LocalVariable
    SUBTYPE OF (Variable);
  Initializer : OPTIONAL Expression;
END_ENTITY;
(*
```

Attributes:

Initializer : OPTIONAL Expression (Explicit)
This expression gives a value to a variable if it exists. Otherwise, the variable has a null value.

The Property Entity

A `Property` is (part of) the definition of an entity. Attribute properties describe material characteristics; constraint properties describe how domains of values are restricted.

```
*)
ENTITY Property
    ABSTRACT SUPERTYPE OF (OneOf(
        Attribute,
        Constraint));
END_ENTITY;
(*
```

The Attribute Entity

An `Attribute` is a material property of an entity.

```
   *)
   ENTITY Attribute
       ABSTRACT SUPERTYPE OF (OneOf(
          DerivedAttribute,
          ExplicitAttribute,
          InverseAttribute))
       SUBTYPE OF (Property);
     Name            : ExpressName;
     Representation : metaTYPE;
   END_ENTITY;
   (*
```

Attributes:

Name : ExpressName (Explicit)
> This is the name of the attribute.

Representation : metaTYPE (Explicit)
> This is the type of the value used to represent the attribute.

The DerivedAttribute Entity

A DerivedAttribute is an attribute which gets its value from an expression.

```
   *)
   ENTITY DerivedAttribute
       SUBTYPE OF (Attribute);
     Derivation : Expression;
   END_ENTITY;
   (*
```

Attributes:

Derivation : Expression (Explicit)
> This expression gives a value to a derived attribute.

The ExplicitAttribute Entity

An ExplicitAttribute is an attribute which gets its value from a persistent data store.

```
   *)
   ENTITY ExplicitAttribute
       ABSTRACT SUPERTYPE OF (OneOf(
          MandatoryValuedAttribute,
          OptionalValuedAttribute))
       SUBTYPE OF (Attribute);
   END_ENTITY;
   (*
```

The MandatoryValuedAttribute Entity

A `MandatoryValuedAttribute` is an explicit attribute which requires a non-null value.

```
*)
ENTITY MandatoryValuedAttribute
    SUBTYPE OF (ExplicitAttribute);
WHERE
  Mandatory : Exists(Representation);
END_ENTITY;
(*
```

Propositions:

Mandatory : Non-optional attribute values must have a non-null value.

The OptionalValuedAttribute Entity

An `OptionalValuedAttribute` is an explicit attribute which allows null as a value.

```
*)
ENTITY OptionalValuedAttribute
    SUBTYPE OF (ExplicitAttribute);
END_ENTITY;
(*
```

The InverseAttribute Entity

An `InverseAttribute` is an attribute whose value is the set of all entity values (instances) which use an entity value of the type (in which this attribute is declared) as an attribute value.

```
*)
ENTITY InverseAttribute
    SUBTYPE OF (Attribute);
  User    : metaENTITY;
  UserRole : ExpressName;
DERIVE
  ValueSet : SET OF metaValue :=
    UsedIn(SELF, User.Name + UserRole);
END_ENTITY;
(*
```

Attributes:

User : metaENTITY (Explicit)
    `Self` must be the type of an attribute in the scope of this entity.

UserRole : ExpressName (Explicit)
> This is the name of the specific attribute in `User` that has `Self` as its type.

ValueSet : SET OF metaValue (Derived)
> This contains the specific instances of the entities that use `Self` in the designated role.

The Constraint Entity

A `Constraint` is a property of an entity which restricts its value domain.

```
*)
ENTITY Constraint
    ABSTRACT SUPERTYPE OF (OneOf(
      UniqueRule,
      DomainRule))
    SUBTYPE OF (Property);
  Label : OPTIONAL ExpressName;
END_ENTITY;
(*
```

Attributes:

Label : OPTIONAL ExpressName (Explicit)
> A label is similar to an attribute name, but a value for it is not mandatory.

The UniqueRule Entity

A `UniqueRule` is a constraint which requires that, in a population of entity values, the specified attribute values are unique.

```
*)
ENTITY UniqueRule
    SUBTYPE OF (Constraint);
  UniqueItems : SET OF Attribute;
END_ENTITY;
(*
```

Attributes:

UniqueItems : SET OF Attribute (Explicit)
> The values of the attributes named in this set are examined across the population of entities in which they appear. Duplication of values is illegal when this rule is in force.

The DomainRule Entity

A `DomainRule` is a constraint which controls the domain of a value in the scope of an entity value or rule.

```
*)
ENTITY DomainRule
    SUBTYPE OF (Constraint);
  Domain : Expression;
END_ENTITY;
(*
```

Attributes:

Domain : Expression (Explicit)
This expression (which must produce a logical or boolean type) determines whether or not the domain restriction is satisfied.

The Import Entity

An `Import` entity identifies declarations made within a specific schema which are to be imported into another schema.

```
*)
ENTITY Import;
   Source    : metaSCHEMA;
   Foreigners : SET OF ImportedItem;
END_ENTITY;
(*
```

Attributes:

Source : metaSCHEMA (Explicit)
This is the schema from which something is imported.

Foreigners : SET OF ImportedItem (Explicit)
This is the collection of things imported from source.

The ImportedItem Entity

An `ImportedItem` is a declaration to be imported into a schema. It optionally has an alias. When the alias is present, the alias replaces the natural name in the scope of the importing schema.

```
*)
ENTITY ImportedItem;
  Item : Declaration;
  Aka  : OPTIONAL ExpressName;
END_ENTITY;
(*
```

Attributes:

Item : Declaration (Explicit)
    This thing is imported.

Aka : OPTIONAL ExpressName (Explicit)
    This name is substituted for the natural name in the importing scope
    if it exists. It acts as an alias.

The Glue Entity

Glue is what holds subtype entities together. That is, when an entity has
several subtypes, a specific kind of glue indicates how those subtypes behave.

```
*)
ENTITY Glue
    ABSTRACT SUPERTYPE OF (OneOf(
        AndGlue,
        AndOrGlue,
        OneOfGlue));
  LeftOperand  : GlueItem;
  RightOperand : GlueItem;
END_ENTITY;
(*
```

Attributes:

LeftOperand : GlueItem (Explicit)
    This is one of the two things held together by glue. It is either an
    entity or a glue (see GlueItem).

RightOperand : GlueItem (Explicit)
    This is the other thing held together by glue. It is either an entity or
    a glue (see GlueItem).

The AndGlue Entity

An AndGlue is a kind of glue means that both of the operands exist at the
same time.

```
*)
ENTITY AndGlue
    SUBTYPE OF (Glue);
END_ENTITY;
(*
```

The AndOrGlue Entity

An AndOrGlue is a kind of glue means that one or the other or both of the
operands exist at the same time.

```
*)
ENTITY AndOrGlue
    SUBTYPE OF (Glue);
END_ENTITY;
(*
```

The OneOfGlue Entity

A OneOfGlue is a kind of glue means that only one of the operands exist at the same time.

```
*)
ENTITY OneOfGlue
    SUBTYPE OF (Glue);
END_ENTITY;
(*
```

The Expression Entity

An Expression acts on values to produce a value result. Expressions are out of the scope of this presentation, so it is not elaborated here.

```
*)
ENTITY Expression;
END_ENTITY;
(*
```

The Statement Entity

A Statement performs some operation or activity (such as looping or testing values). Statements are out of the scope of this presentation, so it is not elaborated here.

```
*)
ENTITY Statement;
END_ENTITY;
(*
```

The metaValue Entity

A metaValue entity holds a value (or instance) of an entity, attribute, local variable, parameter or datatype. This entity is out of scope and therefore is presented as a stub only.

```
*)
ENTITY metaValue;
END_ENTITY;
(*
```

The BinaryChars Function

The BinaryChars function examines a list of characters and returns **True** if every character is a binary digit. Otherwise, it returns **False**.

```
*)
FUNCTION BinaryChars(Str : LIST OF CharSet)
  : Boolean;
  REPEAT i := 1 TO SizeOf(Str);
    IF ((Str[i] <> '0') AND
        (Str[i] <> '1')) THEN
      RETURN(False);
    END_IF;
  END_REPEAT;
  RETURN(True);
END_FUNCTION;
(*
```

Parameters:

Str : LIST OF Charset (Input)

The characters in this list are checked to determine if each is either a '0' or a '1'. If all characters are either zero or one, then **True** is returned. Any other character causes **False** to be returned.

The NamesUnique Function

The NamesUnique function examines a list of names and returns **True** if every name is unique. Otherwise, it returns **False**.

```
*)
FUNCTION NamesUnique(Names : ListOfNames)
  : Logical;

  LOCAL
    SetOfNames : SET OF ExpressName := [];
  END_LOCAL;
  REPEAT i := 1 TO SizeOf(Names);
    SetOfNames := SetOfNames + Names[i];
  END_REPEAT;
  RETURN(SizeOf(Names) = SizeOf(SetOfNames));
END_FUNCTION;
(*
```

Parameters:

Names : ListOfNames (Input)

The names in this list are checked for uniqueness. **True** is returned when every name is unique. Otherwise, **False** is returned.

The ParseOK Function

The ParseOK function looks at a name and returns True if it conforms to what EXPRESS expects for a name. Otherwise, it returns False.

```
*)
FUNCTION ParseOK(Name : ExpressName)
  : Logical;
END_FUNCTION;
(*
```

Parameters:

Name : ExpressName (Input)
> A value of a name is examined. If it conforms to the EXPRESS rules for forming an identifier, True is returned. Otherwise, False is returned.

The NameList Function

The NameList function examines what is in Container and returns the names of the things it finds there. For example, if Container was a schema, it would return the names of all the entities, constants, types, and other things declared in it.

```
*)
FUNCTION NameList(Container : Declaration)
  : ListOfNames;
END_FUNCTION;
(*
```

Parameters:

Container : Declaration (Input)
> This is a declaration which has other declarations inside it (such a metaSCHEMA).

```
*)
END_SCHEMA; -- end of Resource schema
(*
```

Appendix F

Resources

This appendix explains the standard resources of EXPRESS. Resources are constants, functions and procedures which are frequently needed when developing information models. These resources are static: Redeclaration of them is not allowed.

F.1 Standard constants

The numeric constants are assumed to have an infinite number of digits. This may or may not mean that they are exact values, but the effect should be close enough for most of us. Keep in mind, however, that most computer representations of these values will only have 6– 18 (or so) digits.

Constant E _____ Constant

`Const_E` is the number which is the base of natural logarithms (usually denoted by e). Its value contains an infinite number of digits the first few of which are 2.71828...

Indeterminate _____ Constant

The indeterminate symbol ? stands for an indeterminate value. This symbol may be used as the upper bound specification of a bag, list or set, or in an expression to indicate a null value.

Expressions and some EXPRESS functions (e.g., `HiBound`) can produce a null value indicated by ?.

False _____ Constant

`False` is a value of a boolean or logical datatype.

Pi _____ Constant

`Pi` is the familiar ratio between the circumference and the diameter of a circle. The first few digits of this number are 3.1415927..., but there are a lot more of them.

Self _____ Constant

`Self` stands for the current value and may be used within an entity declaration, type declaration or entity initialization.

True _____ Constant

`True` is a value of a boolean or logical datatype.

Unknown _____ Constant

`Unknown` is a value of a logical datatype. It is a logic state which is neither true nor false.

Note: *The difference between* `Unknown` *and* ? *may seem vague. It may seem odd, but if we have a logical variable whose value equals* `Unknown`, *then we know exactly what its value is — it is* `Unknown`! *However, if its value equals* ?, *then we do not know what its value is. In fact, it has no value,* `Unknown` *or otherwise.*

F.2   Standard functions and procedures

This section explains each function and procedure which is part of the EX-PRESS environment. The prototype for each of these standard algorithms shows the type of the formal parameters, and the returned result in the case of functions.

When conditions are noted, the input values are inspected before any attempt is made to act upon them. If the input values do not conform to the required conditions the result will be indeterminate (?).

Note: *ISO 10303: Part 11 does not explain this behavior.*

Abs _____ Function

```
Function Abs (V:NUMBER) : NUMBER;
```

The **Abs** function returns the absolute value of a number.

Parameters: **V** is a number (integer or real).

Result: The absolute value of **V**. The returned datatype is identical to the declared type of **V**.

Conditions: Exists(V)

ACos _____ Function

```
Function ACos (V:NUMBER) : REAL;
```

The **ACos** function returns the angle given a cosine value.

Parameters: **V** is a number which is the cosine of an angle.

Result: The angle in radians ($-\pi \leq result \leq \pi$) whose cosine is **V**.

Conditions: $-1.0 \leq V \leq 1.0$

Example F.1

Here are some of the trigonometric functions in use.

```
ACos ( 0.3 )              --> 1.266103...
ASin ( 0.3 )              --> 3.04692...e-1
ATan ( -5.5, 3.0 )        --> -1.071449...
Cos ( 0.5 )               --> 8.77582...E-1
Sin ( pi )                --> 0.0
Tan ( 0.0 )               --> 0.0
```

ASin _____ Function

```
Function ASin (V:NUMBER) : REAL;
```

The **ASin** function returns the angle given a sine value.

Parameters: **V** is a number which is the sine of an angle.

Result: The angle in radians ($-\pi \leq result \leq \pi$) whose sine is **V**.

Conditions: $-1.0 \leq V \leq 1.0$

ATan _____ Function

```
Function ATan (V1:NUMBER; V2:NUMBER) : REAL;
```

The **ATan** function returns the angle given a tangent value of V, where V is given by the expression $V = V1/V2$.

Parameters:

1. **V1** is a number.
2. **V2** is a number.

Result: The angle in radians ($-\pi \leq result \leq \pi$) whose tangent is V. If V2 is zero the result is $\pi/2$ or $-\pi/2$ depending on the sign of V1.

Conditions: V1 = V2 = 0 is not allowed.

BLength _____ Function

```
Function BLength (V:BINARY) : INTEGER;
```
The **BLength** function returns the number of bits in a binary value.

Parameters: V is a value of a binary type.

Result: The returned value is the number of bits in the binary value. When the binary is declared as fixed length the returned value is the declared length.

Example F.2

This shows how to get the length of a binary value.

```
LOCAL
  n : NUMBER;
  x : BINARY := %01010010 ;
END_LOCAL;
...
n := BLength ( x ); -- 8
```

Cos _____ Function

```
Function Cos (V:NUMBER) : REAL;
```
The **Cos** function returns the cosine of an angle.

Parameters: V is a number which is an angle in radians.

Result: The cosine of V ($-1.0 \leq result \leq 1.0$)

Exists _____ Function

```
Function Exists (V:GENERIC) : BOOLEAN;
```
The **Exists** function returns true if a value exists for the input parameter, false when its value is null. The **Exists** function is useful for checking if values have been assigned to optional valued attributes or if variables have been initialized.

Parameters: V is an expression which results in any type.

Result: True or False depending on whether V has a non-null or null value.

Example F.3

The exists function lets you find out if a variable has a value.

```
IF Exists ( a )  THEN ...
```

Exp ———————————————————— **Function**

```
Function Exp (V:NUMBER) : REAL;
```

The **Exp** function returns e (the base of the natural logarithm system) raised to the power **V**.

Parameters: **V** is a number.

Result: The value e^V.

Example F.4

The exp function

```
Exp ( 10 )  --> 2.202646...E+4
```

Format ———————————————————— **Function**

```
Function Format(N:NUMBER; F:STRING):STRING;
```

The **Format** returns a formatted string representation of a number.

Parameters:

1. **N** is a number (integer or real).
2. **F** is a string containing formatting commands. The formatting string contains special characters to indicate the appearance of the result.

Result: A string representation of **N** formatted according to **F**. The formatting string can be written in symbolic, picture or default form.

Symbolic format

The formatting string can give a symbolic description of the output representation. The general form of a symbolic format is:

`[sign]width[.decimals]type`

- One position is reserved for the sign. `[sign]` determines how the sign of the number is displayed. • When the sign specification is omitted, a space is displayed for zero and positive numbers and - is displayed for negative numbers. • When the sign specification is given as -, a space is displayed for zero and positive numbers and - is displayed for negative numbers (same as omitting the sign specification). • When the sign specification is given as +, a space is displayed for zero, + is displayed for positive numbers, - is displayed for negative numbers.

- `width` gives the size of the display excluding the character set aside for the sign. This is a positive integer number. If `width` has a preceding zero then the display will have preceding zeros; otherwise preceding zeros are suppressed.

- `decimals` gives the number of digits displayed to the right of the decimal point. This is written as a *period* followed by a non-negative integer number.

- `type` is a letter indicating the form of the number being displayed as shown next.

Type	Display
E	Exponential
F	Fixed point decimal
I	Integer

Some examples are given below to show how different formatting commands affect appearance.

Picture format

The formatting string can give a *picture* description of the output string. In the picture format, picture characters correspond to a character in the output display.

Picture Code		Represents
#	(hash mark)	Digit
,	(comma)	Digit Groups
.	(dot)	Decimal Point
+ -	(plus and minus)	Sign
( )	(parentheses)	Sign

Any other character is displayed without change.

Example F.5

Here are some examples of symbolic and picture formatting.

Symbolic Format			Picture Format		
Number	Format	Display	Number	Format	Display
10	+7I	+10	10	###	10
10	+07I	+0000010	-10	(###)	(10)
10	10.3E	1.0E+01	7123.456	###,###.##	7,123.46
123.456789	8.2F	123.46			
123.456789	8.2E	1.23E+02			
32.777	6I	33			

Default format

The formatting string can be empty, in which case the standard output representation is used. The standard representation for an integer number is '7I' and the standard representation for a real number is '10E'. See the description of symbolic representations above.

HiBound _____ Function

```
Function HiBound (V:AGGREGATE OF GENERIC) : INTEGER;
```

The **HiBound** function returns the declared upper index of an array or the declared upper bound of a bag, list or set.

Note: HiIndex *and* HiBound *produce identical results when called with an array as an actual parameter.*

Parameters: V is a variable of any aggregation type.

Result:

1. When V is an array the returned value is the declared upper index.

2. When V is a bag, list or set the returned value is the declared upper bound. If there is no declared upper bound, then ? is returned.

Example F.6

```
LOCAL
  a : ARRAY[-3:19] OF
        SET[2:4] OF LIST[0:?] OF
          INTEGER;
  h1, h2, h3 : INTEGER;
END_LOCAL;
  ...
  a[-3][1][1] := 2;        -- places a value in the list
  ...
  h1 := HiBound(a);        -- =19 (upper bound of array)
  h2 := HiBound(a[-3]);    -- = 4 (upper bound of set)
  h3 := HiBound(a[-3][1]); -- = ? (upper bound of list)
```

HiIndex ──────────────────────────── Function

`Function HiIndex (V:AGGREGATE OF GENERIC) : INTEGER;`

The **HiIndex** function returns the upper index of an array or the number of elements in a bag, list or set.

Note: HiIndex *and* HiBound *produce identical results when called with an array as an actual parameter.*

Parameters: V is a variable of any aggregation type.

Result:

1. When V is an array, the returned value is the declared upper index.

2. When V is a set, bag or list, the returned value is the actual number of elements.

Example F.7

```
LOCAL
  a          : ARRAY[-3:19] OF
                 SET[2:4] OF
                   LIST[0:?] OF INTEGER;
  h1, h2, h3 : INTEGER;
```

```
END_LOCAL;
a[-3][1][1] := 2;        -- places a value in the list
h1 := HiIndex(a);        -- =19 (upper bound of array)
h2 := HiIndex(a[-3]);    -- = 1 (size of set)
h3 := HiIndex(a[-3][1]); -- = 1 (size of list)
```

Insert _____ Procedure

```
Procedure Insert(VAR L:LIST OF GENERIC:G; E:GENERIC:G; P:INTEGER);
```

The **Insert** procedure inserts an element into a list.

Parameters:

1. L is a variable whose datatype is list.
2. E is a value compatible with the datatype of L.
3. P is an integer giving the position in L to insert E.

Result: L is modified by inserting E into L at the specified position. The insertion follows the existing element P, so when P=0 the element E becomes the first element.

Conditions: $0 \leq P \leq SizeOf(L)$

Length _____ Function

```
Function Length (V:STRING) : INTEGER;
```

The **Length** function returns the number of characters in a string.

Parameters: V is a variable of string type.

Result: The returned value is the number of characters in the string. When the string is declared as fixed length the returned value is the declared length.

Example F.8

```
LOCAL
  n : NUMBER;
  x : STRING;
END_LOCAL;
...
n := Length ( x );
```

LoBound _____ Function

```
Function LoBound (V:AGGREGATE OF GENERIC) : INTEGER;
```

The **LoBound** function returns the lower index of an array or the lower bound of a bag, list or set.

Parameters: V is a variable of any aggregation type.

Result:

1. When V is an array the returned value is the declared lower index.
2. When V is a bag, list or set, the returned value is the declared lower bound.

Example F.9

```
LOCAL
    a : ARRAY[-3:19] OF SET[2:4] OF LIST[0:?] OF INTEGER;
    h1, h2, h3 : INTEGER;
END_LOCAL;
...
h1 := LoBound(a);          -- =-3 (lower index of array)
h2 := LoBound(a[-3]);      -- =2 (lower bound of set)
h3 := LoBound(a[-3][1]);   -- =0 (lower bound of list)
```

Log — Log2 — Log10 _____ Function

```
Function Log (V:NUMBER) : REAL;
Function Log2 (V:NUMBER) : REAL;
Function Log10 (V:NUMBER) : REAL;
```

These functions return:

- **Log** returns the natural logarithm of a number.
- **Log2** returns the base two logarithm of a number.
- **Log10** returns the base ten logarithm of a number.

Parameters: V is a number (integer or real).

Result: A real number which is the logarithm of V. The base of the logarithm depends on which function is used.

Conditions: $V > 0$

Example F.10

Here are the log functions in action.

```
Log ( 4.5 )      --> 1.504077...E0
Log2 ( 8 )       --> 3.00...E0
Log10 ( 10 )     --> 1.00...E0
```

LoIndex _____ Function

```
Function LoIndex (V:AGGREGATE OF GENERIC) : INTEGER;
```

The **LoIndex** function returns the lower index of an aggregate.

Parameters: V is a variable of any aggregation type.

Result:

1. When V is an array the returned value is the declared lower index.
2. When V is a bag, list or set, the returned value is 1 (one).

Example F.11

```
LOCAL
a : ARRAY[-3:19] OF SET[2:4] OF LIST[0:?] OF INTEGER;
h1, h2, h3 : INTEGER;
END_LOCAL;
...
h1 := LoIndex(a);          -- =-3 (lower bound of array)
h2 := LoIndex(a[-3]);      -- =1  (for set)
h3 := LoIndex(a[-3][1]);   -- =1  (for list)
```

NVL _____ Function

```
Function NVL(V:GENERIC:GEN1;
SUBSTITUTE:GENERIC:GEN1):GENERIC:GEN1;
```

The **NVL** function returns either the input value or an alternate value in the case where the input value is null.

Parameters:

1. **V** is an expression which is of any type.

2. **SUBSTITUTE** is an expression which has a non-null value.

Result: When V has a non-null value, it is returned. Otherwise, SUBSTITUTE is returned.

Conditions: $Exists(Substitute)\ And\ (TypeOf(V) \equiv TypeOf(Substitute))$

Example F.12

```
ENTITY UnitVector;
   x, y : REAL;
   z    : OPTIONAL REAL;
WHERE
   x**2 + y**2 + NVL(z, 0.0)**2 = 1.0;
END_ENTITY;
```

The NVL function is used to supply zero (0.0) as the value of Z in cases where Z is *null*.

Odd _____ Function

```
Function Odd (V:INTEGER) : LOGICAL;
```

The **Odd** returns true or false depending on whether a number is odd or even.

Parameters: V is an integer number.

Result: When V is odd (...-3, -1, 1, 3, 5 ...) True is returned; otherwise False is returned.

Example F.13

```
Odd ( 121 )  --> TRUE
```

Remove ——————————————————— Procedure

`Procedure Remove(VAR L:LIST OF GENERIC; P:INTEGER);`

The **Remove** procedure removes an element from a list.

Parameters:

1. L is a variable whose datatype is list.

2. P is an integer giving the position of the element in L to be removed.

Result: L is modified by removing an element at the specified position P.

Conditions: $1 \leq P \leq SizeOf(L)$

RolesOf ——————————————————— Function

`Function RolesOf (V:GENERIC) : SET OF STRING;`

The **RolesOf** function returns a set of strings containing the fully qualified names of the users (i.e., any attribute whose datatype is) of the specified value.

Parameters: V is any value of any type.

Result: A set of string values (in upper case) containing the fully qualified names of the attributes whose datatype is the specified type.

When an entity or type is used or referenced then the original schema and the original name, if renamed, are also returned.

Example F.14

This example shows that a point might be used as the center of a circle. The RolesOf function determines what roles an entity value actually plays.

```
SCHEMA ThatSchema;

ENTITY Point;
  x, y, z : REAL;
END_ENTITY;

ENTITY Line;
  start,
  end : Point;
END_ENTITY;

END_SCHEMA;

SCHEMA ThisSchema;
```

```
USE FROM ThatSchema (Point, Line);

CONSTANT
  Origin : Point := Point(0.0, 0.0, 0.0);
END_CONSTANT;

ENTITY circle;
  center : Point;
  axis   : vector;
  radius : REAL;
END_ENTITY;
  ...
LOCAL
  p : Point := Point(1.0, 0.0, 0.0);
  c : circle := circle(p, vector(1, 1, 1), 1.0);
  l : Line := Line(p, Origin);
END_LOCAL;
  ...
IF 'ThisSchema.Circle.Center' IN RolesOf(p) THEN      -- true
  ...
IF 'ThisSchema.Line.Start' IN RolesOf(p) THEN         -- true
  ...
IF 'ThatSchema.Line.Start' IN RolesOf(p) THEN         -- true
  ...
IF 'ThisSchema.Line.End' IN RolesOf(p) THEN           -- false
```

Sin _____ Function

```
Function Sin (V:NUMBER) : REAL;
```

The Sin function returns the sine of an angle.

Parameters: V is a number (integer or real) which is an angle expressed in radians.

Result: The sine of V $(-1.0 \leq result \leq 1.0)$

SizeOf _____ Function

```
Function SizeOf (V:AGGREGATE OF GENERIC) : INTEGER;
```

The SizeOf function returns the number of elements in an aggregation.

Parameters: V is any aggregation.

Result: The returned value for an array is its declared number of elements (that is $n - m + 1$ for an array declared as ARRAY[M:N]). The returned value for a bag, list or set is the current number of elements.

Example F.15

```
LOCAL
  n : NUMBER;
  x : LIST[1:?] OF y;
END_LOCAL;
...
n := SIZEOF ( x );
```

Sqrt _____ Function

`Function Sqrt (V:NUMBER) : REAL;`

The `Sqrt` function returns the non-negative square root of a number.

Parameters: `V` is any non-negative number (integer or real).

Result: The non-negative square root of `V`.

Conditions: $V \geq 0$

Tan _____ Function

`Function Tan (V:NUMBER) : REAL;`

The `Tan` function returns the tangent of an angle.

Parameters: `V` is a number representing an angle expressed in radians.

Result: The tangent of the angle.

TypeOf _____ Function

`Function TypeOf (V:GENERIC) : SET OF STRING;`

The `TypeOf` function returns, in a set of strings, the names of the supertypes of `V`. Those names are qualified by the name of the schema in which the definition of the type was made. Types which are part of EXPRESS (i.e., binary, boolean, integer, logical, number, real, string, array, bag, list and set) will not have a schema name since they are not defined within a schema. The main use of this function is to find out whether or not two types are compatible.

Parameters: `V` is a variable of any type.

Result: The returned set of strings will contain the fully qualified names of the supertypes of `V`. Only upper case letters are used in those names. Neither the bounds nor the base type of aggregations is included in the result. If needed, that information can be determined by using the `TypeOf`, `LoBound` and `HiBound` functions.

Example F.16

In the context of the following schema

```
SCHEMA ThisSchema;
TYPE
  MyList = LIST [1 : 20] OF REAL;
END_TYPE;
...
1 : MyList;
...
END_SCHEMA;
```

the following conditions are true:

```
TypeOf (1)      = ['ThisSchema.MyList', 'LIST']
TypeOf (1[17]) = ['REAL', 'NUMBER']
```

The effects of Use or Reference are shown based on the previous one.

```
SCHEMA ThatSchema;
REFERENCE FROM ThisSchema (MyList AS HisList);
...
1 : HisList;
...
END_SCHEMA;
```

Now we can say:

```
TypeOf(1) = ['ThatSchema.HisList', 'ThisSchema.MyList', 'LIST']
```

UsedIn _____ Function

```
Function UsedIn (T:GENERIC; R:STRING) : SET OF GENERIC;
```

The UsedIn function returns each entity value that uses a specified value in a specified role. *This function pretends that there is an information base, populated with entity values.*

Parameters:

1. T is any value of any entity type.

2. R is a string that contains a fully qualified attribute (role) name. R is converted to upper case letters if necessary.

Result: Every entity value that references T in the specified role is returned in a set.

All relationships directed toward T are examined. When the relationship originates from an attribute named by R, the entity value containing that attribute is added to the result set. When R is an empty string, then every actual use of T is reported. An empty set is returned if T is never used.

Example F.17

This example shows a rule which requires that among all of the points used as circle centers, at least one of them is the origin. Note that this example uses the query expression twice. The inner query scans the Point population to find every use of a point as a center. The outer query finds out how many of those points are at the origin.

```
ENTITY Point;
  X, Y, Z : REAL;
END_ENTITY;

ENTITY circle;
  Center : Point;
  ...
END_ENTITY;
...
(*
This rule finds every point that is used as a circle center
and then it ensures that at least one of the points lies at
the origin *)
...
RULE example FOR (Point);
WHERE
  SizeOf(
  Query( AtZero <* Query(AtCenter <* Point |
  UsedIn(AtCenter, 'ThisSchema.Circle.Center') <> []) |
  AtZero.Center = Point(0.0, 0.0, 0.0)) ) >= 1;
END_RULE;
```

Value _____ Function

```
Function Value (V:STRING) : NUMBER;
```

The **Value** function returns the numeric representation of a string.

Parameters: V is a string.

Result: A number (integer or real) corresponding to the string representation. If the string cannot be converted to numeric form, null is returned.

Conditions: The string is interpreted as an integer literal or a real literal (see 9.7).

Example F.18

```
Value ( '1.234' ) --> 1.234 (REAL)
Value ( '20' )    --> 20    (INTEGER)
Value ( 'abc' )   --> ?     null
```

Bibliography

[A⁺90]   M. Atkinson et al. 'The Object-Oriented Database System Manifesto'. In *Deductive and Object-Oriented Databases*. Elsevier Science Publishers, Amsterdam, The Netherlands, 1990.

[Ash91]   M. J. Ashworth. 'An Interactive Tool for the Population of EXPRESS Models'. In P. R. Wilson, editor, *EUG'91 — First International EXPRESS User Group Conference*, Houston, TX, 17–18 October 1991.

[AW91]   M. Alavi and J. C. Wetherbe. 'Mixing Prototyping and Data Modeling for Information System Design'. *IEEE Software*, 8(3):86–91, May 1991.

[AW92]   M. Ahmed and R. Weems. 'Augmented Role of EXPRESS in Modern Specification Methodology'. In P. R. Wilson, editor, *EUG'92 — Second International EXPRESS User Group Conference*, Dallas, TX, 17–18 October 1992.

[BB90]   F. Bancilhon and P. Buneman, editors. *Advances in Database Programming Languages*. ACM Press Frontier Series. Addison-Wesley Publishing Company, 1990.

[BBJS92]   B. Bruegge, J. Blythe, J. Jackson, and J. Shufelt. 'Object-Oriented System Modeling with OMT'. *SIGPLAN Notices*, 27(10):359–376, October 1992. (Proceedings OOPSLA'92, Vancouver, Canada, October 1992.).

[BCN92]   C. Batini, S. Ceri, and S. B. Navathe. *Conceptual Database Design*. Benjamin Cummings Publishing Company, Inc., 1992.

[Ben86a]   J. Bentley. 'Programming Pearls: A Literate Program'. *Communications of the ACM*, 29(6):471–483, June 1986. (With Special Guest Oysters Don Knuth and Doug McIlroy).

[Ben86b]   J. Bentley. 'Programming Pearls: Literate Programming'. *Communications of the ACM*, 29(5):364–369, May 1986. (with Special Guest Oyster Don Knuth).

[BHB90]   D. Batra, J. A. Hoffler, and R. P. Bestrom. 'Comparing Representations with Relational and EER Models'. *Communications of the ACM*, 33(2):126–139, February 1990.

[Big88]   J. H. Bigelow. 'Hypertext and CASE'. *IEEE Software*, 5(2):23–27, March 1988.

369

[BK85]   E. B. Birchfield and H. H. King. 'Product Data Definition Interface (PDDI)'. In *Proceedings of the 1985 USAF CIM Industry Days*, Texas, April 1985.

[Boo91]   G. Booch. *Object-Oriented Design with Applications*. Benjamin Cummings Publishing Company, Inc., 1991.

[BOS91]   P. Butterworth, A. Otis, and J. Stein. 'The GemStone Object Database Management System'. *Communications of the ACM*, 34(10):64–77, October 1991.

[BP92]   L. Blencke and J. Perlt. 'The EXEP Toolkit'. In P. R. Wilson, editor, *EUG'92 — Second International EXPRESS User Group Conference*, Dallas, TX, 17–18 October 1992.

[BPR88]   M. Blaha, W. Premerlani, and J. Rumbaugh. 'Relational Database Design Using an Object-Oriented Methodology'. *Communications of the ACM*, 31(4):414–427, April 1988.

[Bru92]   T. A. Bruce. *Designing Quality Databases with IDEF1X Information Models*. Dorset House Publishing, New York, 1992.

[Bry88]   M. Bryan. *SGML: An Author's Guide to the Standard Generalized Markup Language*. Addison-Wesley Publishing Company, 1988.

[CERE90] B. Czejdo, R. Elamsri, M. Rusinkiewicz, and D. W. Embley. 'A Graphical Data Manipulation Language for an Extended Entity-Relationship Model'. *Computer*, 23(3):26–36, March 1990.

[CET93]   B. Czejdo, C. F. Eick, and M. Taylor. 'Integrating Sets, Rules, and Data in an Object-Oriented Environment'. *IEEE Expert*, 8(1):59–66, February 1993.

[CG86]   S. Ceri and G. Gottlob. 'Normalization of Relations and Prolog'. *Communications of the ACM*, 29(6):524–544, June 1986.

[Cha92]   P. K. Chawdhry. 'NIAMEX — A NIAM Compiler and EXPRESS Preprocessor'. In P. R. Wilson, editor, *EUG'92 — Second International EXPRESS User Group Conference*, Dallas, TX, 17–18 October 1992.

[Che76]   P. P-S. Chen. 'The Entity-Relationship Model — Towards a Unified View of Data'. *ACM TODS*, 1(1), March 1976.

[CJS92]   B. Chandrasekaran, T. R. Johnson, and J. W. Smith. 'Task-Structure Analysis for Knowledge Modeling'. *Communications of the ACM*, 35(9):124–137, September 1992.

[CKO92]   B. Curtis, M. I. Kellner, and J. Over. 'Process Modeling'. *Communications of the ACM*, 35(9):75–90, september 1992.

[Cla91]   S. N. Clark. 'Building EXPRESS–Driven Applications with Fed-X'. In P. R. Wilson, editor, *EUG'91 — First International EXPRESS User Group Conference*, Houston, TX, 17–18 October 1991.

[Cle92]   P. Clements. 'The Application of EXPRESS Modelling and Tools within an Integration Platform'. In P. R. Wilson, editor, *EUG'92 — Second International EXPRESS User Group Conference*, Dallas, TX, 17–18 October 1992.

[CM87]   N. Cercone and G. McCalla, editors. *The Knowledge Frontier*. Springer-Verlag, 1987.

[Coa92a] P. Coad. 'Finding Objects: Practical Approaches'. *OOPS Messenger*, 3(4):17–19, October 1992. (OOPSLA'91: Addendum to the Proceedings.).

[Coa92b] P. Coad. 'Object-Oriented Patterns'. *Communications of the ACM*, 35(9):153–159, September 1992.

[D$^+$91]   O. Deux et al. 'The O_2 System'. *Communications of the ACM*, 34(10):34–48, October 1991.

[Dah92]   H. K. Dahl. 'The EXPRESS Data Manager (EDM): A Multi-user Database System'. In P. R. Wilson, editor, *EUG'92 — Second International EXPRESS User Group Conference*, Dallas, TX, 17–18 October 1992.

[Dat89]   C. J. Date. *A Guide to the SQL Standard*. Addison-Wesley Publishing Company, 2 edition, 1989.

[Dat90]   C. J. Date. *An Introduction to Database Systems*, volume 1. Addison-Wesley Publishing Company, 5 edition, 1990.

[dC90]   D. de Champeaux. 'Structured Analysis and Object Oriented Analysis'. *SIGPLAN Notices*, Special Issue:15–17, 1990. (OOPLSA/ECOOP'90: Addendum to the Proceedings.).

[dCLF92] D. de Champeaux, D. Lea, and P. Faure. 'The Process of Object-Oriented Design'. *SIGPLAN Notices*, 27(10):45–62, October 1992. (Proceedings of OOPSLA'92, Vancouver, Canada, 18–22 October, 1992.).

[Dev91]   K. Devlin. *Logic and Information*. Cambridge University Press, 1991.

[DPT91]   T. Davis, B. Palmer, and G. Trapp. 'CERC's Expressions – Impressions – Confessions of EXPRESS'. In P. R. Wilson, editor, *EUG'91 — First International EXPRESS User Group Conference*, Houston, TX, 17–18 October 1991.

[EN89]   R. Elmasri and S. B. Navathe. *Fundamentals of Database Systems*. Benjamin Cummings Publishing Co. Inc., 1989.

[EW93]   C. F. Eick and P. Werstein. 'Rule-Based Consistency Enforcement for Knowledge-Based Systems'. *IEEE Transactions on Knowledge and Data Engineering*, 5(1):52–64, February 1993.

[F$^+$92]   J. A. Fulton et al. *Technical Report on the Semantic Unification Meta-Model: Volume 1 — Semantic Unification of Static Models*. ISO TC184/SC4 WG3 Document N175, October 1992.

[FHRK93] M. E. Fayad, L. J. Hawn, M. A. Roberts, and J. R. Klatt. 'Using the Shlaer-Mellor Object-Oriented Analysis Method'. *IEEE Software*, 10(2):43–52, March 1993.

[FK92]   R. G. Fichman and C. F. Kemerer. 'Object-Oriented and Convential Analysis and Design Methodologies'. *Computer*, 25(10):22–39, October 1992.

[Fow65]   H. W. Fowler. *A Dictionary of Modern English Usage*. Oxford University Press, second edition, 1965. (Revised by Sir Ernest Gowers. First published 1926.).

[Ful92a] J. A. Fulton. 'Enterprise Integration Using Semantic Unification'. In C. Petrie et al., editors, *Proceedings of the First International Conference on Enterprise Integration*, Cambridge, MA, 1992. MIT Press.

[Ful92b] J. A. Fulton. 'EXPRESS as a Language for Semantic Unification'. In P. R. Wilson, editor, *EUG'92 — Second International EXPRESS User Group Conference*, Dallas, TX, 17–18 October 1992.

[Gad93]   S. K. Gadia. 'Parametric Databases: Seamless Integration of Spatial, Temporal, Belief and Ordinary Data'. *SIGMOD Record*, 22(1):15–20, March 1993.

[GF92]   M. R. Genesereth and R. E. Fikes. *Knowledge Interchange Format, Version 3.0 Reference Manual*. Report Logic-92-1, Computer Science Department, Stanford University, June 1992.

[Gin91]   M. L. Ginsberg. 'Knowledge Interchange Format: The KIF of Death'. *AI Magazine*, 12(3):57–63, Fall 1991.

[Gol90]   C. A. Goldfarb. *The SGML Handbook*. Oxford University Press, 1990. (Edited and with a foreword by Yuri Rubinsky).

[Gow73]   E. Gowers. *The Complete Plain Words*. Penguin Books Ltd., second edition, 1973. (Revised by Sir Bruce Fraser. First published by H.M. Stationery Office, 1954.).

[GR89]   A. Goldberg and D. Robson. *Smalltalk-80, The Language*. Addison-Wesley Publishing Company, 1989.

[GS90]   P. K. Garg and W. Scacchi. 'A Hypertext System to Manage Software Life-Cycle Documents'. *IEEE Software*, 7(3):90–98, May 1990.

[H+91]   M. Hardwick et al. 'Adding EXPRESS to an Object-Oriented Database'. In P. R. Wilson, editor, *EUG'91 — First International EXPRESS User Group Conference*, Houston, TX, 17–18 October 1991.

[Har92]   M. Hardwick. 'Using EXPRESS to Implement Concurrent Engineering'. In P. R. Wilson, editor, *EUG'92 — Second International EXPRESS User Group Conference*, Dallas, TX, 17–18 October 1992.

[HMMS92] K. Higa, M. Morrison, J. Morrison, and O. R. L. Sheng. 'An Object-Oriented Methodology for Knowledge Base – Database Coupling'. *Communications of the ACM*, 35(6):99–113, June 1992.

[Hol92]   R. Holibaugh. 'Object Oriented Modeling'. *OOPS Messenger*, 3(4):73–77, October 1992. (OOPSLA'91: Addendum to the Proceedings.).

[Hop92]   S. Hope. 'Information Modelling and System Integration with EXPRESS and ORB'. In P. R. Wilson, editor, *EUG'92 — Second International EXPRESS User Group Conference*, Dallas, TX, 17–18 October 1992.

[HPC93]   A. R. Hurson, S. H. Pakzad, and J. Cheng. 'Object-Oriented Database Management Systems: Evolution and Performance Issues'. *Computer*, 26(2):48–60, February 1993.

[HS89]   M. Hardwick and D. L. Spooner. 'The ROSE Data Manager: Using Object Technology to Support Interactive Engineering Applications'. *IEEE Transactions on Knowledge and Data Engineering*, 1(2):285–289, June 1989.

[HSE90]   B. Henderson-Sellers and J. M. Edwards. 'The Object-Oriented Systems Life Cycle'. *Communications of the ACM*, 33(9):142–159, September 1990.

[IDE81]   AFWAL/MLTC, Wright-Patterson AFB, OH. *Integrated Computer-Aided Manufacturing (ICAM) Architecture, Part II, Volume IV — Function Modeling Manual (IDEF0)*, 1981. Report Number: AFWAL-TR-81-4023, Volume IV.

[IDE85]   AFWAL/MLTC, Wright-Patterson AFB, OH. *Integrated Information Support System (IISS), Vol. V: Common Data Model Subsystem, Part 4: Information Modeling Manual — IDEF1X*, 1985. Report Number: AFWAL-TR-86-4006, Volume V.

[ISO86]   ISO 8879. *Information Processing — Text and Office Systems — Standard Generalized Markup Language (SGML)*, 1986.

[ISO87]   ISO TR9007. *Information processing systems — Concepts and terminology for the conceptual schema and the information base*, 1987.

[ISO92a]   ISO 10646-1. *Information technology — Universal multiple-octect coded character set (UCS) — Architecture and basic multilingual plane*, 1992.

[ISO92b]   ISO TC184/SC4 Document N151. *ISO/DIS 10303-11 Industrial automation systems and integration — Product data representation and exchange — Part 11: Description methods: The EXPRESS language reference manual*, September 1992. (Available from ISO and national standards organizations.).

[ISO92c]   ISO TC184/SC4 Document N154. *ISO CD 10303-1 Product data representation and exchange — Part 1: Overview and fundamental principles*, September 1992. (Available from NIST, Gaithersburg, MD 20899.).

[ISO93]   ISO 10303-11. *Industrial automation systems and integration — Product data representation and exchange — Part 11: Description methods: The EXPRESS language reference manual*, 1993. (To be published.).

[Jon86]   C. Jones. *Systematic Software Development Using VDM*. Prentice Hall, Englewood Cliffs, NJ, 1986.

[JvLN+91] U. Jasnoch, U. von Lukas, C. Neuss, R. Peters, and M. Ungerer. 'Xpresso — An Object-Oriented Graphic-Interactive Design Environment for EXPRESS '. In P. R. Wilson, editor, *EUG'91 — First International EXPRESS User Group Conference*, Houston, TX, 17–18 October 1991.

[KC93]   G. M. Karam and R. S. Casselman. 'A Cataloging Framework for Software Development Methods'. *Computer*, 26(2):34–46, February 1993.

[KE88]   T. Koschmann and M. W. Evens. 'Bridging the Gap between Object-Oriented and Logic Programming'. *IEEE Software*, 5(4):36–42, July 1988.

[Ken78]   W. Kent. *Data and Reality*. North-Holland Publishing Company, 1978.

[Ker92]   N. L. Kerth. 'A Structured Approach to Object-Oriented Design'. *OOPS Messenger*, 3(4):21–43, October 1992. (OOPSLA'91: Addendum to the Proceedings.).

[KK91]   T. Kamada and S. Kawai. 'A General Framework for Visualizing Abstract Objects and Relationships'. *ACM Transactions on Graphics*, 10(1):1–39, January 1991.

[KKS92]   M. Kifer, W. Kim, and Y. Sagiv. 'Querying Object-Oriented Databases'. *SIGMOD Record*, 21(2):393–402, June 1992. (Proceedings 1992 ACM SIGMOD International Conference on Management of Data, San Diego, CA, 2–5 June, 1992.).

[KL89]   W. Kim and F. H. Lochovsky, editors. *Object-Oriented Concepts, Databases and Applications*. ACM Press Frontier Series. Addison-Wesley Publishing Company, 1989.

[KM90]   T. Korson and J. D. McGregor. 'Understanding Object-Oriented: A Unifying Paradigm'. *Communications of the ACM*, 33(9):40–60, September 1990.

[Knu83]   D. E. Knuth. *The WEB System of Structured Documentation*. Stanford Computer Science Report 980, September 1983.

[Knu84a] D. E. Knuth. 'Literate Programming'. *Computer Journal*, 27(2):97–111, May 1984.

[Knu84b] D. E. Knuth. *The TeXbook*. Addison-Wesley Publishing Company, 1984.

[Knu86]   D. E. Knuth. *TeX: The Program*. Addison-Wesley Publishing Company, 1986.

[Knu87]   R. M. Knutson. *Flattened Fauna — A Field Guide to Common Animals of Roads, Streets, and Highways*. Ten Speed Press, Berkeley, CA, 1987.

[KS91]   W. Kim and J. Seo. 'Classifying Schematic and Data Heterogeneity in Multidatabase Systems'. *Computer*, 24(12):December, 1991.

[Kun90]   C. Kung. 'Object Subclass Hierarchy in SQL: A Simple Approach'. *Communications of the ACM*, 33(7):117–125, July 1990.

[Lam86]   L. Lamport. *LaTeX: A Document Preparation System*. Addison-Wesley Publishing Company, 1986.

[LC92]   D. Libes and S. N. Clark. 'The NIST EXPRESS Toolkit — Lessons Learned'. In P. R. Wilson, editor, *EUG'92 — Second International EXPRESS User Group Conference*, Dallas, TX, 17–18 October 1992.

[Len90]   M. Lenzerini. 'Class Hierarchies and Their Complexity'. In F. Bancilhon and P. Buneman, editors, *Advances in Database Programming Languages*, ACM Press Frontier Series, chapter 3. Addison-Wesley Publishing Company, 1990.

[LH90]   B. S. Lerner and A. N. Habermann. 'Beyond Schema Evolution to Database Reorganization'. *SIGPLAN Notices*, 25(10):67–76, October 1990. (Proceedings OOPSLA/ECOOP'90, Ottowa, Canada, 21–25 October, 1990.).

[LK92]   R. Y. W. Lau and H. J. Kahn. 'The Use of EXPRESS in the EDIF Information Model'. In P. R. Wilson, editor, *EUG'92 — Second International EXPRESS User Group Conference*, Dallas, TX, 17–18 October 1992.

[LLOW91] C. W. Lamb, G. Landis, J. A. Orenstein, and D. L. Weinreb. 'The ObjectStore Database System'. *Communications of the ACM*, 34(10):50–63, October 1991.

[LLPS91] G. M. Lohman, B. Lindsay, H. Pirahesh, and K. B. Schiefer. 'Extensions to Starburst: Objects, Types, Functions and Rules'. *Communications of the ACM*, 34(10):94–109, October 1991.

[LM85]   W. Lew and P. Machmiller. 'A Case Study in Data Base Integration'. *CIM Review*, 1(2):41–48, Winter 1985.

[LM91]   G. Lehrenfeld and W. Mueller. 'Validation of EXPRESS Models Using Prolog'. In P. R. Wilson, editor, *EUG'91 — First International EXPRESS User Group Conference*, Houston,TX, 17–18 October 1991.

[Loo87]   M. E. S. Loomis. *The Database Book*. Macmillan Publishing Company, New York, 1987.

[MC91]   H. Mak and S. Chan. 'A Data Model for EDIF in EXPRESS'. In P. R. Wilson, editor, *EUG'91 — First International EXPRESS User Group Conference*, Houston, TX, 17–18 October 1991.

[MC92]   H. Mak and S. C. F. Chan. 'An EDIF to STEP Translator using an EXPRESS Data Model'. In P. R. Wilson, editor, *EUG'92 — Second International EXPRESS User Group Conference*, Dallas, TX, 17–18 October 1992.

[MCB90]   M. V. Mannino, I. J. Choi, and D. S. Batory. 'The Object-Oriented Functional Data Language'. *IEEE Transactions on Software Engineering*, 16(11):1258–1272, November 1990.

[McG34]   W. McGonagall. *Poetic Gems selected from the works of William McGonagall, Poet and Tragedian*. David Winter & Son Ltd., Dundee, 1934. (First published in two parts in 1890.).

[Mey88]   B. Meyer. *Object-Oriented Software Construction*. Prentice Hall International (UK) Ltd, 1988.

[Mil28]   A. A. Milne. *The House at Pooh Corner*. E. P. Hutton & Co., 1928.

[MK92]   W. Mueller and B. Kleinjohann. 'The EXPRESS Information Modeling Workbench — A New Approach to Graphical Design Environments'. In P. R. Wilson, editor, *EUG'92 — Second International EXPRESS User Group Conference*, Dallas, TX, 17–18 October 1992.

[Moe90]   S. Moen. 'Drawing Dynamic Trees'. *IEEE Software*, 7(4):21–28, July 1990.

[MP92]   D. E. Monarchi and G. I. Puhr. 'A Research Typology for Object-Oriented Analysis and Design'. *Communications of the ACM*, 35(9):35–47, September 1992.

[MVL92]   V. Misic, D. Velasevic, and B. Lazarevic. 'Formal Specification of a Data Dictionary for an Extended ER Data Model'. *The Computer Journal*, 35(6):611–622, December 1992.

[Nav92]   S. B. Navathe. 'Evolution of Data Modeling for Databases'. *Communications of the ACM*, 35(9):112–123, September 1992.

[Nel91]   M. L. Nelson. 'An Object Oriented Tower of Babel'. *OOPS Messenger*, 2(3):3–11, July 1991.

[Ner92]   J-M. Nerson. 'Applying Object-Oriented Analysis and Design'. *Communications of the ACM*, 35(9):63–74, September 1992.

[NH89]   G. M. Nijssen and T. A. Halpin. *Conceptual Schema and Relational Database Design: A Fact Oriented Approach*. Prentice Hall, Englewood Cliffs, NJ, 1989.

[NKN91]   S. R. Newcomb, N. A. Kipp, and V. T. Newcomb. 'The HyTime Hypermedia/Time-based Document Structuring Language'. *Communications of the ACM*, 34(11):52–83, November 1991.

[NNGE92] T. E. Nagle, J. A. Nagle, L. L. Gerholz, and P. W. Eklund, editors. *Conceptual Structures: Current Research and Practice*. Ellis Horwood, New York, 1992.

[NV82]   G. M. Nijssen and D. Vermeir. 'A Procedure to Define the Object Type Structure of a Conceptual Schema'. *Information Systems*, 7(4), 1982.

[P⁺92]   R. Patil et al. 'The DARPA Knowledge Sharing Effort: A Progress Report'. In *Proceedings of the Third International Conference on Principles of Knowledge Representation and Reasoning*, Cambridge, MA, October 1992.

[PBRV90] W. J. Premerlani, M. R. Blaha, J. E. Rumbaugh, and T. A. Varwig. 'An Object-Oriented Relational Database'. *Communications of the ACM*, 33(11):99–109, November 1990.

[PCKW89] K. Parsaye, M. Chignell, S. Khoshafian, and H. Wong. *Intelligent Databases — Object-Oriented, Deductive Hypermedia Technologies*. John Wiley & Sons, Inc., New York, 1989.

[PDD84]   *Product Definition Data Interface*, 1984. (5 Vols), obtainable from CAM-I Inc, Arlington, Texas, as Reports DR-84-GM-01 through -05.

[PL92]   N. Plat and P. G. Larsen. 'An Overview of the ISO VDM-SL Standard'. *SIGPLAN Notices*, 27(8):76–82, August 1992.

[Pou92]   A. Poulovassilis. 'The Implementation of FDL, a Functional Database Language'. *The Computer Journal*, 35(2):119–128, April 1992.

[RBP⁺91] J. Rumbaugh, M. Blaha, W. Premerlani, F. Eddy, and W. Lorensen. *Object-Oriented Modeling and Design*. Prentice Hall, Englewood Cliffs, NJ, 1991.

[RG92]   K. S. Rubin and A. Goldberg. 'Object Behaviour Analysis'. *Communications of the ACM*, 35(9):48–62, September 1992.

[Roe91]   P. Roesch. 'Exploit — A Graphical Editor for EXPRESS-G'. In P. R. Wilson, editor, *EUG'91 — First International EXPRESS User Group Conference*, Houston, TX, 17–18 October 1991.

[RRHD88] T. Risch, R. Reboh, P. E. Hart, and R. O. Duda. 'A Functional Approach to Integrating Database and Expert Systems'. *Communications of the ACM*, 31(12):1424–1437, December 1988.

[S+90]   M. Stonebraker et al. 'Third-Generation Database System Manifesto'. *SIGMOD Record*, 19(3):31–44, September 1990. (The authors are the members of The Committee for Advanced DBMS Function.).

[SB91]   O. Schettler and A. Bredenfeld. 'XDDL: The EXPRESS-Oriented Data Definition Language of the DASSY Data Model'. In P. R. Wilson, editor, *EUG'91 — First International EXPRESS User Group Conference*, Houston, TX, 17–18 October 1991.

[Sch91]   D. Schenck. 'Five Principles of EXPRESS'. In P. R. Wilson, editor, *EUG'91 — First International EXPRESS User Group Conference*, Houston, TX, 17–18 October 1991.

[SFL+91] S. Y. W. Su, S. Fang, H. Lam, C. S. Chen, and S. Garje. 'An Object-Oriented Rule-Based Approach to Schema/Model Transformation'. In P. R. Wilson, editor, *EUG'91 — First International EXPRESS User Group Conference*, Houston, TX, 17–18 October 1991.

[SGH90]   J. R. Slagle, D. A. Gardiner, and K. Han. 'Knowledge Specification of an Expert System'. *IEEE Expert*, 5(4):29–38, August 1990.

[SH92]   A-W. Scheer and A. Hars. 'Extending Data Modeling to Cover the Whole Enterprise'. *Communications of the ACM*, 25(9):166–172, September 1992.

[Shi81]   D. W. Shipman. 'The Functional Data Model and the Data Language DAPLEX'. *ACM Transactions on Database Systems*, 6(1):140–173, March 1981.

[SHS90]   D. L. Spooner, M. Hardwick, and D. B. Sanderson. 'Engineering Data Exchange in the ROSE System'. In A. Meystel, J. Herath, and S. Gray, editors, *Proceedings 5th IEEE International Symposium on Intelligent Control 1990, Volume II*, pages 972–976. IEEE Computer Society Press, 5–7 September 1990.

[SK91]   M. Stonebraker and G. Kemnitz. 'The POSTGRES Next-Generation Database Management System'. *Communications of the ACM*, 34(10):78–92, October 1991.

[SKL89]   S. Y. W. Su, V. Krishnamurthy, and H. Lam. An Object-oriented Semantic Association Model (OSAM*). In S. T. Kumura, A. L. Soyster, and R. L. Kashyap, editors, *Artificial Intelligence: Manufacturing Theory and Practice*, chapter 17. Industrial Engineering Management Press, Norcross, GA, 1989.

[SLH+92] S. Y. W. Su, H. Lam, M. Hardwick, D. Spooner, A. Goldschmidt, and J. Chida. 'An Integrated Object-Oriented Knowledge Base Management System OSAM*.KBMS/ROSE for Supporting Design and Manufacturing'. In *Proceedings of the Second International Conference on Systems Integration*. IEEE Computer Society Press, June 1992.

[SM88a]   S. Shlaer and S. J. Mellor. *Object-Oriented Systems Analysis*. Yourdon Press, 1988.

[SM88b]   G. H. Sockut and A. Malhotra. 'A Full-Screen Facility for Defining Relational and Entity-Relationship Database Schemas'. *IEEE Software*, 5(6):68–78, November 1988.

[Sny93] A. Snyder. 'The Essence of Objects: Concepts and Terms'. *IEEE Software*, 10(1):31–42, January 1993.

[SO92]   X. Song and L. J. Osterweil. 'Toward Objective, Systematic Design-Method Comparisons'. *IEEE Software*, 9(3):43–53, May 1992.

[Soo91] M. D. Soo. 'Bibliography on Temporal Databases'. *SIGMOD Record*, 20(1):14–23, March 1991.

[Sow84] J. F. Sowa. *Conceptual Structures: Information Processing in Mind and Machine*. Addison-Wesley, Rading, MA, 1984.

[Sow91] J. F. Sowa. 'Towards the Expressive Power of Natural Languages'. In J. F. Sowa, editor, *Principles of Semantic Networks*, pages 157–189. Morgan Kaufmann Publishers, San Mateo, CA, 1991.

[Spi91] P. Spiby. 'An EXPRESS Development Environment'. In P. R. Wilson, editor, *EUG'91 — First International EXPRESS User Group Conference*, Houston, TX, 17–18 October 1991.

[Spi92] M. Spivey. *The Z Notation — A Reference Manual*. Prentice Hall, Englewood Cliffs, NJ, second edition, 1992.

[SS91a] Y-M. Shyy and S. Y. W. Su. 'K: A High-level Knowledgebase Programming Language for Advanced Database Applications'. *SIGMOD Record*, 20(2):338–347, June 1991. (Proceedings 1991 ACM SIGMOD International Conference on Management of Data, Denver, CO, 29–31 May, 1991.).

[SS91b] L. M. C. Smith and M. H. Samadzadeh. 'An Annotated Bibliography of Literate Programming'. *SIGPLAN Notices*, 26(1):14–20, January 1991.

[SS92]   D. B. Sanderson and D. L. Spooner. 'Mapping between EXPRESS and the Extended Entity Relationship Model'. In P. R. Wilson, editor, *EUG'92 — Second International EXPRESS User Group Conference*, Dallas, TX, 17–18 October 1992.

[SSU91] A. Silberschatz, M. Stonebraker, and J. Ullman. 'Database Systems: Achievement and Opportunities'. *Communications of the ACM*, 34(10):110–120, October 1991.

[Sto88] M. Stonebraker, editor. *Readings in Database Systems*. Morgan Kaufmann Publishers Inc., California, 1988.

[Str86] B. Stroustrup. *The C++ Programming Language*. Addison-Wesley Publishing Company, 1986.

[Str88] B. Stroustrup. 'What Is Object-Oriented Programming?'. *IEEE Software*, 5(3):10–20, May 1988.

[SUW91] G. Scholz, M. Ungerer, and W. Wilkes. 'Using EXPRESS for Modeling EDIF — Case Study: The Model of PORT Hierarchy'. In P. R. Wilson, editor, *EUG'91 — First International EXPRESS User Group Conference*, Houston, TX, 17–18 October 1991.

[TK78]   D. Tsichritzis and A. Klug, editors. *The ANSI/X3/SPARC DBMS Framework*. AFIPS Press, 1978.

[Tra93]   G. Trapp. 'The Emerging Step Standard for Product-model Data Ex-
           change'. *Computer*, 26(2):85–87, February 1993.

[Van87a]   C. J. Van Wyk. 'Literate Programming'. *Communications of the ACM*,
           30(7):594–599, July 1987.

[Van87b]   C. J. Van Wyk. 'Literate Programming'. *Communications of the ACM*,
           30(12):1000–1010, December 1987.

[Van88]   C. J. Van Wyk. 'Literate Programming'. *Communications of the ACM*,
           31(12):1376–1385, December 1988.

[Van89a]   C. J. Van Wyk. 'Literate Programming'. *Communications of the ACM*,
           32(6):740–755, June 1989.

[Van89b]   C. J. Van Wyk. 'Literate Programming: Weaving a Language-
           independent WEB'. *Communications of the ACM*, 32(9):1051–1055,
           September 1989.

[Van90]   C. J. Van Wyk. 'Literate Programming: An Assessment'. *Communi-
           cations of the ACM*, 33(3):361–365, March 1990.

[Var88]   M. Y. Vardi. 'The Universal-Relation Data Model for Logical Indepen-
           dence'. *IEEE Software*, 5(2):80–85, March 1988.

[Vos91]   G. Vossen. 'Bibliography on Object-Oriented Database Management'.
           SIGMOD Record, 20(1):24–46, March 1991.

[War89]   P. T. Ward. 'How to Integrate Object Orientation with Structured
           Analysis and Design'. *IEEE Software*, 6(2):74–82, March 1989.

[WBJ90]   R. J. Wirfs-Brock and R. E. Johnson. 'Surveying Current Research in
           Object-Oriented Design'. *Communications of the ACM*, 33(9):104–124,
           September 1990.

[WBT92]   D. L. Wells, J. A. Blakeley, and C. W. Thompson. 'Architecture of
           an Open Object-Oriented Database Management System'. *Computer*,
           25(10):74–82, October 1992.

[WD90]   M. A. Whiting and D. M. DeVaney. 'Finding the Object'. *SIGPLAN
           Notices*, Special Issue:99–107, 1990. (ECOOP/OOPSLA'90, Adden-
           dum to the Proceedings.).

[Web85]   *Webster's Ninth New Collegiate Dictionary*. Merriam-Webster Inc.,
           1985.

[Weg90]   P. Wegner. 'Concepts and Paradigms of Object-Oriented Program-
           ming'. *OOPS Messenger*, 1(1):7–87, August 1990.

[Weg92]   P. Wegner. 'Dimensions of Object-Oriented Modeling'. *Computer*,
           25(10):12–20, October 1992.

[Wen91]   B. G. Wenzel. 'Information Modeling Principles'. In P. R. Wilson, edi-
           tor, *EUG'91 — First International EXPRESS User Group Conference*,
           Houston, TX, 17–18 October 1991.

[Wil91a]   P. R. Wilson, editor. *EUG'91 — First International EXPRESS User
           Group Conference*, Houston, TX, 17–18 October 1991.

[Wil91b] P. R. Wilson. *Modeling Languages Compared: EXPRESS, IDEF1X, NIAM, OMT and Shlaer-Mellor*. Rensselaer Design Research Center, Rensselaer Polytechnic Institute, Troy, NY 12180, May 1991. Technical Report No: 91015.

[Wil91c] P. R. Wilson. 'Overview of EXPRESS-G and EXPRESS-I'. In P. R. Wilson, editor, *EUG'91 — First International EXPRESS User Group Conference*, Houston, TX, 17–18 October 1991.

[Wil92a] P. R. Wilson. 'EUG'91 Meeting Notes'. *SIGMOD Record*, 21(1):90–92, March 1992.

[Wil92b] P. R. Wilson, editor. *EUG'92 — Second International EXPRESS User Group Conference*, Dallas, TX, 17–18 October 1992.

[Wil92c] P. R. Wilson. *EXPRESS-I Language Reference Manual*. ISO TC184/SC4/WG5 Document N40, November 1992. (Available from NIST, Gaithersburg, MD 20899.).

[Wil92d] P. R. Wilson. *Processing Tools for EXPRESS*. Rensselaer Design Research Center, Rensselaer Polytechnic Institute, Troy, NY 12180, December 1992. Technical Report No: 92031.

[Wil93]   P. R. Wilson. 'A View of STEP'. In P. R. Wilson, M. J. Wozny, and M. J. Pratt, editors, *Geometric and Product Modeling*. North Holland, 1993. (To be published).

[WM91]   B. G. Wenzel and S. Mullenbach. 'EXPRESS Version 2: Requirements and Project Proposal'. In P. R. Wilson, editor, *EUG'91 — First International EXPRESS User Group Conference*, Houston, TX, 17–18 October 1991. (Draft report. Version 0.1.).

[WPM90]   A. I. Wasserman, P. A. Pircher, and R. J. Muller. 'An Object-Oriented Structured Design Notation for Software Design Representation'. *Computer*, 23(3):50–63, March 1990.

[YC79]   E. Yourdon and L. L. Constantine. *Structured Design — Fundamentals of a Discipline of Computer Program and Systems Design*. Yourdon Press, Englewood Cliffs, NJ, 1979.

[Yin91]   M. A. Yinger. 'Implementing an EXPRESS Modeling Environment: Smalltalk Meets EXPRESS'. In P. R. Wilson, editor, *EUG'91 — First International EXPRESS User Group Conference*, Houston, TX, 17–18 October 1991.

[You89]   E. Yourdon. *Modern Structured Analysis*. Yourdon Press, Englewood Cliffs, NJ, 1989.

[Zan83]   C. Zaniolo. 'The Database Language GEM'. In *Proceedings 1983 ACM-SIGMOD Conference on Management of Data*, San Jose, CA, May 1983.

[ZW91]   J. Zimmerman and A. Williams. 'Relating EXPRESS to Other Modeling Languages'. In P. R. Wilson, editor, *EUG'91 — First International EXPRESS User Group Conference*, Houston, TX, 17–18 October 1991.

Index

% 131, 133
' 131
(* 130–131
(................................ 131
) 131
*) 130–131
** 131, 196–197
*

    intersection 205
    multiply 131, 196–197
+

    addition 131, 196–197
    string concatenate 204
    union 205
, ... 131
-- 131
-

    difference 205–206
    subtract 131, 196–197
. ... 131, 196
/ 131, 196–197
:<>: 131, 196, 200–201
:=: 131, 196, 200–201
:= 131
: 131
; 131
<* 131
<=

    less than/equal . 131, 196, 200
    subset 198, 204
<> 131, 196, 200–201
< 131, 196, 200
= 131, 196, 200–201
>=

    greater than/equal ..131, 196, 200
    superset 198, 204
> 131, 196, 200
? . 135–136, 138, 210, 354–355, 360

[.............................. 131
\ 131, 196
] 131
{ 131
|| 131, 137, 170
| 131
} 131

A

Abstract supertype 166
Abstract test case 260, 271
Abstract 53
Abstraction 12, 14, 73
Abstract 53, 87, 248, 309, 311
Abs 179, 356
ACos 356
Aggregate 135, 140, 337
    Comparison 201
    Conformant 172
    Dynamic 47, 73, 265, 339
    Fixed 47, 73, 265, 338
    Operators 205
    Value 264
Aggregate 171–172
Aggregation 14, 47
Algorithm 171, 174–175
    Symbol 240
Alias Statement 188
Alias 181, 212
Alias 179, 188
Ambiguity ... 7, 54, 68, 79, 91, 168
AND operator 199
AndOr 53, 87–89, 167, 309–312
And 53, 167, 196, 198–199, 309, 311–312
ANSI/SPARC 73
Array 145–146
Array 47, 247
ASCII 144

ASIM 96–97, 101
    Structure 99
ASin 356
Assignment Statement 188
Assignment
    Compatibility 189
ATan 356
Attribute .17, 34, 43, 125, 156–157,
    260, 345
    Derived 56, 157, 159
    Explicit 157–158
    Inheritance 168
    Inverse 160, 162, 317
    Optional 81, 158, 164
    Redeclaration .. 169, 181, 249,
    256
    Reference 183
    Value 266

B
Bag 146–147, 149
Bag 47
Begin 190
Binary digits 133
Binary 133, 144
    Comparison 200
Binary 43, 111, 239, 241
BLength 357
Block 127
Boolean 135, 143, 198, 201
Boolean 43, 64, 156, 239

C
C (language) 272
C++ 272
Cardinality 17–18, 36, 246, 316
Case sensitive 132
Case Statement 189
Case 189
Categorization 42, 52
Category 13, 34
Chunk 181–183, 186, 202
Circular definitions 154
Circular references 159
Class ..7, 13–14, 16, 41, 43, 47, 270
Classification 166
Collection 145
Communication 6
Comparison 143, 189, 201

Aggregate 201
Binary 200
Entity value 201
Enumeration 201
Logical 201
Numeric 200
String 200
Compatibility 189
    Operator 197
Compiler 107, 118
Complex entity
    Value 267
Compound Statement 190
Concatenation operator 204
Conceptual model 12
Concrete model 12
Constant 153, 334
    Value 268
Const_E 263, 354
Constraint 15, 17–18, 24, 34, 36, 45,
    70–71, 124, 142, 155–157,
    162, 164, 187, 235, 247, 259,
    272, 348
    Behaviour 63
    Cardinality 157
    Checking 116
    Existence 47, 63
    Function 77
    Global 63, 71, 75, 101, 157
    Inverse 48, 160, 162
    Local ..46, 56, 63, 71, 75, 157,
    162
    Property 125, 156
    Rule 124, 176
    Static 125, 156
    Structure 75
    Supertype 52, 87, 167
        Default 167
    Uniqueness 45, 126, 163
Constructor function 170, 185
Context ...58, 69–70, 105, 211, 260
    Schema 212
Context 131
Cos 357

D
DAPLEX 24
Data model 12
Data modeling 10

Database 113–115
Data 6–7
Datatype 124, 139, 154
Declaration 152, 333
    Attribute 157
    Constant 153
    Entity 156
    Formal parameter 171
    Function 173
    Local rule 162
    Local variable 173
    Procedure 174
    Rule 175
    Schema 153
    Subtype 165
    Supertype 165
    Type 154
Default 73, 81, 257, 310
Defined type 149–150, 155
Derive 56, 82
Design goal 235, 259
Difference operator 206
Div 196–197
DML 15
Documentation ..34, 36, 48, 65, 69,
    92, 99, 104
    Embedded . 104–105, 280, 330
    Partitioned 104, 107
    System 118
    Tagged 108
Domain expert 31
Domain 43, 124, 139
DSL 15

E
EBCDIC 144
Editor 117
Eiffel 272
Else 190
End_Context 131
End_Local 173
End_Model 131
End_Procedure 175
End_Schema 152
End_Type 155
End 190
Entity-Relationship 316
Entity .14, 17, 34, 41, 71, 124, 136,
    156, 334, 342

Comparison 201
Complex 156, 170, 181
Modeling 248
Reference 182
Simple 156
Symbol 240
Value 265
Entity 42
Enumeration 51, 149
    Reference 184
    Value 263
Enumeration 248
ER model 16, 18, 26
Escape Statement 194
Escape 193–195
Evaluated set 311
Executable statements 187
Existence 35, 47, 63
Existential dependency 157
Exists 357
Expression 196
    Evaluation 196
    Interval 202
    Query 206
    Syntax 208
Exp 358

F
False 135, 337, 352–353, 355
File 113–114
First-class 63, 89
Fixed 144–145
Formal parameter 171
Format 358
Functional model 24
Function 174, 343
    Call 207
    Reference 184

G
GEM 26
Generalization 13, 42, 52, 86
Generic 139–140
Generic 171–172, 239
Glossary 34
Graphic requirements 236
Graphical model 15, 17, 27

H

HiBound 354, 360, 366
HiIndex 172, 360
Homonym 7, 34, 70, 93
Hypermedia 111
Hypertext 111

I

Icon 15, 17
IDEF1X 20, 25
Identifier 132, 157, 179, 181
Identity 35
If ... Then ... Else Statement .. 190
If 190
IIM 37, 91, 94–96, 99
Import 63, 70, 89, 96, 212, 245, 349
IN operator 203
Independence
      Implementation 72
Independent existence 212, 216
Infinite precision 354
Infix operators 196
Information base 89, 113, 115, 163,
            176, 211, 259, 271
Information model 10, 31
Information modeling . xxiii, 10, 32
Information 5–6
Inheritance .16, 35, 52, 82, 86, 125,
            156, 168
      Attribute 168
      Multiple 168, 312
      Repeated 168
      Rule 169
Insert 361
Instance .. 7, 10, 14, 41, 47, 63, 79,
            87, 115, 259
      Language 260
      Object 260
      Schema 260, 268
Instantiated model 12
Integer division 197
Integer 134, 141–142
Integer 43–44, 51, 179, 239
Integration 37, 86, 91, 96
      Continuity 92, 94
      Core based 95
      Cosmetic 92
      Editorial 92
      Evolutionary 95
      Structural 94

Interface 211, 245
      Chaining 214
      Implicit reference 214
      Specification 212
            Reference 213
            Use 213
Interfacing 89, 100
Interpretation rules 7–8, 10
Intersection operator 205
Invariance 73
Inverse 48
Inverse 47, 317
In 196, 198, 203

K

Key 20, 125
Keyword 131
Knowledgebase 113
Knowledge 6, 31

L

LaTeX ....xxv, 109
Lattice 166, 180
Length 361
Letters
      Case of 128
Lexical model 15, 24, 27
LIKE operator 203
Like 196, 198, 203
Line style 236
List 146, 148
List 47, 247
Literal 133
Literate programming 104
LoBound 141, 361, 366
Local variable 173
Local 173
Log10 362
Log2 362
Logical 135, 143, 198, 201
Logical 43, 156, 239
Log 362
LoIndex 141, 172, 362
Long form 100

M

Meta-model 330
Modeling environment 116
Modeling expert 31

Modeling team 32
Model 260
    Complete 251
    Entity-level 236, 246
    Partial 251
    Schema-level 236, 245
    Subset 58
Model 131
Modulo 197
Mod 196–197
Multiple inheritance 168
Multiple-dimension 146

N

Network model 18
Newline 128–129
NIAM 21, 25
Normal form 16
NOT operator 199
Not 196, 198–199
Null (Statement) 187
Number 141
Number 43, 239
NVL 81, 165, 363
Nym principle 70

O

Object base 271–272
Object identifier ..45, 115, 125–126
Object 14, 41, 270
Odd 363
OID 45, 55
OMT 22
OneOf 53, 88–89, 103, 167, 249, 309,
    311–315
Operator
    AND 199
    Boolean 198
    Comparison 200
    Compatibility 197
    concatenation 204
    Difference 206
    IN 203
    Intersection 205
    LIKE 203
    Logical 198
    NOT 199
    Numeric 197
    OR 199

Subset 204
Superset 204
Union 205
XOR 199
Optimization 37
Optional value 81
Optional 147, 158, 169, 260
OR operator 199
Order of declaration 153
Ordering 47
Or 196, 198–199
Otherwise 189
Out of scope
    Expression 351
    metaValue 351
    Statement 351

P

Parser 117
Partitioning 58, 70, 89
Peer names 179
Permissive 75, 125
Pi 263, 355
Precedence 196
Precision . 8, 73, 115, 142, 198, 268
Prefix operator 196
Pretty printing 117
Principle 101
    Abstraction 73
    Concept 79
        Correspondence 80
        Default 81
        Syntax 79
    Constraint 75
    Context independence 70
    Hierarchy 82
        Data aggregation 82
        Inheritance 82
    Independence 72, 257, 320
    Invariance 73, 82
    Nym 70, 92, 99
    Readability 68
    Reality 78
    Redundancy 79
    Scoping 69
    Simple type 83
Procedure Call Statement 191
Procedure 175, 343
Property 17

Pruning 96, 100, 215
Pseudo-code 78
Pseudotype 140, 171, 340

Q
QL 15
Quality 95
Query expression 206
Query 205

R
Readability 68
Real 134, 141–142
Real 43, 52, 179, 239, 247
Redeclaration
      Not allowed 354
Redundancy 54, 79, 91
Reference 179
      Attribute 183
      Entity 182
      Enumeration 184
      Function 184
      Inter-schema 250
      Type 183
      Variable 185
Reference 63, 70, 90–91,
      96, 99–100, 110, 212, 214,
      244–246, 250, 367
Relational model 15, 18, 20
Relationship 17, 35, 42, 80, 160, 316
      Is-defined-by 161
      Is-represented-as 161
      Isa 86, 160
      Supertype 309
      Symbol 236, 241
Remark 130
      Embedded 107, 130
      Tail 107, 131
Remove 364
Repeat Statement 191
Repeated inheritance 168
Repeat 191, 195
Reserved word 131–132
Resources 354
      Constants 354
      Functions 355
      Procedures 355
Return Statement 195
Return 174, 195

Rogue characters 129
Rogue 128
Role names 246
Role 246
RolesOf 364
Rounding 198
Rule 152, 342
      Domain 164
      Global 175
      Inheritance 169
      Local 162
Rules 124
Rule 71

S
Schema ... 50, 58, 69, 89, 115, 124,
      152–153, 211, 331
      Instance 268
      Symbol 240
Schema 50, 58, 69, 152
Scope 32, 34, 69, 71, 100, 104, 132,
      152, 157, 168, 179
Second-class 63, 90, 99
Select 150
      Value 264
Select 241, 248
Self 155–156,
      159, 161, 164, 177, 182–
      183, 186, 347–348, 355
Set model 18
Set 146–148
Set 47
SGML 109
Short circuit evaluation 196
Short form 99
Side effects 171
Significant digits 142
Simple type .17, 35, 43, 50, 83, 141
      Symbol 239
Sin 365
SizeOf 365
Skip Statement 194
Skip 194
SM language 23
Specialization 13, 34, 42, 52, 70, 86,
      96, 98
Spiby, Phil xix
SQL 26, 73
Sqrt 366

Statement 127, 187
    Alias 188
    Assignment 188
    Case 189
    Compound 190
    Escape 194
    If ... Then ... Else 190
    Null 187
    Procedure call 191
    Repeat 191, 194
        Increment 193
        Until 194
        While 193
    Return 195
    Skip 194
String 134, 144
    Comparison 200
    Matching 203
    Value 263
String ... 43–44, 51, 107, 239, 242,
    247
Structure 33, 58, 63, 75
Subset operator 204
Subset 35, 96, 110
Substring 144
Subtype ...42, 52, 74, 86, 125, 156,
    166
    Pruning 96
Subtype 42, 86
Superset operator 204
Supertype modeling 248
Supertype operator 310
Supertype·relationship 309
Supertype 42, 52, 86, 125, 166
    Abstract 53, 166
    Constraint 87, 167
    Expression 311
Supertype 86
Symbol 17, 24, 131, 239
    Algorithm 240
    Composition 236, 242
    Definition 236, 239
    Entity 240
    Inter-schema 244
    Page reference 242
    Relationship 236, 241
    Schema 240
    Simple type 239
    Type 239

Synonym 34, 70
Syntax
    EXPRESS-I 273
    EXPRESS 220

T
Tan 366
Terminal datatypes 141
Terminal 239–240
Test case 271
Then 190
TIM 37, 91, 94–96
Token 24, 127
True 135, 337, 352–353, 355
Truncation 198
Type lattice 86
TypeOf 366
Type 124, 154, 334–335
    Defined 155
    Modeling 247
    Reference 183
    Symbol 239
    Underlying 155
Type 51, 155

U
Underlying type 155
Union operator 205
Uniqueness ...36, 45, 115, 157, 163
    Name 179
Unique 45, 147–148, 163
Unknown 135, 337, 355
Until 193–194
UsedIn 179, 367
Use 63, 70, 90,
       96, 99–100, 110, 212–214,
       244– 245, 250, 367

V
Value
    Aggregate 264
    Attribute 266
    Basic 262
    Complex entity 267
    Constant 268
    Entity 265
    Enumeration 263
    Select 264
    String 263

Value 368
Variable
      Reference 185
Var 153, 171, 174–175
Visibility 179
Visualizer 118

W
WEB 111

Wenzel, Bernd xix
Where 46, 71, 164
While 193
Whitespace 127, 129–130
Wildcard 203

X
XOR operator 199
XOr 196, 198–199